THE GOTHIC VISIONARY PERSPECTIVE

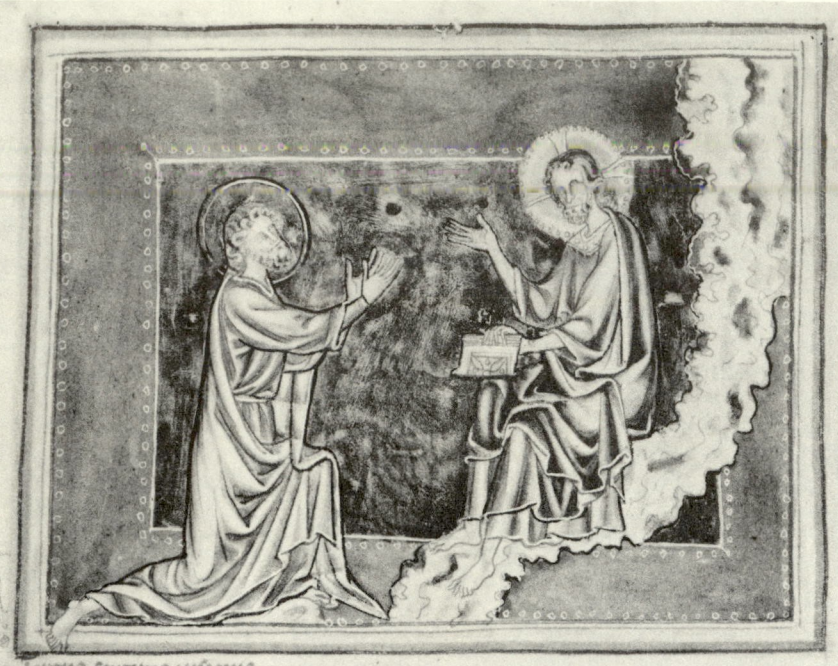

Et dicit in. sle signauerit uba libri p ophetie huf. Tempuf n. pre. Q̄ nō cer noceat adhuc: ej in sordibz e̅: sordescat adhuc: ⁊ uustuf iustam faciat adhuc: ⁊ sc̄o sctificer̄ adhuc. Ecce uenio cito ⁊ merces mea mecum e̅: reddere unicuiq: secdm opa sua. Ego sum. A. ⁊ ō. primum ⁊ nouissim̄. ben apium ⁊ finis. Beati qui lauant stolas su as. ut sit potestas cor̄ in ligno uite: ⁊ p por tas intrent in ciuitate. foris canes ⁊ uenefi ci. ⁊ impudici homicide. ⁊ ydolis seruientes: ⁊ ōis qui amat. Ego iesus misi angelm meū testificari uobis hec in ecclisis. Ego sū radix ⁊ genuf dauid stella splendida ⁊ matuti na. ⁊ spiritus ⁊ sponsa dicunt ueni. Et qui audit dicat ueni. Qui sitit: ueniat. Qui

uult accipiat aq̄m uite gratis. Con testor ego audienti omni homini uer ba prophetie libri huj. Siquis apposue rit ad hec: apponet ds̄ sup illum pla gas scriptas in libro isto. Et siquis dimmuuerit de uerbis libri prophetie li. auferet ds̄ partem eius de libro uite et de ciuitate sc̄a: ⁊ de hijs que scripta s̄ in libro isto. Dicit qui testimoni um phibet istorum etiam: uenio ci to amen. Veni dn̄e iesu. Gratia dn̄i nostri iesu xp̄i cum omnibz nobis amen.

Explicit liber apocalipsi

domini.

At the end of his visions, St. John kneels before Christ. Lambeth Palace Library MS. 209 (mid-13th c.) fol. 39v

THE GOTHIC VISIONARY PERSPECTIVE

by Barbara Nolan

Princeton University Press

Princeton, New Jersey

To Dick

Ion blessis hom alle þat þis boke reden
Wit gode entent, and hor god dreden,
Or heren hit red wit gode wille
In al hor myȝt hit to fulfille;
ffor þis blessing iche mon shulde wirke
To knowe hit & mayntene Holy [Kirke].
Hit tellis of peynes & sorowes sere
Þat here shal falle to cristis dere;
Þoo þat ben trewe & stiffly stonde,
Þei shal be hatid þorwout þo londe—
Of deefe & blinde þat wil not se,
Ne here hor fautes heelid to be.
Herefore crist counfortis his chirche
And biddes hom alle with pacience wirche.
Þis way went I to teche ȝou alle
Hou ȝe shal enter to heuenly halle,
Þere to duelle euere in pees,
In ioye & blis þat neuer shal cees.
                              Amen

Cambridge, Magdalene College, MS. 5
printed in R. H. Robbins, Secular
Lyrics of the Fourteenth and Fifteenth
Centuries *(Oxford, 1952), pp. 259–260*

CONTENTS

LIST OF ILLUSTRATIONS

PREFACE

A CHANCE encounter with a thirteenth-century English illustrated Apocalypse on exhibit in the British Museum first suggested the directions of this book. I had been studying a group of thirteenth- and fourteenth-century French, Italian and English poems concerning eschatological visions when I came upon an illuminated manuscript in its glass case opened to a vision of the New Jerusalem. Closer examination revealed striking similarities between the elegant miniatures in this book and the poems I had been reading. Was it simple coincidence that two artistic modes for treating visions of the eschaton should appear during the same period and should seem to mirror each other in tone and themes as well as narrative method?

My initial question led to further and broader inquiries. It became increasingly clear that novel attitudes toward the vision of the Last Things and the end of time—and new terms for treating it—had shaped both the form and content of some of the finest examples of later medieval art: the sculptural programs, stained glass windows and architectural design of many Gothic cathedrals; ninety or more surviving Anglo-Norman and Latin illustrated Apocalypses—many containing sequences of miniatures of the highest order; Giotto's frescoes of the Last Judgment at Padua; the early thirteenth-century prose *Queste del Saint Graal*; Wolfram von Eschenbach's *Parzival*; the pilgrimage poems of Raoul de Houdenc, Huon de Méri, Rutebeuf, Deguileville, Dante, Langland and the *Pearl* poet; the English play cycles written for the feast of Corpus Christi.

Anyone who examines these masterworks as a group must be struck by a special coherence among them. They are related not only by their interest in describing visions but also by their effort to represent men alive in time approaching the eschaton, imagining the state of beatific joy, participating in the glory of the heavenly court. Galahad's quest for the Grail brings him to a transforming final revelation. Dante's pilgrim reaches the empyrean. The *Pearl* narrator looks on the procession of the Lamb in the heavenly city. Langland's Will experiences a series of dreams which lead him toward Antichrist's coming. Giotto, Fra Angelico, and the cathedral sculptors represent themselves, their patrons, contemporary saints actually present in the heavenly realm. Artists of the illustrated Apocalypses contemporize St. John and describe precisely his human, affective responses as he studies the figures of the eschaton. The actors of the Corpus Christi play cycles used their own time, language and gestures to act out the entire history of salvation from Genesis until their final judgment at doomsday. In a variety of modes, artists had undertaken to examine the ways in which they and their contemporaries might both participate in sacred history leading to the eschaton and perceive the joy of beatitude, and their art asserted that such experiences need not be relegated entirely to life after death.

Above all, a faith that visions were not only possible but probable in this world suggested to theorists and artists the possibility of transforming matter into spirit, of spiritualizing human sight and understanding, of transmuting word and story, stone, glass and contemporary history. Material substances were to be accidental "integuments" for spiritual presence. The model for such transformations may well have been the Eucharist. In that sacrament, as it was redefined by the Fourth Lateran Council of 1215, "a unique and wonderful changing" took place by which the "whole substance of the bread was transformed into the body, the whole substance of the wine into the blood of Christ." Through the forms of art and the visionary possibilities inherent in the soul, the materials of cathedrals might be somehow analogously transubstantiated by intellect and imagination, becoming shimmering models of the _visio pacis_; the verses of a poem might form the precise and luminiscent representation of ecstatic experience, a prelude to the beatific vision itself; a personal history might be raised up and transformed into a segment of salvation history. Never before in the history of Christian art had artists so consciously labored to translate time, space and matter, to devise through the conformations of number and the materials of the created world "models" of divine realities. Gothic architects, painters, sculptors, saints, hagiographers and poets came to see and show the elements of the physical universe and human history as necessary stepping stones to the world of the spirit. The aesthetic theory supporting this transformation affected not only the form of the art object itself, but also its calculated effect on its audience. The form, in all its details, was intended to project a spiritual reality and thereby lead audiences through a process of purification and discovery toward their own transformation. Gothic visionary art was essentially an art of edification in the root sense of that word: the formal construction was to effect spiritual reconstruction, reshaping the souls of observers within the patterns of sacred history in order to transport them even before death into the company of the saved.

In the early stages of planning this book, I had intended simply to set side by side descriptive analyses of several major art works of the later Middle Ages (c. 1150–1400), all of which represent vision as an informing metaphor or outline the way to, and nature of, visionary experience. But I became more and more aware that common spiritual backgrounds must have supported the pervasive and long-lived persistence of the several "arts of vision" once they had been invented during the twelfth century. Because my central emphasis remains with the works themselves, I do not want to argue for causal relationships between the twelfth-century commentaries on the Apocalypse and treatises on vision discussed in Chapter One and the art works examined in subsequent chapters. But I would suggest, at least tentatively, that each of the artifacts I describe—the Gothic cathedral envisioned by Abbot Suger and realized at Chartres, the illustrated Apocalypses, the thirteenth-century French visionary quests, the *Vita Nuova*, *Pearl*, and *Piers Plowman*—can be more fully understood if considered within the context of attitudes toward history, prophecy and vision developed by monastic and clerical writers of the twelfth and early thirteenth centuries. It seems to me that by defining this context we can more clearly perceive the terms that shape the narrative structures and thematic forms of all these visionary works, both in the visual and the verbal arts.

The essays which follow explore a few of the most important moments in the history of a "Gothic visionary perspective." I begin with descriptions of that perspective in its purest forms as it appeared in commentaries and treatises and in the work of some of the twelfth century's most imaginative and influential artists. The commentaries of Rupert of Deutz, Richard of St. Victor and Joachim of Fiore and the architectural ideas of Abbot Suger caught and stirred the imaginations of men of genius. New attitudes toward the process of sacred history, the end of the world, vision, *aevum* (eternal time) and anagogy spurred artists to create powerful and durable new forms of thought and expression. I devote particular attention in the second chapter to the Gothic cathedral and the illustrated Apocalypse. Both these modes reflect the presence and power of new attitudes toward history and vision before the beginning of the thirteenth century.

Through formal design, architect, sculptor and illuminator alike began to assert that divine revelation and human beatitude were to be examined and realized preeminently within the context of history—both mankind's and one's own. They demonstrated that vision belongs necessarily to the working out of God's temporal plan for man. Hence, linear narrative—telling the story of divine revelation and personal salvation from Adam until the Apocalypse—became as central to the artistic form as the representation of visionary experience.

The third chapter is devoted to the *Vita Nuova*. Dante's earliest masterpiece offers us a remarkable version of the visionary perspective filtered through the refined atmosphere of the *stilnovisti* poets. Dante chooses to make linear narrative the principal means for expressing the transformation of disparate experiences into the story of his own salvation. Certainly the *Commedia* is far grander and more total in its achievement of a similar purpose. But I have preferred to study the *Vita Nuova* precisely because of its far smaller compass. It allows us to follow in detail the narrative method whereby Dante translates personal history into a process of beatification through a series of visionary experiences. His method here predicts the *Commedia*. It also exemplifies clearly the kind of double form —a temporally based *historia* shaped by spiritual purpose—which served the best vision poets of the later Middle Ages.

The fourth chapter defines a later medieval mode comparable in its diffusion and public appeal to the Gothic cathedral. Like the rise of romance in France, the emergence of the visionary quest in the early thirteenth century is a phenomenon directly related to the rapid development of the vernacular as a literary language. It is also dependent on the increased importance given to the sacrament of Penance and the consequent need for persuasive manuals of instruction. But above all, the new visionary quest—even in its most pedestrian manifestations—articulates those historical and prophetic interests described in Chapter One. Poets make linear narrative their central concern. In their fictions, they "place" the hero-soul on a temporal course leading through visions to salvation. Perhaps most remarkably, they can insist on the close relationship between personal beatitude and the spiritual transformation of the world. Thirteenth-century vision poets drew on earlier monastic forms as they developed this Gothic mode, but their novel translations of the older conventions led ultimately to three of the finest and most complex compositions of the later Middle Ages—the *Commedia*, *Pearl*, and *Piers Plowman*.

The last two chapters chart the fate of the Gothic visionary perspective near the end of its history. A century and a half—and the vicissitudes of war, plague, charges of heresy—separate the pure impulses of twelfth-century spiritual writers and artists from the writing of *Pearl* and *Piers Plowman*. The visionary quest came late to England, and the two major English examples show the influence of earlier continental efforts. But both the *Pearl* poet and Langland imbue the mode with a distinctly English genius even as they reflect respectively the development and breakdown of earlier dreams.

The fifth chapter offers a close reading of *Pearl*. This detailed analysis may appeal chiefly to those who have followed the scholarly conversation over that very difficult poem during the last century. Those who know its critical history will recognize my considerable debt to other readers in defining the problems which have led to my own discussion. But such close study also serves the argument of this book. It demonstrates how, and in what terms, the *Pearl* poet developed that visionary perspective described in Chapter One. Through form and imagery meticulously arranged, he, like the designers of the cathedrals and like Dante, can still insist that history and time may point the way to the vision of God.

I have chosen to conclude with a discussion of *Piers Plowman* because this long, confusing poem heralds the disappearance of those attitudes toward history and vision which so powerfully shaped the arts of vision in the later Middle Ages. Langland's is an art which reaches with apparent anguish toward the affirmation of a visionary perspective in the face of impossible worldly pressures. The poet draws fully on the conventions of the vision quest only to find that they cannot bring his Will to the spiritual peace enjoyed by his forebears. Yet even at the end of the poem, after the greatest hardships and suffering, Will persists in his dream. An Age of the Spirit—a kingdom of love and brotherhood on earth—still remains a possibility, if only in poetry.

Though a continuous argument concerning the nature and forms of the Gothic visionary perspective unites each of the studies in this book, many readers may prefer not to read from beginning to end. Each of the essays is also intended to exist as an independent entity; this is particularly true of the chapters on the *Vita Nuova*, *Pearl*, and *Piers Plowman*. In an effort to define a "visionary movement" in the later Middle Ages, many examples would have served as well as the ones I have chosen. The early thirteenth-century *Queste del Saint Graal*, Wolfram's *Parzival*, the *Fioretti*, the English Corpus Christi plays have all presented themselves as likely candidates. But the selections I have finally made have the double claim of being central and major examples of the movement and also of seeming especially puzzling, and therefore challenging, to many readers, including this one.

Grateful acknowledgment is made to His Grace the Archbishop of Canterbury and the Trustees of Lambeth Palace Library, the Master and Fellows of Trinity College, Cambridge, the Bodleian Library, Oxford, the British Library Board, the Bibliothèque Municipale, Cambrai, the Stadtbibliothek, Trier, the Biblioteca Vaticana, Rome, and the Pierpont Morgan Library, New York, for permission to publish photographs of materials in their possession; and to the Archives Photographiques, Paris, for permission to use their photographs of French monuments. I would also like to thank the Fulbright Commission, the National Endowment for the Humanities, the American Council of Learned Societies and Washington University for grants in aid of this project over the past ten years.

I take great pleasure in acknowledging particular debts of gratitude, first to my parents without whose interest and help this book could not have been written; to Professors Nancy P. Brown and Madeleine Doran whose example and instruction introduced me to the joys and demands of scholarship; to Professor Morton Bloomfield who criticized a version of my chapter on *Piers Plowman* and who continues to provide a model of humanistic scholarship at its most rigorous and generous; to Professor Chauncey Finch for expert and painstaking advice on paleographical questions; to Professors Douglas Kelly, Stanley Fish, Valerie Lagorio, Peter Riesenburg, Beatrice White, John Grigsby and Mr. Albert Lebowitz who kindly read and criticized portions of my book at various stages; to Professors George Pepe and Stephen F. Brown for their careful correction and refinement of my Latin translations; to Fr. Lowrie Daly, S.J. and Dr. Charles Ermatinger of the Vatican Film Library for their gracious assistance during my work with materials in their care; to Margot Cutter of Princeton University Press and to the Press's readers for meticulous attention to form and substance; and to Mrs. Grace Nicholson and Mrs. Eleanor Van Sant for their preparation of the typescript. Finally, I thank my husband, Richard Ruland, for his close reading, apposite criticism, and constant encouragement during crises of confidence.

St. Louis   BARBARA NOLAN
December, 1975

THE GOTHIC VISIONARY PERSPECTIVE

ONE

NEW DIRECTIONS IN TWELFTH-CENTURY SPIRITUALITY

From Bede to Alexander of Bremen: Tradition and Transformation in Commentaries on the Apocalypse

At least from the time of Eusebius, the whole history of the world from Adam until the Apocalypse had been divided into six ages. The first five ages had already been thoroughly detailed in sacred scripture. The early Fathers, by studying types and antitypes in the Old and New Testaments, had made it clear that there was a progressive improvement in the quality of human time through the course of the Old Testament to the coming of Christ; that is, they demonstrated that the intensity and fullness of the divine presence was greater at the time of the Incarnation than it had been immediately after Adam's fall. The period before Moses was described as the time before the law, and, in terms of human knowledge of divinity, the time in which man knew only the shadows of truth. In this dispensation, man was a "slave." He continued to live as a slave during the age from Abraham until the coming of Christ. This was the time under the law in which he knew truth only through images and figures. Then, with the coming of Christ, the law was replaced by grace, the shadows and figures by the *corpus veritatis*. In the "fullness of time," man encountered truth itself and was infused with saving grace.

But what then? The Fathers called the time after Christ's incarnation the Sixth Age. It would continue until the events of the Apocalypse brought the eternal sabbath. But they were unwilling to assert that God would continue to reveal himself systematically and progressively to his Church. Nor could they suggest that the Book of Revelation, the final prophecy of the New Testament, might describe systematically the progress of the Church step by step from Pentecost until the end of the world. Of this last temporal age St. Augustine, the antique harbinger of the

Middle Ages, says, "Sexta nunc agitur nullo generationum numero metienda propter id quod dictum est: *Non est uestrum scire tempora, quae Pater posuit in sua potestate*" (The Sixth Age is now proceeding, not measured by any number of generations because of that which has been said: "It is not for you to know those times which the Father has placed in his own power").[1] Augustine removes a sense of climax from the day of the Last Judgment by making it only one of all the judgments made by God from the time of Adam's eviction from paradise: "Ideo autem, cum diem iudicii Dei dicimus, addimus ultimum uel nouissimum, quia et nunc iudicat et ab humani generis initio iudicauit dimittens de paradiso et a ligno uitae separans primos homines peccati magni perpetratores" (Therefore when we say the day of God's judgment, we add "ultimate" or "last" because he judges now and he has judged from the beginning of the human race, casting out and separating the first men from paradise and the Tree of Life as perpetrators of a great sin).[2] For St. Augustine and early medieval commentators the possibility of mankind moving progressively *in time* toward total spiritual perfection and knowledge during the Sixth Age was overshadowed by emphasis on the individual soul moving with great difficulty *out of time* toward its own eschaton. The visionary approach to God was personal and vertical rather than social and historical.

Augustine's reluctance to discover a systematic relationship between specific events in contemporary history and God's progressive movement of the pentecostal Church toward the eschaton is eloquently reflected in early medieval monastic commentaries on St. John's Apocalypse. That difficult book of the New Testament—which was to become a favorite subject in later medieval art—had, in its earliest interpretations, been taken for a prophecy concerning the imminent end of the world.[3] Its subsequent fate in commentaries from the early to the high Middle Ages is fascinating in its own right.[4] But its changing fortune has a special relevance for the

---

[1] *De civitate Dei* xxii, 30, *PL* xli, 804; *CCSL* xlviii, pp. 865–866.

[2] *De civ.* xx, 1, *PL* xli, 659; *CCSL* xlviii, p. 699.

[3] See, for example, St. Justin, *Dialogus cum Tryphone*, 81, *PG* vi, 670; St. Irenaeus, *Contra haereses* v, 28–36, *PG* vii, 1197–1224; St. Victorinus, *Scholia in Apocalypsim*, *PL* v, 317–344; and Lactantius, *Institutiones divinae* vii, 14–25, *PL* vi, 779–813.

[4] For an interesting summary of this history in relation to the development of attitudes toward the Virgin Mary, see P. Prigent, *L'Apocalypse 12. Histoire de l'Exégèse* (Tübingen, 1959). The best history of commentaries on the Apocalypse before Joachim of Fiore is that of W. Kamlah, *Apokalypse und Geschichtstheologie.*

development of those arts of vision which are the subject of this book. Here, following the developments from Bede's influential exposition to Alexander of Bremen's, I trace only two aspects of the commentaries: (1) the explicit relationship which the commentator establishes between himself, St. John and the text; and (2) the ties he discovers between the imagery of the Apocalypse, the movements of time and contemporary history. The history of these developments shows, as we shall see, the dramatic emergence among twelfth- and thirteenth-century exegetes of new attitudes toward contemporary time and visionary spirituality which are to be found simultaneously in art and literature—both in the commentator's stance toward his material and in his interpretation of the apocalyptic imagery. Without suggesting a causal relationship between these new commentaries and concurrent developments in the arts, it is interesting to observe that trends in exegesis exactly parallel experiments in church architecture and decoration, book illustrations for the Apocalypse, and most important for our purposes, in literary vision quests, which use the Apocalypse either allusively or as a central subject.

For Bede, whose commentary was to exert an enormous influence throughout the earlier Middle Ages, the Apocalypse was taken to be an "intellectual vision" to be understood chiefly by reference to the exegesis of the Fathers. Bede is a compiler, and, following the advice of St. Augustine, he makes no claim to the privileges of divine illumination.[5] He evokes the rules of Tychonius as a guide for wresting meaning from John's obscure symbolism.[6] And in order to give the narration a manageable order, he divides it into seven parts. His rhetorical learning not only prompted him to organize the parts of the Book of Revelation but also to comment on its form. In his description of the second division, he suggests that his expectations for narrative order have been disappointed. St. John, "according to the custom of this book," interrupts narrative order to recapitulate, to begin again, to plunge into the "midst of time," or to describe the final tribulations.[7] As a scholarly rhetorician, Bede sets himself apart from the text of the Apocalypse both in these formal con-

---

Historische Studien, v. 285 (Berlin, 1935). See also H. Swete, *The Apocalypse of St. John* (London, 1906), pp. cxciii–ccxv.

[5] See Beryl Smalley, *The Study of the Bible in the Middle Ages* (Oxford, 1952) for a brief but precise description of Bede's general attitudes as an exegete, esp. pp. 26–36.

[6] *Explanatio Apocalypsis*, PL xciii, 131–134.

[7] *PL* xciii, 130–131.

siderations and in his humble acknowledgment of the exegetical tradition
in which he labors. He is anxious to find the universal moral significance
of St. John's prophecy and to present its teaching to the lethargic English
as tersely, directly and memorably as he can.[8]

Bede's method of exegesis is to translate each of John's symbolic images,
taken singly, by means of logical analysis. For example, in his interpretation of the Whore of Babylon's purple and scarlet garments, he says:
"In purpura fucus simulati regiminis, in coccino cruentus habitus impi-
etatis demonstratur" (In purple, the red dye [dissimulation] of deceitful
government is demonstrated, in scarlet, the bloody appearance of impi-
ety).[9] Here Bede savors the multivalent figural significances of the scriptural *litera*. To suit his purpose, he first translates "purpura" into a syno-
nym, "fucus," since the latter carries both the literal meaning, "red dye"
and the transferred sense, "face painting," and "dissimulation." From this
transferred sense, he derives his moral interpretation of the purple garment
as deceitful government.[10] Next, he considers the adjective "coccineus,"
derived from the noun "coccum," meaning the berry that grows on the
scarlet oak from which cloth was colored scarlet.[11] No doubt with full
knowledge of forethought, Bede discovers a special relationship of similitude between the berry juice coloring the Whore's clothing and the blood
marring the appearance of the impious. Not only in this treatment of the
Whore's garments, but also in his interpretations of all John's vivid, often
bizarre imagery, Bede is preeminently interested in nouns and adjectives,
not in verbs, in moral essences, not in historical or narrative action, and in
the verbal play which can lead by logic to the inner moral significance
of the Divine Word.

Alcuin, who builds his commentary on Bede's work and that of the
French Benedictine, Ambrose Autpert (d. 778 or 781), gives us an even
clearer picture of early medieval monastic attitudes toward the Apocalypse. Charlemagne's schoolmaster is, if anything, more devoted to authority than his master, Bede. He quotes Bede at length in his prologue,
reminding readers of Bede's seven divisions and Tychonius' rules. He
dutifully rehearses the list of patristic commentators on the Apocalypse—

---

[8] *PL* XCIII, 134.   [9] *PL* XCIII, 183.

[10] In this verbal play, in which the word "fucus" carries in part the meaning
"face painting, make-up," we may see one possible source for a long iconographical
tradition that interprets the Whore of Babylon both as Luxuria, holding a cup of
blood, and Vanitas, holding a mirror and combing her hair.

[11] Cf. Pliny, *Historia Naturalis*, 24, 4, 4, sec. 8.

Victorinus, Jerome, Tychonius, Primasius, and of course, Bede. Enlarging on Bede's description of Revelation's form and the nature and meaning of its imagery, he articulates unequivocally a mode of reading the Apocalypse which characterizes early medieval monastic commentators generally. For Alcuin, Revelation signifies "nothing historical." It is an "intellectual vision" in which the truth of things is manifested directly to the intuition without the mediation of corporeal things or "similitudes" for things. To support his definition of the Apocalypse as "intellectual vision," Alcuin, borrowing from Ambrose Autpert, describes the nonlinear form of the whole book:

> Ordo vero narrationis hic est. Aliquando ab adventu Domini inchoat, et perducit usque ad finem saeculi. Aliquando ab adventu Domini inchoat, et antequam finiat, ad initium redit, et ea quae dimiserat, sive quae dixerat, diversis figuris repetens, ad secundum Domini adventum percurrit. Aliquando incipit a novissima persecutione; sed antequam ad finem veniat, recapitulando utraque conjungit. Aliquando ad enarrandum proposita paululum intermittit, et aliud non ad hoc pertinens interponit; post quod ordine conciso quae coeperat perdocet. Aliquando in ipso genere locutionis sic mutata figura quasi alia permiscet, ut non nil aliud significet quam quod narrare coeperat. Et nota quia rarissime in hac revelatione vel angelus, vel Joannes proprias tenent personas.[12]

(This is the sequence of the narration. Sometimes it starts with the arrival of the Lord and carries through to the end of time. Sometimes it starts with the arrival of the Lord, and before it finishes, it returns to the beginning and by repeating in different figures both what it has left out and what it has said, it hastens to the second coming of the Lord. Sometimes it begins with the last persecution. But before it comes to the end it recapitulates and connects both [beginning and end]. Sometimes in order to narrate, it temporarily abandons its themes and introduces something totally unconnected. Afterward in concise order it teaches thoroughly what it had begun. Sometimes in this kind of style, a figure is changed in such a way that it is confused, as it were, with other things so that it signifies something quite other than what it began to represent. And you should note that very rarely in the revelation do the Angel or John retain their own persons.)

[12] *PL* c, 1089. See Ambrosius Autpertus, *In Apocalypsin*, in *Opera*, ed. R. Weber (Turnholt, 1975), pp. 13–14.

Because the vision is intellectual, Alcuin argues, one cannot expect the linear narrative order proper to history, nor stable images with univocal meanings. John's vision, then, is allegory and not entirely coherent allegory at that. The *litera* must melt as its spiritual meanings are perceived. Bede had noted the apparent disorder of John's narration but had not discussed its implications. Alcuin, on the other hand, seeking a divine rationale for the surface difficulties of the story, had found it in his definition of "intellectual vision." In this way, narrative order, the *sequence* of imagery, the progress of the *historia* could all be subordinated to a moral (and preeminently rational) interpretation of individual images. Furthermore, since John, in Alcuin's reading, "rarely retains his own person," there could be no point in studying his responses to his vision either in themselves or as potential examples intended for the reader.

Bede and Alcuin, as compilers and rhetoricians, were important for the future development of the exegetical tradition. But it was two much less prominent figures, Haimo of Auxerre (fl. 840–870) and Beatus of Liebana (d. 798), whose commentaries enjoyed particularly wide currency from the ninth to the thirteenth century.

As a Spaniard, largely removed from the mainstream of the Carolingian renaissance, Beatus might well have slipped into oblivion—an obscure provincial polemicist—had it not been for the major cycle of illustrations designed to accompany his commentary. The commentary itself, like Bede's and Alcuin's, participated in the Tychonian tradition of allegorical interpretation. But Beatus was also a keen opponent of a local heresy and his interpretation reflects his position. He used his exposition in part to celebrate the divinity of Christ, glorifying the risen, victorious Jesus against those who would make the incarnate Christ merely the adopted son of God. Because the effects of this particular emphasis—and especially the heightening of a traditional monastic reticence before John's mysterious images—were to be transmitted more dramatically through the Beatus cycles of illustrations than through the commentary itself, fuller discussion of Beatus will be reserved for the next chapter. Haimo, on the other hand, who was a direct heir to the central Carolingian tradition, produced a commentary which was to exert a significant influence on the most important twelfth-century exegetes, including Rupert of Deutz and Richard of St. Victor.[13]

[13] The influence of Haimo's commentary on eleventh- and twelfth-century exegetes was extraordinary. See Kamlah, esp. pp. 14, 17, 22–23, 30 and passim. Haimo's identity is open to some question. See C. Spicq, *Esquisse d'une histoire de l'exégèse latine*

Haimo fully assented to the Carolingian exegetical habits of abstraction and allegorization. St. John's visions are, for him, "intellectuale," containing "nihil historicus." Yet a close scrutiny of his commentary also reveals hints of innovation. Without in any way developing its implications, Haimo touches very briefly on the significance of St. John's spiritual experience as an example for holy readers seeking beatitude. In describing John's exile on Patmos, for example, he explains the importance of such isolation for contemplative experience generally:

Ubi quanto magis putabatur vinciri custodia humana, tanto magis humanitatis transcendens, meruit videre coelestia. Et cui certa negabantur spatia terrarum excedere, secreta sunt concessa penetrare coelestia. Et quanto magis destitutus est humano solatio, tanto ei adfuit divinum.[14]

(By however much more he is thought to be held down there by human bondage, so much the more, transcending humanity, he deserves to see heavenly things. And to him to whom it is denied to go beyond defined earthly limits, it is allowed to penetrate heavenly mysteries. And the more he is deprived of human consolation, the more the divine is present to him.)

And again, interpreting the name "Patmos" allegorically, Haimo argues that John's suffering should serve as an example to all the holy, for "quanto magis enim sancti in praesenti vita affliguntur, eo amplius illis secreta coelestia manifestantur" (for the more the holy are afflicted in this present life, so much the more are heavenly secrets shown to them).[15] Indeed, he concludes one cannot possess the kingdom unless he practices such tribulation. To be sure, Haimo speaks only briefly of St. John's experience and even here his chief concern is with the visionary's general allegorical significance for all the faithful. But it may have been precisely such fleeting hints as these, pointing to the personal spiritual significance of Revelation, which made his commentary particularly interesting to twelfth-century exegetes.

The most original of the early commentaries—that of Berengaudus—presents difficulties because it cannot be dated with certainty.[16] It has been

---

au moyen âge (Paris, 1944), pp. 50–51; B. Smalley, *Study of the Bible*, p. 39; Kamlah, p. 14 and n. 24.

[14] *PL* cxvii, 937. Compare Ambrosius Autpertus, *Opera, In Apocalypsin*, p. 9.

[15] *PL* cxvii, 949.

[16] The first editor of Berengaudus' commentary, Cuthbert Tunstall (Paris, 1548) attributed it to St. Ambrose and placed it among Ambrose's work. Tunstall omitted

called the first of the "historico-prophetic" interpretations, and therefore
placed closer to the twelfth than the ninth century. Yet, although Berengaudus' originality sets him apart from the major Carolingian compilers,
he remains essentially of the monastic, allegorical school. For him, as for
Bede, Alcuin, Beatus and Haimo, the universal Church in all times and
places is the general subject hidden in the images of the Apocalypse.

But it is only a short logical step from this omnitemporal concern for
the one, universal Church to a systematic reading of the "sevens" so pervasively present in the Book of Revelation as the seven ages of the Church
from the time before the Flood until the Last Judgment. And Berengaudus was the first to make this connection.[17] "If you look closely," he says,
"you will discover that the holy city of God,"

> . . . quae ex omnibus electis constat, quae ab initio usque ad finem
> tendit, . . . in septem partes divisam. Prima igitur pars ejus sunt electi,
> qui ab initio usque ad diluvium fuerunt: secunda, patriarchae et caeteri
> justi usque ad legem datam: tertia, hi qui sub lege fuerunt: quarta,
> prophetae: quinto, apostoli et qui ex Judaeis crediderunt: sexta vero
> pars est gentium multitudo quae ad fidem venit: septima, electi qui in
> fine mundi nascituri sunt, et contra Antrichristum pugnaturi.[18]

> (. . . which is built from all the elect which stretches from the begin-
> ning even to the end is divided into seven parts. The first part of the
> elect are those who lived from the beginning until the flood; the second,
> the patriarchs and other just men until the law was given; the third,

---

a note at the beginning of the epilogue which directs the reader to find the author's
name in the capitals beginning each of the seven visions (BRNGVDS). That the author's
name is Berengaudus is confirmed by a notation in B.N. MS. lat. 2467 in the original
scribe's hand: "Auctor huius libri Berengaudus appellatur." Berengaudus was first
identified as a Benedictine monk of the Abbey of Ferrières (Maurist Fathers, *Histoire littéraire de la France* v [1740], pp. 653f.). A few scholars have put forward
a date as late as the eleventh or twelfth century for Berengaudus: see esp. R. Lauren-
tin, *Court Traité de Théologie Mariale* (1953), p. 123. R. Weber in his recent edition
of Ambrose Autpert's commentary leaves the question open: "Berengaudus could be
either Berengaudus of Auxerre who lived in the ninth century or his homonym of
the twelfth century who lived in Angers" (xiv). The best summary of the debate
over Berengaudus' identity is to be found in F. Vigouroux, *Dictionnaire de la Bible*,
vol. I, pt. 2 (Paris, 1926), cols. 1610–1611.

[17] Berengaudus makes this leap early in his commentary as he interprets the seven
candelabra and seven stars of Rev. I, 15.

[18] *PL* XVII, 851.

those who lived under the law; the fourth, the prophets; the fifth, apostles and those among the Jews who believed; the sixth part, truly is the multitude of peoples who have come to the faith; the seventh, those elect who will be born at the end of the world and will wage war against Antichrist.)

Once the seven *partes* of sacred history had been invoked as Revelation's specific subject, Berengaudus could read each image of the Apocalypse as a piece in a puzzle, the total picture of which would be the life of the Church in its "seven times."

Berengaudus' interest in the "sevens" of Revelation also led him to divide the scriptural text into seven visions, each of which would be explicated as a separate unit. In addition, he had sought to discover a logical and narrative rationale for the seven visions he had distinguished. Thus, while the first vision describes the form of the whole Church under the figure of the seven churches of Asia, the second, which invites St. John to "ascend," signifies that the faithful must rise up to heavenly virtue in order to perceive the sublimity of the Church more fully. Then, "not unsuitably," the third vision unfolds the opening of the Book with Seven Seals, that is, the Old and New Testaments as they were expounded *after* the founding of the Church by the holy doctors according to the Apostolic faith. Next, "according to the order of reason," the figure of the seven angels blowing their trumpets must signify the holy doctors themselves who expound the scriptures to the elect and reprobate alike while the angels pouring out their vials represent those same doctors, preaching *now* only to the reprobate. Finally, Berengaudus concludes that while all the first five visions describe the general history of the Church, the last two, following the order of time, describe particularly the general resurrection at the end of the world, the damnation of the wicked, the glorification of the just and the life of the blessed after the resurrection.

In his comparison of the "sevens" of Revelation, Berengaudus discovered an intricate network of correspondences whereby John's visions symbolically represent, over and over, the history of the Church leading ineluctably to the coming of Antichrist. Thus the Apocalypse becomes for him as much a story about the passage of time from Adam until the Apocalypse, as of the omnitemporal struggle between the devil and the Church. Berengaudus' special interest in the times of the Church led him to a far more literal and concrete imagination of the "time" of Antichrist and the blessed time after the general resurrection than can be found in either Alcuin or Haimo. Though he does not relate the apocalyptic symbolism specifically to the course of the present time, he prepares the way, suggesting for instance not only that the seven heads of the beast represent the reprobate through whom the devil deceives the human race, but also that "five of the heads have already fallen and that the seventh is not yet come."[19]

But in his treatment of St. John, Berengaudus follows a traditional monastic pattern: John is a minor figure in the narrative, the transparent instrument through whom the vision is presented. He is shown to be awe-struck by his vision and he reveals his "humana fragilitas" when he falls down as if dead in the face of God's immensity:

> Ecce Joannes, qui sibi stare videbatur, viso Domino, cecidit tanquam mortuus; quia unusquisque vir sanctus quantum se ad contemplandam divinitatem Dei altius erexerit, tanta apud se introrsus inferius cadit; quia in comparatione Dei ejus magnitudo quam parva sit, facile perspicit.[20]

(Behold John, who seems to stand before Him, before the vision of the Lord, he fell as if dead; because each and every holy man, as much as he is raised on high for the contemplation of God, so much he falls down into himself; because in comparison to God he easily perceives that his size is tiny. Whence he falls as if dead because in comparison to God he perceives that he is nothing.)

Although Berengaudus must be considered closer to the Carolingians than to the twelfth century in his interests and in his methods, his innovative concern with the Apocalypse as a narrative sequence arranged in seven visions and revealing the course of sacred history are significant enough to set him apart as a link between the early compilers and the writers of original commentaries who were to come.

The only other major commentary now extant produced between the end of the ninth and the beginning of the twelfth century was that of Bruno of Segni (1049–1123), a politically active churchman and counselor to three popes, who finally sought the quiet of the cloister at Monte Cas-

---

[19] *PL* xvii, 999. Berengaudus may owe his treatment of Antichrist in part to Gregory the Great whom he cites as a source and who was himself anti-Augustinian in his anticipation of the world's imminent end.

[20] *PL* xvii, 775.

sino.[21] On the whole, Bruno follows earlier tradition both in his interpretation of St. John and his moralization of the text. But at several points, easy to overlook but nonetheless significant, he develops traditional exegesis in new directions. Though Bruno humbly and sincerely acknowledges the authority of his forebears, he is not loathe to launch out on his own, perhaps in part because he is writing for friends. In both the freedom and fullness of his exposition, he presages the far more daring work of twelfth-century exegetes to follow.

Like Berengaudus, Bruno makes a seven-part division of Revelation corresponding to seven distinct visions. In the orderly procession of these visions, he discovers a striking pattern of recapitulations: each vision but the last, according to Bruno, recounts the progressive history of the Church from its beginnings until the eternal sabbath of the blessed. One of his dominant interests—the centrality of preaching for the Church's development—leads him to find over and over in the figures of the first six visions the successive appearance of good preachers in the face of changing persecutions. For example, in his account of the horses of the first four seals, the white horse signifies the purity of the primitive Church while the red, black and pale horses (or the changing colors of the single horse) demonstrate the series of persecutions from Nero onward in successive times of preaching.[22] Following the curve of history, the fifth, sixth and seventh seals point to the final movements in the Church's history, the concluding periods of preaching, the coming of Antichrist and the eternal sabbath. The seven trumpeting angels likewise mark out stages in the history of preaching, this time particularly against heresy. The trumpet of the fourth angel sounds against the heretics, Arius and Sabellius, while the fifth and sixth angels preach in the time of Antichrist, and the seventh marks the end of all preaching as the action of grace fills all souls with God's praise.[23]

Bruno reserves the last book of his commentary exclusively for the final vision of the New Jerusalem. For him, the heavenly city in all its details signifies the joy of the universal Church omnitemporally practicing virtue, preaching truth and preparing for the eternal sabbath. A few of the sacred figures in this last vision also lead him to imagine aspects of that final state, for example the beauty of wisdom as it will be enjoyed by the blessed:

[21] Prigent, p. 22; Kamlah, p. 16. For the existence of other commentaries on the Apocalypse between the ninth and eleventh centuries, see Kamlah, p. 15, n. 6.

[22] *PL* CLXV, 633–636.   [23] *PL* CLXV, 646–666.

At vero ipsa civitas est de auro munda, quod simile est vitro mundo, quia ipsius civitatis domus, turres et palatia ex illo metallo composita sunt, quod caeteris omnibus clarius et dignius est, per quod sapientiam intelligimus, de qua dicitur: "Sapientia aedificavit sibi domum." Sed quam domum, nisi hanc nobilissimam civitatem? Nusquam ergo in ea tenebrae, nusquam caecitatis ignorantiaeque caligo, ubique aurum fulget, ubique sapientiae luce cuncta resplendent, et se vicissim omnes contemplantes, nihil est in alicujus conscientia, quod ab omnibus non videatur. Unde et vitro mundo hoc aurum simile dicitur, aurum enim et si fulgeat, non tamen videtur quod intra se habet; in vitro autem, si mundum est, nihil est interius quod exterius non appareat. Merito igitur illius civitatis aurum mundo vitro similes perhibetur, siquidem omnia ibi clara et manifesta erunt, et nihil ibi obscurum et tenbrosum, nihil quod insipientium oculos offendere possit.[24]

(But truly this city is of pure gold, which is like clear glass, for the dwelling place of this city, the towers and the roof are made from that metal which is clearer and more worthy than all others, by which we understand wisdom, concerning which it is said: "Wisdom has built a house for herself." But what is this house except this most noble city? Nowhere shadows in it, nowhere the cloud of blindness and ignorance, everywhere gold shines, everywhere all things shine with the light of wisdom, and all those contemplating each other in turn, there is nothing in any consciousness which is not seen by all. Whence this gold is said to be like clear glass, for gold may shine, but what is within is not seen; in glass however, if it is clear, nothing is within which does not appear outside. With reason therefore is it asserted that the gold of this city is like clear glass for here all will be clear and evident, and nothing here will be hidden or shadowy, nothing foolish which could offend the eyes.)

Such imaginations as these are more frequent in Bruno than in earlier medieval commentary generally and may have helped to prepare the ground for the far fuller images of heavenly bliss to be developed in succeeding centuries.

Finally, the bishop of Segni shows more than a passing interest in the nature of St. John's experience as it bears on the reader's. For example, when he describes the evangelist's first stunning vision, he explains John's state and then exhorts his readers to a like response:

[24] *PL* CLXV, 724–725.

Conversus namque ad spiritualem intelligentiam beatus Joannes vidit et intellexit vocem illam, quae cum eo loquebatur. Convertere ergo et tu, quicunque hanc prophetiam intelligere cupis, ut nihil carnaliter sapiens, totus ad spiritualem intellectum rapiaris.[25]

(Having turned around for spiritual understanding, blessed John saw and understood that voice which spoke with him. Therefore you, whoever desire to understand this prophecy, turn around so that, knowing nothing carnally, you may be wholly drawn up to spiritual comprehension.)

And again, as he speaks of St. John being carried to a mountain to perceive the heavenly city, he suggests, by using the first person plural, that his readers may share the visionary's experience:

Et sustulit me in spiritu in montem magnum et altum, per quem ecstasim et mentis excessum intelligimus, in quem nullis aliis quam spiritualibus pedibus ascendere possumus.[26]

(And he carried me in spirit onto a great and high mountain, through which we understand ecstasy and mental rapture, into which we can ascend by no other means than by spiritual feet.)

Yet for all his innovation, Bruno remains firmly placed in his own time, a romanesque writer carefully but freely developing the directions of his Carolingian forebears. His commentary gives only the barest hints of the amazing developments to come in the twelfth century.

In a prefatory letter appended to his *Expositio in Apocalypsim* (written between 1117–1126), Rupert of Deutz, a German monk well educated in Liège and finally Abbot of Deutz, sounded a new note. He proposes not to gather the flowers of earlier commentators but to offer an original interpretation, something other and better than his forebears, the "antiquores patres." Though Rupert frames his daring proposal in a discourse on meekness and develops the metaphor of the Scriptures as a field in order to justify this new plowing, his intention to be original sets his commentary apart. Further, Rupert makes the rationale for his new work his personal experience of the Scriptures' power to excite the soul. "What," he asks, "is Sacred Scriptures but the Promised Land? What it was for those to leave Egypt and to enter into that Land of Promise, that it is for us to leave the shadows of ignorance, and enter into the knowledge of God

[25] *PL* CLXV, 611. [26] *PL* CLXV, 720–721.

through the truth of Scriptures."[27] In this regard, Rupert's commentary is
to be an example. It will show readers how they, too, may find their personal liberation and the beginning of divine wisdom by likewise studying
and grasping God's word.[28]

Rupert is explicit in describing what the reader is to find in the Apocalypse and how he will discover its mysteries:

> Horum omnium temporum, sive de omnibus his temporibus, scilicet de
> praeterito, de praesenti et de futuro, haec prophetia contexitur, quia
> videlicet qualis fuisset, qualis tunc esset, qualis futurus esset Ecclesiae
> status, hac Apocalypsi revelavit huic dilecto suo Jesus Christus, sicut ex
> ipsa serie mirabili, eodem Jesu Christo dante, cognoscere potest lector,
> sive auditor beatus.[29]

> (This prophecy is comprised of all times, or concerning all times, name-
> ly concerning the past, present and future, so that Jesus Christ revealed
> to his loved one [John] what had been, what then was and what the
> future status of the Church would be, just as by that wonderful series,
> the reader or blessed hearer can know, if Jesus Christ grants it.)

Here he explains that we (as well as John) are led into this prophecy by
our leader Jesus Christ. Then "legentes pariter audiamus, foris legendo litteram, intus audiendo mysteria" (when we read let us listen equally: by
reading the letter without, by hearing the mystery within).[30] Implicitly
Rupert puts the reader in John's place and offers him the exciting possibility of experiencing the letter of his vision and simultaneously understanding its mysteries.

Rupert's notion of reading—which gives greater significance to the letter
than heretofore—required a redefinition of "intellectual vision" as Alcuin
had described it. And he does not fail to make the adjustment. Instead of
being a vision which requires no forms or similitudes of things, "intellectual vision" is for Rupert a mode of understanding whereby "mens a
Spiritu sancto illuminatur, ut intelligat, quomodo intellexit Joseph, quid
per easdem imagines significaretur" (the mind is illuminated by the Holy
Spirit so that it understands, as Joseph understood, what is signified

[27] *PL* CLXIX, 825–828.

[28] *PL* CLXIX, 850. This same interpretation is repeated a century later by the Franciscan expositor, Alexander of Bremen, who gives a far more historical and personal
interpretation of the Apocalypse than Rupert.

[29] *PL* CLXIX, 831.   [30] *Ibid.*

through these images).[31] The difference between the two definitions—
Alcuin's and Rupert's—is a subtle one, but it makes a significant difference in the way the images are handled. For Rupert, the apocalyptic
images signal both particular moments in the history of God's revelation
to man through the Old and New Testaments and the mystery of divine
and diabolic power omnipresent in the world. Thus, for example, the
apocalyptic red horse signifies the "bloodied populace of the devil's city,
the city of Babylon." But it also includes particular moments of blood and
death in the course of sacred history: the blood of the just Abel, and of
Zacharias, son of Barach, and the blood of Christ through the actions of
the gentile, Pontius Pilate.[32] Rupert goes on to name the bloodied tyrants
of the early Church, Titus and Vespasian. Likewise, in his discussion of
the pale horse—the heretics—he names the fourth-century heretic, Arius.
Rupert's interpretation of the apocalyptic imagery as signifying particular
historical moments differs substantially from Berengaudus' more general,
schematic exegesis. Unlike Berengaudus, he discovers the dynamic movement of powerful forces through specific historical moments hidden in
John's symbols. And although he himself ties the Book of Revelation more
fully to Old than New Testament history, his historicization of the
apocalyptic images would be carried in new directions in the interpretations of Anselm of Havelburg and Richard of St. Victor, and transformed
by Joachim of Fiore and Alexander of Bremen.

But what is most strikingly innovative is Rupert's discovery of a divinely arranged memory system in the mysterious imagery of the Apocalypse. Framed by his commentary, the Book of Revelation becomes an
intricately organized book of meditation—a systematic guide to spiritual
consolation, and finally, to beatitude. Haimo of Auxerre, who was Rupert's principal model, had, like Alcuin, confessed to bewilderment in
the face of Revelation's apparently repetitive and digressive imagery in
which he could find "nihil historicus." As a consequence, he had tried to
explicate the intellectual meaning of discrete figures, always following the

---

[31] *PL* CLXIX, 852. Rupert's definition may owe its inspiration directly or indirectly
to St. Augustine's distinctions regarding the three kinds of vision. In his *De Genesi
ad litteram* Augustine describes St. John's visions as *both* spiritual and intellectual:
the evangelist perceived his vision through similitudes of things, but then understood
with perfect intellectual clarity the truth contained in the revelation. See *De Genesi*
XII, 9 and 26 in *PL* XXXIV, 461 and 476. See also Ambrosius Autpertus, *In Apocalypsin*, p. 13.

[32] *PL* CLXIX, 943.

Rules of Tychonius, seeking the genus within the species. By contrast, Rupert insists on the importance not only of the images *per se* but of their order. By systematic meditation on the sacred "imagines" "per ordinem" he argues, the blessed reader will be able to draw his soul toward beatitude, conforming it to the seven spirits who stand before the throne of the apocalyptic Lord. If he reads and understands the book aright, such a reader will, like St. John, behold the door of heaven opened to him, inviting him to enter in and converse with the blessed.

That such an experience is within his reader's reach, Rupert confirms as he explicates the opening of John's second vision: Post haec vidi, et ecce ostium apertum in coelo (Apoc. 4). For the reader, as well as John, that "heaven which is opened" signifies "coelestem vitam . . . ad quam nuper resurgendo Christus a mortuis, universam Ecclesiam suscitaverat consurgentem secum, resurrectione prima." Because of Christ's saving death and resurrection, "regnum Dei intra nos est." Thus by the opening of the door, the mysteries of Scriptures are opened, which "to understand spiritually, and to live according to them, is to reign *already* in the kingdom of heaven and to have conversation in heaven."[33]

But in order to "reign *now* in the Kingdom," Rupert argues, the reader must dispose himself properly, and then, opening the Book of Revelation, he must await that inspiration from God which will clarify the mysteries of its images. In the prologue to the second book of his commentary, Rupert defines the kind of preparation he envisions for his ideal audience as they approach St. John's revelations: "With great desire to taste the sweetness of the divine Word, and with humility, we hasten to seek and find so that the door will be opened to us. What we seek is not the milk of babies, but the solid food of the perfecti. For all those things which are contained in that mystery are as strong as wine, and wine, even as the bride of the Song of Songs says, most sweet and excellent, worthy for drinking by my beloved, and for savoring with lips and teeth." "Therefore," Rupert concludes, "we seek so that we may discover, we knock with perseverance so that it may be opened to us."[34] With so urgent and burning a desire, then, the soul may, with John, obey the command, "Ascende huc," that is, as Rupert explains, "in spiritu excedere omnes sensus carnis atque spiritualia videre oculis spiritualibus" (in spirit to pass beyond every sense of the body and to see spiritual things with spiritual eyes).[35]

The commentary of Rupert, then, leads the reader through a meditation following the order of the apocalyptic images to a final discovery—

---

[33] *PL* CLXIX, 903–904.   [34] *PL* CLXIX, 863–866.   [35] *PL* CLXIX, 905.

glimpsed *through* the sacred figure of the heavenly Jerusalem—of the glory of the blessed after the general resurrection. In his exposition, the images have become signs of spiritual progress, leading by ordered stages to the experience of beatitude, which as Rupert suggests, is symbolically present to the readers' spiritual eye (and imagination) in the *picture* of the heavenly city descending from heaven.

With Anselm of Havelburg's exposition of the seven seals, we encounter for the first time a full reading of apocalyptic imagery as specifically symbolic of the progressive order of history leading to the present time.[36] Anselm did not write a complete commentary, and so his work cannot offer us as much information about changing attitudes toward the Book of Revelation as later texts do. But it is nevertheless important as it heralds, early in the twelfth century, what can be regarded as a revolution in the history of Apocalypse commentaries.

For Anselm the seven seals represent clearly definable, successive stages in the history of the pentecostal Church. Of the seals, four have already been opened—indeed, the present age is in the midst of the *status* of the pale horse. In Anselm's scheme of the four horses, we recognize a broad leap beyond Rupert's suggestive interpretation. The white horse signifies the first status of the Church, clear and beautiful with the whiteness of miracles.[37] In the red horse, Anselm discovers the bloodshed of the martyrs which began with St. Stephen.[38] The black horse stands for the poisoned doctrine of heretics—Arius, Sabellius, Nestorius, Eutyches, Macedonius, Donatus, Photinus, Manes.[39] But the pale horse affords the most fruitful field for Anselm. Here he develops a history of holiness in the pentecostal Church, showing its growth in brightness in the midst of blackness—for the horse is pale to suggest a mixture of black and white.

Anselm traces the development of "religious men, lovers of truth, founders of religions," concentrating especially on the late eleventh and early twelfth centuries. With the efforts of men like St. Norbert (1085–1134), founder of the Premonstratensians, "religion, greatly renewed, began to increase, and it has been diffused throughout the world." Anselm also praises St. Bernard of Clairvaux, the Knights Templar who defend Christ's sepulcher against the Saracens, and the congregations of the East-

---

[36] Anselm of Havelburg, *Dialogues*, ed. G. Salet (Paris, 1966). Anselm, probably born in the Rhineland and educated at Laon, became a Premonstratensian under the influence of his teacher, St. Norbert. In one of his letters he mentions Rupert of Deutz.

[37] *Dialogues*, pp. 68–70.   [38] *Dialogues*, p. 72.   [39] *Dialogues*, pp. 77–83.

ern Church which he had visited in Constantinople.[40] From this brief account he draws a most astonishing conclusion, but one which would be in perfect accord with those other twelfth-century writers who also discovered an increase of grace through New Testament history even to their own time:

> Et fit mira Dei dispensatione, quod a generatione in generationem succrescente semper nova religione, renovatur ut aquilae juventus Ecclesiae, quo et sublimius in contemplatione volare queat et subtilius quasi irreverberatis oculis radios veri solis contueri valeat.[41]

(And by the marvelous dispensation of God it happens that, the new religion always increasing from generation to generation, the youth of the Church, as of an eagle, is renewed, whereby it is able to fly higher in contemplation and more subtly to behold the rays of the true sun as it were with unflinching eyes.)

We have only to compare Anselm's sense of history's dynamic movement toward the seventh seal and the eternal sabbath with Alcuin's schematic moralization of John's visions to measure the distance we have traveled. The earlier exegetical cast of mind has been decisively superseded by new historical and spiritual concerns which were to appear in various guises in three major commentaries of the twelfth and early thirteenth centuries—those of Richard of St. Victor, Joachim of Fiore, and Alexander of Bremen.

The importance of Richard of St. Victor (d. 1173) for the development of later medieval spiritual attitudes cannot be overstated.[42] Dante fittingly

---

[40] *Dialogues*, pp. 84–107.

[41] *Dialogues*, p. 104.

[42] Though Hugh of St. Victor's broad and original explorations, including his commentary on Pseudo-Dionysius' *Celestial Hierarchy*, decisively shaped Richard's spiritual thought, the latter's concentrated interest in the visionary ascent to God gave him a special role in later medieval spiritual history. Thus St. Bonaventure places him in the development of Christian thought: Primum maxime docet Augustinus, secundum maxime docet Gregorius, tertium vero docet Dionysius–Anselmus sequitur Augustinum, Bernardus sequitur Gregorium, Richardus seqitur Dionysium, quia Anselmus in ratiocinatione, Bernardus in praedicatione, Richardus in contemplatione (*De reductione artium ad theologiam*, 5, in *Opera theologica selecta*, ed. minor, tom. v [Quaracchi, 1964], p. 221). For a brief history of the origin and development of the school of St. Victor in the twelfth century, and of the relationship between Hugh and Richard, see R. Baron, *Hugues et Richard de St-Victor* (Paris, 1961), pp. 7–50.

honors him in the heavenly sphere of contemplatives and describes him as "più che viro" (*Para.* x, 132). But the "magnus contemplator" also has particular relevance for this study, and his name will appear frequently in the following pages. Richard gives the first full and systematic interpretation of the Book of Revelation as a linear narrative centering upon the quality of John's visions and directed toward the spiritual education of the reader. The experience of John, the seer, becomes in Richard's exposition as central to the narrative as the series of images he perceives. Whereas Bede and his successors in the earlier Middle Ages were concerned with the universal moral significance of discrete images, Richard even more fully than Rupert, attends to the *actions* of Revelation and to the spiritual conditions which accompany John's (and the reader's) progress through a sequence of temporally organized scenes leading to a vision of the heavenly city.

Two simple comparisons will epitomize the changes Richard wrought in the monastic exegetical tradition. In his exposition of Revelation 21, describing the descent of the New Jerusalem, Bede had written: "De coelo descendere ista civitas dicitur, quoniam coelestis est gratia, qua Deus eam fecit" (That city is said to descend from heaven because it is the grace of heaven, where God made it).[43] Beatus gives a longer and likewise moral exposition:

> . . . *et ostendit mihi civitatem sanctam Ierusalem, descendentem de caelo a Deo.* haec est ecclesia, civitas in monte constituta, sponsa agni, quia non est alia ecclesia et alia civitas, quia una est, quia semper in penitentia de caelo descendet a Deo, quia filium Dei imitando in penitentia descendere dicitur in humilitate.[44]

> (*And he showed me the holy city, Jerusalem, descending from heaven from God.* This is the Church, the city built on the mountain, the spouse of the lamb, because there is not one Church and another city, for it is one because the Church by imitating the Son of God in penance is said to descend from heaven in humility.)

By contrast, Richard looks excitedly through John's eyes on the shimmering, bejeweled image of the City and discovers its spiritual meaning emanating from the surface of the figure:

[43] *PL* xciii, 194.
[44] H. A. Sanders, *Beati in Apocalypsin* (Rome, 1930), p. 623.

Agit autem haec septima et sacratissima visio de innovatione futura
elementorum, et glorificatione justorum et coelestium mansionum, atque
bonorum jucunditatem, multiformium figurarum qualitatibus pulchre
describens, et humanum animum ad summi boni appetitum atque dul-
cedinem mirabiliter trahens. Nam si quis etiam solam verborum pulchritudinem in serie visionis hujus diligentius ac studiosius attenderet,
unde semetipsum ad tanti boni concupiscentiam excitaret, perfectissime
reperiret, et tam pulchrae ac jucundae civitatis habitator fieri votis omnibus exoptaret.[45]

(This seventh and most sacred vision tells of the future renewal of the
elements and the glorification of the just and of the heavenly mansions,
and the joy of the good, describing them beautifully with the properties
of multiform figures, and drawing out wonderfully the desire and sweetness of the highest good. For if one would even attend to the beauty of
the words in the sequence of the vision diligently and studiously, then
he would stir himself up to the desire of such good. He would most perfectly perceive it and greatly desire to be made an inhabitant of so
beautiful and joyful a city in all his prayers.)

Furthermore, while earlier monastic exegetes had attended more to discrete images than to John's actions in seeing his visions, Richard makes
understanding that action both literally and spiritually a central concern
in his interpretation. When Bede explains the sentence of Revelation 17:3,
"Et abstulit me in desertum in spiritu," he writes simply: "Desertum ponit
divinitatis absentiam, cujus praesentia paradisus est" (The desert signifies
the absence of divinity whose presence is paradise).[46] What interests Richard, on the other hand, is the import of the verb: What was the "I" doing?
For what reason did the angel carry John into the desert? Hence he explains the same statement, concentrating on the nature of John's experience, and using the "me" ambiguously to signify at once St. John himself,
and the reader: "Et abstulit me in spiritu, ad sublimiora videlicet videnda,
in desertum, ad contemplanda reproborum corda, quae sunt a Deo deserta"
(And he carried me in spirit, namely for a higher seeing, into the desert,
for contemplating the hearts of the reprobate who are deserted by God).[47]

Richard justifies his method of interpreting John's revelations by refer-
ence to his important redefinition of the class of vision into which the
Apocalypse falls. Following Pseudo-Dionysius and his teacher, Hugh of
St. Victor, Richard rejects Alcuin's description of the Apocalypse as an

[45] *PL* cxcvi, 858–859.   [46] *PL* xciii, 182.   [47] *PL* cxcvi, 832–833.

"intellectual" vision. For him, it is, rather, symbolic—an apparition in which "aliquando per signa sensibilibus similia invisibilia demonstrata sunt" (sometimes invisible things are shown forth through signs like things perceived by sense).[48] Richard had criticized the Fathers' habit of bypassing the *historia* in favor of allegorical interpretation in his commentary on Ezekiel.[49] So here, too, he insists on the substantiality and necessity of St. John's images:

> Liquet igitur quod eam tertio videndi modo contemplatus sit, eo praesertim quod liber iste formalibus rerum temporalium plenus sit similitudinibus, videlicet coeli, solis, lunae, nubium, imbrium, grandinum, fulgurum, tonitruorum, ventorum, avium, piscium, bestiarum, animalium, serpentium, reptilium, arborum, montium, collium, aeris, maris, terrae et aliarum rerum, quae modo sensui non occurrunt. Necessarium erat enim nostrae infirmitati quae summa nonnisi per ima, spiritualia nonnisi per corporalia valet capere, non ignota per ignoriora, sed ignota per cognita noscere.[50]

> (It is therefore manifest that he has seen it in the third kind of seeing, especially because the book is full of formal likenesses of temporal things, namely the heavens, the sun, moon, clouds, rains, hail, lightning, thunder, winds, birds, fish, beasts, animals, serpents, reptiles, trees, mountains, hills, air, sea, earth, and other things present to the senses. It was necessary for our weakness which is able to grasp the highest only through the lowest, the spiritual only through the corporeal, to learn the unknown not through the more unknown but through the known.)

Like Rupert and Anselm, Richard insists, too, on the significance of the Apocalypse as a symbolic representation of the history of the pentecostal Church. When he describes the opening of the seven seals, he reads their meaning as *successive* stages in the Church's history:

> Quae vero in septem succedentibus capitulis sequuntur, et septem sigillorum apertione distinguuntur, ad *sequentis temporis redemptionem, et ordinem referuntur.*[51]

> (Those which follow in the seven succeeding chapters, and which are separated by the opening of the seven seals, refer to the redemption and order of the following time.)

---

[48] *PL* cxcvi, 687.   [49] *PL* cxcvi, 527–528.   [50] *PL* cxcvi, 687.
[51] *PL* cxcvi, 760.

He goes on to stress the orderly *historical* arrangement of John's images:

> In quibus videlicet sequentibus electorum virtutes et reproborum in
> electos persecutiones, et patientium tribulationes ab exordio nascentis
> Ecclesiae usque in finem mundi describuntur, *et non simul, et semel,*
> *sed secundum dispositionem, et apertionem sigillorum, et processum*
> *temporum paulatim et succedenter praedicta compleri,* et occulta mani-
> festari multiformiter ostendunt.[52]

> (In what follows, the virtues of the elect and the persecutions of the
> reprobate toward the elect and the tribulations of the patient from the
> beginning of the Church even to the end of the world are described;
> and not altogether or at once, but according to the arrangement, i.e. the
> opening of the seals and the procession of times make it clear that the
> prophecies are gradually fulfilled and the hidden are manifested in a
> variety of ways.)

Not only does Richard find historical order in the imagery of the seven
seals, he also speaks of the process of grace increasing as the course of time
moves God's revelation to completion. When he interprets the red horse
of the second seal as the cruel worldly rulers, red with the blood of martyrs, he adds, "Et cum aperuisset sigillum secundum, id est, cum, *crescente*
gratia, amplius coepisset exhiberi et compleri promissio divina et aperiri et
manifestari quod praemissum, et promissum erat in Scripturis. . . ." (And
when he had opened the second seal, that is, when, with the increase of
grace, the divine prophecy began to be shown forth and to be completed,
and that which had been prophesied and what had been promised in
Scriptures began to be opened up and clarified).[53]

Richard's confidence that the apocalyptic imagery should be interpreted
historically is even more dramatically evident in his reading of the seventh
seal. Rupert and Anselm read the seven seals as symbolic of the stages in
the Church's development leading to the *visio pacis.* And so does Richard.
But they describe the seventh "status" as occurring beyond time, when, as
Anselm writes, "annus jubilaeu instaurabitur, octava infinitae beatitudinis
celebratur. . . ." (the jubilee year will be instituted, the octave of infinite
blessedness will be celebrated).[54] By contrast, Richard allows that marvelous peace to occur within the confines of the world's time. For him, the
seventh seal marks the final time just preceding eternity:

[52] *Ibid.*   [53] *PL* cxcvi, 762–763.   [54] *Dialogues,* p. 114.

In fine visionis describit ea quae contingent in fine temporis. Et cum aperuisset sigillum septimum, id est cum per extremitatem saeculi praesentis inciperet demonstrare in sacra visione jam compleri mysterium humanae redemptionis.[55]

(At the end of the vision he describes those things which will pertain to the end of time. And when he has opened the seventh seal, that is in the last part of the present age, he will begin to show forth in sacred vision the mystery of human redemption now completed.)

He goes on to summarize his historical interpretation of the seven seals, concluding with a brief description of that final time: ". . . de parvi temporis pace, et tranquillitate quae eis post Antichristum in fine mundi, et in his omnibus de justorum probatione, et ad coelestem gloriam praeparatione, et de profunditate coelestium mysteriorum . . ." (. . . of the peace and tranquility of the brief time which is to come after Antichrist at the end of the world, both for the trial of the just in all these things, and by way of preparation for heavenly glory, in the depths of heavenly mysteries).[56]

The most imaginative and innovative effort to describe the meaning of St. John's revelation as it affected contemporary time and involved the contemporary reader was that of Abbot Joachim of Fiore (c. 1135–1202). His is a commentary which carries the directions set by Rupert, Anselm and Richard of St. Victor to their logical conclusion and in the process transforms them. *The Expositio in Apocalypsim,* written near the end of the twelfth century, is at once wholly personal and radically historical. Joachim follows Rupert and Richard in insisting on the centrality of a personal affective interaction between Revelation and the reader. But he takes their argument further: he claims that he himself experienced a marvelous spiritual illumination, as if the stone had been rolled away from Christ's sepulcher. Then as if seeing the apocalyptic imagery as John had, suddenly he understood both the full prophetic meaning of Revelation and its complex symbolic representation of all sacred history from Adam until the Last Judgment.[57] In that moment of illumination, he perceived a system of concordances between the events of Old Testament history and their antitypes in the New Testament which fully accounted for the course of Church history from the birth of John the Baptist to his own time.

[55] *PL* cxcvi, 775.　　　　[56] *PL* cxcvi, 776.

[57] *Expositio in Apocalypsim* (Venice, 1527), fol. 39r-v quoted in M. Reeves, *The Influence of Prophecy in the Later Middle Ages* (Oxford, 1969), p. 22.

Beyond that, he predicted the emergence of a final time, near at hand, not unlike the time of the seventh seal described by Richard of St. Victor. In the time of that *status*, all men would enjoy a heightened spirituality preparatory to the eternal peace of the New Jerusalem. The "Tree of Human History" from Joachim's *Liber concordie* (Fig. 1) is but one example of his extraordinary conceptualization of God's systematic revelation to mankind moving toward its spiritual completion in the present time near the end of the Last Age.

Joachim's grand vision for the course of history posits in a systematic way what Anselm and Richard had suggested, namely an incremental growth in the human knowledge of God extending from Adam until the end of the world. In Joachim's figures, neither the people of God in the time under the law nor those in the time under the gospel had enjoyed the spiritual perspecuity of those who came after the Incarnation and Ascension. For like himself these privileged souls could put together the events of the Old and New Testaments and understand their typological relationships. Further (and of most importance for Joachim) beyond this typological understanding, in the period just preceding the end of the world, man would be given an "anagogical" understanding of divinity. Then before the end of the world he would pass beyond typological understanding of the concordances between Old and New Testament history to perceptual participation in God's glory. For Joachim, this historical process was particularly interesting when viewed as moving mankind towards a sanctified world dominated by the spiritually free contemplative who, within time, would enjoy this clear vision of God.

To explain the emergence of a universal spiritual life in the Church, Joachim developed his concept of the three *status* with emphasis on their relative spiritual values in the progress of history.[58] The first status, he said, was initiated at the time of Adam and made manifest from the time

---

[58] St. Augustine, by way of comparison, describes the three ages, which he calls *tempora* as opposed to Joachim's status, in this way:

Deinde ita quaeritur quomodo quinquagenarius de quadragenario numero existat, qui non mediocriter in nostra religione sacratus est propter Pentecosten (Act. 2) et quomodo ter ductus propter tria tempora, ante Legem, sub Lege, sub Gratia, vel propter nomen Patris, et Filii, et Spiritus sancti, adjuncta eminentius ipsa Trinitate, ad purgatissimae Ecclesiae mysterium referatur (*De doctrina* II, 16, *PL* XXXIV, 48).

For a vivid figural representation of the three *status*, see L. Tondelli, ed., *Il Libro delle figure dell'Abate Giochino da Fiore* (Turin, 1953), 2nd ed., vol. I, Tavola XII.

of Abraham until the time of Ozias. Men in this spiritual "state" under the law were poor slaves. They were dominated by the elements of their world, "non valens adipisci libertatem spiritus quousque veniret ille . . . ." (not yet being strong enough to attain the freedom of the spirit until He should come . . .).[59] The time of the second *status*, begun under Ozias and manifested from the birth of John the Baptist "usque nunc" (until now), was the time "sub evangelio" (under the gospel). Then men were partly freed. Their spiritual liberation extended to the past but not to the future. The third *status*, not yet made manifest, was to occur near the end of the world. At that time, the veil of the letter would be removed and the spirit would emerge "plena spiritus libertate" (in full freedom of spirit). This third *status*, Joachim's most pressing and novel concern in the *Expositio*, although not yet a dominant chord in history, had already begun to present itself. It had been foreshadowed and predicted in the person of St. Benedict whose "precellens claritas" is regarded as an anticipation of the *status* of the Holy Spirit.[60]

Obeying the "decorum of similitude," Joachim taught that each of the three persons of the Trinity presides over one of the three *status*. God the Father was most fully revealed in the First Age, represented in the letter of the Old Testament. The Son was presented to man in the time of the second *status*, described in the letter of the New Testament. But the Holy Spirit, the fullness of the Godhead, would be manifested fully only in that third "time" presaged by St. Benedict in which mankind would possess a spiritual understanding of both Testaments. By means of generation, just as the Father had begotten the Son and the Holy Spirit proceeded from the Father and the Son, so the New Testament was begotten of the Old, and a spiritual understanding would proceed from both Testaments. The three *status* are organically related to one another, with the third spiritual state emerging as the fruit and culmination of the first two.

Like Berengaudus and Richard of St. Victor, Joachim divides the Apocalypse into seven parts corresponding to seven visions. But for Joachim, the seven sections also correspond precisely to the progress of the Church's history from Christ until the end of time:

Sex sunt itaque libri partes et totidem tempora pertinentia ad secundum statum in quarum consumatione iudicata prius meretrice magna que sedet super aquas multas. Capietur bestia et cum illa pseudo propheta ut mittantur simul in stagnum ignis. Quamvis et diabolus qui auctor est

---

[59] *Expositio*, fol. 5r, col. 2.   [60] *Expositio*, fol. 5r, col. 2.

tanti mali claudendus est in abysso ut non seducat amplius gentes usque ad extrema tempora tertii status.[61]

(Thus there are six parts of the book and just as many times pertaining to the second *status* at the end of which the great Whore who sits upon many waters will be judged first. The beast will be captured and with it the false prophet so that they may be sent together into the lake of fire. Moreover, even the devil, who is the author of such a great deal of evil, will have to be closed up in the abyss so that he may no longer seduce people even to the final times of the third *status*.)

The seventh part of the Apocalypse, then, will correspond to the "extrema tempora tertii status" (the final times of the third *status*). Then there will be peace and comfort in Christ's Church and the spiritual Church will be one, dominated by contemplatives "even to the consummation of the world."[62]

In his temporal and spatial figures describing the course of human history, Joachim foresees the entire world as a cloistral utopia governed by monks and representing the final flowering of human spirituality before the Last Judgment. He imagines a moment in history when all political and social values—the entire world and time itself—will be lifted to a divine plane. Then all human action will serve God in preparation for the descent of the New Jerusalem. Joachim's scheme—not wholly unlike those of Anselm and Richard of St. Victor—represents a rich, creative personalizing and contemporizing of St. John's eschatological imagery. In his vision, the world's space and time must finally become the cathedral of man's contemplation as the whole race prepares to enter the heavenly city.

Like Joachim, the early thirteenth-century Franciscan friar, Alexander of Bremen, claims the gift of a special and personal illumination from heaven as the muse for his commentary. In an autobiographical sketch at the beginning of his exposition, he tells us that on a certain Sunday (the same day on which John had received his vision), he had been wrestling vainly with the text of the Apocalypse, hoping to discover in it some prophecy concerning the deeds of the Church. While he was preparing for Communion, the knotty problem continued to haunt him. But then, after he had "received the body of Our Lord Jesus Christ," suddenly he understood the meaning of the Apocalypse fully, "secundum ordinem historiarum."[63] Whereas Richard of St. Victor, and to a certain extent Rupert of

---

[61] *Expositio*, fol. 11, col. 2.   [62] *Ibid.*

[63] Alexander Minorita, *Expositio in Apocalypsim*, ed. A. Wachtel (Weimar, 1955), p. 6.

Deutz, had only suggested the possibility that readers of Revelation might experience spiritual understanding like John's, Joachim and Alexander give testimony to their own participation in the Johannine vision. The exegetical tradition has here been superseded by a personal, divinely sanctioned direct interaction through John's example between the scriptural text and the individual reader.[64]

In this context, it is not surprising that Alexander, like Joachim, finds contemporary relevance for the imagery of the Apocalypse, and particularly for those images that describe the New Jerusalem. For Joachim, the seventh part of the Book of Revelation had symbolized the final time of the third *status*—that last phase of human history in which man would participate "anagogically" in God's Truth. For Alexander the imagery of the heavenly city actually interpenetrates the history of contemporary spirituality. Particularly in the persons of St. Francis and St. Dominic he discovers a kind of holiness which can only presage the end of the world and the eternal sabbath:

> Per istam civitatem designantur fratres Minores, qui secundum historiam vitam apostolorum imitantur, et Praedicatores, qui apostolum Paulum in praedicatione sequuntur. Isti omnes Jherusalem vocantur, quia ad visionem pacis aeternae iam tendunt.[65]

> (The Friars Minor are designated through this city, who imitate the life of the Apostles according to history, and the Preachers, who follow the Apostle Paul in preaching. All these are called Jerusalem because they now tend toward the vision of eternal peace.)

Richard of St. Victor and Visions in the Evening of the World

In Richard's and Joachim's predictions of a contemplative Church near the end of time, they were in part extending an ancient Benedictine ideal to serve the lives of all men living near the end of the Last Age. Benedict's rule had called for the incorporation of all a monk's time in the service

---

[64] But it should be noted that Alexander draws on other commentators for the interpretation of particular images. Rupert of Deutz seems to have been a particular source of inspiration for both Joachim and Alexander. Compare, for example, Rupert's reading of John's place of exile (*PL* CLXIX, 850) with that of Joachim (*Expos.*, fol. 39) and of Alexander (*Expos.*, p. 14). Alexander explicitly acknowledges his debt to Joachim by quoting from his *Concordia novi et veteri Testamenti* (*Expos.*, p. 351).

[65] *Expositio*, p. 469.

of prayer. His days, months and years were to be transformed by their inclusion in the *opus Dei*. And the liturgical works themselves—the reading of Scripture and the divine office, as well as the intellectual and manual labors—were to be performed so as to transvalue ordinary time. In this way, holy men might begin to escape the constrictions of the material world and enter for privileged moments into the angelic life. By such transformation or transvaluation, the "time" and "place" of the cloister could be seen ideally as an imitation and intimation of the angel's visionary state.[66] During the twelfth century, this ideal of an angelic life on earth was not only preached with new urgency; it was also historicized and personalized by spiritual thinkers like Anselm of Havelburg, Richard and Joachim. Several writers gave assurance that the soul might apprehend angelic joy, and that visionary experience might be enjoyed more fully by Christians nearing the end of the Last Age.[67]

Among the most important and long-lived of such descriptions are Richard of St. Victor's *Benjamin Minor* and *Benjamin Major* (1158–1162). For the first time in the medieval Christian West, Richard offered a phenomenology of *personal* vision to be experienced by those who awaited the opening of the seventh seal. St. Augustine had cautioned even the most spiritual of Christians against expecting to enjoy God's presence while still bound to time:

Nam in tantum uident, in quantum moriuntur huic saeculo, in quantum autem huic uiuunt, non uident. Et ideo quamuis iam certior, et

[66] See J. Leclercq, *The Life of Perfection*, trans. L. Doyle (Maryland, 1961), chap. I.

[67] See for example William of St. Thierry, *De contemplando Deo*; Aelred of Rievaulx, *Speculum caritatis*; Hildegard of Bingen, *Scivias*. Twelfth-century writers like William of St. Thierry and Hildegard of Bingen who were indirectly or directly influenced by eastern thought, particularly through the writings of Dionysius the Pseudo-Areopagite and his commentators, emphatically affirmed the possibility of visions in this life. For Hildegard's access to Greek spirituality, see H. Schipperges, *Die Welt der Engel bei Hildegard von Bingen* (Salzburg, 1963), pp. 37–39. For the influence of Dionysian thought and Eriugena's commentary on St. Bernard's illustrious disciple, see William of St. Thierry, *On Contemplating God*, trans. Sr. Penelope CSMV (Spencer, Mass., 1971), pp. 29–30. The general presence and influence of eastern spiritual thought on twelfth-century thinkers, which certainly aroused new interest in the question of visionary experience, is very well summarized by M.-D. Chenu, *La Théologie au XIIe siècle* (Paris, 1957), pp. 274–308. For a brief history of Pseudo-Dionysius, his translators and commentators through the thirteenth century, see H. F. Dondaine, *Le Corpus Dionysien de l'Université de Paris au XIIIe siècle* (Rome, 1953), esp. pp. 24–66.

non solum tolerabilior, sed etiam iucundior species lucis illius incipiat apparere, *in aenigmate* adhuc tamen et *per speculum* uideri dicitur, quia magis *per fidem* quam per speciem ambulatur, cum in hac uita peregrinamur, quamuis *conuersationem* habeamus *in* caelis.[68]

(For they are able to see only in so far as they die to this world; in so far as they live for it, they do not see. And now although the light of the Trinity begins to appear more certain and not only more tolerable but also more joyful, it is still said to appear "through a glass darkly" for "we walk more by faith than by sight" when we make our pilgrimage in this world, although our "community is in heaven.")

But the Abbot of St. Victor wrote his treatises for those who aspired to heights and frequencies of vision undreamed by Augustine. He outlines a *life* lived in expectation of vision, and he promises participation in the divine spirit by means of prayer, virtue, devotion and meditation. The speculative men are those, he says, "qui caelestibus intendunt, qui invisibilia Dei per speculum in aenigmate vident. Qui eopse speculativi dicti sunt, quia nonnisi per speculum et in aenigmate videre possunt" (who study heavenly things and are able to see the invisibilia of God through a mirror in enigma, because they cannot see except through a mirror and in enigma).[69] These are St. Augustine's men of faith. But those for whom Richard wrote his guidebooks were the contemplatives; those "quibus

[68] *De doctrina christiana* ii, 7, in *PL* xxxiv, 40; the translation is that of D. W. Robertson, Jr. *On Christian Doctrine* (New York, 1958), p. 40. It is interesting to observe that the young Augustine, having, as he tells us in the *Confessions*, begun to read certain Platonic books, espoused the Plotinian notion that good men could experience visions of God in this life. Indeed, both Book vii of the *Confessions* and the Cassiciacum Dialogues give evidence that Augustine had himself attempted a graduated ascent to vision not unlike that described by Richard nearly eight centuries later. Augustine later rejected his belief in the possibility of such visions in this life. See especially the *Retractationes I*, 19, 1. By 395 A.D., in his *Expositio epistolae ad Galatos*, Augustine had, according to Fr. Frederick Van Fleteren, "explicitly rejected the possibility of ultimate happiness through the vision of God in this life" (Paper delivered at the 1976 Medieval Institute). I am gratefully indebted to Fr. Van Fleteren for calling my attention to the very interesting question of Augustine's changing attitude toward visionary experience. See especially his essay, "Augustine's ascent of the Soul in Book vii of the *Confessions*: a Reconsideration," *Augustinian Studies* v (1974), pp. 29–72. See also P. Courcelle, *Recherches sur les Confessions de Saint Augustine* (Paris, 1950), pp. 157–174; A. Mandouze, *Saint Augustin: L'Aventure de la raison et de la grace* (Paris, 1968), pp. 688ff.

[69] *Adnotationes mysticae in Psalmos* cxiii, in *PL* cxcvi, 337.

datum est facie ad faciem videre, qui gloriam Domini revelata facie contemplando, veritatem sine involucro vident in sua simplicitate sine speculo et absque aenigmate" (those to whom it is given to see face to face, who, contemplating the glory of God when his face is unveiled, see truth without a covering in its simplicity without a mirror or enigma).[70]

In this raising of the mind beyond itself, the Abbot of St. Victor discovers the transformation of the spirit as it is translated into the heavenly regions:

> Magnitudine admirationis anima humana supra semetipsam ducitur, quando divino lumine irradiata, et in summae pulchritudinis admiratione suspensa, tam vehementi stupore concutitur, ut a suo statu funditus excutiatur, et in modum fulguris coruscantis, quanto profundius per despectum sui invisae pulchritudinis respectu, in ima dejicitur, tanto sublimius, tanto celerius per summorum desiderium reverberata, et super semetipsam rapta, in sublimia elevatur. Magnitudine jucunditatis et exultationis mens hominis a seipsa alienatur, quando intima illa internae suavitatis abundantia potata, immo plene inebriata, quid sit, quid fuerit, penitus obliviscitur, et in abalienationis excessum, tripudii sui nimietate traducitur, et in supermundanum quemdam affectum, sub quodam mirae felicitatis statu raptim transformatur.[71]

> (By the greatness of wonder, the human soul is led above itself, irradiated by divine light and suspended in wonder before the greatest beauty. So vehemently is it shaken by bewilderment that it is utterly torn from its foundation. The more it is cast to the depths in contempt of self by comparison with beauty—shaken by its desire for the highest things—so much the higher and faster will it be raised into the sublime and carried above itself like a lightning flash. With the greatness of its joy and exultation the mind of man is alienated from itself. Drunk with the inner abundance of interior sweetness—utterly inebriated—it completely forgets what is and what it has been. In an excess consisting in self-alienation, it is translated by the fervor of its dance, and in some supernatural feeling, in some state of wonderful happiness, it is suddenly transformed.)

Only superlatives and similes can convey Richard's sense of the soul's visionary dance. As he expresses it, the soul ascends like lightning into *sublimia*. In this heavenly "place," spirit itself is transformed. The result is a

---

[70] *Ibid.*   [71] *Benjamin Major* v, 5, in *PL* cxcvi, 174.

melting of the human soul into the Divine Presence in such a way that the soul becomes foreign to itself. Perhaps the most remarkable aspect of this description is Richard's close analysis of the spiritual tremors which mark the soul's passage beyond itself into the *summa*. His anxiety to delineate the soul's experience *as it passes* into the divine realm contrasts sharply with earlier monastic reluctance to allow, much less describe, affective states of ecstasy.

But what leads a spirit to have such visions? According to the doctor of St. Victor, there are a number of ways to "fashion" the soul in the "form of angelic likeness." Chief among them is simple aspiration accompanied by the practice of virtue, meditation and devotion. Yet the vision itself is a gift. Christ, finally is its cause. In a beautiful passage of *Benjamin Major*, Richard describes Christ's coming in vision to the prepared mind:

Dominum pascimus quando virtutum nostrarum victimis, ampliatoque arctioris vitae proposito, charitatis ejus in nos benevolentiam nutrimus, et accrescimus: *Ecce*, inquit, *pulso ad ostium; si quis aperuerit mihi, intrabo ad ipsum, et caenabo cum illo.* Cum Domino sane apud nosmetipsos comedimus, quando id ejus obsequio libenter impendimus, et in eo ejus beneplacito deservimus, unde illius in nos benevolentiam, unde nostram in ipsum fiduciam augeamus. Ex hac fiduciae accumulatione agitur, ut ad diu cupitam, multumque desideratam gratiam mens praeter spem et supra aestimationem subito animetur. Egredientem vero Dominum prosequimur, quando praeceptae divinitus intelligentiae diligenter insistentes, per id, quo de cognita divinitatis luce miramur, ad altiora contemplanda supra nosmetipsos levamur, et revelantis gratiae vestigiis inhaerentes pereuntem Dominum comitamur. Post egressum autem cum stante Domino stare, est in illo celsitudinis statu revelatae luci per contemplationem diutius inhaerere. Stanti Domino assistit, qui totum humanae mutabilitatis lubricum, ambiguitatisque incertum, alta mentis sublevatione transcendit, et in illo aeternitatis lumine defixus, inspectae imaginis in se similitudinem trahit. . . . In hac mentis sublevatione humana intelligentia saepe illam divinorum judiciorum abyssum ingreditur, et ad futurorum etiam, . . . praescientiam eruditur.[72]

(We feed the Lord when we nourish and increase the benevolence of his love toward us by the sacrifice of our virtues, having fully aimed at a stricter life. "Behold," he says, "I knock at the door; and whoever

[72] *Ben. Maj.* IV, 11, in *PL* CXCVI, 147–148.

opens it to me, I shall go in to him and sup with him." We truly eat with the Lord in our own house when we freely use those things at his good pleasure in which we may become worthy of his good will, whence we increase his favor toward us and our confidence in him. Through this multiplication of faith it comes about that the mind is suddenly enlivened to the long desired and much hoped for grace, beyond hope and above expectation. We truly escort the Lord in his going forth when we diligently tread the path of understanding divinely taught. Through that whereby we wonder at the known light of divinity, we are raised above ourselves to higher things, and we accompany the Lord's passing by the footprints left by his unveiling grace. But to stand with the standing Lord after his departure is to remain still longer in that state of heavenly, revealed light through contemplation. He who stands by the standing Lord transcends all the precariousness of human mutability and the uncertainty of ambiguity by his high exaltation of mind. Fixed on that light of eternity, he draws into himself the likeness of the image he perceives. . . . In this elevation of mind, the human understanding frequently enters into the abyss of divine judgments and is given even foreknowledge of future things.)

In luminous language, Richard describes the interpenetration of the soul with and through Christ. The soul's ecstatic state is for a "time" one of fixity; it rests beyond the flux and chaos of the fallen world. Thus protected, the visionary spirit assumes the divine perspective. It is able to look forward prophetically to its own and Everyman's eternal beatitude. Richard's lucidity, his tense certainty in representing the soul's pure "seeing," bespeaks a new era in spiritual thought and expression—one already suggested by the personalizing direction of twelfth-century Apocalypse commentaries, including his own. The soul, perfected by vision while still alive, may dwell in a spiritual world beyond the change and decay of the material universe. In such a condition, it must serve as a model for all those fallen spirits threatened by mammon on earth.

TWO

ANAGOGY, *AEVUM* AND TWO LATER MEDIEVAL VISIONARY ARTS

ANAGOGY AS A MODE OF EXPERIENCE

As Richard of St. Victor analyzes the cognitive nature of St. John's visions in his commentary on the Apocalypse, he offers a full definition of "anagogical" vision. This concept, which Richard drew both from the *Celestial Hierarchy* of Pseudo-Dionysius, and from Hugh of St. Victor's commentary on that extraordinary work, suggested specific new possibilities for visionary experience not only to saints and mystics in the evening of the world, but also to artists concerned with visions.[1] Abbot Suger would use it in describing his experience of the renovated Abbey of St.-Denis and Dante in shaping the *Commedia*. The newly developed meanings for anagogy helped spiritual writers, saints and artists to discover through symbolic forms, including the images of the Apocalypse, the highest states of bliss available to man in time.[2]

[1] The *Celestial Hierarchy*, which had been twice translated into Latin in the ninth century, and explicated by John Scotus Eriugena, enjoyed extraordinary popularity among twelfth-century spiritual writers. Most important, it provided them with a firm basis for positing a close relationship between material forms and divine ideas. It is not without significance that the royal abbey of St.-Denis was dedicated to Dionysius, "disciple of St. Paul," and the then supposed author of the *Celestial Hierarchy*.

[2] St. Francis of Assisi offers perhaps the clearest example of a saint whose life was represented as a symbolic form leading to visions "in an anagogical manner." Both his rule and the *Actus* (later translated into Italian as the *Fioretti*) outline the concrete historical means whereby an ordinary life may become a manifestation of divine presence. Over and over in the *Lives*, the *Actus*, and the *Fioretti*, Francis is blessed with symbolic vision as the result of an intense but simple attitude of prayer and spiritual attention. As the *poverello*, the "little poor man" of God, his physical form is to be seen as a symbol of God's particular goodness, and in his reception of the stigmata, his body is transformed into a living figure of Christ.

Traditionally anagogy had been defined as the fourth sense of sacred scripture, discoverable through exegesis. It is the eschatological sense, relating the *historia* or *litera* of scriptural texts to eternal glory. More generally, the anagogical sense raises the mind from the visible to the invisible, from things earthly to things heavenly, from the present to the future. It is the sense by which one is able to discover the realities of the heavenly Jerusalem in images of the earthly Jerusalem. Bede, for example, defines the traditional notion of anagogy simply and typically: "Anagogen, id est, sensum ad superiora ducentem, cupiebat videre decorem patriae coelestis domus, scilicet non manufactae, sed aeternae in coelis" (Anagogy, that is, the sense leading above whoever desired to see the beauty of the house of the heavenly fatherland not of course made by hands, but eternal in heaven).[3] But the term "anagogy" could also describe the immediate experience of the "heavenly homeland" and it is in this sense that Richard uses it. Though he quotes from Pseudo-Dionysius and borrows from his teacher, Hugh, he contributes his own close scrutiny of the various kinds of "seeing."

The mystical doctor of St. Victor begins his explication of St. John's revelation by asking how John "saw" the last things. He answers with a description of four-fold vision. At the first level one merely opens his eyes to the exterior visible world: "Visio namque prima corporalis est, quando oculos ad exteriora et visibilia aperimus, et coelum, et terram, figuras et colores rerum visibilium videmus" (The first "seeing" is corporeal, when we open our eyes to the exterior and the visible, and we see heaven and earth, the figures and colors of visible things).[4] But this kind of seeing, Richard tells us, is "infima et infirme" (low and weak). Being "angusta" (narrow) and "hebes" (sluggish), limited to the simple perception of matter, it fails to reach the "remota" (distant) or to penetrate the "occulta" (hidden). Hence, "nihil denique mysticae significationis continet" (it contains nothing of mystical significance).

There is a second kind of corporeal vision of a higher order which does admit of mystical meanings. It also begins with an outward appearance or physical action, but the object perceived contains within it "magna mysticae significationis virtus" (great power of mystical significance). Such for example was Moses' vision of the bramble bush which burned and was

---

[3] *In Hexameron* 1, 4, *PL* xci, 168; quoted by H. de Lubac, *Exégèse médiévale* (Paris, 1959), ii, p. 623. For a full discussion of the two meanings of "anagogy" and twelfth-century developments of the term, see de Lubac ii, chap. 10, pp. 621–643.

[4] *In Apocalypsim, Prologus, PL* cxcvi, 686.

not consumed. For Richard, this sight has extensive spiritual meaning to be discerned or read into the event:

Quid namque accipimus per flammam, nisi Spiritus sancti gratiam? Quid per rubum arborem parvulam, asperam, viridem, floridam, nisi beatam Mariam virginem. . . et Filio Dei carnem in virgine sumente, obumbrante Spiritus sancti gratia, pudor virginalis illaesus permansit.[5]

(For what do we understand by the flame but the grace of the Holy Spirit? What through the little bramble bush, rough, prickly, green, flowering, but the Blessed Virgin Mary. . . . And thus, when the Son of God assumed flesh in the Virgin, overshadowed by the grace of the Holy Spirit, her virginal modesty remained unharmed.)

Because corporeal visions like Moses' could be mere veils for spiritual significance for those who would see, Richard calls them "sublimior et excellentior . . . quam primus" (more sublime and excellent . . . than the first). "Primus a mysterio penitus vacat, secundus coelestis sacramenti virtute redundat" (The first is quite empty through and through of mystery while the second overflows with the power of the heavenly sacrament).

Richard's third and fourth modes of vision are spiritual rather than corporeal and it is these which put the soul in touch with its end. The third mode invites the "oculi cordis" (eyes of the heart) to discover "formis et figuris, et similitudinibus rerum" (by means of forms and figures and the similitudes of things) the "occultarum veritas" (truth of hidden things). In this third, figurative mode, in which both imagination and reason operate, St. John experienced his revelation. As Richard explains it, such images are necessary for our infirmity in order that the unknown might be learned from the known.

The final visionary mode, beyond that experienced by St. John, transcends all integuments. It is the pure and naked seeing of divine reality. This properly speaking is anagogical vision. Richard quotes Pseudo-Dionysius in order to differentiate between the third and fourth kinds of vision and he divides *anagogy* from *symbol* in the following way: "Symbolum est collectio formarum visibilium ad invisibilium demonstrationem. Anagoge, ascensio sive elevatio mentis ad superna contemplanda" (A symbol is a gathering [*collectio*] of visible forms for the demonstration of the invisible. Anagogy is the ascent or elevation of the mind for supernatural contemplation).[6] It is important to notice that Richard had no intention

---

[5] *Ibid.*   [6] *In Apocalypsim*, 687.

of excluding symbols and material forms from playing their part in leading to the purest contemplative experience of God. Rather, he wants to
distinguish the objects formed for spiritual edification (symbols) from the
act of the edified spirit.

Up to a point, Richard respects the limits of vision which earlier exegetes had imposed on St. John and other prophets. But he also sets all the
modes of human sight in analogical order because he wants to allow for
man's ability to "see" God's deepest secrets through the forms of his symbolic language. From St. John's figural revelation (or through it), he suggests, one may ascend by grace to a higher degree. Through and then
beyond all integuments the blessed soul may hope to find the blinding
glory of God "face to face."

AEVUM: THE ETERNAL TIME OF THE VISIONARY STATE

When Matthew Paris recounts a soldier's vision of the earthly paradise,
he uses the phrase *in aevum* as he describes the privileged spirit's delight:

> Unde miles tantam dulcedinis in corde simul et corpore sensit suavita-
> tem, quod vix intellexit utrum vivus an mortuus fuisset; sed hora illa
> in momento transivit. Ibi miles libenter in aevum maneret, si ibi his
> deliciis frui liceret.[7]

> (Whence the knight felt such charm of sweetness in his heart as well as
> his body that he hardly knew whether he was alive or dead. But that
> time passed in a moment. There the knight would willingly remain for
> a while if there he might be permitted to enjoy its delights.)

This same term, *aevum*, served schoolmen of the later twelfth and early
thirteenth centuries in a very different technical sense when they undertook to describe in a significantly full way the durative state of the soul
enjoying visionary experience.

St. Augustine had argued that no relationship exists between the state
of eternity and particular human time. Eternity is the fullness of being;
time, nonbeing. But although doctors of the new schools agreed with
Augustine that time *per se* constitutes nonbeing, they could not accept a
total separation of the two orders of existence. Such a division implied
equally a separation of the world of creatures from that of the Creator.
They, on the other hand, were seeking to explore ever more closely the

---

[7] *Chronica Majora*, ed. H. R. Luard (London, 1872–83), vol. II, p. 202.

ways in which man within time could participate in the experience of divinity. To provide a bridge between time and eternity, schoolmen advanced the term *aevum*, which had been loosely defined by the Fathers, and gave it a new exact definition.[8] *Aevum* came to signify that duration which participates at once in aspects of time and eternity. Though itself a state of unity, immobility and indivisibility—the vision of peace—*aevum* is accidentally related to time and can coexist with it. There can be no proportional analogy between time and eternity since time is successive and has an end, while eternity is complete in itself and admits no succession. Nevertheless a relationship was found to exist between the worlds of God and his creatures through this state of eternal time.

The term *aevum*, thus newly defined, could be used to describe three interrelated but distinct levels of durative experience. (1) Although God as pure essence is eternal, untouched by any shadow of time, his plan for the created world—his archetype—is not eternal but finite. It exists all at once, a whole image containing past, present and future. But it remains accidentally related to the succession of times in the created universe. Because it combines the wholeness of God's unity with the durative qualities of the created world, the archetype subsists in the state of *aevum*.[9] Ordinary human existence, then, imperfectly imitates this archetype, being itself essentially dependent on the succession of times. (2) *Aevum* can also be applied to the state of the angels. As pure spirits, they contain at once all the perfection of essence and existence, but they may also be subject, accidentally, to succession.[10] (3) Finally, and most importantly for us, *aevum* is used to describe the durative state of the human soul when, drawn out of the pure succession of events in earthly time, it is raised up to the realization of its own wholeness and perfection by coming into contact with the divine presence. Through ecstasy, through vision, through theophany, the soul may enjoy for a while the state of perfection and integrity always enjoyed by the angels.[11] In that state, midway between time and eternity, the questing spirit might in some way share God's vision for the whole of time. It could also discover itself in its own spiritual totality. In addition, because this visionary state put the soul in touch with God's archetypal plan for the universe, the information collected by the soul in

---

[8] *Dictionnaire de théologie catholique* [DTC] (Paris, 1913) v, i, 915. For a parallel discussion of *aevum* turned to different purpose, see E. Kantorowicz, *The King's Two Bodies* (Princeton, 1957), pp. 275–284.

[9] See Honorius of Autun, *De imagine mundi* ii, in *PL* cxlxxii, 145.

[10] *DTC* v, i, 914.　　　　[11] *Ibid.*

the state of angelic vision could be and was in fact weighed very carefully in understanding events in the imperfect world of ordinary time.

ART AND ANAGOGICAL VISION

Artists who entered into the newly formulated discussions of vision, anagogy and *aevum* with the materials of their art undertook to create symbolic forms capable of pointing souls toward the full ecstatic experience of God. One of the earliest such figures to articulate a theory of anagogical vision and apply it to his work was Abbot Suger, a contemporary of Richard of St. Victor.[12] For Suger, renovator of the Abbey of St.-Denis, the church building as an artifact was to be an inspired model of divine order and wholeness with power to lift observers into the heavenly realms.[13] This model, informed by human imagination and grace, could openly imitate divine reason—even participate in it—and thus lead the mind and heart by the details of its construction, to appreciate the spiritual work of the divine artificer.

Suger's theory of art was as revolutionary as his alterations of the royal abbey and was to have results as far-reaching and powerful.[14] When the choir of the great Abbey of St.-Denis had been completed, Suger wrote of his reaction:

[12] Erwin Panofsky calls particular attention to Suger's interest in anagogical experience and his application of Dionysian ideas to the design of St.-Denis in the introduction to his admirable translation of the *De administratione* and *De consecratione* (*Abbot Suger on the Abbey Church of St.-Denis*, ed., trans. and annotated by E. Panofsky [Princeton, 1946]).

[13] Thus when Suger describes his scheme for the renovation, he wittily envisions the physical structure in relation to the form of God, the Alpha and Omega, beginning and end: "I implore Divine mercy that He Who is the One, the beginning and the ending, Alpha and Omega, might join a good end to a good beginning by a safe middle (*Abbot Suger*, ed. Panofsky, p. 45). S. McK. Crosby has argued that Suger intended the crypt and choir to symbolize the structure of the universe ("Crypt and Choir Plans at St.-Denis," *Gesta* v [1966], pp. 4–8).

[14] See E. Mâle, "La Part de Suger dans la création de l'iconographie du moyen âge," *Révue de l'art ancien et moderne* xxxv, 1914; idem., *L'Art réligieux au XII*e *siècle* (Paris, 1953), pp. 380–382; W. S. Stoddard, *The West Portals of St.-Denis and Chartres* (Cambridge, Mass., 1952); idem., *Monastery and Cathedral in France* (Middletown, Conn., 1966); L. Grodecki, "La première sculpture gothique," *Bulletin monumentale*, 117 (1959), pp. 265–289; Otto von Simson, *The Gothic Cathedral*, 2nd ed. (Princeton, 1962).

Unde cum ex dilectione decoris domus Dei aliquando multicolor gemmarum speciositas ab extrinsecis me curis devocaret, sanctarum etiam diversitatem virtutum de materialibus ad immaterialia transferendo, honesta meditatio insistere persuaderet; videor videre me quasi sub aliqua extranea orbis terrarum plaga, quae nec tota sit in terrarum faece, nec tota in coeli puritate demorari, ab hac etiam inferiori ad illam superiorem anagogico more Deo donante posse transferri.[15]

(Whence, when the many-colored beauty of the gems had called me from external cares out of delight in the comeliness of God's house, and serious meditation had induced me to concentrate on transferring the variety of holy virtues from the material to the immaterial; then I seem to see myself as if dwelling on some foreign shore of the earth neither wholly in the slime of the earth nor wholly in the purity of heaven. By God's grace I seem to be able to be transported from this inferior world to that superior one in an anagogical manner.)

Here we find Suger describing himself as ascending to a quasi-temporal state of cognitive suspension between earth and heaven in which he can have the best of both worlds. He can enjoy the sensible beauty of human artistic creation and then, through it, he can rise to that higher world of the spirit "anagogically."

If we move from the twelfth to the fourteenth century, and turn from architecture to the poetry of vision, we find Dante (who places Richard of St. Victor in the paradisal sphere of the sun) likewise insisting on symbolic form as a means to spiritual vision. Dante has quite clearly absorbed the new affective mystical theology and can use the term "anagogy" both in its older traditional sense and in the experiential senses developed by his immediate predecessors. He applies both meanings to his poetry. In the *Convivio*, and in his famous letter to Can Grande, Dante defines "anagogical" as the fourth sense, the "suprasensible explication of the letter."[16] But in the *Commedia*, he invites his readers to experience the light of pure contemplation through his verbal form—and he makes his last teacher in the poem St. Bernard, the sublime example of the contemplative "affetto al suo piacer" (*Par.* xxxii, 1). The narrator himself

---

[15] *De administratione, PL* xciv, 1233–34; Panofsky, pp. 62–64.

[16] Epistole xiii, 20–22 in *Le Opere di Dante*, Testo Critico della Società Dantesca Italiana, ed. M. Barbi et al., 2nd ed. (Florence, 1960). All references to Dante will be to this edition.

finally realizes this affective, all-engrossing state of vision in which the senses are deprived of their normal function and the soul is totally absorbed (*Par.* xxx, 49–51):

> Così me circunfulse luce viva;
>   e lasciommi fasciato di tal velo
>   del suo fulgor, che nulla m'appariva.

> (Thus living light engulfed me
>   and left me so wrapt in the veil
>   of its brilliance that I could see nothing.)

In the midst of an ecstatic vision, Dante's pilgrim also recognizes his own highest perfection which both the master poet and Thomas Aquinas,[17] following Aristotle, define as the state of intellectual vision (*Par.* xxviii, 109–111):

> Quinci su può veder come si fonda
>   l'esser beato ne l'atto che vede,
>   non in quel ch'ama, che poscia seconda.

> (Whence one can see how the state of blessedness
>   is based in the act of seeing,
>   not of loving, which comes second.)

At last, in the final canto, the narrator of the *Commedia* is one with God's will, turning in that wheel which moves the sun and the other stars. Fully human, still mortal, still subject to time, the narrator has, at least for the duration of the *Commedia*, participated in a state of understanding analogous to that of the angels and saints in the heavenly court. He has arrived, that is, in the state of *aevum*.

Through retelling his vision as its reporter, the narrator also demonstrates how anagogical vision by way of symbolic form is possible for Everyman along the pilgrimage road of *nostra vita*. In his letter to Can Grande, Dante explained that through his poem (especially the *Paradiso* which is the particular subject of the letter) he wished to lead others along just the route delineated spiritually in the three cantiche; his central purpose, as he says in his letter, is to remove his audience from the world of bondage and sin to the kingdom of vision and light, to their

---

[17] See St. Thomas Aquinas, *Summa Theologiae*, ed. T. Gilbey, O. P. (New York and London, 1969), vol. xvi, 1ª11ᵃᵉ, Q. 3, v–viii and Q. 4, i–ii, pp. 73–95.

own freedom and perfection.[18] The whole poem then is to be studied and imitated as a guide to visionary experience realizable in this life. Readers, depending always on God's grace, may learn to share through the agency of poetic form and words the narrator's ecstatic realization of the "isplendor di Dio, per cu'io vidi/ l'alto triunfo del regno verace" (the splendor of God through whom I saw the high triumph of the true kingdom) (*Par.* xxx, 97–99).

Both for Suger and for Dante, art is to be a model, carefully detailed and proportioned, of divine presence and purpose. For the "seer" who perceives the art work properly, the form in its totality, like God's archetype for the universe, can "symbolize" eternal glory and lead souls to experience the joys of the heavenly Jerusalem. Although these two masters represent the highest reaches of creative genius in the later Middle Ages, they were not alone in the grand effort to symbolize the divine essence by shaping and transforming matter. Painters, architects, poets and saints throughout the Christian West made it their task to imitate the Divine Artificer in material forms, thereby attempting to approach the joy of heavenly blessedness. Their art was to be Richard of St. Victor's symbol or *collectio* of visibilia. Through symbolic representation, they might help their audience or their disciples rise to the state of pure contemplation as Suger had suggested, "in an anagogical manner."

The importance given to "anagogical" vision as it might be experienced near the end of this last age of sacred history both by artists and by spiritual writers like Joachim of Fiore and Richard of St. Victor was without doubt a major factor in shaping later medieval religious art. Whether represented in art or experienced in life, metaphors of vision like vision itself, provided a means through which the contemporary Christian (and his fictive surrogates), like the Old Testament prophets, or Mary at the Annunciation, or the disciples on the road to Emmaus—but now far more fully—might be brought into contact with God's presence. Art like prayer could lead to visions "in an anagogical manner," enlarging the pilgrim's personal sphere and making his life intelligible in the perspective of the divine plan. It could offer an environment neither temporal nor eternal—a half-way house in which ordinary events might be

---

[18] So earlier, Joachim of Fiore had used the Old Testament Exodus of the Jews from Egypt into the Promised Land as a model and metaphor for Everyman's pilgrimage from sin to salvation. See M. Reeves and B. Hirsch-Reich, *The Figurae of Joachim of Fiore* (Oxford, 1972), p. 1 and 1n.2.

seen anew in the light of eternity. By "seeing" models of the heavenly city within time and discovering the route thereto, souls could learn how their own lives might figure in the progressive historical course of human salvation. When Virgil invites the living Dante of the *Commedia* to penetrate the worlds of hell and heaven, the pilgrim's first response is to reject such an august voyage as having little to do with the ordinary fourteenth-century Christian: "Io non Enea, io non Paolo sono" (I am not Aeneas, I am not Paul) (*Inf.* II, 32). He cannot imagine that eternity might be part of his earthly experience. But, because of Beatrice, Dante undertakes the visionary journey while still in the body, reaching not only the third heaven, but the empyrean itself. In the course of his fictive pilgrimage he discovers how all his own time and his temporal experience derive grand meaning from the perspective of his vision. He also recognizes that his visionary experience is the essential means for discovering his own salvation. Within the scope of the *Commedia* as art, the metaphor of vision provides the means for transforming personal into sacred history.

Innumerable visions had been recorded in and out of art before the twelfth century. But usually the visionary had moved in spirit out of time into the world of eternal presence, and in the process had discovered no interaction between the two worlds, only difference. But after about 1100 most discussions of visionary experience, or representations of such experience in art—whether by monks, friars, clerks or laymen—suggest that time and eternity could fuse in vision, that when visions occurred within the framework of personal history they infused human time with new importance. Near the end of this last age, as later medieval art would demonstrate, vision could make individual lives shimmer with the light of divine meaning, and a visionary perspective could unite all of human history with God's plan for revealing himself to man.

Before turning to literary visions of the later Middle Ages, I want to explore briefly twelfth-century innovations in two major areas of the visual arts: the Gothic cathedral as it was conceived by Abbot Suger and developed at St.-Denis and Chartres and the illustrated Apocalypse in its twelfth- and thirteenth-century forms. In a study which is mainly literary, such a priority may appear misplaced. But I examine these two evidences of a new visionary art for two reasons: first, the alterations in traditional iconographical formulas in both these art forms demonstrate dramatically the ways in which artists both expressed and extended ideas to be found in contemporary spiritual writing; and second, as "popular" art forms, available to a lay as well as a clerical public, they teach us how fully the ideas and ideals of twelfth-century writers had been carried beyond the monasteries and schools into the centers of city and castle by the mid-thirteenth century. As such they provide a useful context for understanding similar impulses in the literary achievements considered in succeeding chapters.

ABBOT SUGER, ST.-DENIS AND CHARTRES

Twelfth-century artists were not the first to discover the power and usefulness of eschatological images for inspiring devotion. As early as the third century we can find depictions of figures from St. John's Apocalypse and the apocryphal vision of St. Paul. They appear in early Christian and early medieval art as well as in Romanesque painting and sculpture in the period immediately preceding the invention of Gothic visionary forms, and even simultaneously with them.[19] What is new in the twelfth century is an attitude, a new way of describing the time and space of visionary experience and a new emphasis. Attention is abruptly shifted away from the terrors of the eschaton—a central concern in early monastic literature and art—and toward systematic meditation on the beauty and peace of the heavenly city. Above all, the new art reflects the belief that visions of the heavenly city are possible and desirable for Everyman as an anticipation of eternal beatitude.

The Gothic Cathedral: Earthly Model of the New Jerusalem

For a short time the old and new spirit in cathedral art existed simultaneously in different parts of France. At Autun in Burgundy, the great cathedral of St.-Lazare was begun in 1120 and the sculptor, Gislebertus, was engaged to decorate the west façade and capitals.[20] Between 1130 and 1135 he produced one of the most famous tympana in France, a depiction of

---

[19] For summary histories of Apocalypse illustration, see M. R. James, *The Apocalypse in Art* (London, 1931), pp. 28ff.; W. Neuss, *Die Apokalypse des Heiligen Johannes in der Altspanischen und Altchristlichen Bibelillustration* (Münster, 1931), pp. 271ff. and "Apokalypse," in Otto Schmitt, *Reallexikon zur Deutschen Kunstgeschichte* vol. 1 (Stuttgart, 1937), col. 751–781; Louis Réau, *Iconographie de l'art chrétien* vol. 2, II (Paris, 1957), pp. 663–726; and Engelbert Kirschbaum, S. J., *Lexikon der Christlichen Ikonographie* vol. 1 (Vienna, 1968), pp. 123–135.

[20] For a full discussion of Gislebertus' achievement, see D. Grivot and G. Zarnecki, *Gislebertus, Sculptor of Autun*, 2nd (revised) ed. (New York, 1961). For the iconography and style of the tympanum, see especially pp. 25–56.

the Last Judgment (Fig. 2). Two elements are especially interesting in the Judgment scene: the characterization of Christ the Judge and the relationship drawn between Christ and the Church awaiting doom. Christ is shown as a stern administrator to placate. Around his mandorla are carved the words: "Omnia dispono solus meritos corono. Quos scelus exercet me iudice poena coercet" (I alone dispose all things; I alone reward the deserving. Those who sin, I judge and chastise). As glorified king, Christ in the center of the scene has little active relationship with the creatures around him. He exists in his own dynamic state, separate and apart. The action of judgment is carried out by the angels. Far smaller in size than the Christ figure, the apostles as well as the just and the damned adore, supplicate, or reject an all-powerful God. The human Church and the Christ-Judge belong to separate realms. Man sees Christ but is not united with him. For this iconographical scheme, Gislebertus turned not to St. John's revelation but to the gospels and the Old Testament. He placed emphasis on the limits of sinning man, struggling to attain heaven, judged sternly on his merits, saved only by the grace of a distant magnificent Deity.

Less than a decade later (1140) in the Ile-de-France—domain of the French monarchy—Abbot Suger had completed the "renovation and decoration of the entrance" (west façade) of the royal abbey of St.-Denis. The new west front together with the interior renovation directed by Suger amounted to a revolution.[21] The sculpture for the central tympanum of the west façade represents the Last Judgment as at Autun, but it posits an entirely different relationship between the contemporary Christian and his Judge (Fig. 3). The Christ of Judgment is also the Christ of Calvary. A cross forms the background for the heavenly throne.[22] Angels on either

[21] The precise nature of this revolution is still being examined. Extensive nineteenth-century restorations of the west front have complicated study of its original iconographic and stylistic features. S. McK. Crosby's promised monograph should bring us fuller knowledge of the original design. For work in progress, see S. McK. Crosby, "The West Portals of St.-Denis and the St.-Denis Style," *Gesta*, IX (1970), pp. 1–11; S. McK. Crosby and P. Z. Blum, "Le Portail central de la façade occidental de St.-Denis," *Bulletin monumental*, 131 (1973), pp. 209–266. For early pictures of the west façade, before its restoration, see Jules Formigé, *L'Abbaye Royale de St.-Denis* (Paris, 1960), pp. 78–79, figs. 65–67.

[22] Crosby has discovered that, before the restoration, the figure of Christ was marked by a wound under his breast, the cut of Longinus' sword. Nineteenth-century restorers mistook this gash for an accidental cut or mutilation of the surface. Scarcely visible today, the indention measures 7.25 cm. x 2 cm. (*Bulletin monumentale* [1973], p. 218).

side of the Savior hold the instruments of the passion, reminding the observer of his human history. At Christ's feet, Suger himself is represented, in a pose of supplication but also of filial confidence and adoration, above all, of participation in the experience of blessedness.[23] On his right hand, Christ invites the justified to enter the city; on his left, he condemns sinners to hell. But although the sinful suffer here as at Autun, the sense of awe and fear at a stern judge is replaced by emphasis on the grace given to mankind through the passion. The image of a human Christ as head of his Church receives additional emphasis in the archivolt above Christ's head: the Holy Spirit as a dove reigns above all, then John the Baptist holding the Agnus Dei, then the triumphant Christ of the Ascension.

The sculptor's intricate narrative conflation of Christ's earthly sojourn and founding of his Church with the Judgment scene allows him to show the Savior in a close rapport with the other figures in the tympanum. The apostles are drawn up next to the judging Lord apparently enjoying a heavenly conversation. On Christ's right and below, the souls of the just emerge from their tombs, on his left, the damned.[24] Prophets and kings of the Old Testament, the souls of the just and the damned, a tree of Jesse charting Christ's human lineage all articulate the *process* of sacred history moving toward salvation. The entire composition bespeaks the repose of a saved human race, marred, but not seriously so, by the necessary presence of the condemned souls who contribute to the ultimate glory of God by showing his justice.

To preach the intimate spiritual relationship between Calvary, the observer, and the Second Coming, and to draw the observer himself into the composition, Suger had gilded doors installed below the central tympanum. Eight medallions decorate the doors balancing the painful events

[23] Although this figure of Suger has been much restored, Crosby has shown that it follows the outline of the original (*Gesta*, IX [1970], pp. 4–5 and figs. 6–7). Suger's prayer seems to have been erased from the lintel, but is recorded in the *De administratione* (XXVII):

Receive, O stern Judge, the prayers of Thy Suger;
Grant that I be mercifully numbered among thy own sheep.
(*Abbot Suger*, ed. Panofsky, pp. 48–49)

[24] See Crosby, *Bulletin monumental* (1973), pp. 220–223 for a discussion of the original form of these sculptures in relation to their present condition. Both in the depiction of the apostles and of the souls, Crosby discovers the artist's respect for human anatomy, a true reflection of the novel attitudes which distinguish the new gothic style (220).

of Christ's life against scenes of his miraculous triumph. The Betrayal, the Scourging, the Carrying of the Cross and the Crucifixion are countered by the Burial and Resurrection, the appearance to the disciples on the way to Emmaus, and the Ascension (Fig. 4). Each scene in the series, meticulously conformed to a circular medallion, assumes an eternal aspect even as it portrays a significant historical moment. Above these doors, the observer will find a poem written by Suger which explains the use one should make of the artfully arranged scenes.[25] It is quite simply a call to "anagogical" vision to be achieved *through* history and art:

> Portarum quisquis attollere quaeris honorem,
> Aurum nec sumptus, operis mirare laborem.
> Nobile claret opus, sed opus quod nobile claret,
> Clarificet mentes ut eant per lumina vera
> Ad verum lumen, ubi Christus janua vera.
> Quale sit intus in his determinat aurea porta.
> Mens hebes ad verum per materialia surgit,
> Et demersa prius hac visa luce resurgit.[26]

> (Whoever seeks to bring honor to these doors,
> Wonder not at the gold nor the cost, but at the craftsmanship
>   of the work.
> The noble work shines, but the noble work which gleams
> Let it make minds so shine that they may pass through true lights
> To the true light where Christ is the true door.
> The golden door defines in these [forms] what is within.
> The dull mind rises up, through the material, to truth
> And sunk down before, now is raised up at the sight of this light.)

The skill of the artist shaping matter thus draws the mind to see through human creation, and the finest earthly materials, to Truth itself. It is important to notice that Suger confines this conception of art to a certain kind of making. Only that art work which models itself on sacred history and Christian mysteries can produce true vision. But the Abbot indicates that his own designs possess such power. The inscription above the doors suggests that the possibility of enjoying heavenly vision is open not only to souls emerging from their tombs on Judgment Day but also to the observer

---

[25] Panofsky gives a lucid close reading of this poem in the introduction to his translation (*Abbot Suger*, pp. 22–24).

[26] *De administratione*, xxvii, *PL* xciv, 1229; Panofsky, p. 189.

standing alive and in time in front of the abbey. As Otto von Simson has concluded:

> The last words make it clear that the representation of the resurrection of the dead in the tympanum above did not only have its usual eschatological meaning but was also to convey the illumination of the mind that passes from this world to the vision of God. Suger has tried to define as clearly as possible the "analogical" nature of beauty (its partaking of a mystical prototype) and the "anagogical" purpose of art (its ability to raise the mind to the perception of ultimate truth). The idea, happy, naive, ingenious, of choosing the portal for this initiation into the meaning of his art was typical of Suger. The inner disposition of those who entered his church was to change as they crossed the threshold.[27]

As we have seen, the artistically wrought doors and central tympanum designed by Suger had an explicit spiritual function: to help the soul to a state of vision like that of the blessed at the general resurrection. This vision, like St. John the Evangelist's, had been made possible by the Incarnation and Redemption. Through Christ, man was freed from sin. And through him, as well as his own sacramental purgation and the power of art, the contemporary sinner might rise to participation in the spiritual wholeness and purity represented through the material images. Like St. John's, his vision would be figurative and prophetic. He would understand not only the images but what they meant. The difference was, however, that John, a chosen apostle and saint, had received a canonical vision while alone in exile on the island of Patmos. Suger, on the other hand, was suggesting that such experiences were possible to Everyman and that art could inspire vision. He could hope that thousands of Frenchmen coming through the doors of the abbey would be raised in spirit to the presence of the triumphant Christ and would enter into conversation with the apostles and prophets as a foretaste of the eternal banquet to be enjoyed by the blessed after the Last Judgment.

It was not only the central portal of St.-Denis which presaged a new architectural age and introduced a new theory of art. Suger wanted the entire sculptural program, coordinated with the stained glass windows and the architectural form of the building, to edify the observer and lead him toward vision. Before he describes his renovations of the abbey in the *De consecratione ecclesiae S. Dionysii,* he set the theme for his *libellus;*

[27] *The Gothic Cathedral,* p. 115.

proportion and composition can link God's eternal reason with man aspiring to reach from earth to heaven.

> Divinorum humanorumque disparitatem unius et singularis, summaeque rationis vis admirabilis contemperando coaequat: et quae originis inferioritate, et naturae contrarietate invicem repugnare videntur, ipsa sola unius superioris moderatae harmoniae convenientia grata concopulat.[28]

> (The wonderful power of one unique and supreme reason equalizes the disparity between divine and human by due proportion. Only that same beloved symmetry of a single higher modulated harmony unites what seem mutually repugnant by inferiority of origin and contrariety of nature.)

In an age in love with schools and intellectual disputation, it is not surprising that Suger should find the highest beauty in the mind's rational meditations. Nor should we wonder at the confident leap in his treatise from the realm of human reason to art to the soul's participation *in aevo*. Similar efforts to fuse divine and human, eternal and perishable, visionary and temporal had occupied serious contemporary discourse particularly among commentators on the Apocalypse. To this grand endeavor Suger added a new mode of artistic expression. Through his own meditations on proportion "concerning the contraries" of spirit and matter, Suger tells us how he conceived a concrete artistic form which could perfectly imitate—even embody—the "glorious Knowing" by means of due proportion. Through the agency of such an art form properly perceived, the observing spirit could discover something more precise and personal than the vague platonic ideas. Through form and images, one could enter into affective participation in that definable heavenly state which was to be the reward of the blessed. In the prologue to his "little book," Suger poses the possibility for such an experience. He goes on to explain that he has devised an adequate visual form through God's direction. Finally he demonstrates by example how the observer may expect to read the art and react to it. Speaking first as designer, then as critic, he shows how a divine idea has been realized through the form and ornament of the renovated abbey, arguing that he himself has been merely God's instrument in its making.

[28] *Abbot Suger*, p. 82.

Chartres as Total Environment

Suger's effort to teach participation in the vision of heaven for men still on earth, and to bring together the eternal and temporal kingdoms through art and grace, was immediately accepted and developed by virtually all the master stonemasons of the Ile-de-France. At Chartres in particular we find a full flowering of Suger's ideas, to which a tight intellectual coherence has been added under the influence of the School of Chartres.[29] At Chartres, as at St.-Denis, the central tympanum of the west front is dominated by the Christ-Judge of the eschaton. Though there is no cross to serve as background, Christ's pose is that of teacher as well as judge, his right hand raised in blessing, his left hand on the book with seven seals. He is surrounded by the symbols of the four evangelists while below him sit the twelve apostles. As at St.-Denis, the eschatological scene is not presented in isolation, but is made the culmination of salvation history represented in lucid order on the tympana of the other two portals, the columnar statues, the capital friezes and the archivolts.

To the observer's left, as he faces the great west façade of Chartres, is the portal of the Ascension, reminding him of the triumphant human Christ. Around this image of Christ's victory, the signs of the zodiac show how human time derives its form and meaning from Christ's resurrection, ascension and promise to come again. To the onlooker's right is the Virgin's portal, dominated by the image of Mary in heaven as the glorious Mother of God. Below her, scenes from sacred history depict the nativity, the annunciation of Christ's birth to the shepherds in the lower lintel, then, above, Christ's presentation in the temple. Around this panorama of human triumph and Christian salvation the seven liberal arts sit poised and busy. Here the design emphasizes the relationship by subordination of all human intellectual activity to the miraculous coming of Christ through Mary. Reading upward from the lower lintel to the central image of the

---

[29] Work on the west front of Chartres was completed not long after the dedication of St.-Denis–about 1155. See L. Grodecki, *Chartres* (Paris, 1963), p. 26. See also O. Von Simson, *The Gothic Cathedral*, for a full and illuminating study of the theory of anagogical vision and its application at St.-Denis and Chartres. For a thorough description of Chartres' Royal Portal, with plates, see A. Katzenellenbogen, *The Sculptural Programs of Chartres Cathedral* (Baltimore, 1959), pp. 7–49. Katzenellenbogen discusses briefly the nature of the innovation at St.-Denis and Chartres in relation to earlier sculptural programs as well as the advance of Chartres over St.-Denis (pp. 3–6).

glorified virgin, observers (as well as the sculptured exponents of the liberal arts) discover the major and saving importance of theophany—the simple, joyful revelation of Christ's presence in, for, and through the world. The annunciation, the visitation, the angelic song of the shepherds, Simeon's grace-filled recognition of the child on the altar, comprise a limpid anagogical narrative series, leading the observer through history toward a glimpse of Mary's majestic human presence as queen of heaven.[30]

To emphasize the centrality of Christ's temporal existence, a series of capital friezes depicts successively the events of his earthly history, stretching across the whole width of the west façade. As a sub-structure and historical foundation for this full sculptured narrative of Christ's life, death and triumphant ascension, Old Testament prefigurations appear in the lowest part of the program: dignified columnar statues flanking the doors depict the kings, queens and priests who typified Christ and Mary before their coming.

Binding the entire narrative program into a unity and shaping all its details is the theme of God's evolving, temporally based covenant with man. Successive revelations are represented as the chief means by which men have been brought through time progressively closer to the last vision of the Apocalypse. Christ's coming both historical and eucharistic expresses the highest reach of the covenant, the sacramental link between man and God. The stories of the Last Supper and the disciples of Emmaus at supper with Jesus, the altarlike form of the manager and of the table of Christ's presentation in the temple all point toward the Real Presence of the Eucharistic Christ as Everyman's contemporary link with the Second Coming.

For the observer, the movement of the sculptural program of the west front is both horizontal and vertical, temporal and omnitemporal. The stories of the Old and New Testaments are told in *linear* form, moving across the façade as history. But the viewer's eye also moves upward from the types and figures of Christ, King and Priest, and Mary, Queen of Heaven, to the account of their presence in the world, and then to the events which bring humanity into conjunction with divinity: the heavenly motherhood of Mary, the triumphant ascent of the incarnate Christ to heaven, and the Last Judgment with the resurrection of the dead. Here, as at St.-Denis, the sculptural program traces the whole course of sacred

---

[30] Hugh of St. Victor thus defines "anagogical narration": Cum . . . quod occultum est, vel quod manifestum est . . . pura et nuda revelatione ostenditur, vel plana et aperta narratione docetur, anagogica [demonstratio est]. *PL* CLXXV, 941.

history in order to teach that God's progressive revelation to mankind is both radically historical and visionary. But what is most important, the contemporary Christian has his place in this temporally-based revelation. It is vividly defined in his assumed ability to *understand* all the figures of sacred scripture bound together by the art of the cathedral and to participate spiritually in the grand human procession toward universal salvation.

The north and south porches at Chartres, added in the early thirteenth century, encourage the observer in continued encyclopedic meditation on historical and anagogical themes. Again Christ's coming, his earthly history and his continuing presence in the Eucharist receive central emphasis. The north porch presents Old Testament prefigurations of Christ's priestly and sacrificial roles leading to his incarnation through Mary. The central tympanum celebrates the saving outcome of these prefigurations for the human race: Mary's assumption into heaven and her coronation as the first human being to enter heaven body and soul. Balancing the narrative of the north, the south porch depicts the life of the Church, beginning with Christ the teacher and his apostles, and culminating, like the programs of the west front, in a Judgment scene. Christ is now of equal size with the figures of St. John and Mary on either side of him as he raises his arms to judge the living and the dead. Here he demonstrates a calm benevolence, offering the observer a divinely human perspective.

One of the most remarkable effects achieved by the designers of Chartres is the coordination of the exterior sculpture with the stained glass windows and the interior structure, giving the entire edifice an elegant physical and thematic unity. The observer is led to experience not only the progress of sacred history, but also a harmony and interplay between Old and New Testaments and contemporary life. Over and over, through several media, he is struck by correspondences, repetitions and variations. The minor sculpture on columns offers moral instruction in the virtues and vices, in the fall of man and its consequences. But these moral images must be understood now within the larger spiritual scheme of Christ's saving grace and the promise of his return. By representing the revelation of God from its historical beginnings to its conclusion on the cathedral façades and in the stained glass windows, and by emphasizing Christ's Eucharistic presence, the master craftsmen of Chartres provided an exemplary figural edifice on which to pattern the renovation of the late-medieval soul—a renovation which ideally must lead to the *visio pacis*. The Christian, meditating on the artful images, could move from the history of the Old

Testament to its allegorical realization in the coming of Christ humble
and hidden. Having studied the story of the redemption, he could then
perceive Christ drawing the pentecostal Church to himself through his
sacraments. Finally he is brought to focus on the Second Coming and the
Last Judgment which promise him the eternal vision of God. Though this
ultimate joy would be realized only at the end of the world, the soul might
ascend even before that time "in an anagogical manner" to contemplate
the heavenly Jerusalem, moving from the program of images to the spiritual realities for which they stood. All of the materials of the cathedral—
stone, metal, glass, gems—are designed to lift the spirit into that realm
of pure light and beauty figuratively described by St. John. It is clear from
Abbot Suger's account of his church and Chartres' development of his
ideas, that such temporally modulated edification, leading to anagogical
vision, was the ideal purpose of the sculptural program, as well as the
architectural structure and stained glass windows. But the cathedral itself
is still only a building, a work of art. The spiritual edification which it is
to effect requires the concerted effort of the observer meditating on the
images and relationships among the parts of the artistic model.

Later Medieval Revisions of the Illustrated Apocalypse

Another major art form which elegantly and decisively articulates new
attitudes toward vision, sacred history and the images of Revelation is the
later medieval illustrated Apocalypse.[31] As we have already seen, twelfth-
and early thirteenth-century commentators had significantly revised earlier
monastic interpretations of the Book of Revelation. Writers including
Richard of St. Victor, Joachim of Fiore, and Alexander of Bremen attended far more closely than had their forebears to St. John's cognitive
responses to his visions, even suggesting that the reader might share the

---

[31] L. Delisle, who first classified these manuscripts, found fifty-seven extant examples of the illustrated Apocalypse dating from the thirteenth and fourteenth centuries, which he divided into two families (L. Delisle and P. Meyer, *L'Apocalypse en
français au XIIIe siècle* [Paris, 1901], pp. ii–v and lx–cxlv). Subsequently, M. R.
James extended their list to ninety-two manuscripts of the thirteenth, fourteenth and
fifteenth centuries (*Apocalypse in Art*, pp. 28–44). Since Delisle's classification of
the manuscripts into families, there have been two major efforts at reclassification:
R. Freyhan, "Joachism and the English Apocalypse," *Journal of the Warburg and
Courtauld Institutes*, 18 (1955), pp. 211-244; and G. Henderson, "Studies in English
Manuscript Illumination" II, *Journal of the Warburg and Courtauld Institutes*, 30
(1967), pp. 104-136. See below, pp. 68–83.

visionary's privileged experience; they insisted on the importance of the
literal narrative, stressing the temporal order of the apocalyptic figures
and showing their bearing on the Church's progressive movement toward
the eschaton. In a strikingly parallel way, twelfth- and thirteenth-century
artists illustrating the Book of Revelation undertook temporalized and
personalized transformations of older monastic iconographic formulas.
The new designs reflect a faith that the sacred images of the Apocalypse
could render an imaginative glimpse of the Last Things through their
visible splendor. The apocalyptic figures could be studied not only as a
revelation of the omnitemporal conflict between good and evil, but also
as an historical prophecy describing in succession all the times of the
earthly church—and in particular those climactic last times to which the
contemporary Christian might conceivably be a witness in his own lifetime.

Most importantly, St. John as visionary scribe assumes unprecedented
importance in twelfth- and thirteenth-century book illumination. No longer the static or accidental figure he had been in earlier medieval illustrations, he is drawn into a close narrative relationship with his revelation,
acting as an intermediary between the events of his visions and contemporary readers, guiding their responses by his example. We find one of the
first surviving evidences of new epistemological, narrative and historical
interests in an early twelfth-century German picture cycle.[32] The illustrations in this cycle have a startling freshness about them not unlike the innovations at St.-Denis, heralding a new spirit in the midst of Romanesque
contemporaries. With one foot in an old world, the other in a new, the
artist undertakes to develop a personal and historical framework for the
apocalyptic figures. In his novel manner of portraying St. John, he announces a fresh attitude toward the visionary scribe, one which could be
found almost simultaneously in Richard of St. Victor's commentary on the
Apocalypse, and which predicts major thirteenth-century artistic developments. As with the history of Apocalypse commentaries, we can best approach the specific character of the newly designed twelfth- and thirteenth-

---

[32] Two twelfth-century picture cycles provide evidence of developments in Apocalypse illustration leading to the thirteenth-century Anglo-Norman Apocalypses. Of
these, the better known but less innovative is to be found in Lambert of St.-Omer's
Liber Floridus (Wolfenbüttel, Hertzog August Bibl. Cod. Gud. lat. 1.2). The other
is a full series of illustrations for an abbreviated text of Revelation introducing a
copy of Haimo of Auxerre's commentary on the Apocalypse now in the Bodleian
Library (ms. Bodley 352). See below, pp. 65–67.

century picture cycles for Revelation by examining their earlier medieval forebears.[33]

The Earlier Medieval Illustrated Apocalypse

The earliest recorded cycle of illustrations for the Apocalypse to penetrate northern Europe was the series of "imagines" Benedict Biscop brought from Rome (or southern Gaul) in 674 to use as models for decorating his church at Wearmouth.[34] In Bede's account of Benedict's treasures, one notes the abbot's elation in transporting something of Roman culture to that northern outpost, but more importantly, his expectations for their function among his people. According to Bede, Benedict's pictures—including not only images of the Apocalypse but also of Christ, Mary and the twelve apostles—were intended for the lettered and unlettered alike in order that they might better contemplate the "amabilem . . . aspectum" of Christ's blessed and recollect the grace of the Incarnation with greater care. When they studied the scenes of the Last Judgment "as if it were

[33] The subject is a most complex one, requiring close study of sources, lines of filiation as well as of difference in the two main traditions of picture cycles—those emanating from provincial workshops in the Carolingian empire and those originally devised in northern Spain to accompany the commentary of the eighth-century Asturian monk, Beatus of Liebana (see below, pp. 61–64). For pioneering efforts to approach this problem, see T. Frimmel, *Die Apokalypse in den Bilderhandschriften des Mittelalters* (Vienna, 1885), and W. Neuss, *Apokalypse*. See also D. Miner, Review of Neuss, *Apokalypse*, *Art Bulletin*, 15 (1933), pp. 388–391, and reply by Neuss, p. 393; M. Shapiro, "From Mozarabic to Romanesque in Silos," *Art Bulletin*, 21 (1939), pp. 313–374; and O. K. Werckmeister, "Pain and Death in the Beatus of St.-Sever," *Studi Medievali*, ser. 3, 14 (1973), pp. 565–626.

[34] Just what form these "imagines" took is open to question. T. Frimmel suggested that Benedict brought an illustrated Apocalypse from Rome to England (*Apokalypse*, pp. 8–9). Subsequently, M. R. James, following E. Müntz (*Études sur l'histoire de la peinture et de l'iconographie chrétiennes*), proposed that they were "paintings on boards, ready-made" (*Trinity College Apocalypse*, London, 1909, p. 2). A. Goldschmidt argued that Benedict received an illustrated Apocalypse in Vienne where he would have stopped on his way from Rome to Wearmouth. Goldschmidt believed that this book may have been the model not only for the paintings in Benedict's church, but also for a Carolingian illustrated Apocalypse still extant—Paris, B.N. MS. n.a. lat. 1132 (*An Early Manuscript of the Aesop Fables of Avianus* [Princeton, 1947], pp. 33–35). A less convincing argument is made by F. v. Juraschek, who proposes that the scenes at St. Peter's, Wearmouth, depicted only figures of joy and adoration like those to be found in fifth-century churches in Rome and Ravenna ("Sinndeutende Kompositionsweise der Illustrationen zur Apocalypse im Fruhmittelalter," in *Arte del Primo Millenio*, 1951, p. 192).

before their eyes," they were to remember to judge themselves more diligently.[35] These figures, like the images of Revelation according to Bede's exposition, were to lead the viewer from specific images to their universal spiritual and moral significance. By contemplating them, he would be able to recall timeless invisibilia—the spiritual joy of the blessed, the grace of the Incarnation, and his own and Everyman's sinfulness.

The decorations for Benedict's church have been lost. But we may surmise something of their character not only from Bede's account, but also from two later Carolingian picture cycles which may have derived from late Latin illustrations not unlike the ones Benedict brought to Wearmouth.[36] These two cycles, represented by manuscripts at Trier and Cambrai on the one hand, and Valenciennes and Paris on the other, are markedly different from each other in several respects.[37] Nevertheless they express common attitudes toward the images of Revelation which accord well with Benedict Biscop's didactic expectations. Both cycles have been described as "degenerate," "rude," and "infantine" with good reason.[38] What most strikes the reader at first is the simplicity and relative crudeness of the drawing. There is no doubt that all four manuscripts represent the work not of the court but of provincial workshops, perhaps in northeastern France, and one is tempted to characterize their artists as servile,

[35] *Vita sanctorum abbatum monasterii Wiramutha et Girvum, PL* xcIV, 718. I am indebted to the kindness of Paul Meyvaert for pointing out other instances of Bede's moral attitude toward pictures. See esp. *PL* xcIII, 458–459.

[36] See note 34 above and Frimmel, *Apokalypse*, p. 18.

[37] Trier, Stadtbibliothek ms. 31; Cambrai, Bibliothèque Municipale, ms. 386; Paris, B.N., ms. n.a. lat. 1132; and Valenciennes, Bibliothèque Municipale ms. 99. The Trier and Cambrai manuscripts are closely related to each other: either Cambrai was copied from Trier or both depended on the same prototype. B.N. ms. n.a. lat. 1132 and Valenciennes ms. 99 derive from a common prototype and anticipate a later and much finer manuscript of the same family, the Bamberg Apocalypse (Bamberg, Staatsbibliothek, ms. 140), c. 1000. (For facsimile reproduction of Bamberg, see H. Wölfflin, *Die Bamberger Apokalypse*, Munich, 1921). The Trier Apocalypse is a ninth-century manuscript, the other three, late ninth- or early tenth-century productions. For descriptions of Cambrai, Valenciennes and Paris, see H. Omont, "Manuscrits illustrées de l'Apocalypse aux IXe and Xe siècles," *Bulletin de la Société française de réproductions de manuscrits à peintures* (Paris, 1922), pp. 64–95 and plates xIV–xxxII. For a description of Trier, see M. R. James, *The Apocalypse in Art*, pp. 83–92. The Trier Apocalypse has been reproduced in full: *Die Trierer Apokalypse, Codices Selecti* vol. xLVIII, Graz, 1974.

[38] James, *Apocalypse in Art*, p. 37. But for a more favorable assessment, see F. van der Meer, *Maiestas Domini* (Rome, 1938), pp. 282–288.

uncomprehending copyists and conservators, preserving as best they could fragments and shadows of the early Christian tradition.[39] Yet a closer inspection reveals that these "copyists," like contemporary exegetes, may have reshaped inherited materials to emphasize particular thematic concerns and at the same time to define distinctively Carolingian attitudes toward the imagery and the *storia* of the Book of Revelation.

The process of reshaping is most apparent in the illustrations of the Trier-Cambrai cycle. Here, as James Snyder has argued, the artist's source material was probably an early Christian cycle, perhaps of the sixth century, in which the illustrations, arranged in wide margins along double columns of script, provided a running commentary for the text.[40] The Carolingian illuminator rejected this arrangement and with it a close, fluid integration of figures and text. Instead, he removed the illustrations from their immediate verbal context, translating them into complex, full-page compositions, often drawing several narrative episodes into a single picture. The result is a severing of the originally intimate interplay between text and picture, occasionally in an "impromptu" and "arbitrary" manner, and in more than one case, a distortion of the reading sequence.[41] Another feature of the Trier illustrations which Snyder has also observed

[39] The locus of production for these manuscripts has been much discussed. Most recently, Porcher has argued persuasively that, in the lively exchange of influence between Salzbourg and northern Gaul in the ninth century, manuscripts would have been carried back and forth to be copied. He suggests that this would account for the presence of Italo-Alpine together with British traits in three of the four manuscripts—Trier, Cambrai and Valenciennes (J. Hubert, J. Porcher, W. F. Volbach, *L'Empire Carolingien* [Paris, 1968], p. 181). One of these manuscripts, Valenciennes, is certainly from the abbey of St.-Amand in northeastern France while Cambrai is recorded in Cambrai Cathedral's inventory as early as the tenth century, and Trier, in the inventory of the church of St. Eucharius, Trier, in the twelfth century. It is tempting to imagine that twelfth-century Anglo-Norman or German precursors of the thirteenth-century illustrators found one or more of these easily accessible manuscripts a suitable foundation for their own development of the picture cycle.

[40] "The Reconstruction of an Early Christian Cycle of Illustrations for the Book of Revelation—the Trier Apocalypse," *Vigiliae Christianae*, 18 (1964), pp. 153–154. Frimmel had much earlier proposed that a sixth-century Italian illustrated Apocalypse must have served as the model for Trier (*Apokalypse*, p. 12). For an example of this columnar arrangement, preserved in an eleventh-century Catalan Bible (B.N. MS. lat. 6), see W. Neuss, *Die Katalanische Bibelillustration um die Wende des Ersten Jahrtausend* (Bonn and Leipzig, 1922), figs. 173–183.

[41] Snyder, pp. 149–150. Snyder points out that the illustration of the four horsemen shows a reversal of the order of the horses so that the Pale Horse, sent out last by the Lamb, appears to be the first in the Trier design (Snyder, p. 150 and fig. 2).

is the artist's habit of using "fillers" or repeated images folio after folio, a device which, Snyder suggests, the artist employed to avoid empty spaces in his illustrations.[42]

But if, in addition to recognizing the Trier-Cambrai cycle as a "degenerate" copy of a "stately original,"[43] we place it in its Carolingian context, we can better understand its iconographical design, though we will have no better cause to praise its style. The Trier illustrator who transformed his Roman model was not so much concerned with the details of the sacred *litera* of the Apocalypse as with clarifying its general directions and themes. If his representations of narrative detail are noticeably careless, he attends faithfully to those repeated figures which Snyder has labeled his "fillers." Almost every one of the seventy-four scenes of Trier includes one or more from a group of key images—John, static and motionless, staring out at the audience as a presence; Christ, either in full or half-figure, or merely his hand, directing St. John with a gesture; the seven trumpeting angels represented as a unit, the seven angels with their vials, the Lamb and the One Enthroned.[44] The artist may have been merely filling his pages with these repeated figures. But it is perhaps more likely that he, like Alcuin and Haimo, intended a few symbolic images, iterated over and over, to provide a significant meaning-pattern in a way the narrative details—the often bizarre, visionary *historia* of Revelation—could not. John, standing in the presence of his visions, gazing outward, would then represent all the faithful omnitemporally desiring the *visio pacis*, as contemporary commentators had suggested. Similarly, all the images of divine presence—Christ, the Lamb, the trumpeting and vial-pouring angels, the One Enthroned—could be translated finally into a composite representation of the eternal forces for good conquering whatever evils might present themselves either in the illustrated page or in the world from the beginning to the end of time.

Certainly we should not conclude that the illustrator of Trier had Alcuin or Haimo at his elbow as he worked. Yet, there is a curious coincidence between the attitudes of Carolingian commentators and those of the Trier artist. Most important, both sternly subordinate the narrative process of John's vision, so vividly described in the text to the "intellectual," universal content discernible in discrete images. For Alcuin and Haimo, the vision contains "nothing historical"; for the Trier illuminator, the narrative details are dominated by the constant, repeated figures of

---

[42] *Snyder*, p. 150.   [43] James, *Apocalypse in Art*, p. 37.
[44] See *Die Trierer Apokalypse, Cod. Selecti* XLVIII, fol. 1 ff.

eternal presence and purpose. The very carelessness in his representations of specific narrative action—his ability to superimpose scene upon scene with little attention to temporal or spatial relationships—has the effect, and perhaps an intended one, of drawing the viewer's attention away from the concrete, intricately related image clusters of the sacred text and toward universal meanings to be gleaned from figures separated from the narrative.

The second Carolingian cycle of illustrations for the Apocalypse, represented by manuscripts at Valenciennes and Paris, and apparently based on different models, is likewise abstract and symbolic in its emphasis. The designs for the full-page illustrations of Valenciennes, in particular—more carefully and sparely organized though no better drawn than Trier—tend to be schematic and geometric. The artist represents discrete images drawn from the text, charting a simple mnemonic path through the complex narrative.[45] As in Trier, John acts as a presence signifying constancy, gazing out from the page. Only the representations of demonic power—fanciful coiled and scaled serpents and dragons—seem to have delighted the artist's imagination even as they provided a pointed lesson concerning the strength and energy of the devil.

Both in its symbolic interests, and in its emphasis on the awesome vigor of demonic forces, Valenciennes parallels the much finer, more consciously stylized achievements of the Spanish artists who devised a picture cycle to accompany the commentary of the eighth-century monk, Beatus of Liebana. Although there are significant stylistic differences separating one Beatus cycle from another during a long and rich history from the tenth until the thirteenth century, certain elements of iconographic design and general purpose remain constant.[46] Far more sophisticated than their Carolingian counterparts both as artists and theologians, even the earliest of the illustrators had studied Beatus's long, scholarly exposition on the Apocalypse and had scrupulously followed its allegorizing, universalizing directions. Conforming themselves closely to Beatus's themes, tone and

---

[45] See Omont, pp. 73–84 and pls. XIV–XXXII; F. v. Juraschek, *Die Apokalypse von Valenciennes*, Linz, a.d., Donau, n.d.

[46] For a description and classification of the Beatus Apocalypses, see W. Neuss, *Apokalypse*, pp. 5–61, and "Die Illustrationen der Handschrift von Gerona im Lichte der übrigen Beatus-Illustrationen," in J. Marques Casanovas, C. Dubler, W. Neuss, *S. Beati a Liebana in Apocalipsin Codex Gerundensis* (Olten and Lausanne, 1962), pp. 44–63. See also O. K. Werckmeister (*Studi Medievali*, 14, pp. 565–626) for a suggested revision of Neuss's classification.

substance, they had provided illustrations not only for the text of Revelation, but also for the commentary. The Spanish artists may have been influenced by models similar to those used by the artists of Trier and Valenciennes. But they infused them with new purpose and significance, both in their stylistic transformations and in their careful arrangement of the pictures within the text.[47]

The Beatus commentary itself is a long, scholarly compilation, based, as the author says, on the authority of the Fathers, and intended to make their learning available in brief, easily memorable form.[48] Like the Carolingian commentators, Beatus is deeply indebted to Tychonius whose rules for allegorizing the sacred text he follows scrupulously.[49] Even more than Bede or Alcuin, Beatus takes pains to translate the specific images of Revelation into their general, omnitemporal meaning. Whatever particular significance the individual images might have, their universal import is greater. Indeed, Beatus says, John "miscet . . . tempus nunc praesens, nunc futurum . . . numquam enim separat praesens tempus a novissimo, quo revelabitur antichristus, quia quod tunc visibiliter fit, nunc invisibiliter in ecclesia geritur" (confuses . . . time, now present, now future . . . he never separates the present time from the last in which Antichrist will be revealed, because what will then be visible is now invisibly carried on in the Church).[50] Above all, Beatus uses the sacred text as a point of departure for high theological discourse. With the care of an apologist for an awesome deity, he probes the images of the Apocalypse always with the

[47] Frimmel surmised that Beatus himself had overseen the production of illustrations for his commentary and that the prototype for these must have been a late Latin picture cycle (*Apokalypse*, pp. 40–41). W. Neuss agreed with him (*Apokalypse*, p. 237) and added that this prototype might well have had African elements (p. 241). In her review of Neuss's book, D. Miner confirmed the opinions of Frimmel and Neuss concerning the late Latin model, but, perhaps because of a misreading, opposed Neuss's supposition of African influence. O. K. Werckmeister has lately addressed himself to the problem in his study of the Apocalypse of St.-Sever (*Studi Medievali*, 14, p. 197) but the question of the sources and stylistic developments in the Beatus manuscripts remains to be fully studied.

[48] The Beatus commentary has been edited by H. A. Sanders, *Beati in Apocalypsin* (Rome, 1930).

[49] Of all the commentaries indebted to Tychonius, Beatus most fully depended on him and transmits him most faithfully. See H. L. Ramsay, "Le Commentaire de l'Apocalypse par Beatus de Libana," *Révue d'histoire et de littératures réligieuses*, 7 (1902), pp. 419–447; Sanders, pp. xix–xx; F. Lo Bue, ed., *The Turin Fragments of Tyconius' Commentary on Revelation* (Cambridge, 1963).

[50] Sanders, p. 17.

intention of demonstrating the incomparable glory of God and his Divine Son and indirectly refuting once again the Adoptionist heresy.[51]

In this context, St. John the visionary plays a minor role, distanced, like Everyman, from the awesome grandeur of the Apocalyptic Lord. Representing the whole Church when he falls down before the Lord at the beginning of his vision, St. John is, according to Beatus, "terrified by the trembling fear of his fragility, humility and subjection."[52]

Pondering his own role as glossator, Beatus is likewise most keenly aware of his "humana fragilitas." Like St. John, he cannot hope to understand the mysteries and secrets of God even in part unless he receives the grace of the Holy Spirit. For "vere minime intellegimus, quasi in tenebris palpebras Domini clausas habemus, et nisi spiritus sanctus intus sit, qui doceat, doctoris lingua in vacuum laboret" (truly we understand very little, as if we have our eyes closed in darkness of the Lord and unless the Holy Spirit who teaches is within, the tongues of doctors labor in vain).[53] Before beginning his own contemplative labors, Beatus invokes the Spirit. Then, under divine guidance, he proceeds to delineate the "allegoria" of the sacred images, that is, the "significantia cuiuscumque rei, ut aliud sonet in verbis, aliud intellegas in mysteriis, id est, in secretis et spiritualibus" (the significance of the matter whereby one thing may be expressed in words, and you may understand something else in mysteries, that is, in secrets and spiritual senses).[54] Over and over Beatus reminds his readers of the excessive small-mindedness of man who must divide all his notions of divine matters into genus and species. In awe he refers them to God's arcane beauty, only dimly revealed in the scriptural figures, to the abstract splendor of his majesty, and to the inadequacy of the human idiom to penetrate his mysteries.

The artists who illustrated the Beatus Apocalypses shared the eighth-century commentator's awe in the face of God's mysteries even as they sought to celebrate with him Christ's glorious victory over Satan. Most of the Beatus Apocalypses begin with prefatory illustrations of triumph: the cross of Oviedo as a sign both of power and warning; the dramatic image of the eagle conquering the serpent, emblem of Christ's triumph over the devil; and the figure of the apocalyptic Lord as Alpha and Omega, begin-

---

[51] For a succint description of the Adoptionist heresy, see Casanovas, "Beatus of Liebana," in *Codex Gerundensis*, pp. 31–37.

[52] Sanders, p. 82.   [53] Sanders, p. 73.   [54] Sanders, p. 90.

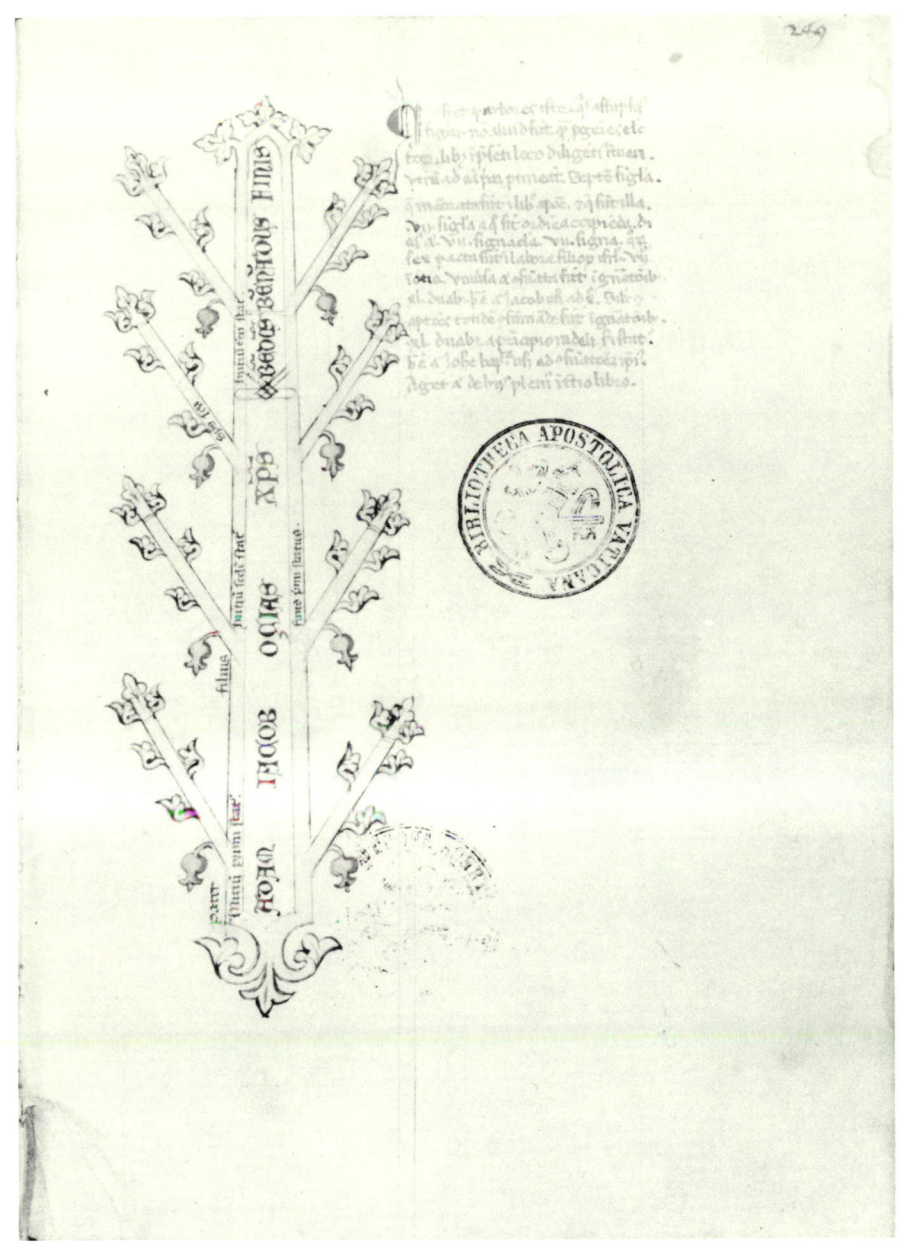

1. Rome, Biblioteca Apostolica Vaticana, MS. Vat. lat. 4860, fol. 289r. Tree of Human History from Joachim of Fiore's *Liber Concordie*

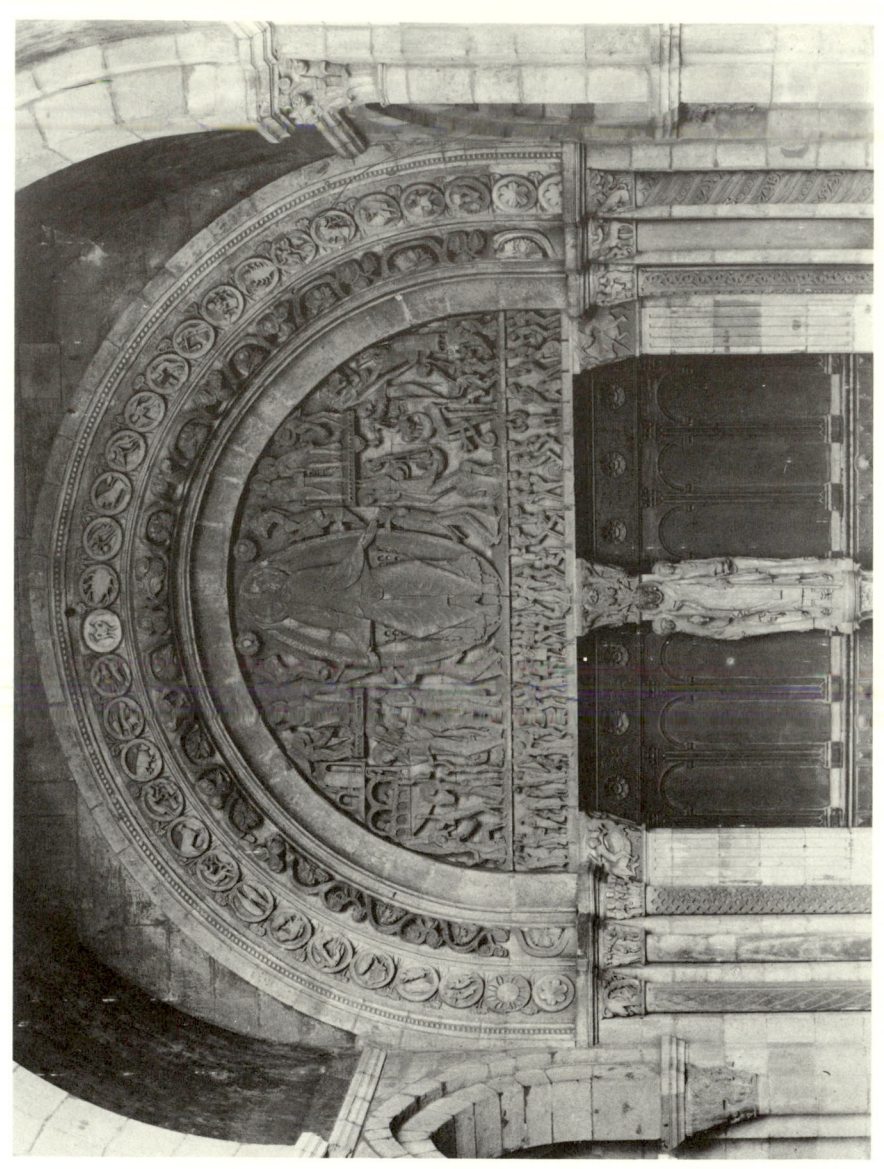

2. St.-Lazare, Autun. Central Portal

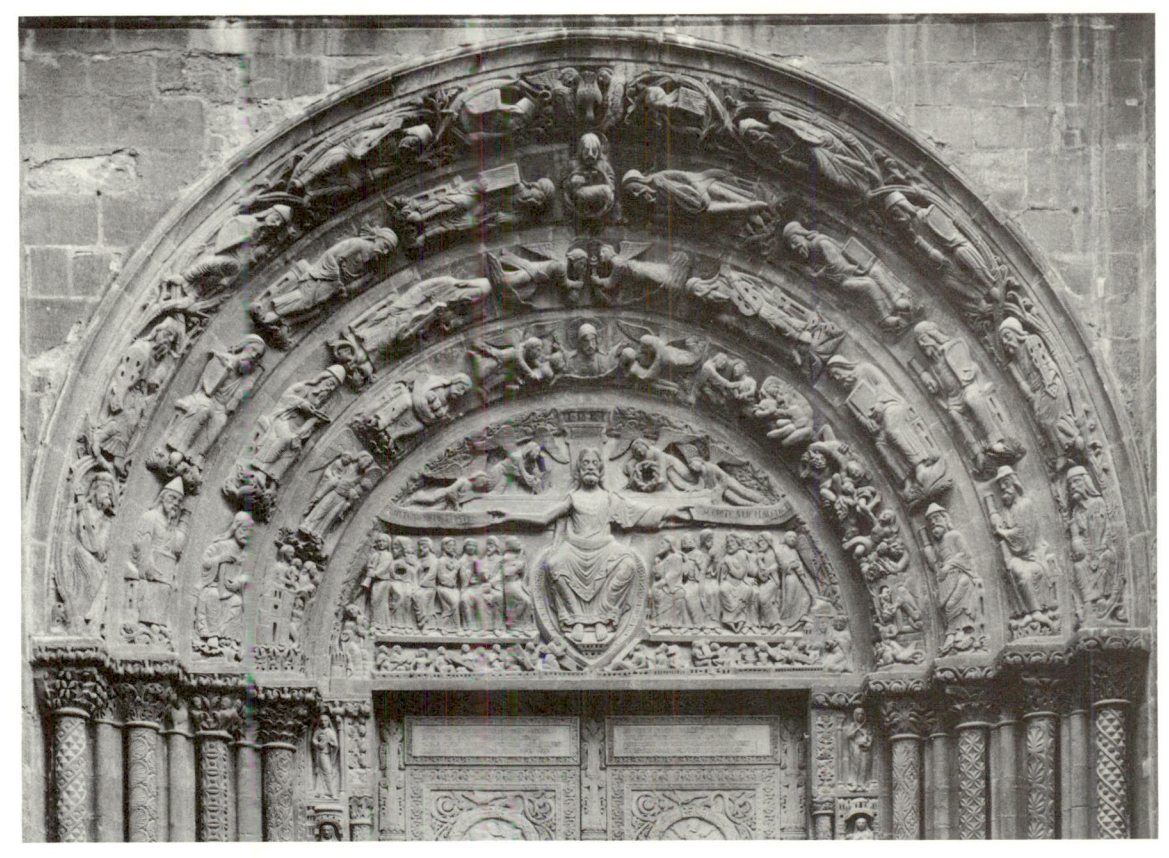

3. Abbey Church, St.-Denis. Central Tympanum

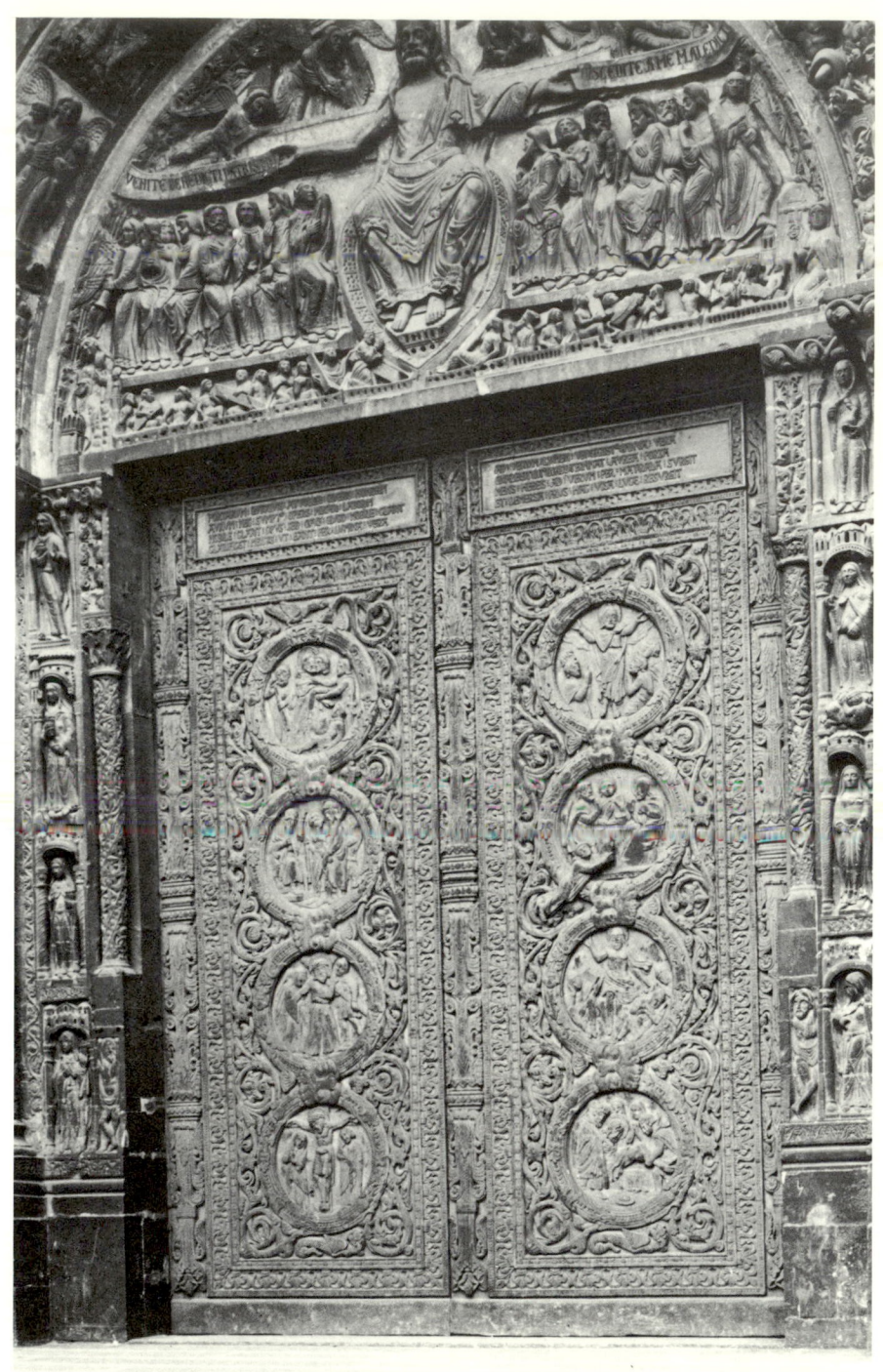

4. Abbey Church, St.-Denis. Gilded Doors

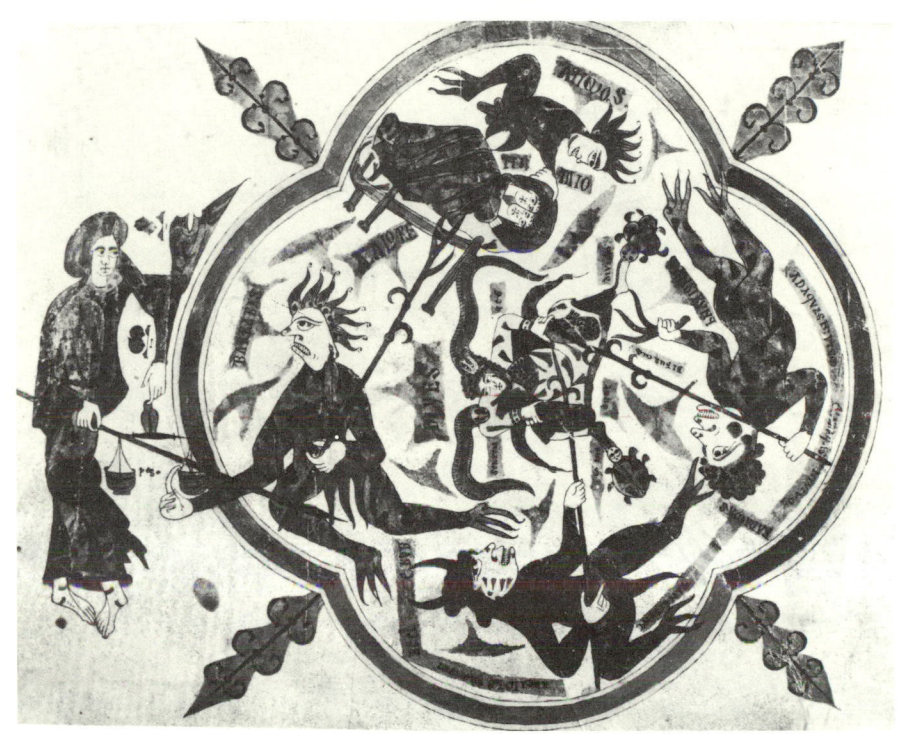

5. Silos Apocalypse (1109). British Library, ms. Add. 11695, fol. 2. The archangel Michael looks upon an image of hell

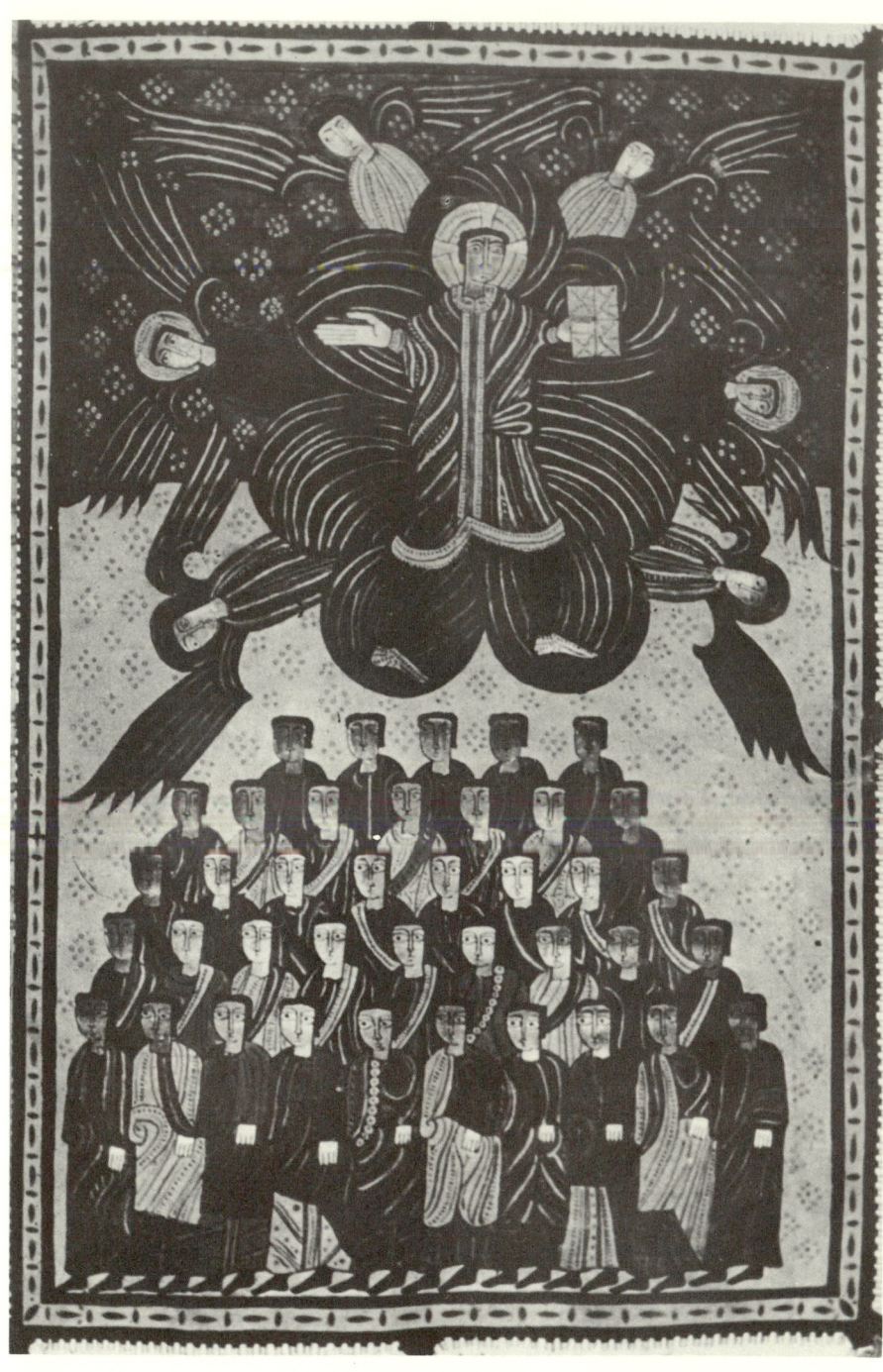

6. Silos Apocalypse (1109). British Library, MS. Add. 11695, fol. 21. The Lord in Glory coming in clouds

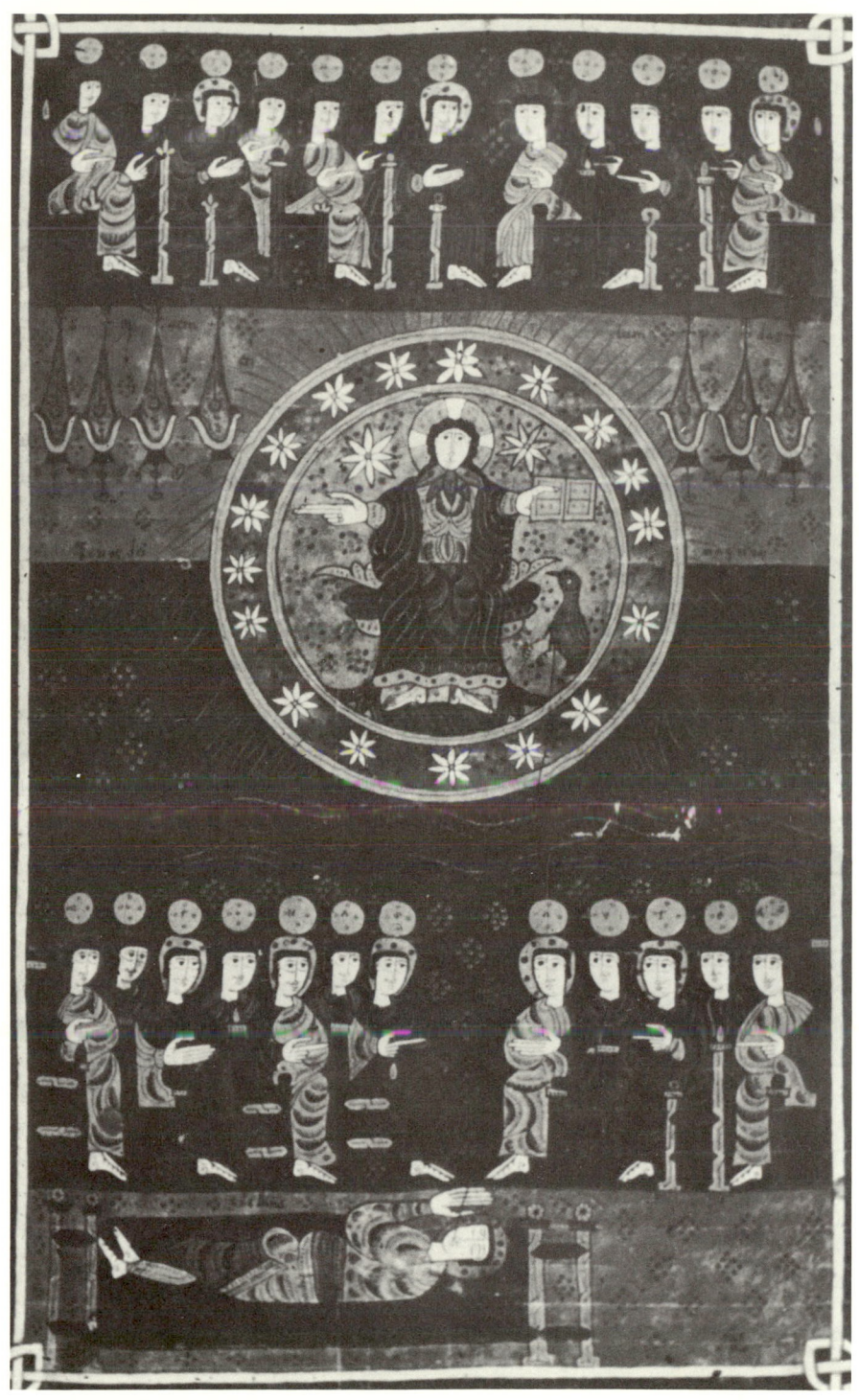

7. Silos Apocalypse (1109). British Library, MS. Add. 11695, fol. 83. St. John's vision of the Maiestas Domini

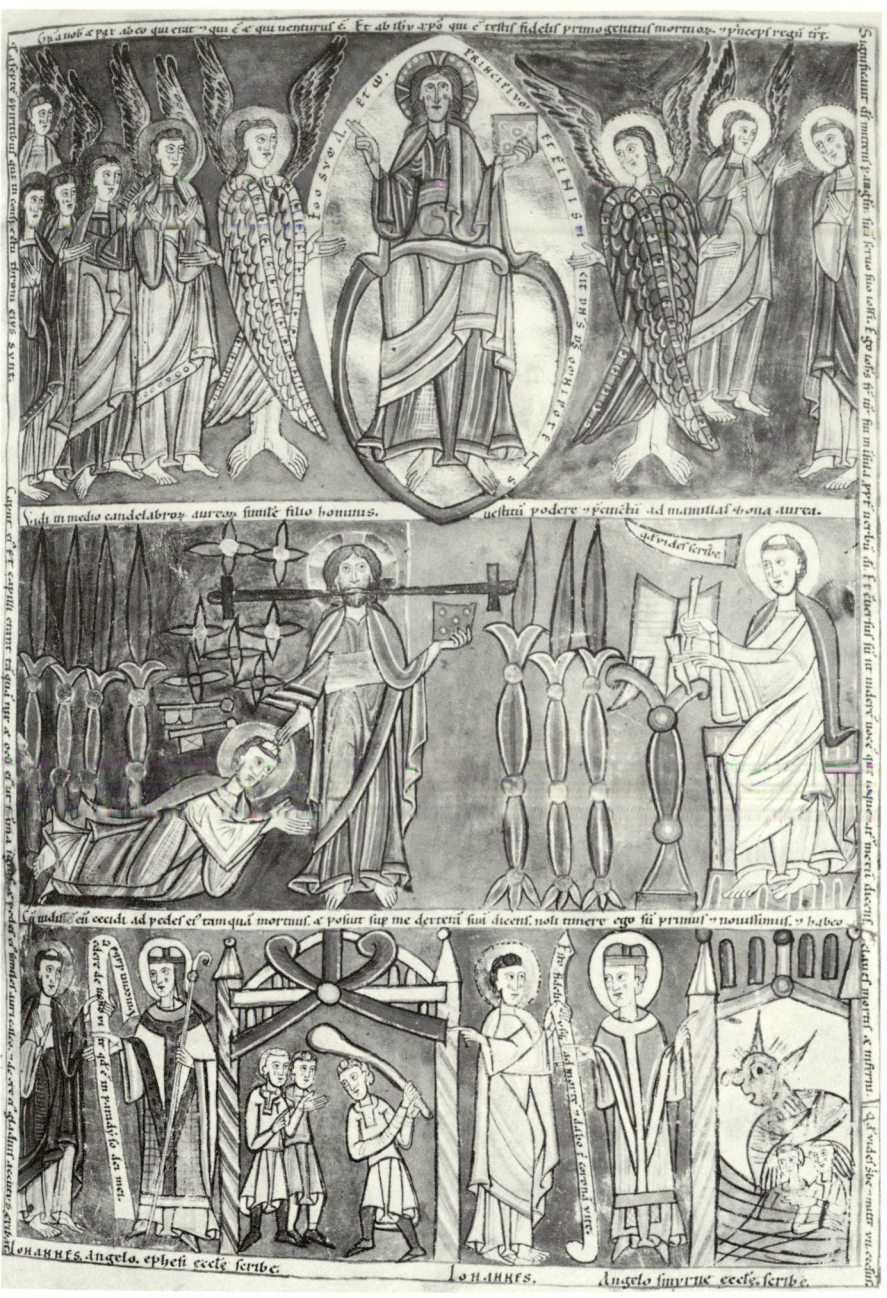

8. Oxford, Bodleian Library, MS. Bodley 352 (early 12th c.) fol. 5. Upper Register: Christ in Majesty; angel announces mission to St. John. Center Register: John at Christ's feet; John as scribe. Lower Register: John addresses Churches of Ephesus and Smyrna

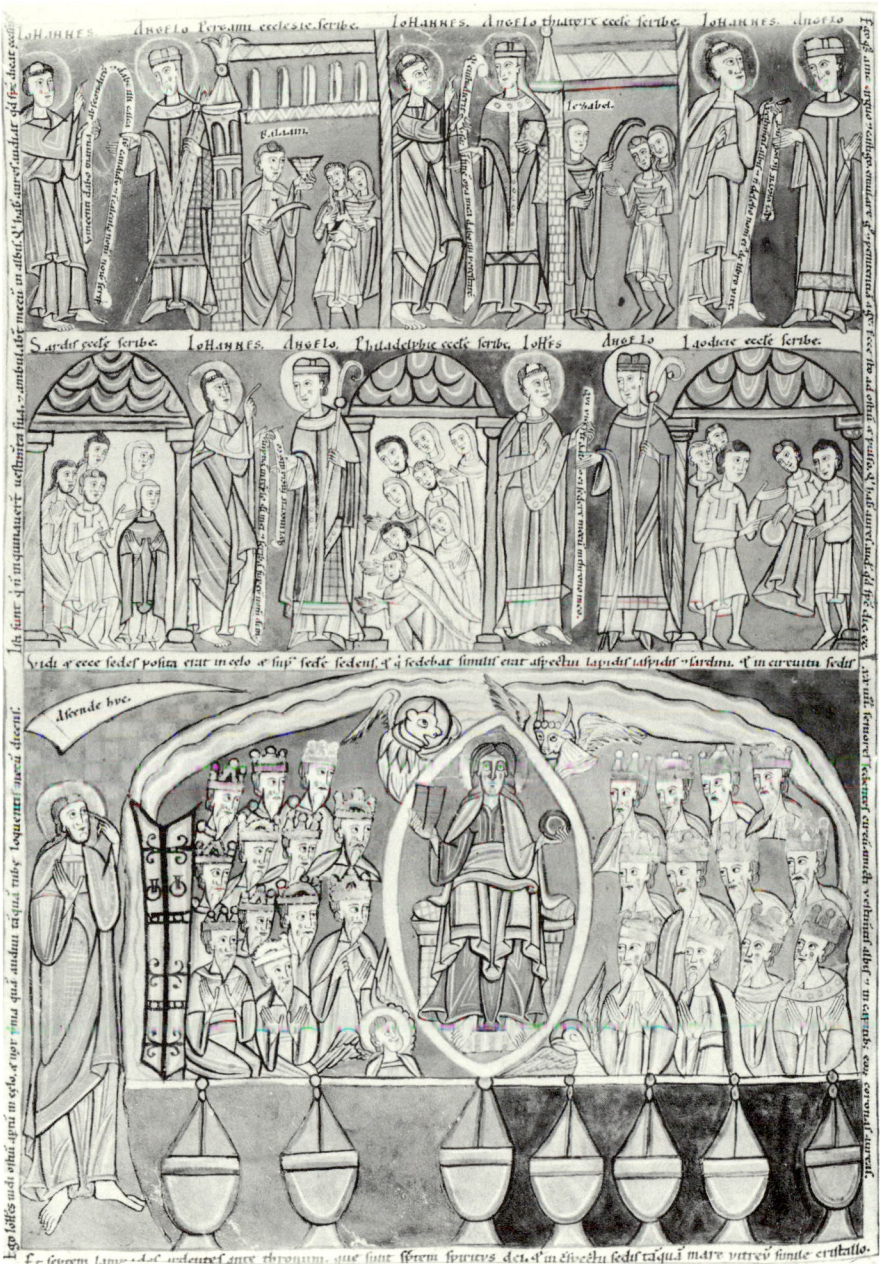

9. Oxford, Bodleian Library, MS. Bodley 352, fol. 5v. Upper Registers: John speaks to the remaining five Churches of Asia. Lower Register: St. John receives the command, "Come up here," as he sees the Lord in Glory

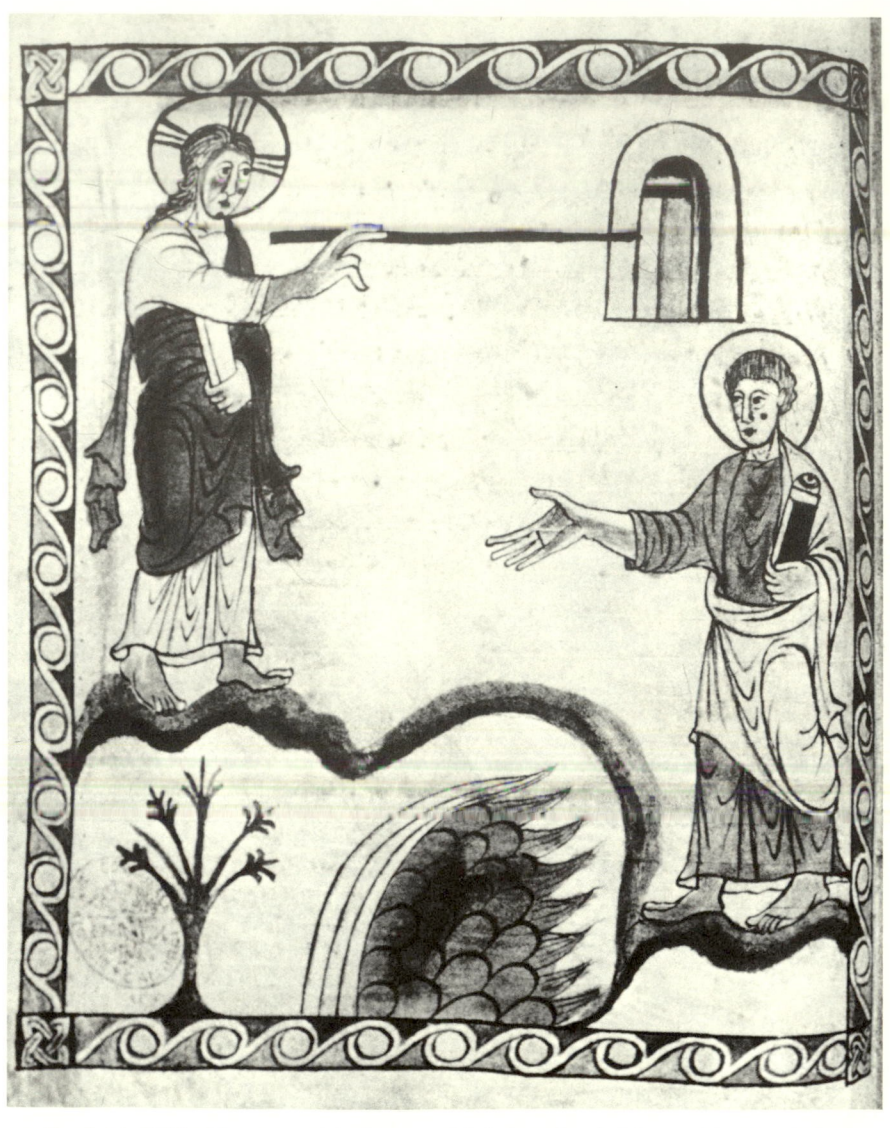

10. Cambrai, Bibliothèque municipale, MS. 386 (9th-10th c.) fol. 9v. The Lord shows
St. John the door to heaven

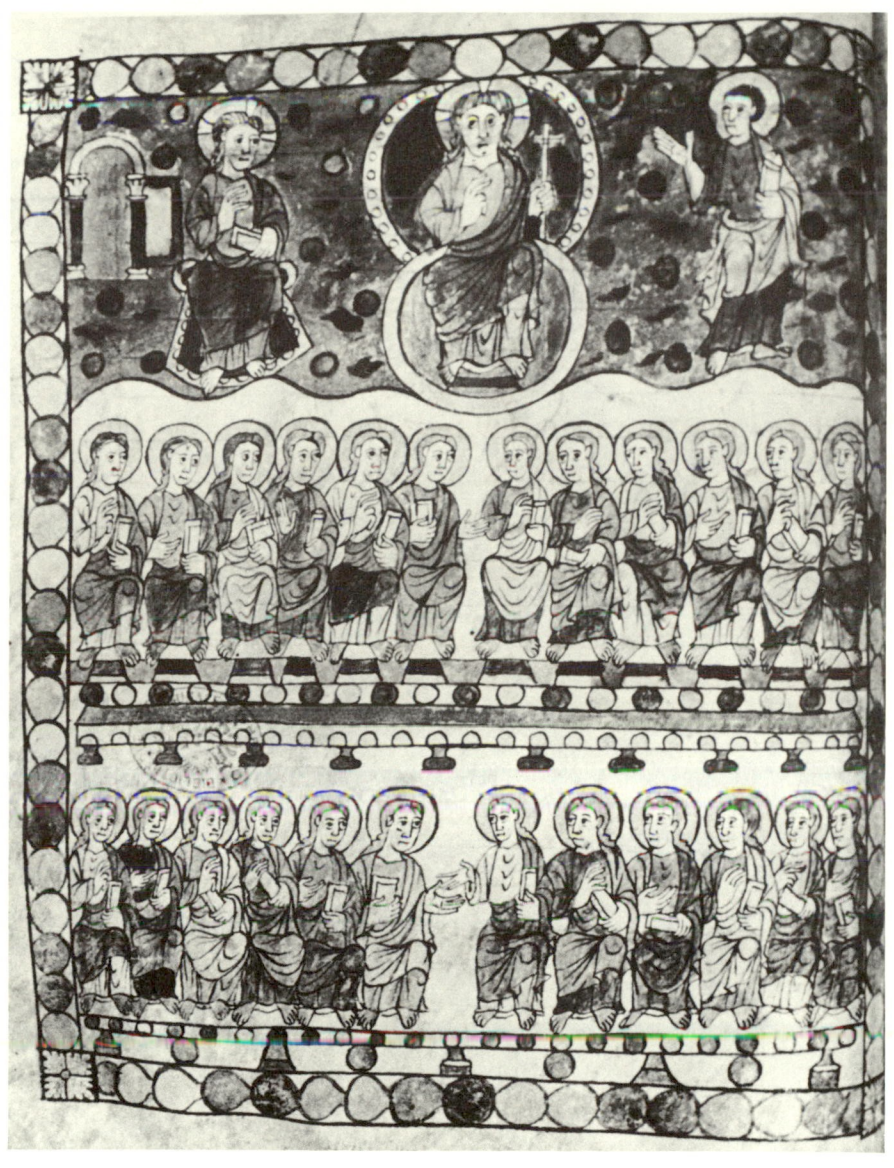

11. Cambrai, Bibliothèque municipale, MS. 386, fol. 10v. Christ, St. John and the elders before the Maiestas Domini

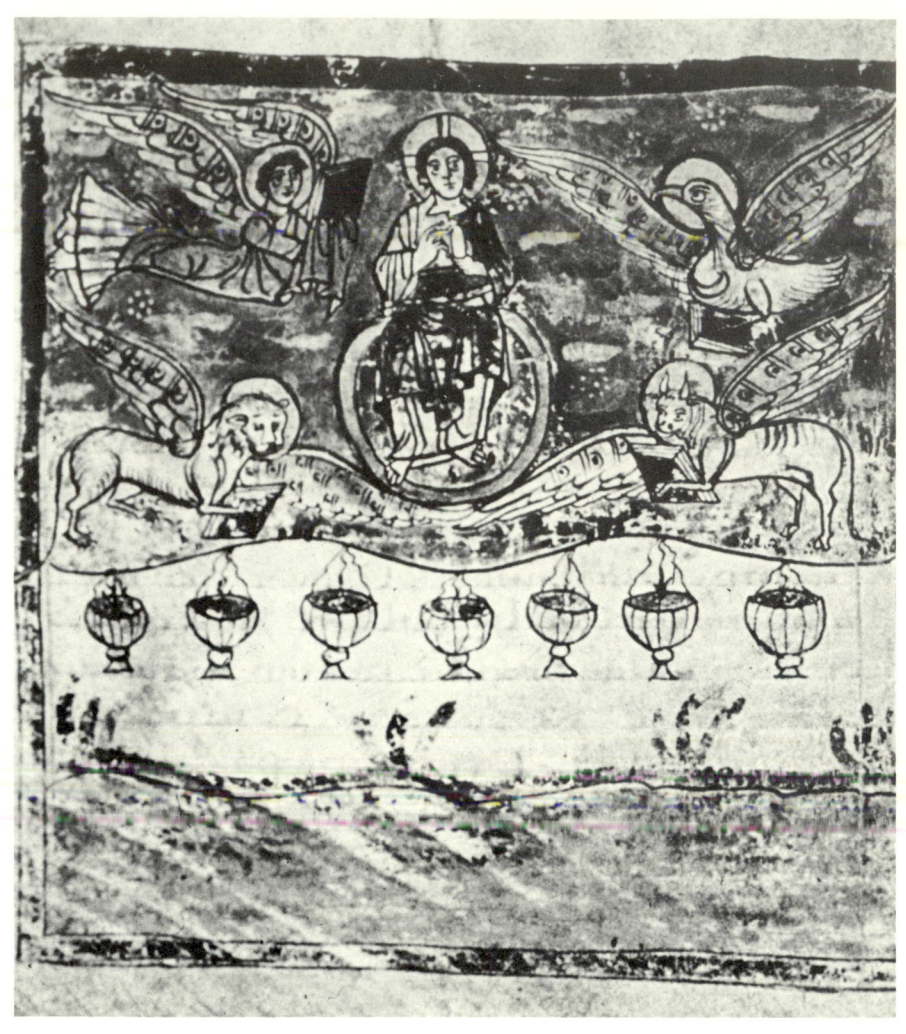

12. Trier, Stadtbibliothek, MS. 31 (9th c.) fol. 15v. The Maiestas Domini

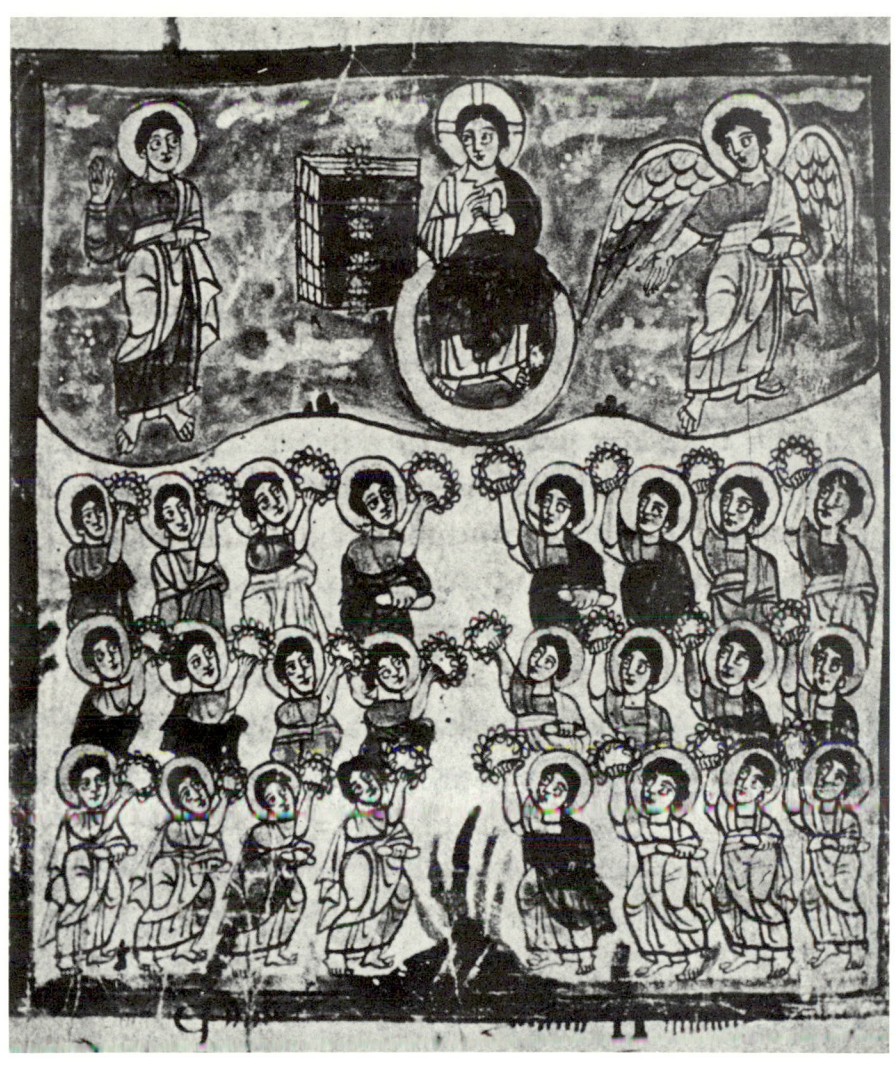

13. Trier, Stadtbibliothek, MS. 31, fol. 16v. St. John, the Maiestas Domini, the book with seven seals, the twenty-four elders

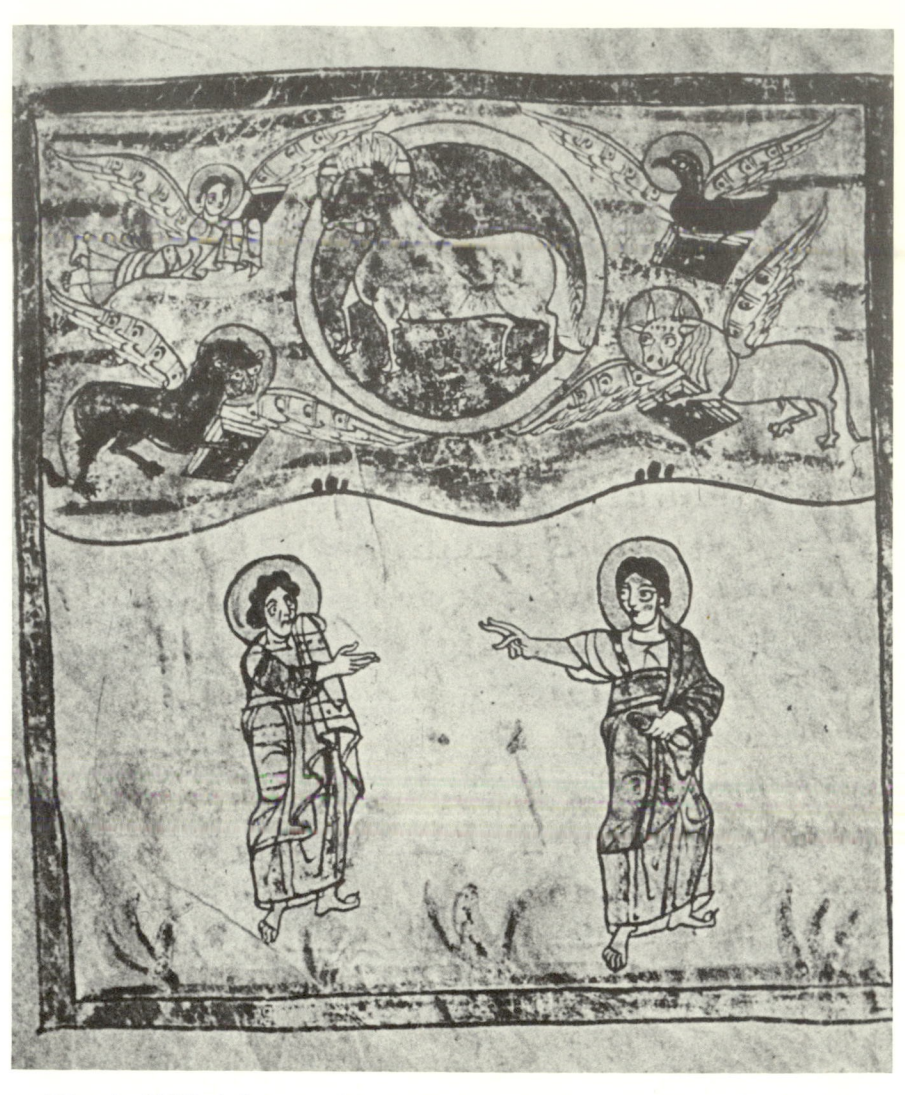

14. Trier, Stadtbibliothek, MS. 31, fol. 17v. The Lamb in glory; an elder speaks to St. John

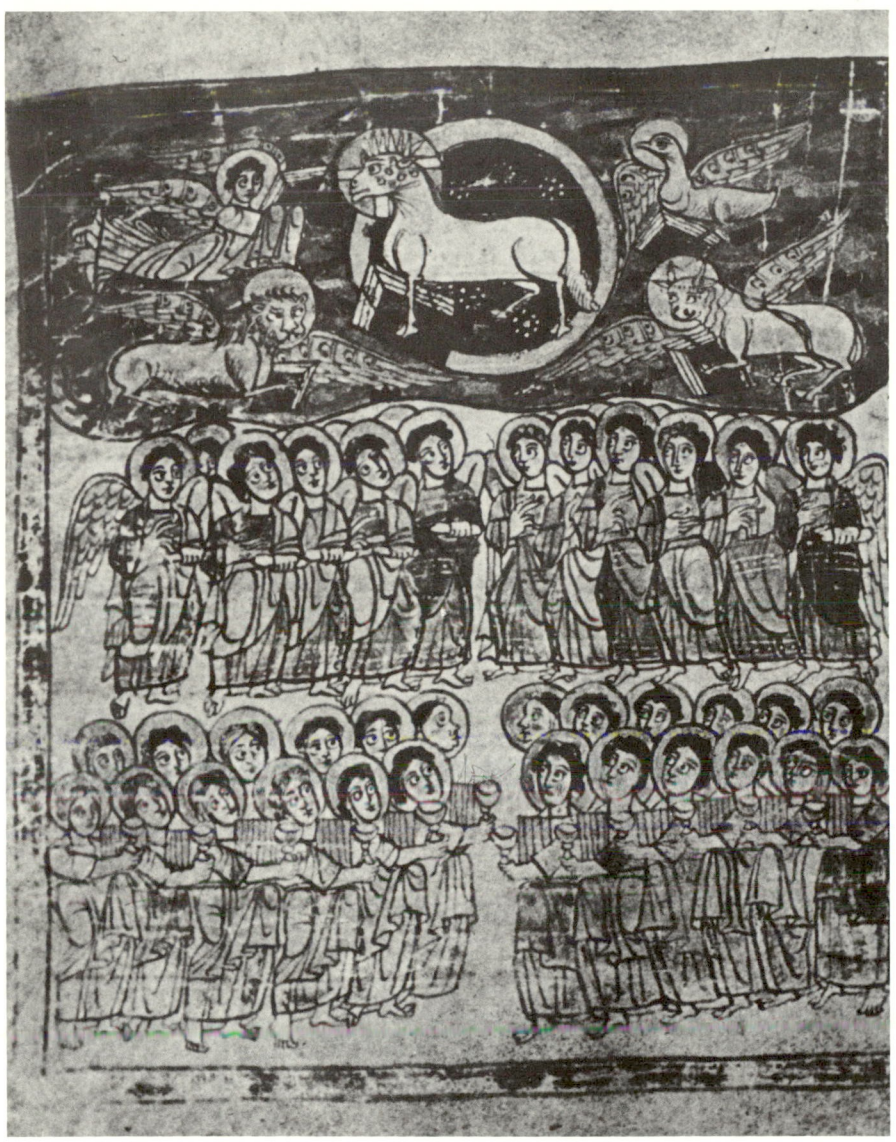

15. Trier, Stadtbibliothek, MS. 31, fol. 18v. The Lamb, the book with seven seals, the symbols of the Evangelists; angels and elders worshipping the Lamb

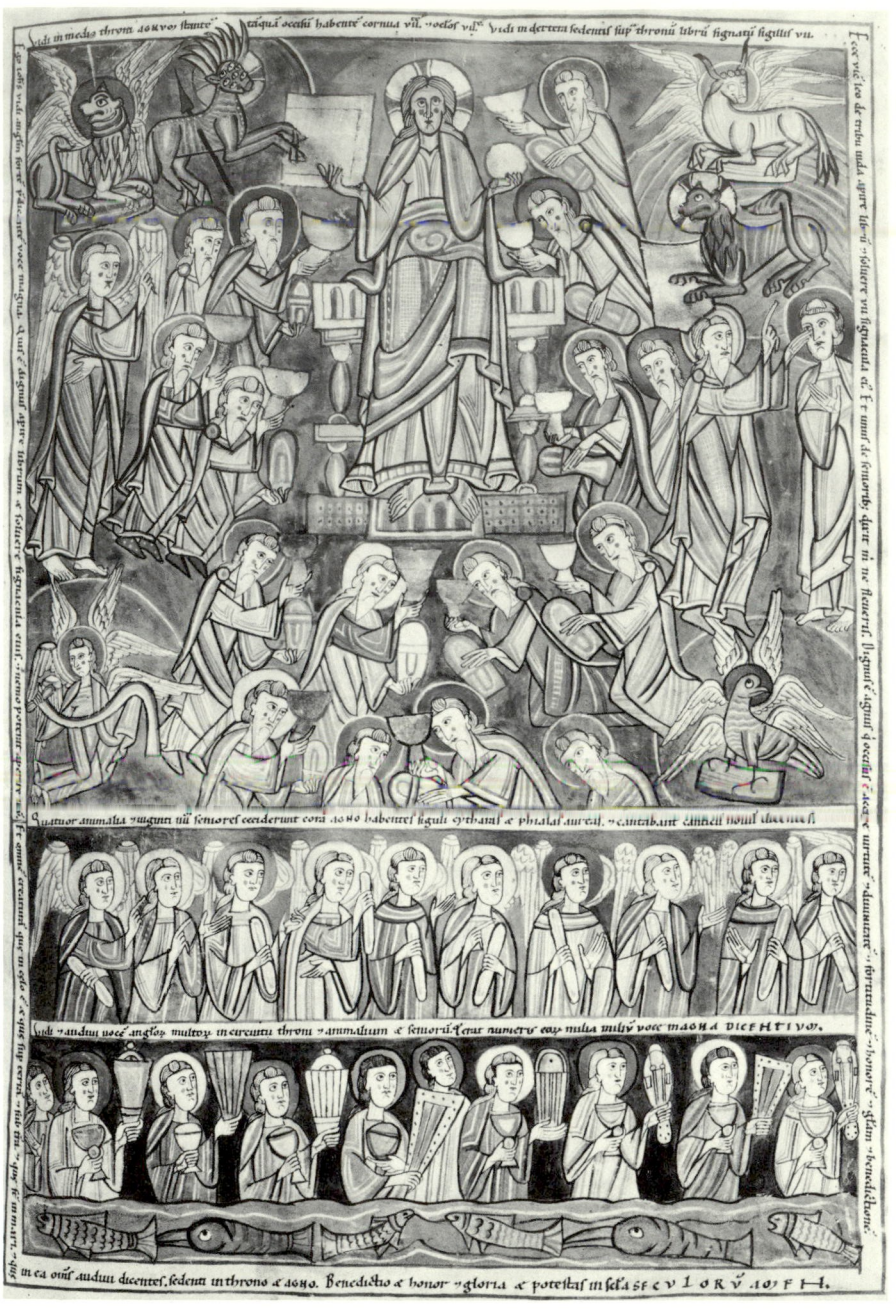

16. Oxford, Bodleian Library, MS. Bodley 352, fol. 6r. The Lamb and the One Enthroned hold the book with seven seals as an elder speaks to St. John. Lower Registers: All creation worships the Lamb

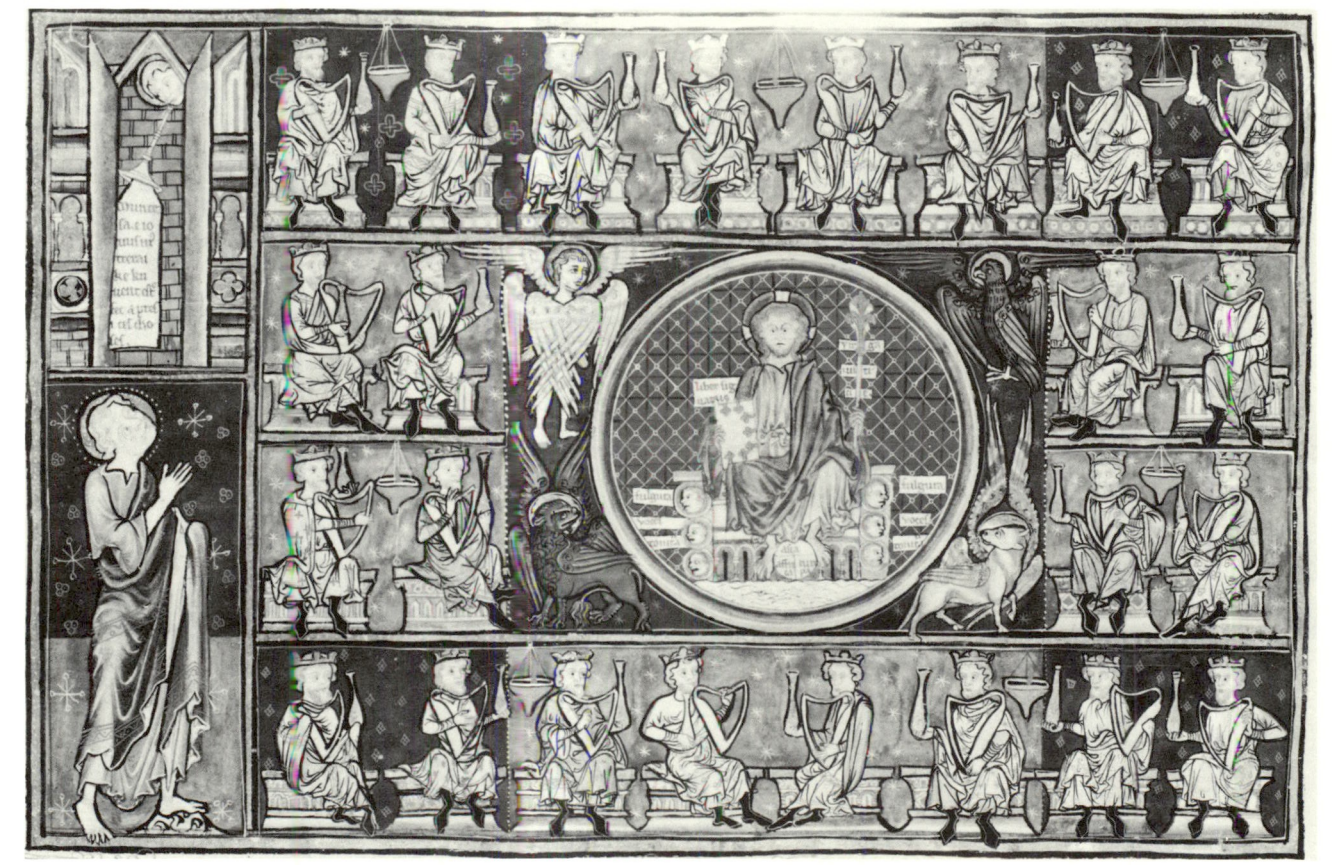

17. Cambridge, Trinity College, MS. R. 16.2 (mid-13th c.) fol. 4. St. John looks upward toward a vision of the Lord in Glory

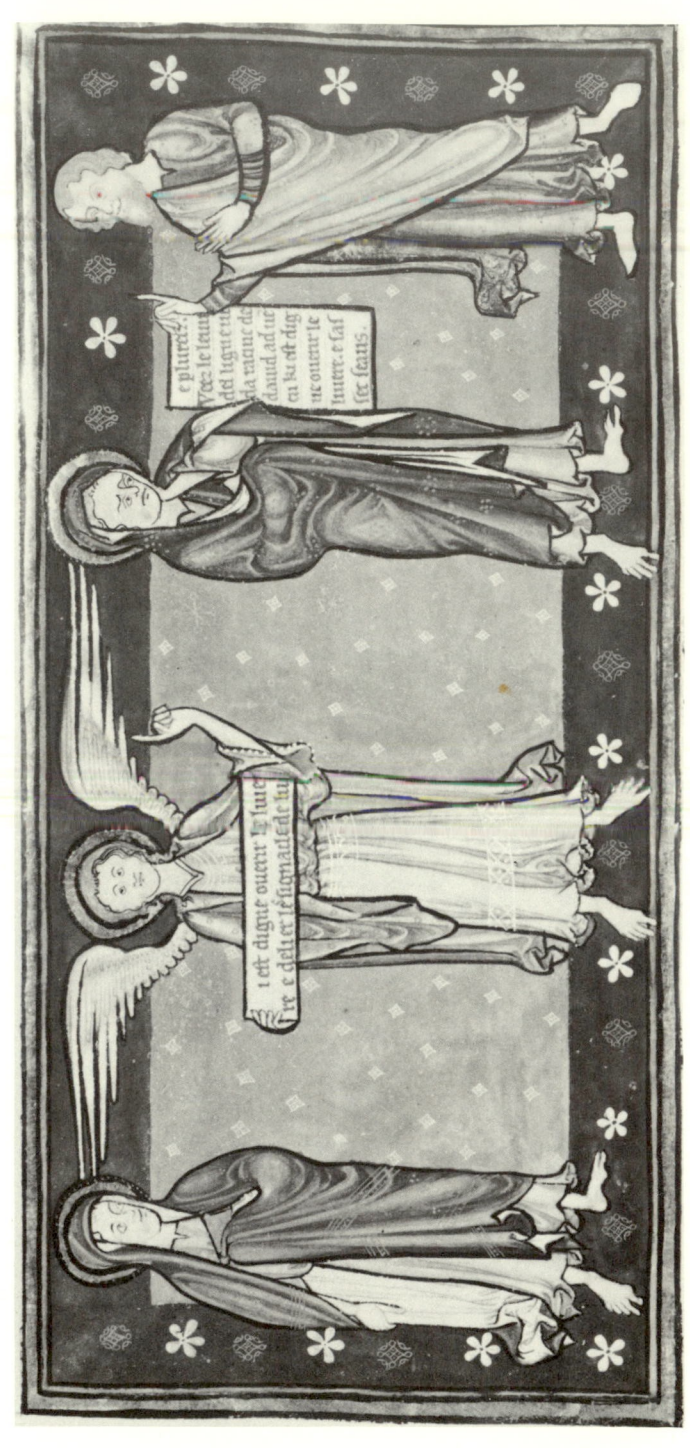

18. Cambridge, Trinity College, MS. R. 16.2, fol. 5r. *Above:* St. John looks on as an angel asks who is worthy to open the Book; an elder advises St. John not to weep. *Below:* John looks on the Lord in Glory and the Lamb, as all creation gives worship

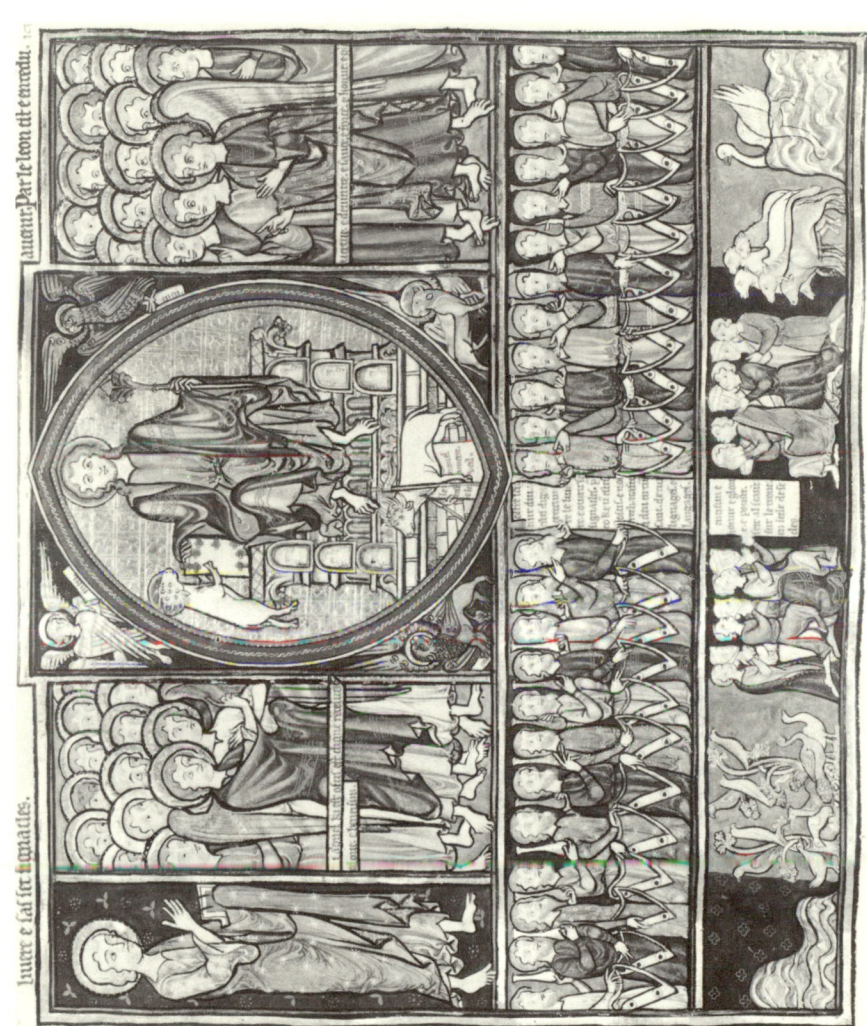

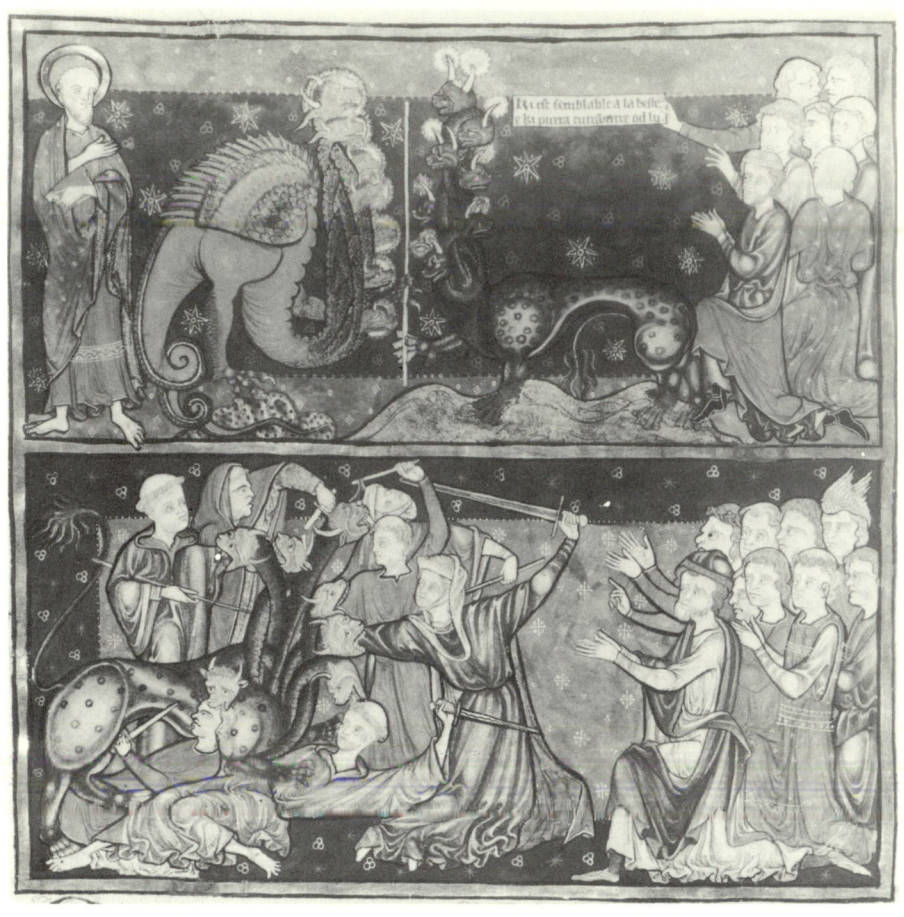

19. Cambridge, Trinity College, MS. R. 16.2, fol. 14v. The dragon gives his power to the beast. Lower Register: The saints make war against the beast

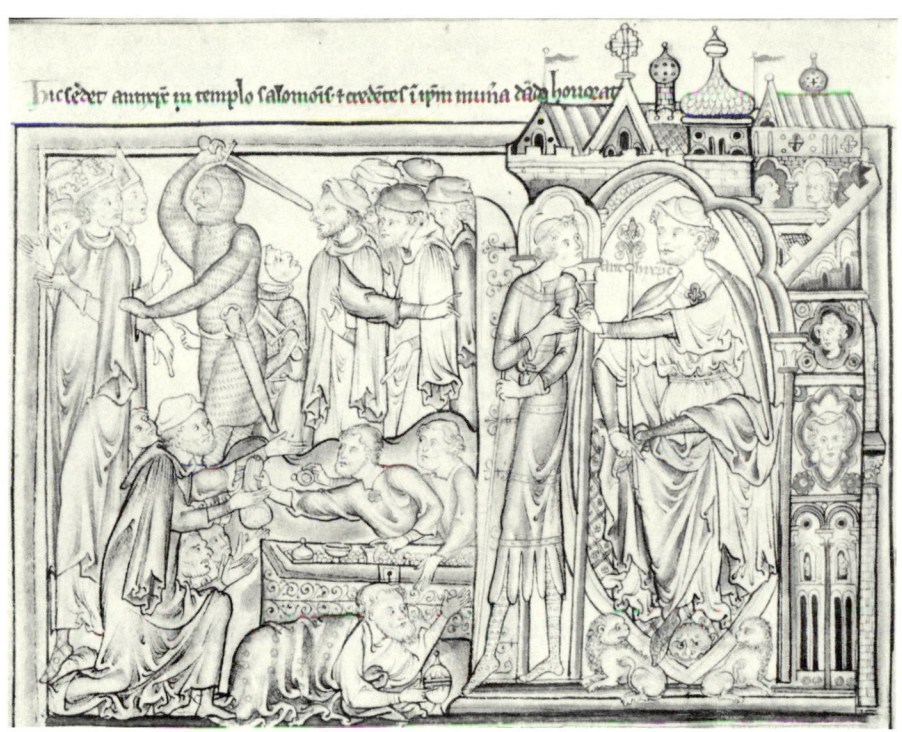

20. Pierpont Morgan Library, MS. Morgan 524 (mid-13th c.) fol. 7v. Antichrist reigns over the people of the world

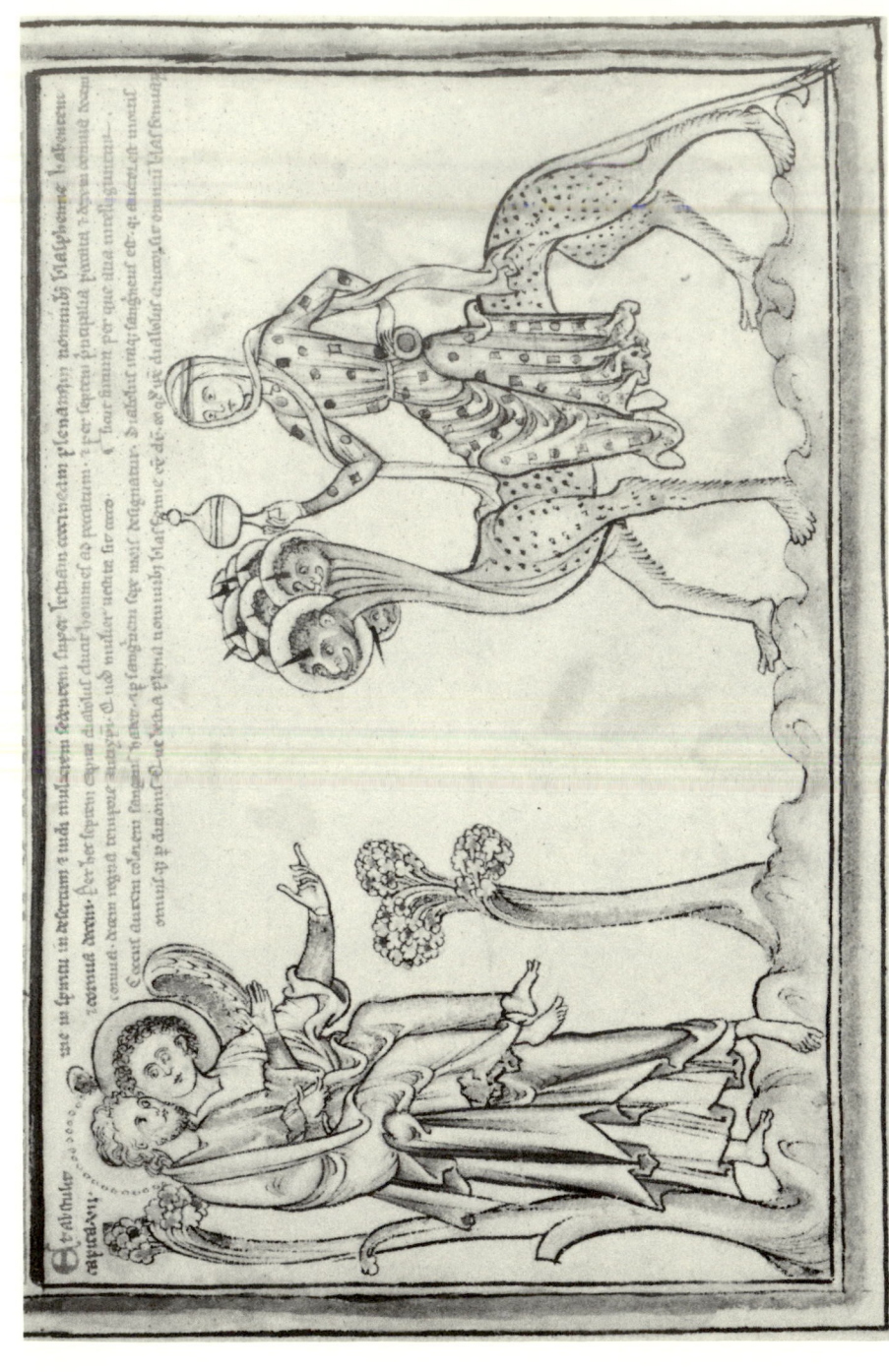

21. Pierpont Morgan Library, ms. Morgan 524, fol. 16v. St. John sees the Great Whore

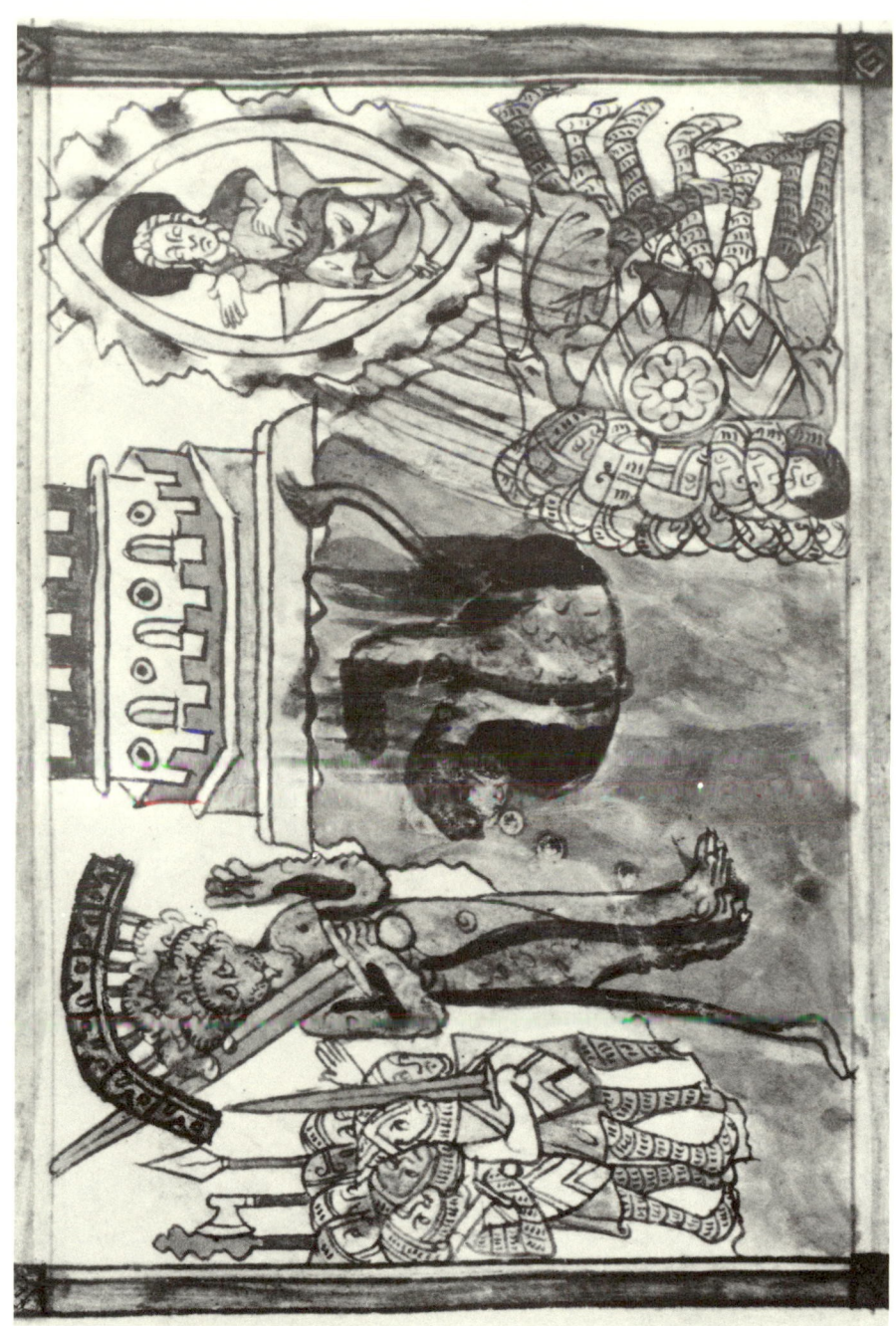

22. British Library, MS. Royal 2 D. XIII (14th c.) fol. 48v. The beast descends into the abyss

ing and end.[55] To this series, two Beatus manuscripts add a miniature depicting the terror of hell, an image which articulates a major theme of the commentary: the importance of penance for sinning man, far from the glorified Lord, ever subject to the prospect of infernal punishment (Fig. 5).[56]

These introductory themes are further developed in the picture cycle illustrating the text and commentary. Arranged at regular intervals in the manuscripts to separate the *storia* from the often lengthy explanations, the Beatus illustrations, like their Carolingian counterparts, represent discrete images drawn from the text rather than the narrative process as it might have appeared to St. John. In their highly stylized treatment of these images, artists would celebrate the glory of the Lord, the Lamb and the blessed, dramatically separating the divine from the human realm by geometric design and color. Thus, in the Silos Apocalypse (1109), the Apocalyptic Lord of Revelation 1:7 appears within a striking black, red and white cloud surrounded by six angels, effecting the illusion of a dynamic, self-contained and containing movement, dramtically emerging from a red background (Fig. 6).[57] By contrast, in the lower register, a group of the faithful gaze upward, motionless, placed against a flat, yellow surface which creates the effect of a space (and a world order) not only below but slightly behind and separated from that of the Lord.

When St. John appears in the Beatus illustrations as the observer of his vision, he is treated as Beatus and most earlier monastic exegetes had viewed him, as a mortal being, sharing the passivity of his fellow creatures in the face of divine glory. In the Silos Apocalypse, as John is invited to witness the Lord's majesty (Rev. 4), the artist describes a glorious vision of eternal joy in the form of a circle encompassing the Lord and his wor-

[55] In the Gerona Apocalypse, the inscription for the cross of Oviedo stresses this theme: *Hoc signum tuetur pius; vicitur inimicus* (fol. 1v). For a discussion of the symbolism of the eagle conquering the serpent, see Casanovas, *et al., Codex Gerundensis,* "Textos Relativos a las Iluminaciones," pp. 81–82.

[56] This illustration appears in the Silos Apocalypse and in the Apocalypse at Turin. See Meyer Shapiro, "From Mozarabic to Romanesque in Silos," *Art Bulletin* (1939), p. 317. Shapiro suggests that this illustration may be related to a lection on the Day of Judgment.

[57] The Silos Apocalypse (1109), preserved in the British Museum, MS. Add. 11,695, has been chosen to illustrate the Beatus tradition both because it provides a clear and stark representation of themes stressed in the commentary, and because it is a strikingly beautiful example of purely Mozarabic developments in the history of Beatus illustration (see Neuss, *Apokalypse,* p. 41).

shipers, bespeaking remarkable power and energy. By contrast, in the lower register, John lies prostrate and motionless on a bed, set apart in his own compartment. (Fig. 7)[58] Interestingly enough, almost as if he were commenting on this very passivity, inherited from his predecessors, the artist adds a second figure of St. John on the page opposite. Just under the *storia* or text describing the vision, an upright, lively figure of St. John hearkens over his shoulder to the *vox domini* represented by a hand, a figure reminiscent of scenes in the Trier Apocalypse and perhaps bespeaking Roman influence.[59] But such commentary is subsidiary, strictly subordinated to a far more central concern for celebrating in color and line the mystery of God's grandeur before whom fragile man can only fall terrified. As the artist of one of the earliest surviving Beatus manuscripts wrote: "Between the marvelous words of his tales, I have painted the ornament, in a series, so that the wise might fear the future judgment and the passing of the world."[60]

If we turn now to twelfth- and thirteenth-century developments in the history of illustrated Apocalypses, we discover significant revisions of older forms and themes. The sacred images have come to be studied and represented as "places" in a coherent linear narrative, specifically designed to teach not only the fear of sin but also the joy of salvation as this state might be concretely expressed through art. At the same time, St. John's expressive responses to his visions occupy more and more attention as he guides his readers sequentially through the series of apocalyptic figures toward a final comforting glimpse of the New Jerusalem. When and where these changes first occurred cannot be charted with certainty, no doubt because time has claimed important evidence. Certainly by the mid-thirteenth century, in two seminal picture cycles produced in English scriptoria, the transformation had been completed, and it is to these codi-

[58] In the Gerona Apocalypse (fol. 107), John is likewise prostrate below his vision. But, to illustrate the visionary's participation, the artist has introduced a thread running from his mouth to a dove (his soul) which is in the Lord's presence.

[59] Fol. 82v. Meyer Shapiro noted the Romanesque quality of this incidental figure of St. John and another on fol. 163v, concluding that their "marginal character . . . corresponds to the limited and superficial role of the new Romanesque forms" in the book (*Art Bulletin* [1939], p. 317 and fig. 4).

[60] Pierpont Morgan Library, Morgan MS. 644, fol. 293: "Inter ejus decus uerba mirifica storiarumque depinxi per seriem ut scientibus terreant judicii futuri adventui peracturi saeculi." For the full text, see Neuss, *Apokalypse*, p. 12. For the date of the Morgan MS., see *Codex Gerundensis*, pp. 45–47.

ces that we must finally turn.[61] Yet one cycle of illustrations executed more than a century earlier, indicates that new attitudes toward the apocalyptic imagery, and a new definition of St. John as seer had already been developed before the mid-twelfth century.

The remarkable picture cycle introducing a copy of Haimo's commentary, now in the Bodleian Library (MS. Bodley 352), has never been fully studied. It has usually been described erroneously as being *in* Haimo's commentary, and its illustrations have been called "rude," "rough," and "archaic."[62] To be sure, the artistic quality of the pictures is uneven. While some of the figures—the apocalyptic Lord, the great-voiced angel, St. John at times—are strikingly angular and forceful in their outline, others are ill-formed or awkward. But if the artist faltered as a draughtsman, he (or his exemplar) was a master of dramatic organization, transforming the symbolic imagery supplied by his predecessors into a vigorous dramatic series. A scene-for-scene comparison of Bodley with the Carolingian Trier Apocalypse suggests close iconographic ties between the two and it is conceivable that the twelfth-century illuminator worked from a Carolingian exemplar.[63] But whatever his immediate source, the result is a

[61] Trinity College Cambridge, MS. R. 16. 2, and the picture cycle represented in three related manuscripts: Bodleian Library, MS. Auct. D. 4. 17, Pierpont Morgan Library, Morgan MS. 524, and B.N., MS. fr. 403. For reasons to be discussed below, I follow G. Henderson and P. Brieger in rejecting Freyhan's argument for a single prototype (Morgan MS. 524). See note 31 above.

[62] M. R. James has twice mentioned Bodley 352: In his introduction to the Trinity College Apocalypse (London, 1909), he notes that he has not looked at the manuscript in detail but that it is "rough German work of the twelfth century" (p. 7). In his Schweich lectures of 1927, published as the *Apocalypse in Art* (London, 1931) he still considered the pictures "rude enough" (p. 42). P. Brieger has been the first to suggest the manuscript's relevance for the development of thirteenth-century Apocalypses (*Trinity College Apocalypse* [London, 1967], p. 8 and fig. 2). For summary descriptions of the manuscript, see Manchester Art Gallery, "Romanesque Art" (Manchester, 1959), p. 11 and pl. 1; O. Pächt and J. J. G. Alexander, *Illuminated Manuscripts in the Bodleian Library* (Oxford, 1966–1973), vol. 1, no. 66 and pl. v, 66.

[63] The lines of filiation from the Carolingian cycles to the twelfth century have yet to be fully traced. Certainly the Bamberg Apocalypse (c. 1000), reproduced by H. Wölfflin (*Die Bamberger Apokalypse* [Munich, 1921]), represents one link but it remains, in its stark, abstract fineness, at a considerable distance from Bodley 352. Nor do the frescoes of the Poitevin church of St.-Savin lead us directly to Bodley (see E. Maillard, *L'Eglise de St.-Savin* [Paris, 1926], pp. 29–41 and figs. 6–10). Bodley should also be compared with the twelfth-century Italian picture cycle in the

thorough-going reorganization of the traditional materials. In place of
earlier generalizing formulas, the Bodley artist has preferred narrative
clarity, economy and focus—the result of grasping Revelation as a temporally modulated story. Instead of the series of discrete tableaus of Trier
or Valenciennes, with St. John as static witness, or the awesome hieratic
figures of the Beatus tradition, the Bodley cycle offers a moving drama
toward which John as seer directs his audience even as he himself engages
in his own visionary experience.

No longer the passive symbolic figure of the faithful he had been in the
Carolingian and Beatus Apocalypses, St. John has entered into a direct,
personal relationship with his revelation—a vital, expressive intermediary
between the events of his vision and contemporary readers. We meet him
at once both in his scribal and his visionary roles. As a scribe, distanced
from the apocalyptic figures, he witnesses himself taking part in his own
spiritual revelation (Fig. 8). Then, as the vision begins to unfold, we are
moved abruptly from his scribal to his visionary experience and the perspective of witness and observer alike becomes both temporal and omnitemporal (Fig. 9). The tensely articulated, elongated figure of John
stands next to the heavenly scene as the scroll above commands: "Ascende
huc." St. John, pointing toward his eye, perceives the apocalyptic Lord,
surrounded by elders in half-figure, as if upon a stage from which a
curtain has been removed for his seeing.[64] While the Trier-Cambrai illuminators had used two pages to describe discrete aspects of this scene—
Christ directing St. John to look upward and the One Enthroned in glory
flanked by John and Christ (Figs. 10–11)—the Bodley artist draws the
two into one complex, focused composition.

In a similar way, Bodley recollects St. John's vision of the Lamb and the
seven-sealed book, to which Trier had devoted four full-page illustrations
(Figs. 12–15), into a single dynamic composition (Fig. 16). As the Lord
and the wounded Lamb hold the book with seven seals, the elders bow
down in worship and all creation sings hymns of praise to God. One might

---

Berlin Beatus (Berlin, MS. theol. lat. fol. 561) and with the Apocalypse cycle in
Lambert of St.-Omer's *Liber Floridus* (Wolfenbüttel, Hertzog August Bibl. Cod.
Gud. lat. 1.2). The provenance of the manuscript may be Germany since the illus-
trations are prefaced by a page, pasted in, depicting a monk with the distinctively
German name Rudolfus (or Rundolfus) offering a book to a "priest of St. Blaise."

[64] In the Bamberg Apocalypse, St. John points to his eye more than once, but there
the gesture does not suggest the intense spiritual tension and concentration to be
found in Bodley, where the same pose is repeated insistently in several scenes.

at first miss the presence of St. John in this grand drama. But we discover him at the right in the upper register, not only observing but participating in the general movement. As the text, written in the frame, explains, an elder is telling John not to weep for there is indeed one to open the great book—the Lamb who was, as it were, killed and is now living.

The Bodley picture cycle here, as throughout, is accompanied by an edited version of the Apocalypse itself, written and sometimes crowded into frames surrounding the illustrations as well as in scrolls within the scenes. The scribe, following upon the work of the draughtsman, used the verbal text to illuminate the order of the illustrations, rearranging and subordinating the sacred *historia* in order to gloss the visual drama unfolded before him. Certainly this picture cycle, accompanied by its skillfully abbreviated text of the Apocalypse, provides clear evidence that the letter of Revelation had already been read and represented as an ordered progressive image series before the middle of the twelfth century.[65] St. John had been individualized, both as seer and scribe, and his experience could be studied as a story related in form to the ordinary time and space of the reader.

The personalizing and temporalizing interests so dramatically apparent in Bodley were to be developed to a high degree of perfection in the succeeding century. Though there were undoubtedly several independent efforts during the course of the twelfth century, paving the way for thirteenth-century achievements, these are now lost to us. From the evidence of the earliest of the thirteenth-century Apocalypses, it seems likely that at least one late twelfth-century codex had united a picture cycle not unlike Bodley's with the historical and spiritual gloss of the enigmatic Berengaudus.[66] This union was a particularly happy one, for, as we have seen,

[65] The Apocalypse illustrations included in the compendius *Liber Floridus* (early twelfth century) corroborate the evidence of Bodley 352 but fall short of the fully developed narrative sense to be found in Bodley. See Peter Brieger, *Trinity College Apocalypse* (London, 1967), figs. 5–10.

[66] Delisle proposed that the common type was established in England or northern France in the twelfth century (*L'Apocalypse*, pp. i–ii). James agreed with him but also observed that "new life" had been infused into the form of the illustrated Apocalypse in the thirteenth century: "I seem to discern that some one person, a person so placed that his work could exercise a wide influence, produced an illustrated Apocalypse which became the standard for succeeding generations. I think he was not independent of one of the currents of earlier tradition; but whatever the material was that he worked upon, he breathed new life into it" (*Apocalypse in Art*, p. 29). More recently, G. Henderson has hypothesized an "older prototype" for Paris, "the model also, in its turn, of Morgan" (*JCWI* [30], p. 113).

the Berengaudus commentary systematized even as it intensified the reading of Revelation as a linear narrative pertinent to the temporal lives of contemporary Christians. If, as Berengaudus had argued, all the "times" of human history were represented in the symbols of the Apocalypse, then the symbols themselves must yield an imaginative understanding not only of earlier periods but also of the reign of Antichrist, the final temporal conflict between God and Satan, and then the joy of the heavenly country after the end of time. In addition, if the symbols which John saw did describe the future *time* of all the world, then his vision could and must be shared by all those who must look forward to the coming of Antichrist, perhaps even in their own lifetime.[67] We do not know when or where the Berengaudus commentary began to act upon the shape of the Apocalypse cycle. But its influence is clear in the two thirteenth-century picture cycles which appear to have served as models for later generations of artists.

The more studied and intellectualized of these cycles is to be found in the magnificent Trinity College Apocalypse (Cambridge, Trinity College MS. R. 16.2).[68] Clearly designed as a book of devotion, Trinity meticulously

---

[67] Both Berengaudus and the Trinity commentary allow this possibility when they explain the meaning of the Beast's number, six hundred sixty-six.

[68] Facsimile reproductions: M. R. James, *The Trinity College Apocalypse*, Roxburghe Club (London, 1909); P. Brieger, *The Trinity College Apocalypse* (London, 1967). The date and provenance of Trinity have been the subject of some dispute. Generally regarded as one of the earliest, if not the earliest of the thirteenth-century Anglo-Norman Apocalypses, it has been dated as early as the 1220s and as late as the 1260s. The most cogent and persuasive discussion is perhaps G. Henderson's (*JCWI* [30], pp. 117–127). On stylistic grounds, he places Trinity between c. 1235 and c. 1265 with a likely guess, c. 1255. He conjectures that the work on the manuscript may have been carried on over a number of years and at a central scriptorium by several hands. This would explain the mixture of styles, older and newer, which makes of Trinity a "transitional manuscript" (Henderson, p. 127). Henderson also shows that R. Freyhan's argument—that Trinity is a revision of an older prototype represented by Morgan MS. 524—is incorrect. Trinity, he concludes, "stands by itself, distinct from Morgan—the cycle, not the manuscript—and equal to it in authority" (135). Independently of Henderson, P. Brieger rejects Freyhan's effort to date Trinity as a deliberate reaction against the Joachite heresy (*Trinity College Apocalypse*, p. 14). Brieger places the manuscript between 1242 and 1250, suggesting, as had James, that it may have been made for Queen Eleanor (pp. 14–15). Trinity has been attributed to a number of workshops—St. Alban's, (A. Lindblom, *La Peinture gothique en Suède et en Norvège* [Stockholm, 1916], p. 184, n. 4); Canterbury (James, *The Trinity College Apocalypse*, pp. 24–25); Westminster (Henderson, *JCWI* 30 [1967], pp. 126–128). Whatever its provenance, it is certainly the product of a first-rate workshop, fully in touch with current artistic and spiritual

organizes illustrations, text and gloss to direct the reader's close meditation. The second prototypical cycle offers a simple, more immediately dramatic reading of Revelation. In this cycle, represented by three extant
thirteenth-century manuscripts—Bodleian Library, MS. Auct. D. 4.17, Pierpont Morgan Library, MS. 524 and Bibliothèque Nationale, MS. fr. 403—
the pictures predominate, providing a vivid account of the events surrounding the eschaton.[69] Because each of these two influential cycles
marks a different stage or development in the marriage of the Berengaudus gloss with illustrations, both must interest us in examining thirteenth-
century visual and intellectual innovations in the interpretation of St.
John's vision.

---

trends, and supported by aristocratic patrons. In this discussion, for reasons which
will become clear below, I follow Henderson in rejecting Freyhan's single archetype,
and in positing Trinity as an independent prototype for later generations of illustrated Apocalypses.

[69] Facsimile reproduction of Bodleian: H. O. Coxe, *The Apocalypse of St. John
the Divine*, Bodl. MS. Auct. D. 4.17, Roxburghe Club (London, 1876); Facsimile of
Paris: L. Delisle and P. Meyer, *L'Apocalypse en français au XIIIᵉ siècle* (Paris,
1900). Bodleian and Morgan are almost identical and one is clearly copied from the
other. Although Bodleian's style seems fresher, more direct and vigorous than the
refined, almost precious drawing of Morgan, it would be difficult to say which depended upon the other. (One might also note Morgan's occasional misspellings of
words. In particular, in a scroll on fol. 5v of Morgan, the scribe has written "parem"
where Bodleian has the correctly abbreviated "ptem" [fol. 7v]. This is the kind of
scribal error which could come from inattention to the copy text.) Both Bodleian
and Morgan are picture books, accompanied by fragmentary pieces of Berengaudus'
commentary in background and scrolls. Although Paris is closely related to Bodleian-
Morgan, it omits the commentary and text, leaving the scrolls blank. The illustrations
occupy only the top half of each page and a French prose gloss, the "non-Berengaudus" commentary occupies the lower halves of the pages. As Henderson has
shown, Paris differs in some significant details from Bodleian-Morgan and should
probably be regarded as an independent production copied from a common prototype and altering its original in the process (Henderson, *JCWI* 30 [1967], pp. 106–
114). All three manuscripts seem to be the product of English workshops. On the
basis of stylistic evidence, Henderson dates Bodleian-Morgan after 1245 while Paris,
which is "stylistically more primitive," may have been produced before 1245, though
it may have been the work of a provincial workshop, not quite current with court
fashions (113–114). It should be observed that Bodleian and Paris include scenes
from the life of St. John at the beginning of the Apocalypse as Trinity shows his
life both at the beginning and end of the Apocalypse illustrations. By thus framing
the visions of Revelation with John's life, the artists could suggest a linear, continuous relationship between personal history and visionary experience. See Brieger,
Trinity College Apocalypse, pp. 6–7.

Whether or not the great Trinity College Apocalypse is based on an earlier model, the designer's interweaving of illustrations, text and commentary bespeaks an original, inventive mind working according to a careful spiritual plan, governed by two principles—one historical and the other anagogical. The picture cycle for Trinity, like that of Bodley 352, seems to be distantly related to Carolingian models. But, like Bodley, its illustrations organize the symbolic imagery into a coherent narrative sequence dominated by the presence of St. John. John as guide emerges in Trinity as a key figure, illustrating for readers the proper response to each of his visions. As a banner unfurls from an angel's trumpet, commanding "muntez la," John looks attentively upward from his compartment (Fig. 17). When he approaches the vision of the Lamb with the seven-sealed book, the artist describes his three-fold reaction, first of question as the angel tells him that no one is worthy to open the book, then of distress before the elder announces the power of the Lamb, and finally of peace, as the visionary points to the Lamb, the book, and the Lord adored by all creation (Fig. 18). Although this complex representation of St. John's vision is less dramatically conceived than that of Bodley, John's expressive presence is more apparent. While the Trinity St. John here and throughout the picture cycle lacks the tense concentration of Bodley's, he assumes a significantly greater affective flexibility. And, in those illustrated Apocalypses which follow Trinity (and Bodleian-Morgan-Paris), he would come to occupy more and more artistic attention, softening into a courtly figure, perhaps so that he might be more closely identified with his aristocratic audiences.

The Trinity illustrations are arranged to coordinate exactly with the progress of the scriptural text. They appear, as in the Beatus Apocalypses, sometimes in the midst of a page, sometimes in close proximity to each other on the same page. Trinity's designer(s) not only organized the pictures to precede and define each stage of the scriptural *historia*; he also infused the apocalyptic images with an incrementally developed historical and spirtual significance by providing an abbreviated version of the Berengaudus commentary. Thus the reader, turning the leaves of Trinity, is offered the experience of confronting moments in John's vision visually first, then reading the accompanying text in the right-hand column, the Berengaudus gloss in the left. Step by step, and page by page, he can follow the course of the revelation with John, understanding through the gloss what the images signify for his own life and times as well as the final times of human history.

One spiritual rationale for this careful organization of the whole book may be found in a slight adjustment which the Anglo-Norman editor made at the beginning of the gloss. When Berengaudus described what the audience of Revelation should draw from their reading, he concluded: "nam nihil proficit eis qui legunt aut audiunt mandata Dei, si non servant ea, quae legunt vel audiunt. Multi namque sunt, qui mandata Dei audiunt aut legunt, sed nihil eos juvat, quia cum corpore praesentes sint, mente sunt absentes" (for it profits those who read and hear the commandments of God nothing if they do not practice what they read and hear. For there are many who hear or read God's commandments, but it does not help them, for they are present in body, but absent in mind).[70] The Trinity scribe not only alters this admonition; he also adds a warning addressed most probably to the audience he anticipated—the noble and wise who may study scriptures in order to flourish in temporal things: "kar lire e oir ren ne valent seinz retenir; kar akeuns aper

nent esscripture pur estre nobles e sages de la gent e pur florir en temporeaus choses. *Le tens est pres*, co est a saver de iudgment" (to read and hear is worth nothing without remembering; for some learn scripture in order to be considered noble and wise by the people and to flourish in things temporal. Time is at hand, that is to say, the time of judgment).[71] What the glossator expects of his noble readers is not only that they should attend to what they read in order to act, but that they should "remember" it because the time of judgment is near. The Trinity Apocalypse must be understood, then, in part as a memory book intended to fix the "places" of St. John's vision—its orderly stages as well as their meanings—firmly in the reader's imagination.

If this was the Trinity designer's goal, his condensation of Berengaudus' gloss served his purpose well.[72] In it, the apocalyptic narrative assumes the character of a carefully devised story, leading the reader through a series of incrementally enriched recapitulations toward an imaginative grasp of the events surrounding the world's end. Whenever the opportunity arises, whether the text dictates it or not, the gloss divides the

[70] Berengaudus, *In Apocalypsin, PL* xvii, 845.

[71] Fol. 2v. The translations of the Trinity gloss are by Marthe Dulong in Brieger, *Trinity College Apocalypse*, "Introduction."

[72] As the following analysis will show, Freyhan's assumption that the Trinity designers selected an "ultra-orthodox" commentary for their "aristocratic picture-book" as a reaction against the Joachite heresy is based on a faulty premise. See Freyhan, *JCWI*, 17 (1954), pp. 223–225.

images of Revelation into seven parts, signifying the seven "times" of the world. Thus, not only the seven angels with trumpets and the seven with vials, but also the apocalyptic Lord of John's first vision, signify the seven periods of sacred history culminating in the Last Judgment. The editor of Trinity builds toward this historically placed eschatological climax by degrees, always reminding the reader of the whole course of time leading to the end.

But, with the progress of the narrative, the commentary dwells more and more insistently on Antichrist's coming. First, after the blowing of the sixth trumpet, the two witnesses, Enoch and Elias appear, representing the two peoples—the pagans and the Jews—who will preach God's word "par tut le tens auntecrist." This first symbolic presentation of Antichrist's time concludes with the angel blowing the seventh trumpet, that is "les seinz precheurs ki sunt a nestre en la fin del munde" (the holy preachers who will be born at the end of the world).[73] Then the scene shifts to the great conflict between the dragon and the virgin. While this image turns us to the omnitemporal struggle between the Church and Satan, it also reminds us, according to the gloss, of the coming eschaton, for the seventh head of the dragon and his tail signify Antichrist. The dragon's confrontation with the virgin prepares for still fuller development of Antichrist's coming with the ensuing narrative of the dragon and the beast. The first of these figures, of course, signifies Antichrist, the second either one or more of his disciples. The commentary, following St. Paul's second letter to the Thessalonians, offers a full picture of the miracles and trickery Antichrist will practice. Simultaneously, the illustrations represent both his worshipers and his opponents (Fig. 19).[74]

Neither gloss nor illustrations neglect the joy of the elect which will issue from the final conflict. A triumphant scene of rejoicing in honor of the Lamb follows upon Antichrist's temporary triumph and presages the concluding scenes of the book—the general resurrection and the vision of the heavenly city. But before this victory can be realized in time (and in the turning of the leaves) further representations of the conflict itself

[73] *Trinity College Apocalypse*, p. 31 [fol. 13r].

[74] It is Berengaudus' commentary itself, and not Martin of Léon or Adso as Freyhan suggested, which provided a complete summary of Antichrist's miracles and treachery. See Freyhan, p. 230. Berengaudus, who explicitly refers to St. Paul's second letter to the Thessalonians, must have given the Bodleian-Morgan illuminators their inspiration for including scenes depicting the life of Antichrist in their cycle. See pp. 80–81 below.

must intervene, punctuated by reminders of divine triumph—the great harvest of the blessed, the elect standing upon a crystal sea, "les seins deu, ki sunt a cumbatre acuntre auntecrist" (God's saints who will battle against Antichrist).[75] Seven angels in turn pour out their vials of destruction, each one representing one of the seven periods of sacred history, and the last signifying the preachers to come in the time of Antichrist. Then, St. John is led to see the great harlot upon her seven-headed beast: the city of the devil riding upon Satan, according to the gloss. While this vivid composition offers an omnitemporal lesson, it also predicts Antichrist's historical coming: five of the beast's heads have already fallen, the sixth signifies the pagans, and the seventh, Antichrist.

At last, at the end of the fifth vision, after besetting all the peoples of the world, Antichrist is defeated by Christ's army and cast into hell's mouth for the last time. The sixth vision, then, opens out to the great Last Judgment, the glorification of the blessed, and the damnation of the wicked while the seventh vision, the heavenly city, Jerusalem, describes particularly the joy of the blessed after the general resurrection. Whatever the reason for Trinity's abridgment of Berengaudus, the result is a new interpretation of the sacred imagery. What is lost in theological richness is gained in specificity. In the new illustrated edition, the images are seen to tell a single story. In a series of overlapping units, recapitulating the history of God's great struggle with Satan through time, the commentary together with the illuminations lead the reader toward a definitive description of the awesome period of desolation and glorification that will mark the end of time.

But what is the place of the contemporary reader in this historical interpretation, and what spiritual purpose should the gloss, the text and the illustrations serve for *his* life? The answers to these questions point to what is perhaps the most distinctive feature of the Trinity Apocalypse and its successors. The gloss places the ideal contemporary reader in the millennium, that thousand-year period of peace which was to herald the brief reign of Antichrist and the subsequent descent of the New Jerusalem. Such a reader, the commentary argues, must participate at once and fully

[75] It is not without significance that the Trinity illustrator pictures contemporary figures in this scene of the "saints who will confront Antichrist." On the sea of glass stand, among others, a Franciscan, a Dominican, a Benedictine, and two noble women. For other instances in Trinity of figures in the costumes of specific religious orders and women engaged in the apocalyptic conflict, see James, *Trinity College Apocalypse*, pp. 24–25 and Brieger, p. 14.

in the City of God in order to avoid being drafted into the army of Antichrist. "Nus dewm entendre par *mil auns*," the gloss preached, "tut le tens de la venu iesu crist treske a la fin del munde" (By a *thousand years* we must understand all the time from the coming of Christ until the end of the world).[76]

The commentary then explains how God had already "tied up" Antichrist during this thousand-year period of peace *now* being enjoyed by the elect:

> Il *lia* le diable ne mie par liens corporaus mes par liens de sa graunt poeste. Nus poum entendre en treis maneres le lier del diable, co est ke li est lie en abisme par la vertue de deu le tut pusaunt treske al tens establie. U ke il seit lie en les queors des mauveis, par les queors des queres abime poet estre entendu, e forsclos des queus as eslus. U ke il seit tenu e destreint ausi cum des liens ke il ne puset tempter ne deceivere les esluz.[77]

> (He *tied* the Devil not by bodily ties, but by ties of his great might. We can understand the chaining of the Devil in three ways: that is that he is chained in the abyss by the power of God the Almighty until the established time; or that, while barred from the hearts of the elect, he is chained in the hearts of the wicked: by those hearts may be meant the abyss; or that he is compelled as by chains, so that he could not tempt or deceive the elect.)[78]

In other words, the righteous, those who have avoided the seven chief vices, are already enjoying a foretaste of heavenly peace in a millennial existence, free from the power of Antichrist. In their own histories, they are participating in God's triumph over the devil even as their own time carries the human race rapidly toward eternity.

The seven deadly sins are typically placed within the narrative framework of the coming of Antichrist, whose spirit is already abroad in the world. Interpreting the apocalyptic image of the beast rising from the sea for instance, the glossator provides both a moral and historical interpretation which are essentially inseparable:

[76] *Trinity College Apocalypse*, p. 47 [fol. 24r]. While this interpretation of the "thousand years" can be found in Tychonius and St. Augustine, Berengaudus' specific, historicized commentary gives it particular point for the contemporary reader.

[77] *Ibid.*

[78] The punctuation of the DuLong translation has been slightly altered here for greater clarity.

La beste est veu munter de la mer, pur co ke auntecrist levera de la cumpainie as reproves. La gent ke auntecrist fra suiet a sai sunt signifie par les *dis cors*. Les *set testes* signifient les sept vices principaus, les queus io voil numbrer solu[m] co ke prudence ordine. Il mist le prem-erein vice idolatrie, co est honur des ydles; le second libidine; le terz ire; le quart orgul; le quint lecherie. . . . Le siste avarice; le setime blasfemie, u descord.[79]

(The beast is seen to *rise up out of the sea* because Antichrist will rise up out of the crowd of the damned. The people whom Antichrist will make his subjects are signified by the *ten horns*. The *seven heads* mean the seven principal vices which I want to enumerate in the way Pruden-tius arranges them. He placed idolatry as the first vice—that is, giving honor to idols; the second is lust; the third, wrath; the fourth, pride; the fifth, luxury. . . . The sixth is avarice; the seventh, blasphemy or strife.)

The glossator will have it both ways: the coming of Antichrist is to be an historical phenomenon, perhaps to come within the time of some of his own readers.[80] But Antichrist has already come spiritually in the guise and presence of the seven principal vices in the world, and, even now, he dominates the damned who will eventually form his army. That is, Everyman can capitulate now to the forces of Antichrist even before his actual appearance, but he can also avoid his power by the watchfulness and prayer the glossator recommends at the very end of his commentary.[81] He then prays that he and his readers may join Christ's army in the grand historical and spiritual conflict both now and in the fullness of time:

Nus doint les armes des vertues, par les queus nus garniz, od lu dustre e baneur, seums defenduz des enemis foreins e de ceus dedeins, ke nus deservuns estre parceneres de la vie pardurable.[82]

(Give us the weapons of the virtues to protect us, so that with Him as leader and flagbearer, we might be defended from the outer and inner enemies, so that we might deserve to be partakers of everlasting life.)

In both these instances, the commentator has personalized and historicized the older Prudentian personified struggle between the virtues and the vices.

[79] *Trinity College Apocalypse*, p. 34 [fol. 14v].
[80] See *Trinity College Apocalypse*, p. 52 [fol. 27v].
[81] *Ibid.*   [82] *Ibid.*

St. John, the glossator, and the reader participate in their own times and in their own ways in the apocalyptic conflict, just as their temporal successors will confront an historical Antichrist to come in the Final Time.

Trinity's concern for the order of history and for spiritual edification in leading readers to imagine the events of the eschaton parallels innovations in cathedral sculpture, and like the cathedral art, it seems to be coupled with the hope of leading readers toward an anagogical experience of the figures. Like Abbot Suger, the illuminators of Trinity sought to create images which could reveal spiritual radiance through material splendor. In this they rejected an earlier monastic reticence before the mystery of divine presence and sought to draw their readers closer to vision. When Beatus commented on the apocalyptic image of Christ's face shining as the sun, he had found more difference than similitude in the comparison:

> Hic facies illius soli comparatur. Indignum est enim et satis humile putare Christum descriptum discoloribus membris aut claritatem eius soli comparatam. Nam si de iustis dicit: fulgebunt sicut sol; quam periculosum est dicere, quod pari claritate fulgeant iusti cum Domino, cum ipse sit suorum claritas.[83]

> (His face is compared to the sun: but it is unworthy and humiliating to think of Christ described with discolored members or His brightness compared to the sun. For if it is said of the Just, "they shone like the sun," how dangerous is it to say that the Just shone with a brilliance equal to the Lord's when He *is* their brilliance.)

Richard of St. Victor, on the other hand, describes St. John's image of Christ's face shining like the sun in its strength as an adequate material representation of divine glory. Through the image, the reader could ascend to a true, anagogical understanding of Christ's brightness:

> Clarissimam ergo creaturam ad exprimendam claritatis suae gloriam posuit, dum faciem ejus sicut solem lucere dixit. Sed quoniam nequaquam hoc sufficere, sed adhuc se plus posse dicere cognovit, cum dixisset, sicut sol lucet, protinus adjecit, in virtute sua. Sol autem in virtute sua lucet, quando circa meridiem nubibus ablatis, aere purificato, per ejusdem aeris spatia clarissimo fulgore splendet. . . . Quia igitur humana intelligentia ad humanitatis ejus gloriam non sufficit comprehendere, nec lingua potest digne manifestare, non simus scrutatores majestatis, ne opprimamur a gloria; scrutemur interim et sanemus, adjuvante gra-

[83] *Beati in Apocalypsin*, pp. 80–81.

tia, nostram infirmitatem, ut ad ejus gloriae mereamur quandoque pertingere contemplationem. Laboremus totis viribus ad illius claritatem lucis meritis pervenire, quae et in omnibus tenebris lucet, . . . et manifestae similitudinis Christi gloriam, secundum virtutem in mente retineamus, ut desiderium illius gloriae quae per istam figurata est, in nobis ardentius accendamus.[84]

(He chose the brightest creature for expressing the glory of His brilliance when he said that His face shone as the sun. But this was not altogether sufficient since he knew that more could be said. So he said, "just as the sun shines" and added "in all its strength." The sun shines in all its strength at noon, free of clouds in the pure air, and shines with the clearest light through the spaces of air. . . . Because human intelligence is not sufficient for man to comprehend His glory, nor can tongue manifest it worthily, nor are we scrutinizers of His majesty, we are overpowered by His glory. But in the meantime, we examine, and we allay our infirmity, sustained by His grace, so that we will be made worthy of His glory when we reach contemplation. We labor with all men to reach the clarity of that Light by merit, which shines in all shadows . . . *and we retain the glory of Christ by a clear similitude according to the strength of our mind, so that the desire for that glory, which is figured through this image, burning more ardently in us will carry us upward* [italics mine].)

With much the same theory concerning images of divine radiance, a Trinity colorist could create a Christ with a face of gold leaf gleaming from the page through which readers might be raised to divine contemplation.[85]

By contrast to Trinity, the second prototypical cycle, best represented in two nearly identical picture books—Bodleian MS. Auct. D. 4.17 and MS. Morgan 524—seems simple and popular.[86] In these small, neat illustrated Apocalypses, the ink-drawn illustrations, arranged two on each page and colored in pale washes, follow one another without any meditative interventions. The elongated, graceful figure of John, with bearded face, mov-

[84] *In Apocalypsim,* PL cxcvi, 709.

[85] Depending on a different means to a similar end, one Franciscan illuminator, Brother William by name, made a drawing of the apocalyptic Lord among the candelabra and then wrote on the back of the leaf: "Nothing more is to be written on this page lest the image be injured, as the parchment is transparent, and it can be seen better if held up to the light." (quoted in P. Brieger, *English Art,* 1216–1307 [Oxford, 1957]), p. 161.

[86] See note 69.

ing through his story, occupies still greater attention than it had in Trinity and his expressive responses to his visions are more varied. The images thus organized in orderly procession tell their own story, relying for elucidation and specificity on fragments of Revelation and the Berengaudus gloss written in backgrounds and on scrolls. With the text wholly subordinated to the illustrations, the image series presents a clear, coherent linear narrative, which leads the reader to consider especially the coming and defeat of Antichrist within imaginable time.

The Trinity designers had followed Berengaudus' interest in the times of the world and Antichrist's advent to provide historical depth and richness for their visual images; but the illustrations themselves illuminate the letter of the Apocalypse. In Bodleian-Morgan, on the other hand, Berengaudus' concern for Antichrist provided the artists with a key for reshaping and reorganizing the visual materials (and interrupting the course of the text) to articulate as clearly as possible the historical significance of St. John's prophecy. Perhaps responding to popular demand, or the preaching style of the new orders, the designers of Bodleian-Morgan interpret Revelation principally as a direct, pointed account of the temporal events which will surround the eschaton.[87]

[87] B.N. MS. fr. 403, the third mid-thirteenth-century illustrated Apocalypse using this cycle, carried this emphasis further by joining the pictures with a new commentary, one which insistently studied the interpenetration of contemporary time and the events of the eschaton. Urgent admonitions to good preachers and holy prelates concerning the necessity of penance and virtue are coupled with pervasive reminders that Judgment is at hand and that the disciples of Antichrist are already abroad in the world. For an edition of this commentary, see Delisle and Meyer, *L'Apocalypse en français*. See also John Fox, "The Earliest French Apocalypse and Commentary," *Modern Language Review* 7 (1912), pp. 445–468; Gunter Breder, *Die Lateinische Vorlage des Altfranzösischen Apokalypsenkommentars des 13. Jahrhunderts* (Paris, B.N. MS. fr. 403), *Forschungen zur Romanischen Philologie*, 9 (Munster, 1960); Olwen Rhys, *An Anglo-Norman Rhymed Apocalypse with Commentary* (Oxford, 1946). This last version of the "non-Berengaudus" commentary is especially interesting for two reasons: (1) its audience is clearly defined as a group of Benedictine nuns; and (2) it describes the text and commentary on the Apocalypse as a memory book neatly divided into seven visions:

> Apres tut cest fet sa narraciun
> E fet sun livre, ke est parti en set visiun
> Si ke l'en puet chescune par sei entendre;
> E des chapitres ki veut la cunte rendre,
> Vint e deus i a par acunter—
> Plus ne meins n'i seut huem user;

Yet, although the effect of this cycle is significantly simpler and more direct than Trinity, the intellectual rigor of its design is not inconsiderable. Indeed, it seems clear that these English artists, perhaps working from a model which had already united Berengaudus with illustrations, infused the cycle with their own lucid but limited reading of Berengaudus to suit the temper of their time. Paring away all but the essential historical dimension of Berengaudus, Bodleian-Morgan streamlines and simplifies so that the meaning of the images can be direct and univocal for the reader.

The cycle begins in a traditional manner with the seven churches of Asia and St. John at the feet of the apocalyptic Lord. Brief glosses clarify both the omnitemporal and temporal meaning of the images: the seven churches signify the Catholic Church and their angels are the rectors of the Church. In a scroll, Christ declares to John, "noli timere," announcing his role as comforter both for the evangelist and the reader setting out on their visionary way. In the scenes that follow—the visions of the One Enthroned, the Lamb and the opening of the book with seven seals— Berengaudus' gloss provides a sound historical foundation on which to build toward images of Antichrist's coming. The elder who explains to St. John how the book will be opened represents, according to the gloss, the prophets who foretold Christ's coming. The angel who asks who is worthy to open the book signifies the ancient fathers. And the opening of the seven seals, one by one, marks out the stages of Old Testament history from the time before the Flood until the birth of Christ. In these initial visionary sequences, symbolizing past history, John's responses are vividly delineated. His personal, engaged attention provides certain guidance for readers peering into the meaning of what they see.

With the vision of the angels blowing their seven trumpets, the historical meaning of the images is incrementally enriched. Each of the seven angels, the gloss tells us, recapitulates a period of sacred history as the seven seals had done, but now there are signs of the coming end of the world intruding upon the scenes. While the angel blowing the first trumpet signifies the doctors before the law, the thunder mentioned by the text and visually represented, signifies the world's consummation by fire; the lightning, the virtues of the apostles; the earthquake, the conversion

---

Merche(r)z serunt od les visiouns
Sus en margene par devisiouns.
Des ci orrez la signifiance od l'estoire.
Bien eit ke les mettra ben en memoire!
(Rhys, p. 3)

of the Jews. In addition, the fourth, fifth and sixth angels signify New Testament history, including the defense of Christ's church against heresy and the age of martyrs. Before introducing the seventh angel, who signifies those holy preachers to be born at the end of the world, the artist intrudes his most striking innovation. Like Trinity, Bodleian-Morgan follows Berengaudus in depicting the two witnesses, Enoch and Elias, as preachers in the time of Antichrist. But he develops their significance by adding five scenes describing the life, triumph and death of Antichrist.[88] To introduce this sequence, the designer must have drawn on a later section of Berengaudus' commentary in which Antichrist's miracles and trickery are described (Fig. 20).[89] His motivation seems clear. As the maker of a good story, he perceived the obvious interconnections between the life, death and miraculous resurrection of the witnesses imitating Christ's actions and the miracles of Antichrist, who according to Berengaudus, had only seemed to rise from the dead, parodying Christ. Furthermore, since the witnesses were, in Berengaudus, preaching against Antichrist, it would contribute verisimilitude to represent Antichrist himself at this point in the narrative, though the scriptural text had not explicitly called for him.

Bodleian-Morgan's history of Antichrist concludes, fittingly, with his

[88] The models for this sequence were undoubtedly devised in the twelfth century if not earlier. The image of Antichrist holding his sword of power and authority in his right hand is similar to the Antichrist sitting on Leviathan in Lambert of St. Omer's *Liber Floridus* (ed. A. Derolez, *Lamberti S. Audomari Canonici Liber Floridus*. Codex Autographus Universitatis Gandavensis [Ghent, 1968], p. 131 [fol. 62v]). The *Liber Floridus* also contains Methodius' letter concerning Antichrist's coming which, like Berengaudus' commentary, quotes St. Paul's second letter to the Thessalonians as its authority. A cycle of illustrations describing Antichrist's miracles and overthrow was also contained in the now destroyed manuscript of the *Hortus Deliciarum* of Herrade of Landsperg, written and painted about 1150. (See James, *Trinity College Apocalypse*, p. 56)

[89] *In Apocalypsim*, PL xvii, 970: Faciet namque miracula Antichristus arte diabolica, facient et discipuli ejus: sed eorum miracula falsa erunt, et non vera, sicut dicit Apostolus: "Cujus adventus erit secundum operationem Satanae, in omnibus virtutibus et signis et prodigiis mendacibus (2 Thess. 2: 9)." Non enim credibile est, ut eos quos Deus excaecaverat, aut debilitaverat, sanitati possint restituere: sed eos tantummodo, quos ipsi laeserint, laedentes in occulto, sanantes in aperto. Sed et ipse Antichristus in tanta claritate se hominibus demonstrabit, ut ab insipientibus credatur Deus, sicut dicit Apostolus: "Ita ut in templo sedeat, ostendens se tanquam sit Deus (*ibid.* 4)." The close correlation between this text and the illustrations in Bodleian-Morgan make it certain that Berengaudus was a chief source of inspiration in shaping the scenes of Antichrist's life.

death by the power of God's anger. Now the artist returns to the text of Revelation. The seventh angel blowing his trumpet provides a closing frame for the Antichrist narrative, signifying the preachers at the end of the world. Then, in the scene of adoration which follows, Christ's ultimate triumph and glory is marked by the "Confessio regum."

With Antichrist's life and death fully depicted and standing as the historical culmination for all the forces of evil in the narrative, the succeeding sequences fall easily into place. The dragon's confrontation with the virgin and conflict with Michael are provided with no gloss. Implicitly, these are to be understood entirely within the context of Antichrist's historical coming. So, too, the series of illustrations depicting the dragon from the sea and the beast from the land further develop the theme of Antichrist's dominion over the sons of earth. In the interpretation of these images, as of all the illustrations the artist and/or scribe depended on the authority of Berengaudus; but his pressing concern for the *time* of Antichrist's coming led him to search the gloss for signs of this time, and to stress them both in his illustrations and in the backgrounds of the pictures.

Yet, as in Trinity, an interest in Antichrist is ineluctably coupled with a concern for the triumphant joy of Christ and his blessed. Christ's command to John at the beginning, not to fear, is answered more and more fully in the last third of the Bodleian-Morgan picture book by images of comfort and joy. The triumph of the Lamb on Sion and depictions of the great harvest precede the final sequence of destruction—the seven angels pouring out their vials, the Whore of Babylon reigning and then condemned by God's judgment (Fig. 21).

The last movement of the narrative begins with a gentle, expressive image of the heavenly banquet in the New Jerusalem. Swiftly, then, the illustrations, unaccompanied by any gloss, survey the triumphant conquest of Satan by the One Faithful and True upon his white horse, the dragon's thousand-year incarceration, his brief return and final damnation. Finally, freed from fear entirely, St. John is allowed to perceive the heavenly Jerusalem and its lord. The last scenes of Bodleian-Morgan represent John led by an angel toward the Lord in a distant mandorla, then, remarkably, kneeling before his savior who speaks directly to him, his hand gracefully poised in admonition. These scenes require no gloss for the illustrator has already established their historical framework. St. John, as visionary and guide, has indeed shown all his readers "þe way to heuenly hall" as that path is to be perceived by all Christians living in the evening of the world and approaching the eschaton. The interpretive directions for the Book of Revelation explored by the designers of Trinity on the one hand, and Bodleian-Morgan on the other, met with immediate approbation in succeeding generations of Apocalypse illustrators. One or both cycles, in one way or another, affected nearly every visual representation of apocalyptic imagery in the later thirteenth and fourteenth centuries.[90] Artists and glossators would add their own embellishments and modifications—illustrations for the gloss as well as the text of Revelation in the Abingdon Abbey Apocalypse (c. 1262);[91] a versified version of Revelation together with the "non-Berengaudus" commentary in seven illustrated Apocalypses of the later thirteenth and fourteenth centuries;[92] elegant tapestries transforming the miniatures into finely woven, full-size figures.[93] So well-suited to their time and the needs of their audiences were Trinity and Bodleian-Morgan that they could provide patterns for two centuries, absorbing specific alterations and attracting new commentaries, but continuing to articulate a basic lesson: St. John as leader and guide would show his readers how to prepare their souls and their imagination for their own and the universal eschaton through a series of temporally ordered figures.

Like the sculptural programs of St.-Denis and Chartres, these illustrations were to serve as guides for memory, fixing the "places" of St. John's spiritual pilgrimage in the reader's mind. Through John's example, the audience, turning the pages of the book, might perceive an intimate rela-

[90] For the history of the illustrated Apocalypse in England after Trinity and Bodleian-Morgan, see G. Henderson (*JCWI* [1967]) and *idem*, "Studies in English Manuscript Illumination: III," *JCWI*, 31 (1968), pp. 103-147.

[91] B.M. MS. Add. 42555. This is an especially interesting English Apocalypse which stresses the time of Antichrist's coming and its meaning for the moral life of the contemporary Christian. It seems highly probable that William Langland knew this, or a book like it, and that its iconography and commentary affected his making of *Piers Plowman*.

[92] Cambridge, Magdelene College MS. 1803; B.M. MS. Royal 2 D. XIII; Copenhagen, Bibl. Roy., de Thott. MS. 89; Maclean, now FitzWilliam Mus.; Cambridge, Corpus Christi Coll., MS. 20; B.M. MS. Add. 18633; Toulouse, B.N. MS. 815. For a description of these manuscripts, see P. Meyer, "Version Anglo-Normande en vers de l'Apocalypse," *Romania* 25 (1896) pp. 174-257. For an edition of the versified Apocalypse and non-Berengaudus gloss, see O. Rhys, *An Anglo-Norman Rhymed Apocalypse* (Oxford, 1946).

[93] The fourteenth-century Angers tapestries of the Apocalypse designed by Hennequin of Bruges for Louis of Anjou. See *L'Apocalypse d'Angers*, ed. R. Planchenault, Caisse Nationale des Monuments Historiques et des Sites (Paris, n.d.).

tionship between their own time and place and the course of sacred time figured forth in St. John's revelation. It is not necessary to insist on direct influence in order to suggest that thirteenth- and fourteenth-century poets closely parallel contemporary artistic interest as they likewise chart their readers' way from sin toward salvation through a series of visionary "places."

THREE

THE *VITA NUOVA*: DANTE'S BOOK OF REVELATION

The earliest recorded critic of the *Vita Nuova* (1291–93) was Dante himself. In the *Convivio*, brought to its partial completion thirteen years or more after his *libello*, he places his youthful effort within the context of his subsequent intellectual growth.[1] It is, he argues in the *Convivio*, an adolescent work, "fervida e passionata" (i, 1, 16). Yet the older poet does not reject his juvenilia, and indeed, he discovers a continuity between the perceptions recorded in the *Vita Nuova* and those he had subsequently acquired by diligent study: "I was by natural ability, not by study, already seeing many things as in a dream" (ii, 12, 14). What Dante does not tell us, of course, is precisely what "things" he means. Nor does he explain the richly ambiguous phrase, "as in a dream," though earlier in the *Convivio* he had suggested that it is "dreams" which give us evidence of our immortality (ii, 12, 4).

Of all Dante's works, none has provoked a wider spectrum of critical readings than his earliest. As the story of a first love cast in the literary language of thirteenth-century *stilnovisti* poets, it has served biographical critics who find in it a literal account of Dante's relationship with a certain Bice Portinari. Others, observing the retrospective double structure of the narrative—the story retold through poetry and prose and at the same time reshaped—have described the *libello* as a book of devotion or a saint's life which casts Beatrice in the role of mediatrix of divine grace. At the farthest extreme, the *Vita Nuova* has been read as a sustained per-

[1] For the dating of the *Vita Nuova* and the *Convivio*, see B. Nardi, *Nel Mondo di Dante* (Rome, 1944), pp. 3–4 and 20–36. But see also L. Pietrobono, "Intorno alla data delle opere minori," *Giornale Dantesca* XLII, pp. 50–52. All quotations from Dante's works will be based on *Le Opere di Dante, Testo Critico della Società Dantesca Italiana*, ed. M. Barbi *et al.*, 2nd ed. (Florence, 1960).

sonification allegory, the story of Everyman's encounter with grace or theology.[2]

We should wonder neither at the variety nor number of readings given to Dante's first work. It is not only difficult in itself; it is complicated by the poet's own comments concerning it in the *Convivio*, and his further development of the figure of Beatrice in the *Commedia*. Did the master poet experience a transforming enlightenment through the intellectual pursuits described in the *Convivio* which caused him to devalue his *libello* and revise his image of Beatrice in the *Commedia*? Or should the *Vita Nuova* be recognized as part of a continuum, perhaps even reworked by Dante to serve as a prologue for the *Commedia*?[3] Such critical dilemmas as these, which the *libello* has posed for readers particularly in this century, may finally be due to limitations in the work itself. Yet its undeniable genius—and its particular usefulness for this study—lies, I believe, in Dante's development of a visionary voice never before so self-consciously or confidently sounded in fiction—one which would serve him far more fully in the *Commedia*.

The thirty-one poems of the *libello*, including two imperfect *canzoni*, around which Dante's narrator builds his elaborate prose commentary depend, as we might expect, on the familiar lyric "I" of *fin amor* poetry elegantly modulated by generations of provençal and Italian writers. This voice, at once individualized and general, was the shared property of all who sought fraternity in the inheritance of Guillaume of Poitou, and

---

[2] For critical bibliography, see M. De Bonfils Templer, *Itinerario di Amore* (Chapel Hill, 1973), pp. 162–172. J. E. Shaw has provided a useful survey of evidence for an historical Beatrice and has also assessed the value and limitations of strictly allegorical interpretations in *Essays on the Vita Nuova* (Princeton and Paris, 1929), pp. 163–227. Studies which have been particularly helpful for this study in its final form are the following: A. Marigo, *Mistica e Scienza nella Vita Nuova di Dante* (Padua, 1914); Shaw, *Essay on the Vita Nuova* (Princeton, 1929); A. Sciaffini, *Tradizione e Poesia*, 2nd ed. (Rome, 1943); C. S. Singleton, *Essay on the Vita Nuova* (Cambridge, 1949); D. De Robertis, *Il Libro della "Vita Nuova"* (Florence, 1961); V. Branca, "Poetica del rinnovamento e tradizione agiografica nella *Vita Nuova*," in *Studi in onore di Italo Siciliano* (Florence, 1965); N. Mineo, *Profetismo e Apocalittica in Dante* (Catania, 1968); and R. Hollander," *Vita Nuova*: Dante's Perceptions of Beatrice," *Dante Studies* xcii (1974), pp. 1–18.

I would like to thank the Dante Society of America for permission to reprint parts of two earlier versions of this chapter which appeared in *Dante Studies* LXXXVIII (1970) and xcii (1974).

[3] See Nardi, *Nel Mondo di Dante*, pp. 3–20.

Dante had certainly explored its nuances thoroughly.[4] But the "I" of the prose commentary is quite other. From the very beginning of his little book of memory, the narrator speaks with the assurance, the richness, the particularity of one who has been privileged with a special and unique spiritual experience. The revelations he recounts and interprets are essentially rooted in his own history and have led him to discover absolute spiritual truths—truths which, he suggests, have a fundamental bearing on the final destiny of Everyman.

The voice that dominates the *Vita Nuova*'s prose was not Dante's invention. Heretofore it had been used preeminently by prophets of sacred scripture—Ezekiel, Isaiah, Jeremiah, John the Evangelist—by monastic historians attesting the visionary experiences of special souls chosen as examples for pilgrim man, and by hagiographers assuring readers of the veracity of miracles actually witnessed by them or their informants: "Et qui scripsit, expertus est hoc in seipso" (And he who wrote this had experience of it himself).[5] By appropriating this magisterial voice for his own less certainly sacred revelations and meditations, Dante's narrator insists on the true prophetic meaning inhering in all the images he has drawn from memory and collected in his book. Readers may add their own glosses to the poet's if they wish, he suggests. But above all they must understand that the series of images he presents and examines have had an overwhelming bearing on his own discovery and definition not of the idea but of the true experience of beatitude. In a highly personal, self-consciously literary way, Dante undertakes in the *Vita Nuova* to show how material forms—human events, the changing figure of Beatrice and the languages of poetry—have led him, like certain prophets and saints, to catch a glimpse of eternal joy. The questing narrator exploring his own extraordinary visionary history argues that personal experience can—indeed must—participate in the ineluctable progress of human history toward an eschatological conclusion. Better than many a spiritual treatise, the account of his discoveries demonstrates how one may learn to perceive his own space and time anagogically. In addition, it offers us a luminous example of the double structure—narrative infused with spirit-

---

[4] For Dante's manipulations of this conventional voice, see the recent invaluable edition with commentary of the collected lyrics by K. Foster and P. Boyde, *Dante's Lyric Poetry*, 2 vols. (Oxford, 1967).

[5] *Vita Beati Fratris Egidii* in *Scripta Leonis, Rufini et angeli Sociorum S. Francisci*, ed. and trans. R. Brooke (Oxford, 1970), p. 348.

ual meaning—which would characterize the best vision narratives of the later Middle Ages.

THE DOUBLE STRUCTURE OF THE *Vita Nuova*

As Aristotle had taught the later Middle Ages, memory is the particular gift of mankind. Although some animals have memory, they cannot preserve, polish and return by reason to images received by the senses. It is the glory of man alone to use and develop his power of memory and by that means to find continuity, integrity and purpose in his life. Brought to its highest pitch, the faculty of human memory can transform ordinary events and simple history into an art of living imitative of heavenly perfection. Dante begins the story of the new life with these assumptions about memory. But he carries his readers far beyond the rhetoricians' manuals to a dramatic representation of the high art of a singular human memory discovering sacred meaning in personal history. His narrator, who is both a lover and a prophet-scribe, explores the images held in his memory. As he follows the historical course of the images, he records his gradual transformation from a typical courtly lover, limited by the temporal succession of events, into a prophet chosen to teach the way to beatitude. Because the narrator who tells the story of his transformation has already become a prophet, he undertakes the task of shaping the lover's story into a thirteenth-century book of revelation.

As a lover, the narrator of the *Vita Nuova* recreates his responses to the presence and image of Beatrice. His actions in the beginning of the book are those of the stumbling courtly lover, enchanted and stunned beyond speech by his lady's presence. Because of his love, he swears fealty to the god of *fin amor*, swoons, writes poetry. He is by turns frustrated and jubilant. Most important, in the early stages of his love, whether in joy or woe, he is ineluctably bound by time and place, that is, by the circumstances of his history. When he sees Beatrice, he is lifted into esctasy; when she rebukes him, he suffers indescribable torment. Without the possibility of seeing her, he is like a dead man. But in the course of the conventional love story, he begins to discover patterns which, though not easy to interpret, suggest that the history of this love is no ordinary one, that it must eventually transcend the limitations of time and space.

By degrees, the all-embracing truth becomes clear. The history of the lover's spiritual relationship with the Beatrice of his mind is also the record of his progress towards salvation. As the narrator begins to write the *Vita Nuova,* he has already recognized that, for him, Beatrice is beatific grace recreating him in the image of man redeemed, "tutti i termini della beatitudine" (III).[6] His sanctification has come neither from the sacraments nor prayer but from his vision of the miraculous little girl and his subsequent meditation on her. He has discovered that his personal history in Florence over the course of fifteen years participates by imitation in the cosmic history of salvation.

In order to show both the historical steps to beatitude and its achievement, Dante's narrator speaks alternately with the voices of the lover-poet and of the prophet. The lover's drama proceeds historically from an experience of wonder, which introduces him into the world of sanctity, to a final glimpse of heavenly bliss, the "mirabile visione" defying description (LXII). But the book is set down by a narrator who has already lived through the whole story.[6a]

Because in the course of his experiences he has gradually acknowledged

[6] Those critics who argue for a secular reading of the *Vita Nuova* must ask the question whether Dante really meant "beatitude" when he said it or whether he intended that quite specialized term to be taken in an unusual, general, non-spiritual way. The plain literal evidence of the *libello* seems to argue in the opposite direction. In addition, as we shall see, the carefully constructed imaginative visions alluding to scriptural prophecies, the images of Beatrice's ascent to heaven, her appearance among the angels, her characterization as a miracle, the product of the Trinity, all suggest that for Dante the experiences described in the *Vita Nuova* pointed his way directly to truths about the actual heaven of human salvation. To be sure, his claim was extraordinary. But if we do not read the *libello* this way, we must needs explain away a great deal of "ornamental" imagery and finally discount the book as a pretentious fable. On the other hand, if we take Dante at his word, then we are bound to see that his pervasively allusive imagery precisely fits an important class of medieval figures—those which were designed to show through the colors of poetry truths bearing on man's final destiny. For a brilliant discussion of this class of images, see R. Tuve, *Allegorical Imagery* (Princeton, 1966), pp. 1–55 and esp. pp. 17–18.

[6a] In the *Vita Nuova,* Dante's poet lover begins as an aesthete exploring his own artistic and spiritual history for the sake of an elite coterie of like-minded love poets but emerges as an ethically oriented Everyman figure presaging the narrator of the *Commedia.* The "I" narrator who dominates the retrospective prose of the *libello* has become an example of one sanctified by love and privileged with an absolute vision which does, in fact, have relevance for Everyman. Whether or not, as Nardi has suggested, the end of the *Vita Nuova* was reshaped, the *libello* as a whole demonstrates the transformation of the narrator from an earthly lover to an ethical exemplar for mankind seeking the wisdom of beatitude.

his responsibility as prophet, the narrator must not only tell his miraculous story; he must also teach his readers how to interpret and use his prophecy. They must learn to see (1) that their own history, like the history of revelation recorded in sacred scripture, involves given, personal encounters with divinity which can lead to salvation; and (2) that in order to translate personal history into divine revelation, interpretation by reason is necessary.

To teach his lessons, the prophetic scribe of the *libello* first of all subtly aligns the story of his love for Beatrice with the pattern, discovered by scriptural exegetes, of man's gradual growth in the love and knowledge of God through the Old and New Testaments to the present, a pattern fully outlined in contemporary spiritual treatises. He begins with enigmatic, figurative visions and phantasms of an *Amore* who ambiguously suggests both secular and sacred meaning, and concludes with an anagogical vision. Secondly, as he moves through the images retained in his memory, he reflects in reasoned prose on the meaning of what the lover has seen and recorded at each stage in the development of his relationship with Beatrice. By setting down the images, he insists that historical time is the essential condition for moments of revelation, the necessary environment in which experiences of divinity occur and are marked by memory. But by interpreting the images, he shows that experience alone is not enough to move a man toward salvation; by itself it can produce neither art nor a purpose to shape human life. The final step must be a single universal judgment growing out of many reflections upon experience.

Dante's Book of Memory and Medieval Memory Theory

Dante's narrator begins his "little book" with a proem in which he proposes to explain the relationship between the images of memory, chronologically arranged, and rational judgment which will discover the new life.[7] Setting himself the task of writing out the "words" found in the book of his memory, as if he were copying manuscript, he will begin at a large red letter placed very near the beginning of his temporal existence in the world. He must begin there, following the necessary curve of natural memory. But he is also going to edit, interpret and discover meaning.

---

[7] Charles Singleton was the first to call attention to the importance of chapter 1 as a proem setting forth the central metaphor of the "Book of Memory." In my own study, I am deeply and gratefully indebted to his insightful and penetrating work. See note 2 above.

Indeed, he tells us, it is the *sententia* which must be discovered above all. One may, with discretion, leave out certain experiences inscribed in the annals of memory. But the meaning, the primary concern of the artificer, the seeker after truth and the scientist of wisdom, must be found. If all the experiences are not recorded, "at least their sentence" will be set down. At this point, the reader can only guess what the "new life" will be, perhaps using his knowledge of the familiar Christian theme of the rebirth of man into the life of Christ.[8] But he is prepared by the proem to expect that all the images recorded in the book will contribute in some way to his understanding of that "vita nuova."

To clarify further the relationship between remembered images and his art, the narrator uses the metaphor of "words" in the proem. The "words" of the book of memory are literally no more nor less than remembered images of times, places, persons and things, all of them subject to the failings of memory and to death. But when the scribe copies out these images, he turns them into literal words and into art.[9] The images retain the freshness of actual experience. But their symbolic transformation by the scribe gives them a permanence and purpose beyond their reference to past experience. As symbols, they can carry both narrator and reader from images toward truth, from the role of lover to that of prophet and saint, from moments of wonder to a state of wisdom fully experienced. The "symbol" or model made of words artfully arranged, which is the finished *Vita Nuova*, like Suger's choir at St.-Denis, provides a symbolic means for transporting the spirit from images of earthly beauty to a vision seen "in an anagogical manner."

When, in his prologue, Dante's narrator separates the ordinary course of memory from reasoned interpretation of remembered images, he fol-

---

[8] If the "new life" is not to be construed in its strictly Christian sense, then it should be understood as an analogously transformed state. The prose narrative of the *Vita Nuova* demonstrates that Dante's narrator believes himself at least provisionally sanctified by love and brought into contact with spiritual perfection in an absolute sense. For other possible meanings of the "vita nuova," see Shaw, *Essays*, pp. 55–72; DeRobertis, *Il Libro*, p. 23. See also J. A. Scott ("Religion in the *Vita Nuova*," *Italian Studies* xx [1965], pp. 17–18), who admits a theological significance but limits its function to "ornament."

[9] Dante's scribe is more closely related to the image of St. John the Evangelist as a copyist describing his own visions than to images of ordinary monkish scribes at work (see Fig. 8). The similarity between Dante's narrator and contemporary depictions of St. John is not, I think, accidental, but extends both to details of imagery and to the prophetic purpose of both books.

lows a common classical and medieval rhetorical distinction, at the same time establishing the terms of his double structure—the visionary image series and interpretive commentary. As a special gift of human nature, natural memory makes experiences possible by storing up images. It gives continuity to past, present and future. But the higher, more spiritual discipline by which remembered experiences can participate in the life of morality is not natural but artificial. Both classical and medieval definitions of the "artificial memory" relate it directly to "art." Aristotle calls it judgment which is the cause of art: "Art arises when from many notions gained by experience one universal judgment about a class of objects is produced."[10] Albertus Magnus separates simple remembering from the higher discipline of reminiscence: "Those wishing to reminisce [i.e. wishing to do something more spiritual and intellectual than merely remember] withdraw from the public light into obscure privacy: because in the public light the images of sensible things are scattered and their movement is confused. In obscurity, however, they are unified and moved in order."[11] Boncompagno makes a similar distinction between the natural and artificial memory in his popular *Rhetorica Novissima*, written at Bologna in 1235. Natural memory, he says, is a gift of nature by which "we recall past things, we embrace present things, and we contemplate future things through their likeness to past things"; artificial memory is the "auxiliary and assistant of natural memory . . . called 'artificial' from 'art' because it is found artificially through subtlety of mind."[12]

Judgment, subtlety of mind, the act of spirit and intellect, art: these are the terms used by rhetoricians to describe the artificial, highly selective memory which unites remembered experience with the act and art of human life. Both for Aristotle and the medieval theorists, the "art of memory" involved the imposition of *theoria* or *scientia*, knowledge of causes, upon experience. It imposed a nontemporal significance on what, in the flow of natural memory, could only be temporal, the ordering of

---

[10] *Metaphysica*, trans. W. D. Ross in *Works of Aristotle*, vol. viii (Oxford, 1940) Book A, 981a.

[11] *De Bono* in *Opera Omnia*, ed. H. Kühle, C. Feckes, B. Geyer, W. Kübel (Aschendorff, 1951), p. 108; quoted in Frances Yates, *The Art of Memory* (Chicago, 1966), p. 68. I am indebted to Yates's remarkable book for my introduction to medieval theories of memory.

[12] *Rhetorica Novissima*, ed. A. Gaudentio, *Bibliotheca Iuridicia Medii Aevii*, ii, (Bologna, 1891); quoted in Yates, p. 58.

past, present and future. Exercising this art of memory, Dante's narrator
will examine his historical experience of love. Meditating on his store-
house of images and poems, he will lead his readers by degrees to observe
a pattern, nonlinear, spiritual and abstract, imposed on those images
drawn from personal history. Interpreting the contents of his memory,
image by image, he will transform remembered experiences into an art
of salvation. He will shape the *Vita Nuova* into a dramatic representation
of this transformation, recording the completed art as it appeared in the
act of becoming.

The First Stage: Apparitions and Enigmas

With chapter II of his book, which records the first stage in his drama of
discovery, the narrator carefully analyzes the human imaginative experience of wonder, significantly a child's awakening to love. He remembers
the moment when he first saw Beatrice and emphasizes, first of all, the
sensible origin of the miracle: "lo spirito animale, . . . ne la quale tutti li
spiriti sensitivi portano le loro percezioni, si cominciò a maravigliare
molto" (the animal spirit . . . into which all the sensitive spirits bring their
perceptions began to marvel exceedingly).[13] Although the narrator (in his
role as philosophical scribe) informs the reader that the little girl has since
become the lady of his mind—a symbol existing both as wonder and wisdom, image and concept—he insists on the image of her concrete temporal
reality as the basis for later symbol-making. But the reader does not yet
know what the full significance of the image will be. He must participate
in the drama of translation from eye to mind, following in the path of
the lover's discovery, but also listening to the scribe's knowledgeable, gradual revelation of meaning.

Through his analysis of wonder's workings, the narrator directs the
reader's attention to those elements in the sensible experience which raise
it above the casual, making it extraordinary and preeminently worthy of
transference to the house of memory. Trembling, marveling, weeping, the

---

[13] For the technical meaning of the "spiriti" and their movements, see F. Flamini,
"Un passo della *Vita Nuova* e il *De spiritu et respiratione* di Alberto Magno," *Ras-
segna bibliografica della letteratura italiana*, 18 (1910), 168–174, and De Robertis,
pp. 32 ff. Modern readers may find this anatomical description of the boy's physical
responses to love disconcerting. For Dante it seems to emphasize both the reflective,
learned quality of his commentary and his desire to stress the extraordinary, concentrated nature of his experience.

"spirits of the sensitive organs" recognize that the image of the little girl is miraculous. They tell him in Latin that this is no ordinary image but an apparition, an epiphany: "Apparuit iam beatitudo vestro."[14]

Because this is a revelation, not only the image but its temporal circumstances take on a special importance. The narrator, in his role as philosopher, indicates that the total environment in all its concreteness has momentous significance. At the moment of the miracle, the young boy was at the end of his ninth year, the girl at the beginning of her ninth year. These facts would seem irrelevant under other circumstances. But because the image shimmers with spiritual possibilities overwhelming both to the lover and the scribe, its temporal environment is equally significant. The moment of time in the boy's life, privileged, given, reverberates with meanings yet unknown. The sensitive spirits realize at once that the special quality of this image and its timing must be preserved and understood. No longer part of the process of change and decay, the complex phantasm must be caught up into the memory, rescued from disintegration and studied in its causes. Awed by its mystery, the boy of nine records the moment of wonder in his memory.

The reader who ponders this initial exposition must surely wonder at the clear disjunction between a simple historical event—a meeting between two children—and the absolute divine significance with which the poet's "spiriti" and language invest it. His extravagant interpretation must at first suggest the hyperbole of secular love lyrics. But Dante's choice of philosophical prose to introduce us to the event, as well as his tense, repeated insistence on the miraculous nature of this "apparition," guides us to explore more deeply the nature of "sight" which is here described.[15]

[14] Dante here suggests tentatively what will become a dominant argument of the completed *libello*—that is, that this human love with its grounding in sense experience as well as reason, and its powerful sexual or at least sensuous dimension, is not opposed to divine love but is part of a single and singular human power which draws man both toward his fellows and toward God. See Marigo, p. 50: "L'unità pertanto della *Vita Nuova* sta in questa storia psicologica e mistica in cui la passione amorosa, secondo S. Tommaso, principio e fondamento di tutte le passioni, ha la parte essenziale. Nè è propriamente l'*amor* che posa sul desiderio sensibile, ma la *dilectio*, in cui han parte sempre la ragione e la volontà ben diretta, e che, ancor meglio affinata, diverrà la *charitas* cristiana."

[15] For Dante's repeated and pointed use of the verb "apparire," see G. Lisio, *L'arte del periodo nelle opere volgari di Dante Alighieri e del secolo XIII* (Bologna, 1902), p. 142; A. Sciaffini, *Tradizione e poesia*, 2nd ed. (Rome, 1943), pp. 96–98; A. Rossi, "Dante nella prospettiva del Boccaccio," *Studi Danteschi*, xxxviii (1960), pp. 69–72; R. Hollander, "Vita Nuova. . . ," *Dante Studies* xcii (1974), p. 4. But

The narrator himself proposes a gloss. As if he had a palimpsest before him, he imagines the marvelous apparition of Beatrice superseded by the intimidating power and sovereignty of Amore. Amore, the narrator tells us, springs from the force of imagination. But he is also ordered by the "fedele consiglio de la ragione" (II, 9). It is not surprising that this pointed and morally significant conjunction of reason and imagination as well springs for the lover's apparitions parallels definitions of the modes of corporeal vision in current spiritual treatises, notably in Richard of St. Victor's *Benjamin Major*. In the first and weakest mode of seeing, Richard declares, "nihil ratiocinando quaeritur, sed totum secundum imaginationem ducitur" (nothing is sought by reasoning, but everything is deduced according to the imagination).[16] But in the higher kind of imaginative contemplation to which Dante's first encounter with Beatrice must belong, images are constructed by ratiocination and according to reason. The figure of Beatrice, then, is "vero in imaginatione secundum rationem" (truly in the imagination according to reason).[17]

---

see also E. G. Parodi, review of Lisio in *BSDI* x (1903), p. 72 and C. Segre, "La sintassi del periodo nei primi prosatori italiani" in *MALinc* 8th ser., vol. IV (1952), p. 167, both of whom argue that Dante's verbal repetitions derive from the limitations of the still-infant vernacular tongue.

[16] *Benjamin Major*, II, 11, *PL* cxcvi, 89. It is important to note that Richard does not distinguish between "apparitions" and "visions." He is concerned rather with all grades of human perception and he classifies every order of "seeing" according to its degree of spiritual clarity and purity. A number of critics have insisted that Dante intended to make a sharp distinction between "imagini" and "visioni." But a close study of all the numinous experiences recorded in the *Vita Nuova* argues rather for a broader, more flexible notion of vision not unlike Richard's. See particularly *In Apocalypsim*, I, in *PL* cxcvi, 686–689. It is not necessary to suppose that Dante already knew Richard of St. Victor's writings when he framed the visions of the *Vita Nuova* according to an order of spiritual ascent surprisingly like Richard's. The close description of imaginative and intellectual visionary experience in literature, hagiography and spiritual treatises in the century and a half separating Dante from Richard attests to a remarkable and remarkably homogeneous interest and skill in that art. See for example the several descriptions of visions in the *Queste del Saint Graal* (1220) in the thirteenth-century lives and legends of St. Francis, especially the *Actus* (later translated as the *Fioretti*) and the treatises on spiritual ascent by St. Bonaventure, especially the *Itinerarium mentis in Deum* and the *De triplici via alias Incendium Amoris*, both trans. by J. de Vinck, *The Works of St. Bonaventure*, I (Paterson, N.J., 1960).

[17] *Benjamin Major*, II, 11, *PL* cxcvi, 89. De Robertis observes that it is this conjunction of love and reason which raises the *Vita Nuova* above the aspirations of courtly love literature and gives the story a universal significance: "In questo sotto-

Unlike conventional conversions, this young boy's imaginative initiation into spiritual understanding—his transforming apparition—comes not from poring over the pages of sacred scripture nor from prayer and penance. Nor does grace enter the stream of memory as it did for St. Augustine, from an unknown, unimagined source.[18] On the contrary, it enters through senses open to experience. An image, realized as extraordinary in a moment of wonder and then shaped by reason, baptizes the soul into the new life of grace. By properly responding to a given, personal, sensible event, the narrator moves toward transcendence. Experience radically human and immediate is to be the source of blessedness.

The reader cannot but marvel at the special faith which allows such an apparition to occur. In an important sense, both the lover and the scribe effect the miracle by storing up and returning to the experience through memory and reason, celebrating their belief that moral and spiritual truth are discoverable through time and temporal moments. Dante the lover, having been awakened to wonder by an image which appears to him in particular time and space, undertakes an adventure. Where the adventure will lead he does not know; but his faith and reason teach him that it will have significance. The literary and spiritual exploration is spurred by the certain expectation that all images, all time, all places find their meaning in the divine scheme for the creation and salvation of the world. With this same faith, the lover as scribe is able to undertake the transformation of images into symbols. He will move with full confidence through his art of words toward knowable, absolute, eternal causes.

The third chapter of Dante's *libello* begins with a second illustration of the mode of imaginative apparition recorded in II. Once more, nine years later, Dante encounters "questa mirabile donna" and once again, we are told, she *appears* to the lover. With his wonted spiritual insight, the narrator leaps from the "apparition" to its theological significance narrowly conceived. In her greeting he perceives "li termini de la beatitudine" (chap. III).

This second, precisely defined bridging of the temporal and eternal must not be discounted as merely part of the rhetorical baggage of contemporary love poetry. For Dante, the lover's intellectual acuity as he infuses an

---

fondo razionale ripose il valore esemplare del libro, la possibilità di fare assurgere la favola sentimentale a significato universale" (*Il Libro*, p. 36). See also J. E. Shaw, *Essays on the Vita Nuova*, p. 82.

[18] For St. Augustine's profound and very different account of the relationship between memory and knowledge of divinity, see *Confessions*, Books X–XI.

image perceived in the phenomenal world with a strictly anagogical purpose is a necessary precondition for moving to higher modes of visionary experience and finally to the inexpressible vision of heavenly bliss.[19] Thus, Richard of St. Victor praises precisely that mental activity which Dante's narrator has twice celebrated in his apparitions of Beatrice:

> Miranda procul dubio memoriae capacitas, sed non minus mirabilis intelligentiae vivacitas. . . . Quidquid enim sensus attingit, cogitatio parit; quidquid imaginatio format, ingenium investigat, memoria conservat. Horum omnium notitiam intelligentia capit, et cum liberuit in considerationem admittet, vel in contemplationem adducit.[20]

> (The capacity of memory is wonderful, but no less miraculous is the liveliness of intelligence. . . . For whatever sense perceives, thought brings forward; whatever imagination forms, mental power investigates, memory conserves. Intelligence seizes the notation of all things, and whenever it pleases it will summon them for consideration or draw them into contemplation.)

In this second apparition, Beatrice speaks to Dante for the first time, "saluting" him, giving him salvation through her greeting. But only the narrator's word choices ("salute" and "dolcissimo salutare") lead to this spiritual meaning; the reader must draw his own conclusions while the lover, following the thread of history proceeds to relate his vision.

After he has caught a glimpse of Beatrice in the street, the narrator tells us, the young hero retires to the solitude of his room where, falling into a "sweet sleep," he has a most wonderful vision.

The sleeping lover's "maravigliosa visione" has three parts:

(1) Like Ezekiel's, it begins with the appearance of a cloud the color

---

[19] Dante had learned a great deal from the love lyrics of Guido Cavalcanti and the more spiritualized poetry of Guido Guinizelli and used their example masterfully. But by the time he came to the writing of the *Vita Nuova*—that is, after Beatrice's death on 8 June 1290—he had moved clearly beyond their influence toward the articulation of a new idiom, as M. Marti has so well shown: "La morte di Beatrice è l'avvenimento più importante nella storia psicologica dello stil nuovo dantesco, poichè quella morte è sostanzialmente una trasfigurazione; è soprattutto un supremo idealizzamento teso verso il simbolo e l'allegoria . . . Beatrice . . . diventa, con la propria morte, una luminosa immagine spirituale, una 'figura,' secondo la terminologia di Erich Auerbach . . . et ha via via assunto l'emblematico valore d'un assoluto" (*Storia dello Stil Nuovo*, vol. II [Lecce, 1972], pp. 429-430). See also Marti, II, pp. 421-435.

[20] *Benjamin Major, PL* cxcvi, 130-131.

of fire within which a figure appears. As he looks, Dante recognizes Amore, "a lordly man" who says in Latin, "Ego dominus tuus" (I am your Lord). The scribe will tell us later that his images of Amore have been merely rhetorical personifications—ways of expressing a felt sense of truth rather than truth itself. Nevertheless, now, for the lover, he is immediate and visionary rather than rhetorical. He is all the lover has and consequently he seems perhaps even more real than Beatrice. The young man cannot yet come directly to Beatrice, the source of love. Instead he must reach toward her through the mediation of an awesome, all-powerful deity for whom he feels the greatest reverence. Amore in Dante's first major figure is, in fact, very like the God of the Old Testament, revealing his essence by figurative, partial means, suggesting by types and signs the course of future history.[21]

Indeed, this first image of the dream—the figure of the fearful lord in the midst of a cloud of fire—appears to be designed in direct imitation of Old Testament revelations like that of Ezekiel:

> Et vidi, et ecce ventus turbinis veniebat ab aquilone; et nubes magna, et ignis involvens, et splendor in circuitu ejus: Et de medio ejus quasi species electri, id est, de medio ignis (1, 4).

> (I saw a storm wind coming from the north, a vast cloud with flashes of fire and brilliant light about it; and within was a radiance like brass, glowing in the heart of the flames.)[22]

It calls to mind, too, the Johannine apocalyptic figure drawn from Ezekiel:

> Et vidi, et ecce nubem candidam, et super nubem similem Filio hominis sedentem. (Apoc. 14: 14).

> (Then as I looked there appeared a white cloud, and on the cloud sat one like a son of man.)

For Dante, the cloud of fire, alluding as it does to scriptural prophecy, invests the "segnore" of his own vision with a supramundane divinity and immortal power transcending human fragility (in striking contrast to the narrator in his present state of confusion).

(2) In the vision's second movement, this lord, like the God of some Old Testament visions, perplexes rather than enlightens by his elaborate sym-

---

[21] See A. Marigo, *Mistica e Scienza*, pp. 42–43; D. DeRobertis, *Il Libro*, pp. 42–43; J. A. Scott, "Religion . . . ," p. 19.

[22] Translations from the *New English Bible* (Oxford and Cambridge, 1970).

bolic action. In his arms, he seems to hold a sleeping person, naked except for a lightly draped red veil. The sleeper, Dante realizes, is "la donna de la salute"—the lady of greeting (and of salvation).

(3) Finally, in a bizarre concluding sequence, Amore forces a fearful Beatrice to consume the heart (Dante's) which he holds in his hand. Weeping, he carries her off toward heaven.

This "maravigliosa visione" of chapter III is best characterized as enigmatic. Its difficulty is acknowledged by the narrator himself who disclaims understanding of it, but only *at this point* in the narrative, for, he says, "ora è manifestissimo a li più semplici" (III, 15). So it is a dream which ultimately can and must be interpreted. In addition, the vision occurs while Dante sleeps. Hence we are assured that the bodily senses (*oculis carnis*) are not operative. The imagination has reproduced aspects of sensory experience, but these have been reorganized into a complex dream configuration. The dream images are in some respects *like* the "apparition" of Dante's ninth year and that which has occurred just before this vision. But they have been reconstructed in such a way that they must lead both the dreamer and the reader to ponder mysteries not yet comprehensible to reason.

If we look to Richard of St. Victor to help us place such enigmatic visions in the hierarchy of spiritual experience, we find an explanation which satisfactorily suits the case. In the first stages of visionary love, Richard writes:

> Saepe . . . Dominus descendit de coelis, saepe visitat sedentem in tenebris et umbra mortis, saepe gloria Domini inolet tabernaculum foederis. Sic tamen praesentiam suam exhibet ut faciem suam minime ostendat. . . . Suavitas itaque ejus sentitur, sed species non cernitur. Adhuc nubes et caligo in circuitu ejus. . . . Nondum namque apparet in lumine. Et quamvis appareat in igne, magis tamen in igne accendente quam illuminante. Accedit namque affectum, sed nondum illuminat intellectum.[23]

> (Often . . . the Lord descends from the heavens, often he visits sitting in the darkness and shadows of death, often the glory of the Lord makes sweet the tabernacle of the covenant. Thus he shows his presence so that he reveals his face very little. . . . His sweetness is felt, but his form is not discerned. Clouds and mist surround him. . . . And he does not yet

[23] *De quatuor gradibus violentae charitatis*, PL CXCVI, 1218.

appear in the light. And although he may appear in fire, it is rather a blazing than enlightening fire. For he inflames the affection but does not illumine the intellect.)

Richard further classifies such visions as belonging to the lower order of spiritual revelation: ". . . quo formis, et figuris, et similitudinibus rerum occultarum veritas obumbratur" (that by which the truth of hidden things is covered in forms and figures and similitudes).[24]

Placing Dante's "visione" in this category illuminates its position and function in the *libello*. The forms and figures of the dream are meant to be difficult to interpret only before they are understood in the context of the subsequent narrative. Nor is their meaning grand, rich or deep. In its form, this vision represents quite precisely the partial, limited, mediated way in which the narrator, at this point in his history, is able to perceive the spiritual destiny toward which he is being miraculously drawn.

If we assume that this is, in fact, an enigmatic, limited vision in Richard's sense, then interpretation for those who know the whole *libello* is quite simple. We may begin with the second part of the dream—Beatrice's eating of Dante's heart. This strange and dramatic communion first appeared in a sonnet written by Dante independently of the later *Vita Nuova* and circulated among "trovatori" perhaps to win entrance to their circle.[25] In that poem, the lady's consumption of her lover's heart is presented as a riddle inviting interpretation. Foremost among the readings that Dante actually received for his sonnet was Cavalcanti's. Guido suggested that the lover's consumed heart signified that he had saved his beloved from death. Cino da Pistoia, another of Dante's contemporaries, proposed that through this symbolic action, the lover would make his heart fully known to his lady.[26]

When Dante comes to explain the consumption of the heart in the *Vita Nuova*, he rejects these readings. But before he presents his poem again for interpretation, he fills out the symbolic and historical details of the dream, so that the eating of the heart may be more specifically interpreted. The lady is recognized as Beatrice, "la donna de la salute," and her figure, as well as the action of eating, are represented in spiritualized, refined im-

[24] *In Apocalypsim, PL* cxcvi, 687.

[25] In this discussion of the relationship between Dante's sonnet and the later prose description of the vision in the *Vita Nuova*, I am indebted to K. Foster and P. Boyde's valuable commentary in *Dante's Lyric Poetry*, ii, pp. 22–23.

[26] See Foster and Boyde, i, pp. 14–17, for the poems of Cavalcanti and Cino da Pistoia.

agery and language. Though nearly naked, veiled lightly in a crimson
cloth, the lady in Amore's arms is not presented as carnally attractive.
Rather, her physical presence, distanced by the aura of the dream as well
as the scribe's swift, delicate description gives way to a spiritual atmosphere. Within this context of spiritualized eroticism; the eaten heart must
surely signify the lover's total subjection to love, not to a carnal passion,
but to the "donna de la salute" and to a spiritual love of the highest order
as the later narrative will make clear. The subsequent history demonstrates
in a full, rich way that this symbolic eating means sanctification—not the
lady's, as Cavalcanti's reading had proposed, but Dante's own, as the *libello* will demonstrate.

That Beatrice's communion is to signify Dante's beatification is further
suggested by the third and final part of the dream: Amore, weeping, carries Beatrice, *in whom Dante's heart now resides*, toward heaven. Here, as
many critics have agreed, Dante presents a prophecy not only of Beatrice's
death but also of her translation with his heart into the heaven of the
angels.[27]

If this last movement in the vision dimly adumbrates future events to
be fully realized as history later in the narrative—Beatrice's death and
Dante's spiritual transubstantiation—so, too, do the first and second. The
grand and awesome Amore who gains dominion over the lover in the
dream's first part, will have his allegiance in history as well, but in a far
more complex way than the vision alone can express. Further, the spiritual
union symbolized in Beatrice's eating of Dante's heart—the vision's second movement—will be studied in the ensuing narrative in a way far
transcending the limits of the enigmatic visionary image. Likewise, Beatrice's death and assumption into heaven will yield an absolute transforming significance for Dante's spirit, but one which will be discovered only
later.

The details of this *somnium*, then, presented as they are early in the
story of discovery, are, in Richard of St. Victor's terms, more "blazing"
than "illuminating." The symbolic events perceived in the dream are limited, static and mechanical, presaging but not presenting meanings and
events to be discerned later. Only with experience will the questing narrator absorb love so fully into himself that he can abandon the visionary
Amore as a rhetorical fabrication. Only when he has abandoned his need

[27] See especially C. S. Singleton, *Essay*, p. 14, and M. DeBonfils Templer, *Itinerario*, pp. 30–44.

for Beatrice's physical presence will he fully grasp the spiritual meaning of his consumed heart. Finally, when he confirms the truth of the "new life" after Beatrice's actual death, he will replace Amore's tears for a dead lady with the joy and confidence of spiritual understanding and the affirmation of the highest spiritual goals.

When the lover "thinks of" his puzzling vision just after it has happened, he anticipates in a limited way the methods he will later employ as a scribe. He muses about the time of the vision, but without discovering its significance:

> E mantenente cominciai a pensare, e trovai che l'ora ne la quale m'era questa visione apparita, era la quarta de la notte stata; sì che appare manifestamente ch'ella fue la prima ora de le nove ultime ore de la notte (III, 8).

> (And now I began to reflect, and I found that the hour in which this vision came to me was the fourth of the night; and it was clear that this was the first of the last nine hours of the night.)

Then, still thinking, he proposes to write a poem both to stabilize the experience and to discover its meaning by offering it for public consideration. His motivation is twofold: to give harmony, design and permanence to the event, and to discover its significance, motives which are very like the scribe's in the later *libello*. But there is an important difference in method and understanding. While the poet-lover had moved out of time to capture the moment, the scribe has restored the moments to their temporal context in order to show how the whole history—the pattern of experiences preserved in images and poems—participates *through its temporal order* in divine truth, the revelation of God to man. In his poem, addressed to love-imprisoned souls and gentle hearts, the lover gives no indication of the relationship between his vision and the temporal history of his love. He makes no mention of the initial apparition of Beatrice nine years earlier, and even more significantly, no mention of the conclusion of his recent vision, the assumption of his lady into heaven. The scribe, by contrast, understands that it is precisely historical beginnings and eternal conclusions which give meaning to moments of vision. If the lover had not been awakened to wonder at the age of nine, he would not have rediscovered Beatrice at eighteen, nor would he have retired to the solitude of his room prepared for a vision. And if, after her death, Beatrice were not to be assumed into heaven, there would be no goal for the narrator's quest beyond the failings of memory and the finality of death, no eternal reason for him to love or live. To note a Pauline analogy central to the *Vita Nuova's* art: "If Christ be not risen from the dead, then is all our faith in vain."[28] Precisely this faith shapes the scribe's perspective as he retraces the events of the book of his memory; but it is a faith yet unconfirmed in the lover.

Left at the end of the third chapter with the vision and without the informing wisdom of the scribe, the lover must do the best he can with his miracle and with his overwhelming response to the experience of heavenly bliss in Beatrice. His heart has been consumed by his beloved in his vision. But he is not yet able to understand that heart in its altered state nor to comprehend the beatitude represented by a Beatrice who has ascended into the heavens in his enigmatic vision. In this state of confusion, temporarily deprived of the scribe's shaping power, he is forced to examine his new identity, to find some sort of stability for himself. What else can he do when, having been wholly transformed, he can no longer predict the actions of his new self even in the most familiar situations?

His sonnet reflects his first impulse in this search for understanding. He turns to convention to find a community of fellow lovers and a vocabulary already established to deal with his experience. With graceful ignorance and in desperation, he asks those with experience of love to interpret his vision. In so doing, he seems to want to deny the uniqueness of his introduction to blessedness, something he will come to accept later in all its grandeur.

While the reminiscing scribe will finally turn to a highly structured art form to preserve the stages of his spiritual history, the lover tries to find his pattern in earthly, transitory forms which he will ultimately have to discard. Nevertheless his choice of the idiom of the *dolce stil nuovo* for his quest shows that his instincts are sound: he has the capacity to become a philosopher of love. Yet he will have to come gradually to an art adequate to the needs of describing the beauty of a heavenly lady and making his love really eternal. Beatrice, within the courtly tradition, can be no more than an earthly lady, glorified by a metaphoric halo which must ultimately be buried with her in the dust. But if she is literally heavenly beatitude—and vision will eventually yield that interpretation—then her eternal condition must be expressed by an art surpassing that of even the best poets of earthly love.

[28] For a penetrating discussion of the centrality of Beatrice's death, see C. S. Singleton, *Essay*, pp. 6–24.

Having begun, by means of his sonnet, a friendship with Cavalcanti, the foremost poet of the sweet new style (chap. III), the lover accepts in art and deed the dominion of the courtly Amore and enters upon the life of the ideal young lover. By participating in the rituals described in secular love poetry, he hopes to draw closer to his lady and to an understanding of the love-passion in himself. Unlike the prophetic, philosophical scribe, he pays no attention to the meaning of time in relation to his love and proceeds to conform his actions to those of the lover within the tradition represented by Cavalcanti. Moving out of time into a dreamlike world, in secrecy and disguise, through the composition of difficult, indirect love poems, weeping, sighing, he admires his Beatrice, but always from a distance.

Yet from time to time, and only by intimation, there are reminders to the reader, if not to the lover, that his love is no ordinary one, that it has a connection with a pattern of time, place and eternity not yet fully understood, and unlimited by the courtly tradition. The young lover sees Beatrice in the company of ladies listening to a discourse on the Virgin Mary, "la regina della gloria" (chap. V); in composing a list of the loveliest ladies of Florence, he notices that Beatrice's name appears, as if by design, as the ninth (chap. VI). In a poem, ostensibly written to express grief for the departure of the disguise-lady designated by Amore (chap. VII), he uses Jeremiah's words of grief over the loss of Sion to describe his exile from Beatrice, comparing his emotion to that of the Old Testament prophet.

Then a young lady, a friend of Beatrice's, dies (chap. VIII). The lover's two poetic responses to her death define the earthly limits of his courtly art. With his earthly rhetoric he can represent Amore, villainous death, the "gaia sembianza" of the lady as immediate, passionately felt realities. But the reality of a heaven of salvation he can deal with only at a distance. After condemning death, immediate and personified, the poet can only point with a kind of intellectual poignancy toward salvation as the means of union with the blessed lady. His understanding within the courtly tradition is limited to things of the earth and to earthly responses. Yet in his reference to salvation there are adumbrations of the need for another perspective. He knows now that death comes to ideal ladies, to friends of Beatrice, even, to Beatrice. But the lover is not yet ready to draw conclusions or to act on the inferences of what he has experienced or written.

Chapter IX marks a turning point in the lover's quest for stability and understanding through the art of courtly love as it introduces a second *imaginazione*.

This next vision of Amore comes to Dante when he is traveling away from Florence, in a group, but nevertheless isolated in thought by his grief at leaving Beatrice. His precondition of spiritual withdrawal, we are told, precipitates the apparition: "*E però* lo dolcissimo segnore . . . apparve come peregrino. . . ." (chap. IX, 3). The narrator is awake. Yet, as if in a trance, he perceives the form of his Lord, dressed "leggeramente" like the "donna" of III, and in "vili drappi." The Pilgrim Amore, thus imagined, appears distressed. But the dreamer also notices that his lord's eyes are turned to "uno fiume bello e corrente e chiarissimo"—a river whose clarity and energy provide a sharp contrast to the murky gloom of narrator and "segnore" alike.[29] So changed in appearance is the grand god of chapter III that it is tempting to accept Professor Musa's recent argument and assign this second appearance of the lord to the "lesser aspect" of love.[30] Yet the details that Dante gives, as well as the form, argue for an incremental continuity in the development of the lover's visionary experience rather than a disjunction.

Like the *somnium* of III this *imaginazione* is partly constructed of allusive symbolic materials for which analogues can be found in contemporary devotional literature and in scriptural revelation.[31] Certainly, the image of Amore duplicates the poet's own sense of himself, and the apparition encourages interpretation as psychological allegory even as it demonstrates the narrator's growth in self-understanding.

But it is also more than that. Its form closely parallels the design of the prophet Daniel's vision along the river Tigris:

Ego Daniel lugebam trium hebdomadarum diebus. . . . Die autem vegesima e quarta mensis primi, eram juxta fluvium magnum, qui est Tigri, et ecce vir unus vestitus lineis, et renes ejus accinti auro obryzo. . . . Vidi autem ego Daniel solus visionem: porro viri, qui erant mecum, non viderunt. (x, 2–7)

[29] The river is, of course, the Arno. But Dante's language invests it with a sacramental significance within the context of the narrator's visionary experience.

[30] M. Musa, *Dante's Vita Nuova* (Bloomington and London, 1973), pp. 110–111.

[31] For a contemporary account of Christ appearing as a pilgrim in a vision, see the *Revelations of Mechthild of Magdeburg*, trans. L. Menzies (London and New York, 1953), p. 197.

(In those days I, Daniel, mourned for three whole weeks. On the twenty-fourth day of the first month, I found myself on the bank of the great river, that is the Tigris; I looked up and saw a man clothed in linen with a belt of gold from Ophir round his waist. . . . I, Daniel, alone saw the vision, while those who were near me did not see it.)

In both Daniel's and Dante's apparitions, the experience occurs in the presence of others and is preceded by great spiritual sadness. In both, the divine figure appears as a man beside a river. But Dante, who had the task of constructing a vision for less certainly sacred purposes than Daniel's, creates a more self-conscious, patently symbolic scene. In particular, he heightens the significance of the river by setting its shining clarity in sharp contrast to Love's sad demeanor. Dante's river here seems to share the significance which exegesis had assigned to Daniel's (and Ezekiel's) river:

Et Danieli et Hiezechieli, qui in Babylone erant iuxta flumina, futurorum sacramenta panduntur super aquas, immo in aquis purissimis, ut baptismatis potentia monstraretur.[32]

(To both Daniel and Ezekiel who were in Babylon next to rivers, the sacraments of the future are spread over the waters, in fact in the purest waters so that the power of baptism might be shown forth.)

For Dante, this river likewise seems to function as a sign of the future—a symbolic boundary or eschaton—promising the "new life." Beatrice, who is to be Dante's "remedium salutis," is now absent save in the lover's imagination. In her place, for the time being, the god of love seems to be a sign of salvation in his pointed glance at the shining river—the appropriate sacramental, he suggests, for a baptism into the new life.

That Amore is here dressed as a pilgrim reminds us that Dante the lover is himself a pilgrim away from his beloved. But it also introduces the larger theme of religious pilgrimage—the journey from the Old Jerusalem to the New—and recalls other literary visions depicting pilgrims passing from bondage to freedom.

In sum, we may conclude of this *imaginazione* that it is of an order of enigmatic, sacramental, visionary experience similar to that of chapter III though far clearer. It also draws Dante himself into closer relationship

[32] St. Jerome, *Commentariorum in Hiezechielem*, in *Opera*, Pars I (Turnholt, 1964), p. 6.

with the "dolcissimo segnore" through their mutual suffering and even suggests an identity of the two in the final lines of the sonnet:

> Allora presi di lui si gran parte,
> ch'elli disparve, e non m'accorsi come. (IX, 12)

> Then, I took so much from him
> that he disappeared—I didn't see how.[33]

Yet in the midst of this movement toward identification, there is still the distance of dominion and servitude. Amore has advised the lover to take a second lady as a disguise for his true love. This he does (chap. x), only to discover for himself the dangers of such disguises. Beatrice is displeased and her displeasure sharply recalls the narrator to his proper object. Realizing that too much devotion to replicas keeps him from meriting the greeting of his beloved, he turns to an encomium for his lady (chap. xi). He explains in conventional fashion the way in which his sensible spirits are transformed by love at his beloved's salutation. Though couched in the conceited physiological language of his masters in the sweet new style, the lover's discussion nevertheless indicates a new ability to articulate the extent of Beatrice's power and worth. Her blessedness is of such a quality that it has many times passed and overflowed his capacity. Moving from images to the reality of his lady's presence, he comes to the humble realization that the fullness of Beatrice's grace would have been too much to bear without the disguises provided by Amore, that until he could grow up to her love, it had been necessary to depend on the inadequacies of the action and rhetoric of secular love.

What is especially interesting in this praise of Beatrice and in the account of his own eyes trembling in love is that he now chooses prose rather than verse. Though the images are those of the sweet new style, the mode of expression is discursive, philosophical. It is as if the lover, having actually *lived through* the art of the new literary style in the drama of his own historical actions, is aware that he must move finally from lyrical, artful moments of refined sensibility to the exploration of a philosophy of

---

[33] Translation of Foster and Boyde, I, p. 37. The poems which precipitate the prose elaborations of both III and IX were originally intended as conventional "riddle" poems to be unraveled by fellow poets. Now within the historically and anagogically oriented context of the *Vita Nuova*, Dante specifies their significance to support his sustained argument concerning his narrator's literary and spiritual transformation.

love capable of relating the art of human love to eternal truth. For all its undeniable beauty, the eternity expressed in the poems of the *stil nuovo* is finally an illusion. Though the art may continue, the lovers whom it describes as well as their passions must at last fall short of eternal salvation in any real, theological sense. For the love of an ideal lady to shape life in a totally meaningful way, it had to include death and resurrection into a new life, to encompass, that is, a theology of Christian salvation.

It is precisely this realization of the limitations of the poetry of *fin amor* which from the beginning had caused the scribe to provide the lover's songs and sonnets with an historical framework. By reducing the passions enshrined in the courtly poetry to their historical context, the scribe acknowledges that history inevitably carries all men, including lovers, to death and then beyond it. Because of the exigencies of time, he suggests, there must be another style, another pattern, another ritual more complete to account not only for the highest human love, but also for the love that lives beyond death.

The lover, too, implies this realization when, after praising Beatrice as the fire of his purification in chapter xi, he concludes: "Sì che appare manifestamente che ne le sue salute abitava la mia beatitudine" (So it appeared clearly that in her salutations dwelt my beatitude). It is a monumental claim, a commonplace hyperbole in *stilnovisti* poetry, but also, as the lover will learn, the literal truth. To gain the fullness of divine wisdom he must, as the scribe knows, return to history and the unfolding of his life in grace.

In the intensity of his response to Beatrice, he recognizes her as the source of charity and humility, "una fiamma di caritate." Having been sacramentally purified by her, he is prepared for his third vision of Amore in chapter xii.

THE SECOND STAGE: VISIONS IN REASON ACCORDING TO IMAGINATION

As we confront the vision recorded in chapter xii, we are drawn into a new order of spiritual perception. Thus far, the images depicted in *visioni* and *imaginazioni* have posed interpretive problems for reason, the lord's words have been clear enough. But now there is a dramatic alteration. Amore is simply dressed in white clothing. It is not his appearance but the riddle of his words which must be untangled. "Fili mi," he says, "tempus est ut pretermictantur simulacra nostra" (xii, 3: My son, it is time

that our simulacra be given up). And again, "Ego tanquam centrum cir-
culi, cui simili modo se habent circumferenti e partes; tu autem non sic"
(XII, 4: I am as the center of a circle to which the parts of the circumference
bear an equal relation; but you are not so). What does Amore mean by
"simulacra"? and what are we to make of his geometric definition of
himself?

We can find help in answering these questions if we turn once again
to Richard of St. Victor. In his several definitions of the degrees of vision
and love, he describes the contemplative passing from those visions that
occur in the imagination according to reason (III and IX) to those that
take place in the reason according to imagination.[34] In this higher visionary state, the "seeing" of divine presence is to be abstract and logical
though the abstract perception may be represented by images. As an example of such contemplation, Richard adduces the image of the circle as
a way of grasping divine wisdom:

> Dei siquidem sapientia cum sit, . . . simplex et una, modo praescientia
> dicitur, modo scientia nominatur, nunc eam praedestinationem dicimus,
> nunc dispositionem vocamus. Sic res una a nobis diverso modo distin-
> guitur ut a nostra exiguitate qualicunque modo, vel ex parte capiatur.
> Scientia est qua omnia cognoscit. Praescientia qua ab aeterno omnia
> praevidit. Praedestinatio qua ab aeterno omnes sive ad vitam, sive ad
> mortem praeordinavit. dispositio qua omnia ubique incessanter dis-
> ponendo nihil inordinatum relinquit. Hos nostrae considerationis modos
> quasi in circulum flectimus, quando in omni divinae sapientiae ordina-
> tione initium cum fine concordare videmus.[34]

(The Wisdom of God, although it is simple and one, is called Foreknowledge in one instance, Knowledge in another, now we call it
Predestination, again we call it Disposition. Thus one thing is distinguished by us in a variety of modes so that it can be grasped at least in
part in one way or another through various modes by our little reason.
Knowledge is that by which He knows all. Foreknowledge is that by
which He foresees all from Eternity. Predestination is that by which he
foreordains everyone from all Eternity either to life or death. Disposition is that by which, disposing unceasingly everything everywhere, He
leaves nothing unordered. We shape as it were those modes of our con-

[34] *Benjamin Major*, *PL* CXCVI, 101.

sideration into a circle when we perceive that in every ordination of divine wisdom the beginning agrees with the end.)

Dante's Amore offers the narrator a similar lesson. In his lordly philosophical Latin, he teaches Dante that divine understanding emanates from the circle's center while the lover is able to perceive truth only from various points at the circumference. The vision provides a cryptic prophetic inscription pointing toward the final form of the narrative. Even as the narrator stumbles through his linear, temporally bound process of discovery, Amore knows the whole story. He knows that Beatrice must die in order to lead Dante toward heaven. And he knows that Dante will finally be able to accept his heart in its transformed state so that he can ascend to a closer, fuller vision of his own beatitude through love. The narrator must wait through time and experience for that more complete spiritual perception. But the lord's advice that he abandon "simulacra" indicates that he is moving systematically heavenward.

The word "simulacra" used here by Amore is usually taken to signify those screen-ladies to whom Dante had been directing his feigned attentions and it certainly includes the meaning of "simulato amore." But if we understand the entire vision of chapter XII as marking the narrator's ascent to a higher order of spiritual perception, we are also bound to interpret the term technically. In the Old Testament, *simulacrum* had several connotations, but always it appears in contexts describing idols or vain appearances which are mistakenly worshiped in place of the true God. Thus in the prophecy of Isaiah as the Lord's voice promises the coming of the Good Shepherd, it declares:

Cui ergo similem fecistis Deum? aut quam imaginem ponetis ei? Nunquid scuptile conflavit faber? aut aurifex auro figuravit illud, et laminis argenteis argentarius? Forte lignum et imputribile elegit artifex sapiens: quaerit quomodo statuat *simulacrum*, quod non moveatur. (LX, 18–20)

(To whom then will ye liken God? or what likeness will ye compare unto him? The workman melteth a graven image, and the goldsmith spreadeth it over with gold and casteth silver chains. He that is so impoverished that he hath no oblation chooseth a tree that will not rot; he seeketh unto him a cunning workman to prepare a graven image, that shall not be moved.)[35]

[35] Translation from the Cambridge *Holy Bible* (London and New York, n.d.).

When Bede explicates the descent of the New Jerusalem after the destruction of Babylon, he uses the word "simulacrum" to describe the illusion or idol of worldly glory which is to be replaced by eternal bliss:

> Post ruinam Babylonis civitas sancta, quae sponsa est Agni, supra montem posita videtur. Lapis enim praecisus de monte sine manibus comminuit *simulacrum* gloriae mundanae, et cretit in montem magnum, orbemque implevit universum.[36]

> (After the ruin of Babylon, the holy city, the bride of the Lamb is seen upon a mountain. For the stone cut from the mountain without hands has diminished the image of earthly glory, and has waxed large in the great mountain and has filled the whole world.)

And, as Richard of St. Victor describes the higher, spiritual modes of vision, he insists that all phantasms or "simulacra" be discarded:

> Nihil hic prosunt imo multum obsunt suorum *simulacrorum* tam copiosa multitudo.[37]

> (Here simulacra, whose supply is so abundant, do no good; in fact they cause harm and stand in the way.)

It is with these connotations of the misleading or inadequate image which the texts of Isaiah, Bede and Richard suggest that Dante's use of *simulacrum* should be understood.[38] Here, in chapter xii, as the narrator moves to a new level of spiritual perception, he is told to abandon "*nostra* simulacra," that is, to give over those vivid, mysterious *imagines* for which Amore himself has been responsible.

This technical interpretation of the term *simulacrum* seems to be confirmed in the subsequent narrative (1) by Dante's stern rejection of the "vana imaginazione" of chapter xxiii; (2) by his scholastic explanation of all rhetorical personifications in chapter xxv; and (3) by the nature of the subsequent visions (xxiv and xlii).

The god of love goes on to give a warning: "Non dimandare più che utile ti sia" (xii, 5: Do not ask more than is useful). He indicates that, like the God of the Judaeo-Christian tradition, he is the omniscient custodian of past, present and future.[39] He weeps with compassion for the in-

---

[36] *Explanatio Apocalypsis, PL* xciii, 195.

[37] *Benjamin Major, PL* cxcvi, 109. [38] See also Shaw, *Essays,* p. 84.

[39] See Shaw's excellent discussion of Amore's self-definition in *Essays,* pp. 77–108, and especially p. 96.

evitable death of Beatrice to come but does not allow the lover to understand his meaning completely. To signal the importance of his role as the
center of past, present and future events, he appears at the ninth hour.
But though both lover and reader take note of the importance of the hour,
they cannot yet interpret its significance. This advance in knowledge has
enriched the mystery but the lover has still to enter into the heart of it.

The poem which the lover addresses to Beatrice is cast in a new form.
It is not a sonnet or a canzone, but a *ballata*, a round dance, symbolic of
perfection and heavenly joy (Dante will use a round dance again for the
saints in the *Paradiso*).[40] Heretofore the poet had addressed himself to
sympathetic lovers or other ladies. But this *ballata* addresses itself to Beatrice. The god of love had given permission for a new directness in the
poet's addresses to his lady, but he had also issued a warning not to speak
to her in the second person: "Make these words an intermediary, as it
were, since it is not decorous that you should speak directly." The *ballata*
is to be a conveyor, a word symbol representing Dante's love for Beatrice.
It will carry the love to its source, just as the *Vita Nuova*, artfully arranged by the scribe, conveys, though imperfectly, his love for beatitude to
its source in the New Jerusalem. The parallel is important to recognize
both for understanding the function of the prose and verse of the completed book and for following the lover's gradual awareness of the purpose of words in moving from the love of a lady present to his eyes to a
spiritual love, imaginatively and rationally perceived.

Significantly, the scribe calls the reader's attention to the poet's artifi-
ciality in speaking to his own *ballata* as if it were an animate being. Why
should a *ballata* be treated as a substance apart from the poet when it is
the poet himself who has given the poem its words? This is the question
the scribe invites the reader to ask. But instead of answering directly, he
makes the problem more mysterious by suggesting that if the entire chapter including the *ballata* is very difficult to interpret, the explanation for
it, to be presented later, will be even more difficult. The scribe's interrup-
tion reminds the reader of the form of the book. *At this point*, the lover
must use the device of an artificial address to his poem. To leave the poem
out would falsify a stage in this spiritual history; to clarify its meaning
would distort the form of the book. The lover writing his poetry is bound
at this point by his limited understanding of the difference between the

---

[40] See the discussion of Dante's use of the round dance by A. H. Lograsso, "From
the *Ballata* of the *Vita Nuova* to the Carols of the *Paradiso*: A Study of Hidden
Harmonies and Balance," *Dante Studies* LXXXIII (1965), pp. 23–48.

substance and the accidents of love. For him now the indirect address to Beatrice through the poem is the necessary way for him to reach her. The use of the colors of rhetoric at this stage is absolutely essential because the lover is to know and express his love only through figures and images.

When the explanation of the relationship between figurative language and truth comes finally in chapter xxv, it is more than a scholar's exercise presented as a digression. The scribe, looking back, reduces Amore, so real and powerful for the young lover seeking his Beatrice, to a fabrication. But that reduction required a learning process both for the lover and the reader. Only with time and the detachment of spiritual contemplation could the scribe compare his early poems with classical poetry and comment on the limitations of all poetry to express truth. The scribe's intervention in the narrative following the *ballata*, together with his scholarly explanation of the nature of poetry in chapter xxv, make explicit that the form of the book is a gradual unveiling of meaning through time, or, put another way, a progressive temporal growth in understanding of the meaning of beatitude and salvation.

To return to the progress of the *libello*, the next four chapters (xiii–xvi) draw the reader further into the drama of the young lover. In carefully ordered steps, he both epitomizes the agony of his love-passion and moves in a new direction already foreshadowed by the *ballata* and the visionary advice of Amore. The scribe is scarcely in evidence; but the lover is learning by painful, concentrated experience the detachment which will finally effect his transformation into the prophet who examines the conceptual significance of all the images held in his memory in the light of reason and truth.

In chapter xiii, the lover presents a psychomachia; opposing thoughts contend concerning the nature and value of his love. His conclusion, that "madonna Pietà" can resolve his mental paradoxes, that is, that a love requited by Beatrice will release him, he soon learns is misguided. The next chapter, xiv, provides an encounter with his beloved. In the face of her overwhelming beauty and graciousness, his senses, like his mind in the preceding chapter, are cast into confusion. It is the failure of the senses, transformed and as if dead, that makes him aware that he is not capable of looking at Beatrice; he is not worthy, as Amore had warned him, of addressing himself directly to his lady. His poems in these four sections are poems of frustration and death. Having seen Beatrice and swooned, he laments to his friend: "I have set my feet in that part of life in which one can proceed no farther if he intends to return." The lover realizes he can go no farther in the direction of loving his lady as a real, physical presence. Beatrice is his paradise. But to attain her as a present reality, he must die. Constrained to continue his life in time, though he has been transformed, he must find an object for his passion which will give him life and peace. He must no longer seek to *see* Beatrice. Yet his love will go on. Fortunately, as his senses have deserted him, and last of all his eyes, he has become aware of his faculties of imagination and memory. It had been his imagination which had created his desire to see Beatrice. But now that desire must be directed toward a new goal which might bring resolution to the soul in distress and provide permanence for his great love.

For such a solution Amore has already given directions. Words must be the intermediary. At last the lover is to be released from the conventional idiom of Cavalcanti and the power of the god of love. His imagination, which, after all, had first given life to his lord and had chosen Cavalcanti's language as its own, now finds a new purpose in designing his own vocabulary to define love. The whole gamut of courtly love commonplaces has been explored and has been found inadequate. But the grandeur of a love that cannot find satisfaction in the sight of his beloved must not be allowed to die. Since his senses are insufficient to support his feelings, he must turn to memory and imagination, and must use the image of Beatrice, not her presence, to understand and teach the fullest meaning of his love.

THE NEW LANGUAGE OF BEATRICIAN LOVE

Chapter xvii is a plain statement of the lover-poet's new resolution. Having addressed three sonnets directly to his lady (contrary to the advice of Amore) and having found only frustration in that idiom, he rejects it: ". . . credendomi tacere e non dire più, però che mi parea di me assai avere manifestato, avvegna che sempre poi tacesse di dire a lei, a me convenne ripigliare matera nuova e più nobile che la passata" (xvii, 1: . . . believing that I should keep silence and say no more of this, since I thought I had sufficiently indicated my state to her and since I should never address my poems to her again, it became essential for me to take up a new theme, one more elevated than the last). There has been a rectification of the will in Thomistic terms. The "good" which heretofore had been the sight of Beatrice is now recognized to consist in words praising his beloved, springing from his interior image of her. The grander theme leads the lover away from his own condition toward his new role as a teacher of truth. He is moving very surely now toward becoming the scribe who will be the inspired author of the *Vita Nuova*, the laureate of beatitude.

As the reader has come to expect, the narrator embarks on his new effort spurred by a dramatic historical situation. A group of ladies, having observed his discomfiture in the presence of Beatrice, asks him the purpose of his strange love. He explains that though formerly he had sought the sight of his beloved, now his bliss lies within his own power, "in quelle parole che lodano la donna mia" (in those words that praise my lady). But his powers are weak, for the words which praise his lady require a whole new order of language: "e pensando molto a ciò, pareami avere impresa troppo alta matera quanto a me, sì che non ardia di cominciare; e così dimorai alquanti dì con disiderio di dire e con paura di cominciare" (xviii, 9: thinking a great deal about this, it seemed to me that I had chosen too high a theme for myself, so that I did not dare to begin writing, and for several days afterwards I remained desiring to write and fearing to begin). The desire to write overcoming the fear to begin, he will be performing, in miniature, what the mature scribe has achieved in his *libello*. He will be tracing with words the image of his beloved impressed in his memory, the "material" for his poems of praise. The scribe of the finished book had undertaken in a parallel way to copy out images held in the memory to define and praise the "new life." It is no wonder, since the lover and the scribe must finally be one character, that the *historia* of the *Vita Nuova* should include the steps in the lover's learning how to be the prophet-scribe.

The lover's first effort as a free agent, governed by his own poetic power to define love and no longer a slave under the dominion of the awesome Amore, is justifiably the most famous poem of the book, *Donne ch'avete intelletto d'amore*. The image of Beatrice, pale as a pearl, a marvel proclaimed by the angels who see her light shining from earth, "la speranza de' beati," has such beauty that it can be compared in its concentration of imagination only with the opening scene when the little boy first saw his beloved. The same sense of awed reverence at a miracle sent by God, seen rationally and philosophically, dominates the tone and imagery. The speaker of the poem "thinks," "reasons," "treats of" his subject in order to clear his mind and to teach. Beatrice's face holds the essence of love, not only for the speaker but for all who seek love. She has been universalized by reason. Both philosopher and prophet, the narrator now declares with wisdom the wonder of Beatrice. He has assumed the task of teaching others to see and understand the beauty of the giver of blessings.

Nevertheless, though he has come far in understanding, the poet still does not fully grasp the part Beatrice must play in his actual salvation. He has Love ask: "Cosa mortale/ Come esser pò sì adorna e sì pura?" (vv 43–44: A mortal being/ How can she be so adorned and so pure?) The answer, of course, is that Beatrice belongs in heaven. As beatitude, her flesh is only the outward, accidental manifestation of the bliss of salvation. In presenting the image of Beatrice in heaven as salvation and as heavenly bliss, could the narrator but know it, he is delivering a prophecy. Only in time will he learn the literal truth of the image. But for now, though unconsciously preparing his spirit and his scribal capacities for such a reality, he still speaks through the colors of poetry and does not go beyond the "dress of praise" to substantial truth.

With even greater assurance, the sonnets of the next two sections imitate the method to be used by the prophetic scribe in composing the *Vita Nuova*. Asked by "ladies with an understanding of love" to define love, he reaches back to the images of his own experience and, universalizing them through the power of reason and the art of judgment, he presents two carefully reasoned poems of definition and praise. The anguish of the earlier poetry is gone. The lover has established a new perspective, scholarly and detached, from which to analyze those images which had heretofore been studied only in the context of their immediate dramatic occurrences. To emphasize his detachment, or perhaps to strengthen it in himself, he prefers third person references to Beatrice, using her as his example of the power of beauty to awaken love in gentle hearts.

Chapter xxi concludes with an important explication of an image in the second of the two sonnets which predicts not only the conclusion of the *Vita Nuova* but also the *Paradiso*. In the sonnet, the narrator had called the image of Beatrice's smile a "novo miracolo e gentile." As commentator, he explains that the memory cannot contain the "mirabile riso," for memory cannot retain visions of the ineffable. It will be precisely this conclusion in anagogical vision which Dante will use in the *Paradiso*, as also in chapter xlii of the *Vita Nuova*. Already the lover-poet is studying carefully the role of memory in relation to the vision of beatitude, a relationship essential for Dante in structuring both his finely wrought *libello* and the great *Commedia*.

In chapter xxii, the scribe reengages the lover in the flow of his own history in order to introduce the next stage in his transformation and beatification. The lover as poet has demonstrated his freedom from the exigencies of past time. He has been released from the necessity of seeing Beatrice and can dwell freely on her image, refined and spiritualized, retained in his memory as the essence not only of earthly but of divine love. But what of the future? Amore much earlier had expressed his own perfection (an exact paraphrase of current definitions of the Christian God) as the capacity to comprehend all time, past, present and future from a point at the center. So for the narrator to grasp the essence of love itself, he must somehow arrive at that center of vision.

But at this stage, the future, subject to time and the unpredictable unfolding of events, still remains unknown to him. Yet if all his past, present and future is to be a vehicle for salvation, then unpredictability is simply a question of perspective. Like those Hebrews waiting for the Messiah, like Isaiah, the lover cannot imagine the reality of redemptive grace in all its fullness though prophecy has been given to him.

DEATH AND TRANSLATION

Events conspire to prepare the narrator for such an understanding. First, there is the death of Beatrice's father, willed by the "Lord of Glory who did not refuse death for Himself." Then, in chapter XXIII, as he lies ill in his bed, the lover dreams of the death of Beatrice.

The quality of this *fantasia* parallels that of Amore's first formal appearance (III). It is the *ninth* day of Dante's illness and he is thinking about Beatrice. With his eyes closed, he perceives striking images of mourning— the darkening of the sun, the stars colored "as if they were weeping," mourning women, and the announcement that the "mirabile donna" has died. Then, in the heavens, he sees angels singing "Osanna in excelsis." Earlier in his history, the narrator would surely have taken such a fantasy as significant, requiring interpretation. This *imaginazione* far more directly than the earlier visions shimmers with Christological significance, reminding the reader of the natural events surrounding Christ's death as well as those to come at the end of the world. Yet Dante forcefully rejects it. It is "la erronea fantasia," "lo fallace imaginare," "questa vana imaginazione." Perhaps the poet's rejection of this dream both in his prose and in the canzone is, as Professor Singleton has suggested, a narrative device designed to arouse suspense. But it seems more likely, given the meditative, retrospective voice of the narrator at other key points in his history, that here, too, we are listening to the judgment of the reflective scribe.

He rejects this imagination because the lover's understanding has passed beyond such image-filled dreams and, more importantly, because the subject of the delirious dream runs counter to the theme of his *libello*.

Because the *fantasia* is the product of imagination uninstructed by reason or Amore, Dante, following his Lord's advice in the abstract "true" vision of XII, may be rejecting the partiality of this new "seeing" as a mere *simulacrum* of Truth. With similar ruthlessness in chapter XXV, he denounces all those rhetorical colorings with which his imagination had invested Amore at the beginning of the *libello*. He insists that it is the "true understanding" which must be pursued by denuding the words of their figurative garb. In similar terms Richard of St. Victor had devalued all corporeal visions as the visionary approaches anagogical perception despite his insistence on their importance for earlier stages in the ascent:

Sed quantum interesse putamus inter imaginationem et rationem, nisi quantum est inter dominam et ancillam, inclytam et ignominiosam, eruditam et fatuam?[41]

But do we not think that there is as much difference between the imagination and the reason, as between the mistress and the handmaiden, the famous and the ignominious, the learned and the foolish?

But the matter of Dante's dream provides the strongest reason for its rejection. It is, after all, a depiction of Beatrice's death—albeit in the image of Christ's—a subject which the *Vita Nuova* has been specifically designed to transcend. This *libello* is to be a book in praise of life and love in which death can finally play no central part. Hence, despite the fact that this "erronea fantasia" does predict Beatrice's actual death as had the vision of III, the event itself must be studied only as the necessary prelude to her assumption and glorification. Surely the death must be admitted. But it is significant that Dante gives his fullest account of it in this false imagination, this delirious dream. By refusing the dream a place in his spiritual progress, the scribe firmly subordinates death to the triumph of the spirit and the power of love—the two grand themes which have become the dominant subject of the *libello* from chapter XVII onward.

In the lover's next vision (XXIV) Amore makes clear the true and correct direction prescribed for his servant's spiritual education into bliss. Dante's new and properly joyful "imaginazione" follows upon meditation

[41] *Benjamin Major, PL* CXCVI, 110–111.

(a necessary practice for the philosophical scribe) and in it Amore instructs his heart to recognize once more his singular election to blessedness. With a renewed lightness and strength, briefly lost in his delirium, Dante then sees his living Beatrice preceded by a young woman, Giovanna, who is also called Primavera because of her beauty. Guided by Amore, Dante, penetrating the spiritual significance of what he sees, recognizes in Giovanna an image of John the Baptist crying out in the wilderness "parate viam Domini." And then the "Lord"—Beatrice—appears, the blessed lady who is Love. The narrator's implied comparison between Beatrice and Christ is extraordinary. Yet, for him Beatrice *is* essentially Christ's instrument for the lover's redemption. Nor is the claim blasphemous; Dante and his audience could believe quite firmly that Christ was present in history among them in certain privileged contemporary Christians "in similitude though not in sublimity" preparing the souls of the faithful for the Second Coming.[42] Beatrice, like Galahad, or like the St. Francis of the *Actus* and the *Fioretti*, is portrayed in the poet's hagiography as an image of Christ, representing His grace in the thirteenth century.

This *imaginazione* of xxiv, then, in which the narrator both perceives his lady shimmering with divinity and understands her sacred meaning, demonstrates just how fully he has moved toward the highest forms of spiritual love and anagogical "seeing"; that is, toward those orders of experience which require no vivid images or complex interpretations. In chapter xxiv, the poet gives no description of Amore's outward appearance. Indeed, he declares, love has become so much a part of him that his heart no longer seems to be his. In a parallel way Richard describes that "sweet conversation of God in the soul" which produces a transformation of the heart and unites it to the Savior:

> quorum virtute et auditu corda liquescunt, liquescendo deficiunt, et deficiendo perficiuntur. Dura in illam unitatem concurrunt, quam suis Salvator orat et optat in Evangelio: *Ut sint*, inquit, unum sicut, ut *nos unum sumus.*[43]

> (by the power and hearing of those [conversations], hearts are liquified, and, being liquified, they fail, and failing, they are perfected. Firm they rush into that unity which their Lord prays for and desires in the Gospel: That they may be one, He says, just as We are one.)

[42] *Queste del Saint Graal*, ed. Pauphilet (Paris, 1921), p. 38.
[43] *De gradibus charitatis, PL* cxcvi, 1208.

The Poet as Prophet

If the Beatrice of Dante's vision is a sign of Christ, the narrator has become her witness, apostle and prophet. As the world becomes more and more aware of the "miracolo" who is Beatrice, he takes on the task of presenting her image to those who must have faith without seeing her; he must be her evangelist: "I undertook to speak words in which I would explain her miraculous and excellent effects; so that not only those who could see her with their senses, but others might know of her whatever words can express" (xxvi).

But the way to beatitude for man in time is not without backsliding and digression. Though Dante has become the evangelist for a spiritualized Beatrice, he cannot rid himself of his senses entirely or of his natural attachment to her human existence. Chapter xxvii, which returns the reader to the lover's personal feeling for and response to Beatrice, reflects a much earlier time when the lover required her presence for inspiration. Before he can go beyond the first stanza of his new poem, history breaks in with a far greater dilemma. The prophetic phantasms of Beatrice's death are answered by the announcement that she has in fact died, carried away by the God of Justice under the banner of the Virgin Mary. The abortive canzone of xxvii serves as a reminder that the lover in the process of transformation remains human and vulnerable. It prepares for the uncertainties of the concluding movement of the *Vita Nuova* in which the narrator, drawn closer and closer to his scribal role, meditates on and attempts to absorb the significance of Beatrice's death for his life. He could capture dramatically and present in a finished, carefully chosen style the fumbling uncertainty of the young lover confronted with the beauty of Beatrice. But the death of Beatrice, much closer in time to the writing of the *Vita Nuova*, is still fresh in the scribe's experience. Yet because he has learned in the course of exploring his book of memory that meditation on past experience together with judgment have the capacity to define goals and bring spiritual peace, he attempts the transformation of death into life.

The three chapters dealing directly with the event of Beatrice's death (xxviii–xxx) are the most crucial for the whole book and illustrate the scribe's understanding of his lady's capacity to give salvation through death. Having arrived at the central moment in the history of his new life, he speaks with detached assurance of Beatrice's miraculous significance. Because he, like St. John in the Apocalypse, is writing not about the death of his Messiah (that can be left to other writers), but about her eternal presence, which is the grace of his salvation, he eschews a meditation on her death. Instead he refers the reader to his initial intention, recited in the proem: to record the history of the "new life."[44] Just as Christ's death and subsequent triumph over it lay at the center of the Book of Revelation, the cause and measure of all the other actions of the visions, so in the *Vita Nuova* Beatrice's death is central to the prophetic purpose of the whole book. Without her physical death and assumption into heaven, there would have been no new life. It is the total victory of her spirit over matter and the forces of earth which introduces the scribe, finally, to his own beatitude.

The philosophical scribe makes Beatrice's theological significance in his life explicit in chapter xxix. With scholarly detachment and with the audacity and confidence of a visionary, he explicates the meaning of the number nine. Heretofore nine had been associated with time—the hours, days, months, years related to the development of his life in love with Beatrice. Now by an act of judgment, reflecting upon images held in his memory, he translates time into symbol. Noticing that the date of her death is universally related to the number nine, he concludes that Beatrice *is* the number nine, the miraculous product of the three persons of the Trinity. This explanation, significantly placed between the announcement of Beatrice's death and the narrator's address to the bereft princes of the earth (xxx), deftly negates death through the presence of God's miraculous power. Just as Christ's death, paradoxically a miraculous triumph, removed the necessity of a second death for mankind, so has Beatrice's death promised the narrator his salvation.

As if to set the last movement apart, the narrator offers a second prologue, a quotation from Jeremiah's lamentation over the bereft city of

[44] The narrator's position as he reflects back on Beatrice's death and glorification from the perspective of the completed book parallels that of the special disciple, recorded in thirteenth-century lives of St. Francis, who saw the saint in a vision carried up to heaven and glorified: "Unus autem ex fratribus et discipulis eius, fama non modicum celebris, cuius nomen nunc existimo reticendum, quoniam dum *vivit in carne* non vult tanto praeconio gloriari, vidit animam sanctissimi patris recto tramite in *caelum conscendere super aquas multas*. Erat enim *quasi stella* quoque modo lunae immensitatem habens, solis vero utcumque retinens claritatem, a *candida* subvecta *nubecula*" (Thomas of Celano, *Vita* i [1228] in *Analecta Franciscana* x [Florence, 1941], p. 86). Like St. Francis's disciple, Dante hopes not to be overpraised in this world because of his privileged experience.

Jerusalem. A new Jeremiah, bound to earth and time though a prophet of the heavenly city, he mourns over Florence bereft of its savior. Now that Beatrice has actually gone to the New Jerusalem, he finds that his image-making powers can no longer provide him with material. As he has already pointed out, the beatific vision transcends imagination, and therefore memory. Through the remainder of the book, he is concerned with finding a new idiom to approach as nearly as possible the unimaginable wonder of Beatrice in heaven. His efforts are not entirely successful. But in his quest he demonstrates an increasing awareness of his responsibility as a scribe of the new life which, though ineffable in its final significance, remains chartable as an historical phenomenon.

In the sections immediately following the record of Beatrice's death and assumption, the narrator seems to lose courage. An apparent return to the emotional confusion of the early chapters characterizes both the poetry and the prose. The narrator has, in effect, become a wanderer, his eyes cast down on the solitary, desolated city, his heart turned toward the heavenly city where his love lives. Though he is aware of the beauty and peace of Beatrice's new state "nel ciel de l'umiltate, ove'è Maria," he is equally aware of his own situation in the city emptied of its beatitude. But it is important to recall that the narrator has already put all of this material within a scriptural framework by using Jeremiah's lament over the earthly Jerusalem as his leitmotif. He is in fact enacting the response of Everyman to his exile and to the limitations of the life of pilgrimage. He is marking dramatically an acute awareness of the distance between the earthly and the heavenly Jerusalem. As if to emphasize the weakness of man in exile, the narrator records his brief loss of direction, his attraction to the lady at the window as an earthly substitute for the heavenly lady. She, like the earlier disguise ladies, is an obstruction, too easily distracting him into something like idol worship.

Ascent to Anagogical Vision

Yet, in spite of himself, because he is the principal actor in a miraculous history, a vision is given to him which bridges the gap between heaven and earth. As we have come to expect, the vision occurs about nine o'clock. To return full circle and recall the moment when he first embarked on the new life, the image of the vision is that of Beatrice at that first wonderful meeting, dressed as she had been then, in crimson. His tears, as he retraces the memory of his love, are no longer self-pitying but penitential. His penance leads him to a new role. He becomes a pilgrim moving toward the heavenly city, wanting as a prophet of the new life to bring all dedicated pilgrims with him. As a pilgrim spirit ("peregrino spirito"), he is able to be with his lady, and finally through vision he reaches the limit of words. What he has seen in the final transcendent vision recorded in section XLII surpasses his capacity to relate.

With these last three sections of vision, the scribe indicates, he has found the purpose of his life: to write of his lady as no woman has been written of before. But he has also reached a new beginning for which he has yet to find the proper idiom. History knows that the *Commedia* charts the confident discovery of that idiom.

From the scribe's perspective at the end of the *Vita Nuova*, the whole history recorded in the book of memory has the character of a series of figures divinely given, all of them teaching the way to salvation by stages through time. At the center is the image of Beatrice who inspires a supernatural love, dies and is borne to heaven. Just as St. John writing his Apocalypse depended on the resurrection of Christ as the source for faith in a second coming and eternal peace, so the prophet of the *Vita Nuova* depends on the apotheosis of Beatrice. Both the evangelist and the scribe, servants of God, are given a unique teaching function through their revelation; not only must they see and hear, but they must write down and teach their visions.

Dante's final *visione* (XLII) represents a completion of the movement from imaginative apparitions (now seen as "simulacra") to a fully spiritual vision:

> Appresso questo sonetto apparve a me una mirabile visione, ne la quale io vidi cose che me fecero proporre di non dire più di questa benedetta infino a tanto che io potesse più degnamente trattare di lei.

> (After this sonnet, there appeared to me a wondrous vision in which I saw things which made me determine not to say more of this blessed one until I could more worthily treat of her.)

This final vision of chapter XLII is, in Richard of St. Victor's terms, "anagogical," that is, an ascent or elevation of the mind for contemplation on high. Just as Richard's contemplative soul is required to pass through enigmas and clouds—the orders of imaginative vision—first guided and then governed by reason before reaching true contemplation, so Dante's "segnore" has directed the lover through a series of carefully graded visions to "ascend above himself" to a vision of Beatrice. It is a vision which must lead him ineluctably not only to Beatrice but also to the "faccia di colui qui est per omnia secula benedictus" (XLVII, 3). The conclusion is totally in keeping with the anagogical structure of the *Vita Nuova*. The narrator has moved the reader steadily toward an understanding of perfect beauty and joy and therefore the work must end with a new beginning—a new vision and a new realization which forbids either the narrator himself or the reader from looking backward or repeating earlier stages of the ascent.

FOUR

THE LATER MEDIEVAL SPIRITUAL QUEST: THROUGH TIME TO *AEVUM*

From the beginning of the thirteenth century onward, a number of writers in the vernacular experimented with a narrative quest which carries a pilgrim on a visionary journey toward an eschatological conclusion. Raoul de Houdenc's *Songe d'Enfer* and *Voie de Paradis*,[1] Huon de Méri's *Tournoiement Antechrist*, Rutebeuf's *Voie de Paradis* all represent narrators traveling through visionary realms and all share common thematic and stylistic elements. Like the illustrated Apocalypses of the thirteenth century, these narratives were descended in part from older monastic forms and tradition. And like their pictorial counterparts, they reflect fundamentally new attitudes toward their principal theme, the quest for salvation.

In this chapter I want to probe the emergence and characteristics of a later medieval anagogical mode to which three of the greatest poets of the Middle Ages lent their genius. By no accident, the spiritual quest came into being during that same period of self-conscious prophecy and visionary exploration which produced St.-Denis, Chartres and the Trinity College Apocalypse. Though scholars have long referred to the medieval "dream vision," the "pilgrimage" and the "quest," the particular elements of visionary narrative as they appear after 1200 are nowhere conveniently outlined. Perhaps the devices and conventions have seemed too obvious or common for description. Yet precisely because they are common, they

[1] Raoul's authorship of the *Voie de Paradis* is contested. For a history of the debate and possible solutions, see A. Micha, "L'Auteur du *Songe de Paradis*," *Romania* 68 (1944–1945), pp. 316–360; and V. Kundert-Forrer, *Raoul de Houdenc* (Zurich, 1960), pp. 110–121. For the sake of convenience, I have called Raoul the author of the *Voie*. The poem certainly belongs to the early thirteenth century and it is in that capacity that it serves my argument. But it is important to recognize that the question of authorship is by no means settled.

merit our close scrutiny. And this is especially true when they are studied beside similar impulses and directions in other contemporary arts. Each masterwork in the mode must be set "sengeley in synglere." But each of them also reveals its mythos and purpose more richly when placed within the context of its formal relatives. This chapter will be devoted to a study of origins and developments. It will generalize from particular cases in order to suggest qualities and limits which practitioners imposed on the mode. In the last two chapters, I shall undertake readings of two of the finest manifestations of the spiritual quest—*Pearl* and *Piers Plowman*.

Literary Visions before 1200

Before examining those conventions which came to characterize the new mode, we should recall the central form of vision narrative developed chiefly by monastic historians and hagiographers before the thirteenth century. The numerous accounts of visions which appeared between the seventh and the thirteenth century usually took their details and shape from the apocryphal Apocalypse of St. Paul. These Pauline visions provided materials for meditations that would inspire fear of hell and awe for God and lead the soul toward conversion.[2] Conversion would then encourage those blessed with visions, as well as those hearing or reading them, to intensify their life of asceticism, penance and prayer.

To explore fully the monastic writers' preference for the Pauline rather than the Johannine Apocalypse would carry us beyond the scope of this chapter; for our purposes, it is sufficient that their choice bespeaks a general monastic reluctance to venture easily or comfortably into the secret world of God's eternal mysteries, a reticence noted earlier in Beatus and his illustrators. It seemed much truer to general human possibility to recount visions which taught a single, easily grasped moral lesson. The Pauline Apocalypse had not won official credence and had been roundly condemned by St. Augustine. He had pointed out that the real journey

[2] Monastic emphasis on hell's punishments is evident not only in adaptations of the Pauline Apocalypse, but also, as Professor Silverstein has noted, in editions and abridgements: "The forty-seven codices in which the Latin redactions of the Apocalypse of Paul are extant not only testify by their multiplicity and by the diversity of their provenance, to the widespread popularity of the vision in the later Middle Ages, but also exhibit a strong preoccupation with the horrors of Hell-torment to the virtual exclusion of the less impressive joys of Paradise" (*Visio Sancti Pauli*, ed. T. Silverstein, London, 1935, p. 40).

of Paul to the third heaven was an indescribable contemplative experience while the apocryphal one was imaginative and corporeal. But it was precisely as imaginative and corporeal that it served the monastic writers' purposes. Terrifying images of hell's punishments were presented in visions to the lower spiritual or imaginative faculties of sinful man. By "seeing" the horrors of hell drawn with vivid intensity, souls could be led to repent their sins and labor ever more diligently to perfect their life of asceticism and prayer within the walls of the monastery. Contemplation of God's glory or a mystical grasp of heaven's joy had no part in these powerful literary revelations. They were intended rather to effect a moral reformation in the conduct of earthly life.

Thus, for example, Bede recounts how Drihthelm was taken up into the vivid other world of the Pauline hell and heaven.[3] Upon rising from the grip of death, he declared that he could no longer live the life he had been used to. Having divided his property, he abandoned his wife and "all worldly responsibilities," and joined the monastery of Melrose. There he undertook the most extreme ascetic regimen. He would often plunge into the icy river "for severe bodily penance" and remain immersed "while he recited psalms and prayers for as long as he could endure it, standing motionless with the water up to his loins, and sometimes to his neck. When he returned to the shore, he never removed his dripping, chilly garments, but let them warm and dry on his body." Onlookers, asking how he could bear such cold and suffer such austerity, would receive the simple answers, "I have known it colder," and "I have seen greater austerity."[4]

Such extratemporal visions as that of Drihthelm were usually presented within the larger context of a holy history or a saint's life. The visions were always treated as true and were used by historians and hagiographers not only to demonstrate the holiness of their recipients but also to show mortal man's inevitable sinfulness. Their structure was simple: images of the horrors of hell were amassed, followed by glimpses of the joys of heaven. The visionary, responding to the heat and cold of hell with terror, and guided by an angelic host, learned that the punishments of hell were caused by specific sins. By the time his vision was over, he had realized the need for a total reform of his moral life through prayer and penance within the cloistral peace of the monastery. When this same sort of vision was used as the basis for a homily, as it often was, it was treated in essen-

---

[3] Bede, *Historia Ecclesiastica* bk. v, chap. 12, ed. C. Plummer (Oxford, 1896), p. 310.

[4] *Historia* v, 12, Plummer, p. 310.

tially the same way, as "a sampull . . ./ Þat he that woll hit vnderstand/ In hart he schall be full dredand/ For hys synnis yf he woll drede/ And clanse hym her of his mysdede. . . ."[5]

Furthermore, whether they occurred in histories, saints' lives or sermons, the recorder of these visionary experiences never recommended them as helpful to the pure contemplation of God's glory. Once a monk or saint had learned through his vision to "love the delights of paradise" and "fear the pain of hell," he could turn with diligence to the steep penitential climb up the Lord's mountain. Visions of the other world could serve as a catalyst to higher spiritual experience by moving the soul to comprehend the enormity and eternity of its final reward or punishment. Then, through meditation on Christ's humiliation, through holy reading, penance, and prayer, some few cloistered souls might begin to perceive the "mysteries of Christ." But even that very small number of perfect Christians could receive the light of contemplation only "as in a mirror and in the manner of an enigma."[6]

In sum, the monastic visions were simply constructed "anagogical happenings," occurring outside the course of ordinary time and history and describing the afterlife of good and evil souls. The images used were not

---

[5] These lines begin an English translation of the *Visio Tundali*, a vision which was supposed to have occurred in 1149 (in *The Visions of Tundale*, ed. W. B. Turnbull, Edinburgh, 1893). A similar warning introduces an English homily on St. Paul's "Visions of the Pains of Hell":

> Þe soules of synners, as I þe telle,
> fallen doun þer, in pyne to dwelle,
> Þer to take and resseyue so
> As þei on eorþe deserueden to.
> Be war of þis, I sei, beo-fore,
> As God seide in þe gospel þore (71–76).

(in *The Minor Poems of the Vernon MS.* pt. 1, ed. Carl Horstmann [London, 1892], p. 251).

[6] Thus Dom Leclercq summarizes Bede's program for the contemplative life:
The contemplative life ("speculative") is the desire to see the Lord's face, with the choirs of angels, and to rejoice with the blessed spirits in the eternal vision of God's glory. Here below, through meditating on the humiliation of the savior, through holy reading, fasting and prayers, some come to perceive all the light which shines in the mysteries of Christ. High contemplation depends on God's grace which appears when He wishes it, not by the good will of the soul who looks for it. This light of divine contemplation is given only to a very small number of very perfect Christians; yet they receive it for a time "as in a mirror and in the manner of an enigma" and at the price of an immense labor: through the faith which purifies the heart (*La Spiritualité du moyen âge* [Paris, 1961], p. 89).

mysterious or figural, and it was not difficult to ferret out their moral significance. Nor did the images or the visions as a whole have immediate prophetic significance; that is, they were not directly related to God's historical prophecy concerning the end of the world, the coming of Antichrist, and the descent of the New Jerusalem, but rather to the immediate earthly moral life of the visionary, his conversion and repentance.

THE BEGINNINGS OF THE LATER MEDIEVAL SPIRITUAL QUEST

The emergence of new forms of vision narrative in France early in the thirteenth century parallels the invention and development of the French *romanz*. By about 1220, religious poets in both these novel modes had established directions in literary fiction which would shape the art of the next two centuries. Professor Hans Robert Jauss's brief analysis of the French poetry of our period—the time of ferment and creativity which produced the prophecy of Joachim of Fiore, Richard of St. Victor's phenomenology of vision, St.-Denis and Chartres—testifies to the nature and extent of the new poetry:

> In France, a new allegorical poetry in the vernacular appeared between 1180 and 1240; le *Conte du Graal* of Chrétien de Troyes, at the apogee of Arthurian Romance, on the one hand, and the *Roman de la Rose* . . . on the other will serve as the limits of our study . . . . This epoch is, in effect, testimony to a decisive evolution; . . . One passed gradually from an allegorical explication attached to the text to a religious poetry with an allegorical form which turns on the distinction between spirit and letter to give Christian doctrine an "imaged representation."[7]

Like twelfth-century commentators on the Apocalypse, writers *en romanz*, whether secular or religious, began to concern themselves with the representation of events moving in time, linked causally to one another through the actions of heroes, and bound to a particular landscape. But while the matter of "history" was essential, it had to be infused with mean-

---

[7] Hans Robert Jauss, *La Génèse de la poésie allégorique française au moyen âge (de 1180–1240)* (Heidelberg, 1962), p. 9. Professor Jauss's inquiry into the origins of a new sort of allegorical poetry in France between 1180 and 1240 has not only made clear the newness of works as diverse as Chrétien's *Conte du Graal* and Guillaume de Lorris' *Roman de la Rose*, but has also helped to identify the qualities of that novelty. His essay together with Eugène Vinaver's *Rise of Romance* (Oxford, 1971) have called attention to the creation of vernacular narrative forms "composed" in a manner unknown in religious or secular literature before the twelfth century.

ing. French writers distinguished between the *conte* and its didactic end, and they insisted on the necessity of both. Chrétien de Troyes, Guillaume le Clerc, Raoul de Houdenc, Huon de Méri, the authors of the *Perlesvaus* and the *Queste del Saint Graal* all spoke of, or implied, a central distinction between the *matere* and its *sens*, between the *conte* and its *entendement*. Yet for these writers, this distinction by no means negated the value of the story or poetic composition; rather the *historia* was elevated, infused as it was with a moral or spiritual value which matter alone could not claim.[8]

The new double form thus conceived required of the audience a kind of imaginative and meditative activity preeminently demanded by the narrative and parabolic Word of sacred scripture. Reading from cover to cover, or listening from beginning to end, one could derive a special pleasure from discovering the secrets of an historically based "allegorical" narrative in which a spiritual plan shaped the story and carried history beyond the mere narration of events. As Hugh of St. Victor had done concerning the letter of sacred scripture, Chrétien de Troyes suggested the importance of the *conte*, even as he emphasized the necessity of superimposing a learned commentary. His method allowed the audience to discover meaning only *in and through the narrative*. Just so, according to twelfth-century exegetes and cathedral builders, God had chosen to reveal the destiny of the human race by telling his story episode by episode, ineluctably binding his revelation to the unfolding of history. For the artist, the new forms represented a compromise with the limits of human language and creaturely experience, but also a glorification of their possibilities. Being a human product, like the golden doors at St.-Denis or stained-glass windows without sun, the *estoire* or *conte* could not yield its meaning by itself. But the writer, through his talent and spiritual acuity, could infuse his verbal form with meaning or "bon entendement"—truths which the matter alone could never teach but which could be "built into" the tale to be discovered there by the attentive reader.

One spiritual vision quest which dramatically demonstrates these developments early in the thirteenth century is Huon de Méri's *Tournoiement Antechrist*.[9] Huon is not a brilliant poet, but he had a remarkable knack for recognizing and imitating the most important literary trends of his

---

[8] For a lucid discussion of this complex new mode of literary composition, see Douglas Kelly, *Sens and Conjointure* (The Hague and Paris, 1966), pp. 36–39.

[9] Huon de Méri, *Le Tournoiement de l'Antéchrist*, ed. G. Wimmer (Marburg, 1888). All subsequent line references to Huon's *Tournoiement* will be to this edition.

own time. A Benedictine monk at the Abbey of St.-Germain-des-Prés in Paris, Huon wrote the *Tournoiement* about 1234, looking back with admiration to the masterpieces of Chrétien de Troyes and to the great success of Raoul de Houdenc's visions of hell and heaven. He was also clearly aware of an increasing popular interest in, and new attitudes toward, Antichrist's coming, to be found, for example, in the commentaries of Joachim of Fiore and Alexander of Bremen. Acknowledging the importance of Chrétien's new style and Raoul's eschatological substance, Huon undertook to combine a personal *conte* with the familiar Latin form of the Prudentian soul struggle. Then he added a cosmic dimension by incorporating an apocalyptic vision of Antichrist's coming. In his composition, the old-fashioned personification allegory and the scriptural figures of Revelation are merged and at least partly transformed through the character of a first-person narrator to whom Huon assigns a central position.

Huon first identifies himself both as a self-conscious maker interested in current "news," and as a visionary with a new revelation to report. As a "maker," he claims to imitate Chrétien; as a visionary, Raoul de Houdenc. Having explicitly established these literary precedents, the poet gives way to his narrator's voice and experience. The narrative proper begins with Huon's hero, an Everyman figure borrowed from the romances, leaving the King's war against the British partisans. Abruptly he enters the Arthurian forest of Broceliande, led, against his better judgment, by his heart.[10] Once within the forest, after a miraculous thunderstorm (perhaps adapted from Chrétien's *Yvain*), he encounters a Moor, *Bras-de-fer* (Iron Arms), no doubt one of those Moslem invaders who, Alexander of Bremen had predicted, would be the harbingers of Antichrist. Together with his dubiously qualified guide, the narrator becomes a witness to the arrangements being made for a tournament between Christ and Antichrist. With all the magnificence of medieval ceremony, tents have been set up and a banquet prepared—a banquet, Huon tells us, very like the one Raoul de Houdenc attended in his dream of hell.

As the poet moves his narrator toward climactic conflict, he martials all the Prudentian virtues and vices, and more, to serve his spiritual purpose. He neatly ensconces the moral psychomachia within the context of a con-

---

[10] Like *Amant* in the *Roman de la Rose*, Huon's narrator is idle and therefore a likely object for Cupid's arrows. At least from the time of Ovid's *Ars Amatoria*, idleness had been regarded as a state useful for falling in love. Both Huon and Guillaume de Lorris, with their rationalist, moralist bent, make those who embrace *Oiseuse* prime targets for a painful fall.

temporary French political controversy, the confused heart of a chivalric narrator, and most important, an apocalyptic battle. Just as the French counts and their king have waged war against one another, and the narrator's passion and will are sinfully pitted against reason, so Antichrist will combat Christ. In this complex *conjointure*, Huon has woven political, personal and eschatological conflicts into a polyphonic narrative where all the struggles within the state and the soul are shown as aspects of the cosmic, apocalyptic encounter between Christ and Antichrist.

In following Prudentius, Huon develops a long and often tiresome procession of the vices and virtues. But he never allows his audience to lose sight entirely of his wandering narrator. For nearly twenty-five hundred lines, the hero is a passive witness to his vision. But then, when the god of courtly love appears, he returns to the center of the action and succumbs to love's darts (which identifies at last his moral weakness and the spiritual reason for his being shown the tournament of Antichrist). Fortunately, however, reason, contrition and confession come to his aid and save him from joining Antichrist's forces. He accepts the kindness and unguents of *Contricion*, passes through confession, and emerges to find that *Bras-de-fer*, the Moor, has disappeared. Before him he sees the glorious vision of the New Jerusalem.

In his treatment of the narrator, who draws together history, romance, personification allegory, and eschatological vision, Huon provides a splendid example of the conjunction of romance techniques with elements of the older vision narratives, a combination which prepared the way for the grand figural dream quests of the late thirteenth and fourteenth centuries. Following Chrétien and also imbued with monastic methods for explicating sacred scripture, he understood the importance of composing a lively *historia* or *estoire* from which a *sens* could be extracted. Arranging the images of his narrative in an order governed not only by a logical or thematic moral scheme but also by the order of personal history, he required his audience to do their own meditative glossing, sometimes assisted by the narrator or his guide, sometimes by the poetic voice.

It is Huon's personalization of his narrator which illustrates the most significant thirteenth-century innovation in the making of vision narratives. Earlier monastic visions were often recorded in the first person. But there the narrator is usually treated as a transparent instrument through whom the reader might catch a glimpse of the other world and its inhabitants. In Huon's poem, on the other hand, the narrator is the hero of a romance as well as a wandering visionary, and he perceives his revelation of the apocalyptic conflict through the filter of political and personal history. Like earlier visionaries, he is converted by his experience and becomes a penitent sinner on the road to salvation. But his monastic ancestors had been shown heaven and hell *before* turning to a life of penance. By contrast, Huon's hero is converted during the course of his vision. A gradual spiritual awakening takes place as the allegorical and figural images unfold before his (and the audience's) eyes. Personal conversion to grace through a vision treated as an historical event has become the center of the poetic process.

In this shift of focus, Huon's morally complex, fallible hero resembles contemporary artists' depictions of St. John not only in his relationship to his vision but also in his function for the audience. Like St. John, Huon claims to be reporting his vision as a true event and he writes the revelation down after the fact. Consequently, while the visionary narrator within the story witnesses the event as if for the first time, the poet-reporter can direct the readers' responses to the images and scenes before them with the help of his retrospective meditation and glossing. The figure of the poet looking back and writing provides the narration with the possibility of a spiritual significance to be gleaned in stages by the audience.

In addition, while the older monastic visions had been largely limited to St. Paul's images of the punishments of hell and shadowy glimpses of the joys of heaven set in an atemporal scheme, Huon's *Tournoiement*, patterned after Raoul de Houdenc's *Voie* and *Songe*, draws freely on St. John's eschatological figures. Huon expects his audience to understand them as the necessary conclusion to the narrator's quest for God. This is no minor change. The introduction of St. John's mysterious images provides a cosmic dimension which gives teleological purpose and historical density to visions of the other world. Personal history is extended and mythologized by its association with the history of the world's end. The narrator who sees hell and heaven and also confronts Antichrist becomes involved through his vision with the grand movement of sacred history. His moral choices align him historically with or against Christ.

In their most basic theme—the conversion of fallen man to a life of penance and grace—the new vision narratives introduced during the late twelfth and early thirteenth centuries did not differ greatly from their monastic predecessors. In one way or another, they adapted narrative conventions established by earlier writers: a sinning visionary, an other-worldly guide, revelations concerning the supernatural world, and the narrator's education into his own guilt and consequent need for divine grace. But, as Huon's *Tournoiement* suggests, both in the treatment of the theme and the manipulation of traditional narrative elements, the new writers made major additions and alterations which transformed the older vision structure.

Poets of the allegorical renascence who used the informing metaphor of visionary experience undertook to describe the entire course of a human life both as personal history and as a progressive movement toward salvation and the vision of God. Between a verbal beginning and conclusion, writers strove to encompass specific time and space within the visionary perspective of the end of time. The hero-narrator of the tale learned within the confines of his own history to live morally and sacramentally for the sake of his spiritual end in the New Jerusalem. Likewise the audience, provided with help through grace, might be turned to a reassessment of their own earthly life and that of the human race by following and understanding the narrator's visionary experience.

Structural Elements of the Spiritual Quest

The earliest examples of the new spiritual quest make their most immediate practical purpose clear. They were written for use during Lent, particularly Holy Week, and were intended to move souls toward confession as the fee for entering Paradise. Near the beginning of Raoul de Houdenc's *Voie de Paradis* (c. 1210), the guests in the House of Charity admonish the narrator:

> Va si tien ton chemin errant
> Vers la meson Contriction.
> Apres querras Confession
> Et se tu pues ces .ii. avoir
> Tu porras bien de si savoir
> Que, se foiz ne defaut en ti,
> Ne t'i avons de rien menti,
> Que droit en paradis iras,
> Ne ja chemin n'i mariras;
> Si vendras enz tout a souhait. (ll. 117-126)[11]

[11] Raoul de Houdenc, *La Voie de Paradis*, in A. Jubinal, ed., *Œuvres complètes de Rutebeuf*, 2nd ed., vol. 3, 1874, pp. 195-234, ll. 117-125. All subsequent line references to Raoul's *Voie de Paradis* will be to this edition.

(Go, betake your wandering way
Toward Contrition's house.
Afterward seek Confession
And if you are able to obtain these two,
You should know well
That, if faith is not lacking in you,
We have told you no lies,
You will go straight to Paradise,
Nor ever lose the way.
And you will enter within according to your desire.)

Happily, Raoul's meditative quest is successful. He arrives in the heavenly court and hears Christ's greeting, "Raoul, bien l'as fet" [968] (Raoul, you have done well). Likewise, Huon's *Tournoiement*, as we have seen, leads an imprudent narrator away from the thorns of love through confession to the vision of Christ's triumph. This purpose accords with the traditional function of monastic vision literature. The new allegorical writers were also no doubt greatly influenced by the Lateran Council's decree on penance made in 1215.[12] Once annual confession had become compulsory for all Christans, friars and clerks began to provide copious manuals and sermons teaching the faithful how to approach the sacrament. They circulated a great body of literature dealing with the virtues and vices and reminding sinners of their eschatological consequences.

It seems clear that the need for instruction in examination of conscience invited not only preachers but poets to provide penitential exercises for religious and lay audiences. Certainly the new vision quests, written in the vernacular, had as one central motive just the sort of meditative self-examination required by the friar's manuals on confession. Every religious quest, from Raoul's *Voie de Paradis* and Huon's *Tournoiement Antechrist* to Langland's *Vision Concerning Piers the Plowman*, moves a wandering visionary between the two poles of need and fulfillment, sin and salvation. The artist's further concern, toward which he directs his persuasive art, is

---

[12] See C. J. Hefele and H. Leclerq, *Histoire des Conciles* v, 2 (Paris, 1910). For subsequent developments and effects of the Council's proclamation on penance, see E. Arnould, *Manuel des péchés* (Paris, 1940), pp. 6–25; J. Grigsby, ed., *The Middle French Liber Fortunae* (Berkeley, 1967), p. 17n.; Morton Bloomfield, *The Seven Deadly Sins* (Michigan, 1952), pp. 91–92; H. G. Phander, "Some Medieval Manuals of Religious Instruction in England," *JEGP*, xxxv (1936), pp. 243–258; Rosemond Tuve, *Allegorical Imagery* (Princeton, 1966), p. 80.

clearly to lead the *audience* from confusion to confession and purgation preparatory to the vision of God. The new allegorists took as their spiritual purpose or principle of organization the one described by Dante in his letter to Can Grande and reiterated by Boccaccio in his commentary: to draw souls from misery to bliss. Or put another way, to discover for readers or listeners an answer to Will Langland's query: "how shall I win salvation." Dante's study of the way to bliss and Langland's of the road to human perfection are only logical extensions of the purpose of Raoul's and Huon's and Rutebeuf's poems: to represent for the meditative soul the temporal, narrative route to spiritual transformation through examination of conscience, confession and contrition. Only from this three-fold sacramental action, however conceived, extended and embellished, could human perfection and human beatitude proceed.

If one were to formulate a rulebook for writing vision quests, he would want to include the structural elements of the narrative, the metaphor of vision and the commonplaces associated with it, the motif of the quest, the allegorical, symbolic and apocalyptic imagery provided by tradition and imagination, the character of the sinful narrator, and the mental geography of "houses" and "places." But his main concern would certainly be the ways in which these elements could be combined persuasively to effect the salvation of the audience. All the parts of the poem, drawn from several thoroughly familiar sacred and secular traditions, should lead the reader or listener toward his own spiritual edification and purification through his participation, interpretation and understanding of the narrative.

The "marriage of matter and meaning, of narrative and commentary," characteristic of the new literature *en romanz* was precisely suited to such penitential meditation. The narartor's fictive *historia* was to take place in a visionary realm where material and spiritual, concrete and abstract coexist in a complex verbal context. Properly manipulated, the figurative tale of the pilgrim's progress could engage the reader in a challenging and exacting rhythm of imaginative discovery. The allegorical sense, hovering over and giving purpose to the literal, would spiritualize the story, establishing its intimate metaphoric connection with Everyman's earthly quest for salvation and his need for sacramental conversion to the Edenic state of Adam before the Fall. Readers who attended properly to the narrator's pilgrimage might find in it a mirror of their own halting progress toward spiritual purification and the vision of peace. The stylistic and narrative elements which the quest writers chose in making their penitential meditations effectively contributed to the construction of a double form in which a literal and allegorical sense are manifestly apparent in the poetic process.

THE FUNCTION OF THE PROLOGUE

In later medieval treatises on poetry, the importance of the prologue for literary compositions was discussed at length. Dealing with narrative order, theorists emphasized the value of diverging from the natural course of events in order to underline a single theme. Geoffrey of Vinsauf suggests that, in order to make the theme stand out, the poet might place a proverb or an example of his *sententia* at the beginning, preceding the story.[13] John of Garland recommends that the introduction contain a summary of the whole poem.[14] Whether or not the new vision poets attended to the theorists, they typically chose to give their prologues thematic purpose. Proper interpretation of the introduction reveals the symbolic structure and spiritual function of the whole composition in miniature. Particularly after Guillaume de Lorris's *Roman de la Rose*—a secular version of the vision quest—the prologue came to serve two important purposes: it introduced the pilgrim and established a setting and/or theme prefiguring or predicting the narrative to come.

In courtly love songs, the symbolic imagery of paradise had become a standard topic for introductions.[15] It was Guillaume's genius not only to adapt the typical exordium of the lyrics and romances to his prologue as well as the vision proper, but, in the adaptation, to force examination of the setting in terms of the narrator's spiritual state and situation. Courtly singers had used a paradisal environment of sweetness and light as a static background for their songs of joy or lament. In the *Roman de la Rose*, on the other hand, the May setting of the prologue constitutes a dynamic, thematic statement foreshadowing the narrator's discovery both of the wonders and the thorns of love.[16] Later religious poets, using the secular vision as a model, adapted the garden setting of Guillaume's prologue in

[13] *Poetria Nova*, vv. 125–133 in E. Faral ed., *Les Arts poétiques du XIIe et du XIIIe siècle* (Paris, 1924).

[14] T. Lawler, ed., *Poetria Parisiana* (New Haven and London, 1974), p. 73.

[15] Roger Dragonetti, *La Technique poétique des trouvères dans la chanson courtoise* (Bruges, 1960), pp. 190–191.

[16] Guillaume's description of May at the beginning of the *Roman* emphasizes not only the sweetness of the season but also its transiency. May lasts only a brief time. The trees are covered with new leaves, but the poet reminds us that it has not

a variety of ways, depending on their needs and their own inventiveness. Often the demands of the theme resulted in significant alterations of the conventional setting.

Rutebeuf, in his *Voie de Paradis*, borrowed the general form and some of the wording for his prologue from the *Roman de la Rose*. But he introduced important changes to suit his religious subject. The setting is March, not May, although the details of the flowering trees and new blossoms remain in imitation of Guillaume and also perhaps of Chrétien's *Conte du Graal*. But the central image—the farmer going out to sow his seed—is Rutebeuf's own contribution, an emblem explicitly related to Easter, the feast of the death and resurrection of Jesus:

> Mi marz tout droit, en cel termine
> Que de souz terre ist la vermine
> Ou ele a tout l'yver esté
> Si s'esjoïst contre l'esté,
> Cil arbre se cuevrent de fueille
> Et de flor la terre s'orgueille
> Si se cuevre de flors diverses,
> D'index, de jaunes et de perses,
> Li preudon, quant voit le jor né,
> Reva arer en son jorné;
> Apres arer, son jorné same:
> Qui lors semeroit si que s'ame
> Moissonast semence devine,
> Je di por voir, non pas devine,
> Que buer seroit nez de sa mere,
> Quar tel moisson n'est pas amere. (1–16)[17]

---

always been so: "Li bois recuevient lor verdure/ qui sunt sec tant come yver dure" (53–54: The woods *recover* their green leaves,/ which have been dried up as long as winter lasts). Following the prologue, the narrator, a young man of twenty at the moment he falls asleep, enters unsuspecting into the season and state of love. Within the vision, the transitory May of the prologue is transformed into a dream-time of eternal delight. But the progress of the story brings the narrator to a new understanding of earthly love as it was symbolized by the springtime of the opening lines. By the end of Guillaume's poem, the young lover has enjoyed the moment of falling in love and endured the pangs of unrequited love. The garden setting of the prologue is to be seen finally as a careful and ironic combination of the temporal and eternal, an image of a fallen Eden, which must inevitably have an end, as it had a beginning.

[17] E. Faral and J. Bastin, ed., *Œuvres complètes de Rutebeuf*, vol. I (Paris, 1959), pp. 341–342. All subsequent references to Rutebeuf's *Voie de Paradis* will be to this edition. For the Lenten function of this poem see *Oeuvres*, p. 337.

(Exactly in the middle of March, at that time
When the worm issues forth from under the ground
Where it has been all winter
And rejoices at the coming of the summer,
Those trees are covered with leaves
And the earth boasts of flowers;
It is covered with various blossoms,
Blue, yellow, violet-blue.
The landholder, when he sees the day dawn,
Goes out to plow in his land,
After plowing, he sows all day.
He would sow in such a way that his soul
Would reap the divine harvest;
I speak the truth, not a guess,
He would be fortunately born of his mother,
And such a harvest is not bitter.)

The thematic intention of this prologue is clearly conveyed in the emblematic picture of the sower whose divine seed symbolizes Christ's redemption. The allegorical seed sown at the beginning of the poem bears its eschatological fruits at the end when Rutebeuf recounts the resurrection of Christ and the founding of the New Jerusalem:

Quant Jhesus fu resuscitez,
Lors fu fondee la Citez
Le jor de Pentecouste droit,
A ce point et a cel endroit
Que Sainz esperiz vint en terre
Por fere aus apostres conquerre
Le peuple des Juys divers. (833–889)[18]

(When Jesus arose,
Then the city was founded,
On Pentecost, right
At the time and place
That the Holy Spirit came to earth,
To make the Apostles conquer
The various people of the Jewish race.)

[18] *Œuvres*, p. 370.

Rutebeuf's combination of the courtly setting of the *Roman de la Rose* with explicitly religious symbolism prepares us directly for the prologue to *Pearl*.

Another famous borrower from the prologue of the *Roman de la Rose* was Guillaume de Deguileville in the last of his *Pèlerinages*.[19] He, like Rutebeuf, altered some of the details to emphasize his *senefiance*. The poem begins in a garden of delights. Then, because the *Pèlerinage* is to be about the Fall and the Redemption—Adam and Christ—Guillaume adds details to relate his garden to the paradise of the first parents: the trees bear "pommes et autres fruis." In the midst of singing birds proper to paradise, the narrator sits down at the foot of an apple tree. The May setting of courtly love poetry, adapted by Guillaume de Lorris, has here been brought together with the image of the primordial apple of the knowledge of Good and Evil in order to emphasize the spiritual directions of the vision proper. Should his audience have failed to notice the connection, Guillaume explicitly announces that the emblems relate the prologue thematically to the subsequent vision.

In general, then, the prologue to visionary quests establishes themes, often presented through a symbolic setting, and introduces a narrator about to embark on a spiritual journey. The setting may be parabolic in terms of the subsequent story; or it may be directly and explicitly allegorical, as in Deguileville's *Pèlerinage Jhesucrist* and Rutebeuf's *Voie de Paradis*. The second element of the prologue, the characterization of the narrator, receives more or less attention depending on the poet's skill as well as the centrality of the pilgrim's development to the progress of the narrative.

Narrator, Vision and Audience

For the character of their first-person narrator, quest writers depended, either explicitly or implicitly, on the authoritative model of the prophet St. John, to whom the angel had said, "Write what you see on a scroll." These literary pilgrims shared with the evangelist the purpose of prophecy as defined by St. Thomas, "to instruct the human race in whatever is necessary for salvation."[20] But they usually lacked the privileged certainty of

[19] *Pèlerinage Jhesucrist*, ed. J. J. Stürzinger (London, 1897), ll. 30–31, p. 2.

[20] Thomas Aquinas, *De veritate* q. 12. a. 2c, quoted in Synave and Benoit, *Prophecy and Inspiration* (New York, 1961), p. 62.

the scriptural prophets. Rutebeuf's visionary insists he is a "rude worker." Dante protests that he is neither Aeneas nor Paul. Langland's Will is "unholy of works." The desolate *Pearl* narrator's "wreched wylle" wars with reason. Echoing Boethius' forlorn philosopher, all these fictive pilgrims are portrayed as lethargic and self-ignorant, not chosen for vision because they are holy and elect but because they are Everyman in need of consolation and spiritual guidance. Alone they would not find heaven or the spiritual acuity proper to souls near the end of the Last Age. Only through the power of vision and the authoritative guide provided for their edification can they realize the allegorical sense of their quest[21] and envision spiritual peace.

These willing but ineffectual narrators introduced in the prologue offered poets perhaps their most flexible device for innovation and experimentation. Through the fallible "I" they could provide one point of view —one way of "seeing" the visionary world. Then, using their art and their audience's judgment, they could also suggest alternative perspectives, juxtaposing them with the pilgrim's in order to underscore the difficulties of perceiving divine meaning aright. In this way, poets were able to engage readers in a conspiracy of superior knowledge, complimenting their perspicuity by allowing them to see more than the narrator. Both Raoul and Huon practice a subtle art of irony in thus managing their visionary pilgrims. But the master who brought the technique to a point of perfection was Guillaume de Lorris. His handling of the narrator in relation to his dream world and his audience's reason exerted so powerful an influ-

---

[21] Here and throughout this discussion, I am using the term "allegory" in the strict sense which Rosemond Tuve has derived from medieval practice, particularly from Christine de Pisan. According to Christine, "allegory" had to do more with the human quest for the heavenly city than with descriptions of moral actions *per se*. The allegorical meaning was addressed to the reader as a spiritual being. "The Good Spirit reads in figures the reminder of its true condition as a creature, sometimes seeing its need for rescue, often seeing in the figures a repetition of the news of its way of deliverance or some definition of the nature of this deliverance" (*Allegorical Imagery*, p. 40). All of the works studied in my book are first and foremost "allegories" in this sense. The explicit goal of the narrator's journey is an eschatological one through which he transcends his earthly sinfulness and discovers, if only momentarily, the proper end of his and Everyman's existence. Tuve's distinction between "allegorie" and "moralization" offers one of the most useful ways yet presented for understanding the various kinds of images and figures employed by writers of medieval religious quests. See especially her chapter 1, "Problems and Definitions," pp. 3–55.

ence on later poets that an understanding of his method is an essential preparation for approaching all subsequent questing narrators.

From the beginning of the *Roman de la Rose*, Guillaume assigns not only his lover but also his audience a vital, fully defined dramatic function. During the first half of the poem, readers watch with amusement the narrator's witless foray into the Garden of Love and his ensnarement. As they watch, they are detached from and superior to the narrator. But once the lover has pledged fealty to the God of Love, he, like the audience, becomes aware of the meaning of his dream world. Then, the role of the audience changes. No longer detached from the narrator's vision, they share with him the irony of an untenable situation. Both the narrator and the audience understand the meaning of the personified world, but neither can do anything to make a happy conclusion possible. In those vision quests like the *Roman de la Rose* which depend heavily on the spiritual condition of the narrator in relation to his experience, the audience must be aware simultaneously of two visions. They are expected to see both the visionary world as it is seen by the stumbling narrator and the same world in its universal or spiritual significance. They, together with the poet and often with a guide or guides, observe with ironic detachment and amusement (and sometimes sympathy) the disparity between the two visions.

Besides drawing the audience into the dramatic structure of the composition, the juxtaposition of the "I" narrator and his dream world has an important thematic purpose. The conjunction of the concrete, naively literal narrator with an allegorical or symbolic vision provided an effective means for meshing time and eternity. As Curtius has said with regard to the *Commedia*: "Timelessness and temporality are not only confronted and related, they are also merged and so interwoven that the threads are no longer distinguishable."[22] For those living near the end of the Last Age, this aspect of "timelessness" included all history and metahistory as seen from the divine perspective, that is, *in aevo*. History began with the Creation and Fall and continued, by way of the Redemption, to the final harvest of saints. In the spiritual quest, the whole span of salvation history had to become a part of the "I" narrator's experience. The events from Adam's fall to the Apocalypse comprise an underlying structure which is ultimately incorporated into the vision and life of Everyman. Guillaume de Deguileville's poems begin with the prenatal existence of the narrator

[22] Ernst Robert Curtius, *European Literature and the Latin Middle Ages*, trans. M. A. Trask (New York, 1953), p. 366.

and carry him to his judgment before the throne of God; in the *Pèlerinage Jhesucrist*, emphasis is centered on the perfect pilgrim who atones for the sin of Adam and makes final judgment possible. In *Piers Plowman*, Will discovers the whole course of sacred history woven into his visionary world. He also explores its meaning in terms of contemporary society and the possibility of an apocalyptic age of the spirit. In *Pearl*, the narrator begins to understand how and why man fell and regained paradise.

The Guide in a Visionary World

As a direct source of instruction in the visionary way to salvation, poets provided narrators with a guide to help them through the dream world. These guides patterned on Boethius' Philosophia, had the responsibility of leading the pilgrim as well as the audience from worldly delusion to conversion and the vision of the New Jerusalem. Far more than a literary personification, Boethius's Lady Philosophy had become for the later Middle Ages a character as tangible as Boethius himself. In at least one translation of the *De consolatione*—the tenth- or eleventh-century Provençal *Boeçi*[23]—characteristics of an ideal human lady had already been imposed on the supernatural figure drawn by Boethius. In Alain de Lille's vision of Natura, the personified guide had been transformed into an ideal queen, dressed in a damask tunic, with golden hair, clear calm eyes and a nose "neither out of measure nor unduly prominent." By the thirteenth century, the lady guide of supernatural visions, under the influence of courtly song and romance, had been distinctly humanized, providing a model for Beatrice and the Pearl Maiden as well as Deguileville's Grace-Dieu and Langland's Holichurch.

The manner in which the lady introduces herself to the narrator in his visions has its roots in Boethius. Philosophia appears at the head of the bed, from nowhere. Alain's lady, Natura, descends "from the inner palace of the impassable heavens." Beatrice comes down to Dante on a celestial chariot. Langland's Holichurch descends from a castle. The Pearl Maiden mysteriously sits at the foot of a cliff.

The appearance of the wondrous guide elicits a stock reaction on the part of the narrator. Caught up in a mindless stupor, he is struck with silence and fear in the face of his cure and salvation. In the prototypical story, Philosophia reprimands Boethius for swooning and explains his

---

[23] Christophe Schwärze, *Der Altprovençalische "Boeci"* (Aschendorff, Münster, 1963).

sickness: "he is in a lethargy, the common disease of deceived minds; he hath a little forgot himself but he will easily remember himself again, if he be brought to know us first." Dante, recognizing Beatrice, is struck dumb. Deguileville's pilgrim, meeting Grace-Dieu, falls "ynto a maner drede,/ for vnkonnynge and lewdenesse." Long Will says of Holichurch simply that he was "aferd of her face." *Pearl*'s jeweler stands "as hende as hawk in halle," silent and awestruck in the presence of his maiden. As she draws the narrator from self-conscious fear to a discovery of the fear of God and the beginning of wisdom, the guide leads him and his audience to seek the allegorical sense of their quest.

THE CONSTRUCTION OF THE FABLE

Poets heightened the effect of a double form—the *estoire* and its *sens*—by explicitly separating the fictive making or "fable" from the narrator's original visionary experience. In his *Songe d'Enfer,* Raoul de Houdenc, as retrospective poet, speaks of the fable he has *constructed* to record his narrator's dream: "Raouls de Houdaing . . . cest fable fist de son songe" (677–678). Rutebeuf reminds his audience from time to time that he is creating a fable in his *Voie de Paradis.* He will "devise" the way Envy looks ("Deviser vous vueil sa devise" [292]).[24] Envy is "reposte" and "mise" in her place, removed from her niche in Ovid, Rutebeuf suggests, and somewhat altered by being set in this new context. Guillaume de Deguileville goes to some length to describe the kind of creative reporter he is, first taking up his pen the night after his dream and writing it down, and then correcting and shaping his composition twenty-five years later, polishing and arranging it "as any man will who wants to make something properly." Even Langland, a poet not well-known for his interest in artful construction, considered his poem a "making." Imaginatif chides Will for his poetry: "Thou medlest the with makynges and my𝈰test go sey thi sauter . . . for ther ar bokes ynowe/ To telle men what Dowel is Dobet, and Dobest both,/ And prechoures to preue what it is of many a peyre freres." To this Will answers that he finds solace in his making, and, calling his work "play," he compares it with the play of holy men who "pleyden, the parfiter to be . . ." (B. XII, 16–25).[25]

By thus separating their constructions from actual visions, poets could

24 *Voie,* p. 351.
25 William Langland, *Piers Plowman,* ed. W. W. Skeat (Oxford, 1886), vol. I, p. 366. All subsequent references to *Piers* will be to this edition. Skeat's medial dot has been omitted throughout.

make the fable serve as a stable commentary on the visionary experience in process. It was to be studied in its own right and offer the audience a second level of experience and understanding. Hence the narrator's naive perception of his vision would be effectively countered for readers trained in Christian doctrine by the authorial voice, the directions of the guide, the shape of the figural imagery and the form of the composition. The result would be a fine balancing of the poet's "making" against the pilgrim's literal sense of his *historia*.

The Places of Vision

Once he had chosen the form of the visionary quest, the poet's first task was to create a whole fiction based on images of place, space and character that would provide a satisfactory context for the soul in meditation. Explanations of meaning and direct lessons may interrupt the narrative movement. But the reader, like the narrator, is to remain firmly fixed in the figural landscape just as he would in following any romance, stopping from time to time for instruction at a knowledgeable hermit's lodging.

To provide a geography for the meditating mind, the poet fictionalizes (temporalizes) the relationships among the spiritual states and sacramental actions connected with penitential conversion. He invents and disposes "places" to help his audience memorize the process of salvation. Through his series of "historically" linked illustrations the poet means to recommend the virtues and warn against the vices by imposing their character firmly on the reader's memory. Langland even goes to the length of providing clever alliterative memory structures for his audience in which virtuous actions are coupled, for example, with parts of a manor house.

A simple example from Raoul's *Songe d'Enfer* will illustrate one very popular and obvious way of formulating the mental realm of visionary experience. Having made his way to a tavern, the narrator encounters *Yvrece* (Drunkenness) and her son, *Versez* (Pouring). *Versez* is portrayed as an English muscleman. Constrained to play with him, the wandering pilgrim is thrown down, retreats, returns and is assaulted again until *Versez* gets the "better of his head." Then he is flattened to the ground where he lies as if wounded until *Yvrece* persuades him to visit the *Chastiau-Bordel*. To give his audience a memorable figurative lesson on the relationship between drinking, drunkenness and lechery, Raoul locates a series of dramatic events in a city tavern and bordello and adds tension through the lively battle between the dreamer and *Versez*. Later poets using similar techniques further developed and embellished the mental geography of the journey, addressing themselves more and more elaborately to the audience's imagination. They built on the device of dramatic suspense and used it to tantalize audiences into gradual recognition of complex symbolic figures; and they developed more and more fully the personal relationship between the narrator and the places and events of his visions.

Even Dante's mental geography of hell, purgatory and heaven, complex and intricate as it is, serves the same purpose and functions in much the same ways as the geographies of Raoul and Rutebeuf, Deguileville and Langland—though of course Dante does a good deal more. Frances Yates is quite just, I think, in suggesting that the whole *Commedia* can be read as a systematic meditation directed to memory: "it could be regarded," she says, "as a kind of memory system for memorizing Hell and its punishments with striking images on orders of places. If one thinks of the poem as based on orders of places, in Hell, Purgatory and Paradise . . . it begins to appear as a summa of similitudes and exempla, ranged in order and set out upon the universe."[26] In the environment of notable and singular figures carefully placed in an imaginary landscape, the narrator visits each scene, reflects on it, and sometimes forms his will on the basis of a rational interpretation of it. (Often such interpretation is neglected by the narrator and left to the good judgment and prudence of the audience.) When, with the help of his guide or guides, he has correctly interpreted a sufficient number of the scenes and understood in some part the geography and inhabitants of the visionary landscape in the light of eternal judgment, he is allowed to approach the New Jerusalem.

For all religious-quest writers the invention of a visionary landscape provided the necessary "places" through which the hero or narrator might move through and from his earthly life toward his vision of heaven. During the twelfth century *romanciers* had evolved one of the most durable metaphoric vocabularies to suit such a purpose. The vaguely defined geography of Arthurian romance, with its vast pathless forests punctuated by hermitages, mysterious ships and magical castles, marvelous storms and wonderful creatures, provided an exotically abstracted mythic landscape within which Everyman might be set to win his way to spiritual transformation. The Galahad of the anonymous *Queste del Sainte Graal* ventures into the deep forests and wastelands of the Kingdom of Logres and comes finally to the transcendent vision of grace at the castle of Corbenyc. Huon

[26] Frances Yates, *The Art of Memory* (Chicago, 1966), p. 95.

de Méri's confused and less certainly holy narrator enters the forest of Broceliande to find a tournament about to take place between Christ and Antichrist—a tournament in which he finds himself intimately involved, but initially on the wrong side. The landscape of most visionary quests provides similarly abstracted settings. The writer could place his questing narrator explicitly (rather than implicitly as the *romanciers* did) in a land between heaven and earth, a landscape which bore an important resemblance to earthly landscapes but also shared in the abstraction or spirituality of the divine realm. The fictional "places" were to serve as metaphors for the mental states of the spiritual pilgrim who travels with his eyes closed by day and open by night—open, that is, to the presence of grace made visible to the spiritual or cleansed eye.

The Seasons of Vision and Visionary Time

To reinforce and bind together the visionary places, spaces and kinships of their fictive "constructions," writers relied on the coherence of a special sort of fictional time. A temporal setting is the necessary starting point for most visions, and the narrator usually establishes the time of day and/or year when the visionary pilgrimage began. Raoul's vision of heaven takes place at night while he sleeps, after he has finished a prayer asking God to show him the "right way." Rutebeuf's poem begins "exactly in the middle of March" when seeds are sown and when Christ, the divine grain, fell into the earth to rise again to new life. Dante's great other worldly pilgrimage starts on Holy Thursday evening in the year 1300 when twilight has fallen on earthly work. The *Pearl* narrator's quest starts in August in a "hyȝ seysoun," at the harvest when the wheat is ready to be taken into barns. Will Langland sets out in a "somer seson" when the sun is "soft." Guillaume de Deguileville's vision begins "on a tyme . . . fro Crystyes berth a thousand yer,/ Thre hondryd, . . ./ And over ten"[27] as he lies asleep. This temporal precision most obviously gives the fiction a particularity and credibility, ties it to the narrator's (and Everyman's) diurnal life, and establishes a "time" which can anticipate the temporally organized sequences within the dream. It also provides a frame for the vision, allowing the poet to make clear the distinction between the waking world and the world of dreams, similar though the two may appear to be and thematically related though they often are in these works.

[27] John Lydgate, trans. *The Pilgrimage of the Life of Man*, ed. F. J. Furnivall (London, 1889), ll. 211–213, p. 6.

The explicitly spiritual "time" within the dream (*in aevo*) related to but not identical with the narrator's temporal existence outside his vision serves to make visionary discussion of the waking world both appropriate and pointed. In the *Songe d'Enfer*, for example, *Tricherie* (Treachery) asks Raoul how affairs are progressing for his disciples on earth. Raoul willingly responds that traitors can be found flourishing in Poitou, and Treachery gloats:

J'ai toz les Poitevins norris:
Se il s'acordent a mes dis,
Biaus amis, n'est mie merveille. (85–87)[28]

(I have raised all the Poitevins,
And if they accord themselves with my teaching,
Good friend, it is no miracle!)

Such an encounter provides a prototypical pattern for a particular kind of social criticism, anticipating the satire of two later masterpieces, the *Commedia* and *Piers*. Freed from the usual limitations of particular existence, the personal prejudices and biases of a partisan in the world's activities, Raoul finds amnesty in the fictional universalized time of the dream. Whatever is said about particular evils in the world can be related to spiritual certainties—eternal evil and the judgments of Doomsday. Social criticism in a visionary environment assumes an objectivity, time scale and truth which the best poets are able to put to extraordinarily effective religious and satiric use.

The metaphor of visionary time also serves a major structural purpose in controlling the audience's perception of the poem and their approach to interpreting its meaning. As he moves through the visionary landscape of his "historical" pilgrimage, the dreamer reinforces the temporal, linear movement of the narrative. He can rise to the level of total spiritual perception of his environment only by pausing in his linear progress to reflect and remember. But he is not often allowed this meditative luxury and so fails to learn all he might from his dreams. The audience, on the other hand, may both delight in the linear narrative and return to reflect on the whole art work as a fixed form. In this they share that pleasure recorded by St. Augustine as he describes his reading of the Psalms:

I am about to repeat a Psalm that I know. Before I begin, my expectation is extended over the whole; but when I have begun, how much soever

[28] *Songe*, p. 179.

of it I shall separate off into the past, is extended along my memory; thus the life of this action of mine is divided between my memory as to what I have repeated and expectation as to what I am about to repeat; but "consideration" is present to me, that through it what was future, may be conveyed over, so as to become past. The more it is done again and again, so much the more the expectation is shortened, and the memory enlarged: till the whole expectation be exhausted, when that whole action being ended, shall have passed into memory.[29]

At first, the listener or reader participates in the dreamer's visions step by step, just as Augustine followed the words of the Psalms. Drawn into the complexities of the imaginative scene, he shares the narrator's confusions and questionings. But having experienced this anguish, elation, and halting movement toward transformation, he may return to enjoy the retrospective view articulated by the voice of the poet and the form of the composition. Through meditation, through gradually enriched understanding of the symbolic import of the imagery, through perceiving beginnings and endings as part of a larger scheme represented by the form, the reflective audience can begin to discover the full visionary meaning of the narrative scenes. The poet uses and even exaggerates time and "temporal" narrative in his representation of the pilgrimage partly to show both narrator and reader that time is necessary for transformation but also to demonstrate that visionary experience can carry both of them beyond ordinary historical, literal order. Just as the dream narrators have subsequently become poets in order to return to their visions and record them, so too the listener or reader is expected to return to the poet's composition, at least in memory, in order to understand the rational and spiritual orders which have dictated its narrative construction.

The Vision of Peace

As we have seen, a great many vision quests of the later Middle Ages shared narrative conventions: a basic story, stock characters, techniques for ironic and persuasive effects and the cosmic background of sacred history had all become part of the form by the early thirteenth century. But many of these literary conventions could also be found in the form of the complaint and in the secular romances. What distinguishes the religious visionary quest—what is, in a sense, its motive force—is its use of the fig-

[29] St. Augustine, *Confessions*, trans. E. P. Pusey (New York, 1949), p. 267.

ures, the text and/or the spirit of St. John's visions of the last things. With St. John as their venerable predecessor, vision poets could freely and authoritatively direct their narrators to the heavenly city.

There had been, of course, a rich tradition of visions from Plato, through the Scriptures and the Church Fathers, including Augustine, Bede, and Gregory the Great, which to some extent served the needs of the new forms. The secular visions of Cicero, with Macrobius's commentary, and Boethius's *De consolatione* also provided useful materials for verification and technique. Macrobius in particular provided a theoretical basis not only for visions like Cicero's *Dream of Scipio*, but also for the scriptural dreams of Ezekiel, Pharaoh and Joseph. According to Macrobius, dreams caused by a combination of a natural psychological state and divine influence, like Scipio's dream, or directly by God, like the scriptural dreams, were to be accepted as true if they were oracular, prophetic and/or enigmatic.

But none of these authorities shared the esteem accorded the visions of St. Paul and St. John. The use of Scripture as a means of verification had been a commonplace of impeccable authority in all kinds of didactic literature since the beginning of the Christian era. By using scriptural images a writer presented his thesis not as *causa probabilis* but as *veritas*. The scriptural visions which carry prophets to heaven provided a special case of such verification for the vision poets. Under their aegis they might deal with the truth of things not seen or heard since the foundation of the world. Almost all the new religious vision quests culminate in the pilgrim's arrival in St. John's city of the New Jerusalem, or at some point near that end. The arduous pilgrimage route traversed by the dreamer on his way to the heavenly city then functions as a personalized spiritual commentary on the Book of Revelation. The poet shows the meaning of the eschatological *figurae* by glossing them in terms of the narrator's personal history and his movement toward salvation. Having seen the New Jerusalem at the end of his *Voie de Paradis*, Raoul de Houdenc acknowledges his exemplar in St. John, whom he calls simply, "li saint." Deguileville and Dante appeal to St. Paul as well as to Ezekiel and St. John for authority and imagery. Just before he enters the heavenly city in the *Pèlerinage de l'Ame*, Deguileville's pilgrim is reminded by his angelic guide that St. Paul could not find words to describe his singular vision, a fact echoed by the narrator of *Pearl*. While Dante's paradisal "place" is unlike St. John's, its figural representation of perfect peace and beauty parallels the evangelist's figures of the city in spirit. Deguileville and the

Pearl poet paraphrase St. John, freely reusing his images in fresh contexts to represent their pilgrim's goal.

The Proper Reading of Visionary Quests

Taking into full account the "double" form of the visionary quest, John Lydgate gives directions for an ideal reading in the prologue to his translation of Deguileville's *Pèlerinage de Vie Humaine*. His advice might well be applied to all examples of the form:

> And that folk may the Ryhte weye se
> Best assuryd to-warde ther passage,
> lat hem be-holden in the Pylgrymage,
> Which callyd ys pylgrymage de mounde,
> In the wych fful notably ys founde,
> Lernyd, and tauht, *who can well construe*,
> What folk schal take, & what they schal eschue.
> In thys book, *yf that they rede yerne*,
> Pylgrymes schal the verray trouthe lerne,
> yff they sette ther trewe dyllygence
> To understonde clerly the sentence,
> What hyt menyth, & the moralyte;
> *Ther they may, as in a merour*, sc
> holsom thynges, & thynges full notable. (74–87, italics mine)[30]

According to Lydgate, the reader must in some way identify with the pilgrim-narrator of the quest: he must have a high spiritual goal in mind and desire to reach it. Secondly, he must read, "yerne" that is, *earnestly, zealously, vigorously*. Not only is the work to affect him; he is to affect the work by the diligence with which he penetrates its meaning. If he exerts "trewe dyllygence" he will discover the meaning and morality of the poem. Finally, his means of penetration is to be a "seeing" and a "beholding." This last requirement, that the reader is to "see" the poem, bears importantly on the development of visionary spatial and temporal metaphors. For the poetic narrative is to present images in which the beholder will find the likeness of "thynges holsom and thynges full notable." Only if he *sees* the images properly will he begin to understand the difference between good and evil, something he will grasp fully on the Day of Judgment. For

[30] Lydgate, *Pilgrimage*, p. 3.

the matter of the vision quest, as Lydgate and his predecessors conceived it, is precisely the good and evil of the created world seen in the light of the eschaton. But the casual reader will not grasp this matter properly. He will be unlikely to perceive the wholeness, clarity and unity of the subject through the poetic construction "as in a merour." Lydgate's ideal reader, on the other hand, will fully appreciate the economy of the lengthy visionary quest:

> To every pilgrim, vertuous of lyff,
> The mater is so contemplatyff;
> In all the book ys not lost a word. (119–121)[31]

If the poem is properly meditated, the entire narrative will be recognized as a coherent whole, every word and every image being necessary for the completion of the subject. Such a claim is extravagant indeed, particularly when applied to the wandering poems of a Deguileville or a Langland. Yet, assuming the good will, imagination and diligence of an audience adjusted to the poet's intentions and expectations, the most popular visionary quests of the later Middle Ages clearly strove to present a complex, temporally based figurative meditation on the salvation process aimed at adding new richness of meaning to the ordinary histories of fallen men.

Such a method of reading by no means encouraged dismissal of the literal story. Nor did it suggest that once the "meaning" had been found, the audience would abandon the literal for the spiritual. On the contrary, even in the earliest examples of the visionary quest, the artful construction of the literal *conte* enabled it to convey a good deal more than any conceptual translation of it could, Raoul de Houdenc, for instance, in his description of the horror of hell, creates a banquet hosted by an infernal lord. The narrator, sitting on two heretics, sees elegant courses being carried in: "De larons murtriers a plentex/ . . . Ti estoit chascuns toz vermaus/ De sanc de marcheanz mordris" (472–475: plenty of murderous robbers,/ . . ./ each one all red with the blood of murdered merchants), and then, "old fat whores" who cause the banqueters to "lick their fingers with delight" for "les putains qui lor puoient dont il amoient mult le flair" (484–485: the whores smelled and they liked the odor).[32] The obvious moral sense is a warning to the audience to beware of robbery, murder and lechery. But Raoul achieves much more with his fiction. Not merely comic and satiric, as it may first appear, the scene attempts to render the extravagant horror of hell, shown through the metaphor of the

---

[31] *Ibid.*, p. 4.   [32] *Songe,* p. 193.

cannibalistic banquet, the grease-fat whores, the bloody murderers. Here grotesquerie, presented as literal story, approaches Raoul's notion of hell in a way no fact, statement or doctrine could. No matter what moral or *sententia* the reader or listener attaches to the figure, he must remember and ponder the narrative details as well if he is to perceive fully the reasons for avoiding the pains of hell. This is surely the kind of reading Dante intended and for which Boccaccio asks in his commentary on the *Commedia* when he calls attention to the literal subject: "the state of the soul after the death of the body simply taken is the subject because from that and through that all the process of the present work is rendered intelligible (*intende*)."[33] In a somewhat different but related way, the meaning of *Pearl* is to be sought first and foremost by grasping the import of the literal story, and particularly the details of the beautiful landscape. The silvered leaves, the jeweled paths, the stream with its bed gleaming like stained glass, all are efforts to lead the narrator (and audience) toward the beauties one might expect to find in heaven. The literal images leap over the usual material and didactic limits of rhetorical figures to present anagogical mysteries obliquely by means of simple analogy.

Of course, not all the imagery of the literal story requires such close attention. Many of the images in visionary quests invite immediate and quite simple translation, sometimes directly provided by the voice of the poet. Yet even when such explicit teaching interrupts the narrative we do not lose the sense of the linear fictional context, the mental geography of places, houses and valleys operating in its own visionary time scheme. The gloss for the vision deepens and enriches our perception of the scene, impressing its importance on the mind even as the figure is impressed on the memory.

The Test of Truth

Poets of vision quests demanded yet another judgment from their audience: the reader had to assess the truth of the entire fiction thus artfully constructed. In his *Songe d'Enfer*, Raoul de Houdenc, like his successors, Guillaume de Lorris, Dante, Langland, and the *Pearl* poet, urges his audience to consider the truth of his "dreams":

En songes doit fables avoir;
Se songes puet devenir voir,

---

[33] Boccaccio, *Il Comento*, p. 3.

Dont sai je bien que il m'avint:
Qu'en songant un songe me vint
Talent que pelerins seroie.
Je m'atornai et pris ma voie
Tout droit vers la cite d'Enfer. (1–7)[34]

(In dreams there must be fables;
But dreams can come true,
Whereof I know well that it happened to me
That while in dreaming a dream there came to me
The wish to be a pilgrim.
I got ready and took my way
Straight toward the City of Hell.)

Near the end of his *Voie de Paradis*, Raoul suggests one possible method for truth-testing. The substance of his vision, he says, can be set beside truths outside the poetic construction, historical, doctrinal and scriptural. Raoul's narrator, like the jeweler of *Pearl*, awakens from his vision full of sorrow because he has not actually been in paradise but has only dreamed it. But he finds consolation by comparing his vision to another kind of truth:

Qui de paradis veut aprendre,
S'il me veut oïr & entendre
Et il en veut la joie avoir,
Il porra bien de si savoir
Qui j'en dirai vérité pure,
Selonc ce qu'en dist l'Escripture,
Quels il est & de quel bonté,
Si com li saint l'ont raconté. (1034–1041)[35]

(Whoever wishes to apprehend Paradise
And wishes to hear and understand me
And wishes to have its joy,
He should well know
That I shall speak pure truth
According to what Scripture says,
What it is and of what goodness,
Just as the saints have recounted).

---

[34] *Songe*, pp. 176–177.   [35] *Voie*, pp. 224–225.

If the poem can be verified by sacred authority, then the poet's personal dream of paradise assumes substance and significance as a model for all those who aspire to visions and to salvation. Shriven souls may take comfort in a provisional dream of heaven with the full confidence that after their death they will in fact be caught up into the heavenly court for an eternal life of joy after the Day of Judgment.

The motif of truth-testing had yet another effective use for Dante and Langland in their prophetic explorations of a millennial age of the spirit to come on earth before the Last Judgment. The explicitly apocalyptic idealism fostered by prophets and saints, artists and historians during the later twelfth and early thirteenth centuries had become less and less congenial to the Church as the thirteenth century wore on. Successive sacred commissions had condemned those who dared to temporalize the Church's course into measurable ages and argue that the end of the Last Age was to be spiritually superior to all preceding times. The commission of 1319, in examining Peter John Olivi's teaching, declared as "far-fetched and sometimes heretical" the idea that St. Francis of Assisi was the angel of the sixth seal and that his doctrine of poverty represented a renewal of Christ's gospel preparatory to the Last Judgment.[36] The Church's concern stemmed in part from its need to defend itself against the threat of a millennial Church built in love and wisdom rather than wealth and power.

But in art, where the visionary movement had early found eloquent and orthodox expression—in Gothic cathedral sculpture and architecture, in the grail stories, in popular hagiography—millennial optimism continued to enjoy a safe haven. Unlike theological disputation, art erected a symbolic curtain between man and his visions of heaven by the very materials it used, its modes being essentially figurative and suggestive. And no form of literary expression afforded greater scope for continued exploration of vision and the promise of a millennium than the *alienum eloquium* of the visionary quest. Both Dante and Langland, taking sanctuary in a popular and thoroughly familiar form, set their narrators on a course of penitential conversion which could lead them out of the confused fallen world of the sixth age into a time of perfect spiritual peace on earth. In the best vision quests of the later Middle Ages the question of truth assumes the importance of a major theme, challenging readers to contemplate the complex

[36] Marjorie Reeves, *The Influence of Prophecy in the Later Middle Ages* (Oxford, 1969), pp. 159–160.

relationships between personal history, exemplary fictions of visionary experience, and the actual historical movement of all mankind toward universal joy in the heavenly city.

Important differences separate minor from major achievements and distinguish masterpieces from each other. But these variations, significant as they are, are perhaps more fully appreciated by looking first to the visionary poets' shared interest in creating a duality of letter and spirit, narrative and meditative form through which to lead readers on their quest for salvation. Dante, Langland, the *Pearl* poet, building on the work of poets like Raoul de Houdenc, Huon de Méri, Rutebeuf and Deguileville, as well as Guillaume de Lorris and the secular *romanciers*, demand a subtle reading from their ideal audience. Although they permit readers with limited spiritual sight and hearing their portion of entertainment in the plight of a lively, engrossing narrator, they will not have those with light barks test the deep waters. But for those willing to exert memory and imagination and test spiritual acuity, the best poets of the form devised a systematically ordered series of discoveries intended to effect conversion and to suggest as far as art is able a visionary perception of the world and of divine love.

In the next chapters, I have chosen to look closely at two late masterpieces in the form of the visionary quest. In one way or another each refuses to fit tidily into the mold I have just described. It is true, as Peter Dronke has recently reminded us, that "form at its best is something intrinsic, it is controlled and guided by the poet's own conception of his intentions, not by a set of extrinsic rules."[37] But it can only be helpful, in coming to terms with any masterpiece, to know, at least in part, what rules had already been established by the practice of recognized poets—what narrative inventions had already been made and were available for adoption and adaptation. For although *Pearl* and *Piers Plowman* must each be recognized as unique moments in literary history, our understanding and enjoyment of them can be enriched if we set them within the framework of important formal similarities.

[37] Peter Dronke, *Poetic Individuality in the Middle Ages* (Oxford, 1970), p. 64.

FIVE

PEARL: A FOURTEENTH CENTURY VISION IN AUGUST

Perhaps half a century separates Dante's final paradisal vision from the writing of the Middle English *Pearl*. During that time, the Thomistic twining of reason and faith, sense and spirit which had so fully supported Dante in his search for God no longer obtained. Both on the Continent and in England, theologians and philosophers began to posit the unknowability of God and to prefer the study of human will; or they reverted to an older Augustinian and monastic awe for an omnipotent deity. William of Ockham and his followers defended the power of free will to *merit* heaven, while neo-Augustinians like Gregory of Rimini and Thomas Bradwardine argued that God could only be known and gained through faith and grace.[1] The "O Altitudo" of Bishop Bradwardine's teaching in particular celebrated the unimaginable wonder, goodness, mercy and justice of God at the expense of sinning, graceless man.[2]

Pearl, probably written between 1360 and 1390, may seem at first to reflect this fourteenth-century change of emphasis and to support Bradwardinian conservatism.[3] Only fifty years or so before, Dante had dared to use

---

[1] For discussion of these changes and of the controversy over grace and free will which occupied fourteenth-century English theologians, see Paul Vignaux, *Justification et prédestination au XIVe siecle* (Paris, 1934); Gordon Leff, *Bradwardine and the Pelagians* (Cambridge, 1957); Heiko Oberman, *Archbishop Thomas Bradwardine* (Utrecht, 1957); and J. A. Robson, *Wyclif and the Oxford Schools* (Cambridge, 1961).

[2] Bradwardine's long treatise *De causa Dei*, ed. Henry Savile (London, 1618) reflects the author's deeply felt personal involvement in his theological argument. Closely reasoned defense of God's grace frequently concludes in an impassioned prayer of praise for his goodness.

[3] A connection between the *Pearl* poet's theology and that of Bishop Bradwardine was first suggested by Carleton Brown in 1904 ("The Author of the *Pearl* Considered in the Light of his Theological Opinions," *PMLA* xix [1904], pp. 115–153).

the traditional form of the visionary quest to carry his pilgrim to spiritual heights hitherto undreamed by poets. His *Commedia*, the "poema sacra" to which heaven and earth had set their hand (*Para.* xxv, 1–2), leads its narrator to sing of Beatrice as he had promised in the *Vita Nuova*, and to "see" substantial love in the empyrean. Through Beatrice the pilgrim is "transhumanized" so that he can gaze finally on the source of his being. Like Richard of St. Victor's spiritual treatises, *Benjamin Minor* and *Benjamin Major*, the final canticle of the *Commedia* is a guidebook to the highest forms of contemplation. In the last cantos of *Paradiso*, Dante joins Richard, St. Francis, St. Bonaventure and a handful of later medieval writers who could convince their readers, if only momentarily, that mortal man might rest, while still alive, in pure beauty and perfect peace. The *Pearl* poet, on the other hand, allows his dreaming narrator only a conventional "sight" of the New Jerusalem, paraphrasing St. John. After building toward an ecstatic climax, the poet disappoints expectations and leaves his readers with a grudgingly resigned pilgrim still awaiting his own beatitude.

Yet a host of critics have suggested that the poem taken as a whole transcends the narrator's limited discoveries. The larger poetic form seems to reach toward a spiritual "seeing" of the heavenly kingdom not unlike Dante's at the end of *Paradiso*. A secret "cnawyng," veiled and hidden, implied rather than demonstrated in the literal story, appears to be the poem's central organizing principle. But the existence of differing interpretations particularly during this century indicates that the reader of *Pearl* may share or surpass the dreamer's favored experience in a variety of ways.[4] The form of the poem is riddling, figural and parabolic. Meaning

---

Brown suggested that the *Pearl* poet not only followed but also went beyond both Bradwardine and orthodoxy in his teaching. His suggestions touched off a mild scholarly controversy.

[4] The problem of *Pearl*'s meaning has been explored from several perspectives and with a wide range of solutions. Many of the interpretations overlap but few agree on major interpretive questions. The poem's first recorded reader, James, the Bodley librarian, provided what remains in its way a definitive description. *Pearl*, he wrote in his catalogue, is a "vetus poema Anglicanum, in quo sub insomnii figmento multa ad religionem et mores spectantia explicantur." Since then, scholars have sought to examine (or sometimes reject) those larger religious and moral purposes to which James alluded. Early editors emphasized the elegiac and apparently autobiographical elements of the poem: Morris (1864); Gollancz (1891 and 1921); Osgood (1906). W. H. Schofield (1904 and 1909) first insisted that the whole poem must be read *spiritualiter*. His spirited arguments paved the way for a variety of allegorical interpretations: R. M. Garrett (1918); J. B. Fletcher (1921); W. K. Greene (1925); Sr.

does not come immediately or easily as it would if the poet had elected to teach directly. Only in the very last stanza does he speak in his own authoritative voice, and then only fully to those who have paid the closest attention.

In this chapter I want to follow the questor's story as one dimension of a larger form or poetic purpose which lies behind and beyond it. Attention to the poet's manipulation of the traditional quest form, his meticulous arrangements of symbolic images, scriptural parables and eschatological figures, and his numerical composition, may, if we take heed, lead us to pass gradually through history. Then we may be in a better position to understand how fully the *Pearl* master has used and developed the double form proper to the later medieval visionary quest.

THE PROLOGUE: I (STANZAS 1–5)

Pearl apparently begins as a tender, anguished love elegy as the bereft jeweler remembers how his "privy pearl" slipped away from him into the grass. The narrator's grief, a pearl, and a "spot" occupy the foreground of the proem (st. 1–5). In the speaker's hyperbolic rhetoric, his lost love is no mere human but an inimitable round pearl. As a perfect sphere, she had been an image of pure joy and total being for him. In her he had once found "al [his] hele." But now she is simply and absolutely gone.[5]

M. Madeleva (1925); and more recently M. P. Hamilton (1955) and Sr. M. V. Hillman (1961). Several modern and contemporary readers, following Osgood's early suggestion that the poem is "almost allegorical," have argued for the importance of the story without denying its larger meanings: E. V. Gordon (1953); S. de V. Hoffman (1960); A. C. Spearing (1962 and 1970); A. R. Heiserman (1965); P. M. Kean (1967); and Ian Bishop (1968). Study of this critical history provides, at least, a fascinating testimonial to *Pearl*'s rich ambiguities.

[5] Such transformations of ladies into gems was a commonplace in medieval love poetry. One Latin lyric, for example, uses just the conceit employed by the narrator of *Pearl*:

> I have seen many pearls, precious, exquisite, and of diverse kinds; but there is one Pearl who exceeds the rest as the moon outshines the stars; this precious Pearl has value of herself, not polished by a craftsman's hand. Whoever touches her glows with love, and, as men say, she has great worth because of her virtue. May our bishop protect her—for she can assuage the fever in men's blood. She is not taken from a treasure hoard, nor has he, who is Limoge's golden light, set her in gold. This Pearl is no stone, but a living creature. . . . (Peter Dronke, *Medieval Latin and the Rise of European Love Lyric* [Oxford, 1968], pp. 384–386.)

As his "wreched" will wars with reason over the profound loss, he falls into a swooning sleep on the "huyle" where the pearl had "trendeled doun."

In these opening stanzas, the narrator (who is also the protagonist) responds in five quite different ways to his tragedy. As a judge of jewels and a lover of pearls, he despairs (st. 1). Then, in the midst of his mourning (st. 2), songs waft through the air to him. Roused to anger, he condemns the earth for marring his pearl. He is indignant at the aesthetic impropriety of foul earth as a setting for his beautiful jewel. Next, full of hope, he imagines his pearl's rebirth (st. 3): earth assumes a creative new role, for through it the pearl will give birth to spices. When he returns to the same garden in August (st. 4), the jeweler praises the place. It has become a worthy setting for his pearl because of its flowering herbs and perfumes. Finally, overcome by sweet odors in stanza 5, he swoons and falls where the pearl was buried in earth.

As he records his responses to the changing scene the narrator reveals a good deal about himself. He is preeminently a lover of artful beauty, of himself, and of another creature. He thinks he has understood the fullness of joy in union. And he suffers heavily under its loss. He is also a jeweler. His love has grown out of a capacity to appreciate what pleases his senses, as well as his sense of form. This death, like all deaths, is aesthetically unfathomable. Beauty has been destroyed. That ordered radiance which had given him the impression of eternal being is now lost in the grass. But by the same token, though the pearl is gone, the jeweler can still recognize beauty. His spirit is eased by the mysterious presence of aesthetic delights other than the lost pearl: songs, nature's rebirth, a hill decorated with colorful herbs, a sweet perfume suffusing the grave site. The mourner is caught up in the most profound turmoil. But his instinctive appreciation for beauty and wholeness indicates that he has potential for new discoveries. He may be capable, then, of finding that perfect love, beauty and joy which transcends all earthly sorrow, including death, and is to be found, as Dante had shown, in the eternal peace of God's kingdom.

Initially the poet encourages the reader to see the loss in just the terms the narrator has chosen. The pearl is a source of total security, a perfect refuge figuring forth the universal human dream of complete joy and wellbeing. By contrast, the "erbere" is all that evil destructive matter which has marred his jewel. It is the cause of change and has deprived the narrator of "al [his] hele." No one will fail to appreciate the ancient philosophical distinction between pure spiritual good and material destructive evil which emerges in the jeweler's rendition of his catastrophe. Nor will anyone question his values in preferring union with his pearl to the suffering of his loss, *caused* by earth.

The Jeweler Judged

But now let the reader distance himself from the immediacy of the narrator's grief to follow more scrupulously the details of the "speche." In the light of a more reflective reading, he will discover that the "I," not the "pearl," is the real subject of the jeweler's grief. Full of self-importance and self-pity (like the lover of the early chapters of the *Vita Nuova*), he looks chiefly *at himself* as he moves from scene to scene. The first stanza focuses on his own ability to judge:

> Oute of oryent, I hardyly saye,
> Ne proued I neuer her precios pere. (3–4)
>
> . . . .
>
> Quere-so-euer I jugged gemmeʒ gaye,
> I sette hyr sengeley in synglere. (7–8)

Though his ostensible purpose is a eulogy for the lost pearl, the narrator turns it into a complaint of injustice and an expression of his own misery:

> I dewyne, fordolked of luf-daungere (12)
>
> . . . .
>
> Ofte haf I wayted, wyschande þat wele,
> Þat wont watʒ whyle deuoyde my wrange
> And heuen my happe and al my hele,
> Þat dotʒ bot þrych my hert þrange,
> My breste in bale bot bolne and bele; (14–18)
>
> . . . .
>
> Bifore þat spot my honde I spenned
> For care ful colde þat to me caʒt;
> A deuely dele in my hert denned,
> Þaʒ resoun sette myseluen saʒt.
> I playned my perle þat þer watʒ spenned
> Wyth fyrce skylleʒ þat faste faʒt; (49–54)
>
> . . . .
>
> My wreched wylle in wo ay wraʒte. (56)

Syntax works to intensify our impression of the jeweler's self-absorption. Concentrating attention on his loss, he allows the pearl, as well as the garden setting, to slip into prepositional phrases and subordinate clauses. The jeweler assumes the role of judge, creating the value of the gem for his audience. This situation will be reversed only at the end of the journey when God becomes mediator and judge: "syþen to God I hit [the Pearl] bytaȝte" (1207).

The third stanza of the prologue alone escapes the narrator's domination. In place of the "I" we find an impersonal meditation on the familiar scriptural figure of new fruit springing from dead grain:

> For vche gresse mot grow of grayneȝ dede;
> No whete were elleȝ to woneȝ wonne. (31–32)

The poet allows his jeweler to utter truth in this stanza but does not provide him with understanding. Then we are returned abruptly to the dominant, grieving "I" (st. 4). The narrator makes only the most tenuous effort to discern connections between the emblematic imagery of stanza 3 and the miraculous flowering herbs he now finds blossoming on the garden's "huyle." His grief seems to have been eased in the beauty of the pearl's dwelling place. But relief results from an impulsive and fleeting response to setting.

In the last stanza of the prologue (5), the grieving jeweler still occupies center stage, acknowledging his willfulness but unable to correct it. At the end of his impassioned outburst in the fifth stanza, he tells us that his reason has failed to gain mastery over his grief; he refuses the comfort of Christ. His will is wholly concentrated in his sorrow.

In the midst of this consuming passion, the pearl, the green "erbere," the flowering herbs, the August wheat, the songs and perfumes—all the details of the garden scenes of the prologue—are distanced from the reader's vision by the very presence of the speaker and his profound feeling. The effect is an illusion of concrete detail and clear history which is belied by our incapacity to determine exactly when, why and where the accident occurred or, in fact, exactly who or what has been lost. Yet it is precisely through this riddling vagueness that the poet can draw his reader's attention to the wider meaning in the jeweler's story and eventually clarify its significance for Everyman's salvation.

To the astute reader who examines the narrator's *conte* scrupulously, his self-absorption in telling his story should reveal the familiar figure of the spiritually naive vision questor dressed in a new costume. In a most subtle manner, the *Pearl* poet has adapted the character of the narrator of the *Roman de la Rose*, the *Vita Nuova*, and the *Commedia*, in order to look closely at his besetting flaw: love of self and pride of life. "O superbi cristian," the repentant Dante had cried, defining the nature of his own sin,

> miseri lassi,
> che, de la vista de la mente infermi,
> fidanza avete ne' retrosi passi;
> non v'accorgete voi che noi siam vermi
> nati a formar l'angelica farfalla,
> che vola a la giustizia sanza schermi?
> Di che l'animo vostro in alto galla,
> poi siete quasi entomata in difetto,
> sì come vermo in cui formazion falla? (*Purg.* x, 121–129)

> (Oh proud Christians, miserable wretches
> who, infirm in the visions of the mind,
> have faith in backward steps.
> Do you not see that we are worms
> born to form the angelic butterfly
> that flies up to Justice without defense?
> Say how your spirit aspires so high:
> When you are as defective insects,
> like a worm in whom form is imperfect.)

Pride's particular effect is, of course, blindness to man's true nature and destiny, the sin also figured and studied in the lover of the *Roman de la Rose*. There the action of self-love is encapsulated in the narrator's vision of Narcissus' well. As Professor Fleming has noted, the narrator's action involves a "projection of self-love upon an external object (the rose), one of the *choses* in the garden."[6] Like *Amant*, the jeweler of *Pearl* enjoys seeing himself in states of profound feeling. For him the five little scenes of the prologue are like a mirror in which he can watch himself mourning. Unable to see Christ or heaven in the glass as an exemplary pilgrim would, he looks finally at his own hands, clenched in anguish, and then he falls asleep.

Such a harsh reading of the narrator's speech may seem at first crass or indelicate. Yet it is fully justified by the subsequent narrative and its lessons. From a purely human point of view, the narrator earns all our sympathy. But from a divine perspective he outrageously commits "the synne of pride, fro the wyche the goode speryte shulde kepe hym." In his con-

---

[6] John Fleming, *The Allegory of the Roman de la Rose* (Princeton, 1970), p. 95.

demnation of justice, death and fortune, he well deserves Origen's query to the proud:

> Whereof it is that erth and asshes prydeth hyme, or how derre a man rayse hym in arogance, when he thynketh whereof he is comyn and what he sall become, and in how frele a vessel his lyff is all naked and in what harlotrees he is plonged en . . . .[7]

In terms of God's judgment, then, the poor jeweler is no more or less than a *figura* of self-love. As such, he, like his confrères on other visionary pilgrimages, requires purgation through self-examination, contrition, confession and a willingness to amend his life.

"In on erbere": the letter transformed

Once the narrator has been identified as prideful Everyman, the details of the garden scenes and the image of the pearl begin to yield the poet's symbolic purpose. And this is particularly true if the reader imagines them as a series of figural illuminations. Just as later medieval painters and sculptors shaped their symbols by framing them in stories, the *Pearl* poet has provided his major symbolic images in the prologue with their own significant history, touching on and glossing the narrator's. By attending to the historical progress of these first garden-and-pearl images, the reader will begin to understand their spiritual import and prepare to appreciate their intricate congruence with the stages of the visionary quest and spiritual instruction to follow. With admirable reticence, the English master, like Dante, avoids an explicitly allegorical prologue. Instead, he meticulously places and develops his symbolic scenes in the first five stanzas, arranging them like a series of miniatures to adumbrate the form and direction of the subsequent composition.

"History," wrote St. Bernard,

> is a garden and it is threefold. For it includes three periods: first the Creation of both heaven and earth; then the Reconciliation; lastly, the Restoration. The Creation is the sowing and planting of the garden; the Reconciliation is its burgeoning when the heavens dropped down from above in dew and the clouds rained down the Righteous One, and so the earth opened and brought forth the Saviour, by Whom the Reconciliation of heaven and earth was brought about. And the Res-

---

[7] Christine de Pisan, *The Epistle of Othea to Hector or the Boke of Knyghthode,* trans. Scrope, ed. G. F. Warner (London, 1904), p. 28.

toration is still to come, at the end of the age; for then there will be a new heaven and a new earth, and the good shall be gathered from among the wicked, as fruits from a garden, to be laid up safely in the barns of God.[8]

The *Pearl* poet's "erbere" has a history very like the cosmic, changing garden here described. While the scenes of the prologue may seem at first quite particular, a closer look suggests those mysteries and ambiguities often associated with myths and fairytales. The *certain* (*on*) "erbere" (st. 1), the "huyle," (st. 4) (which Luttrell has argued would have been a familiar feature of a real medieval garden),[9] and the specific time of year, "Auguste in a hyȝ seysoun" with its homely adverbial qualifier, "quen corne is coruen wyth crokeȝ kene" (st. 4) may give the illusion that a singular situation is being evoked. But closer scrutiny reveals that the garden is not entirely English or earthly in character. The mysterious songs (st. 2), the emblematic picture of dead grain springing to new life (st. 3), the flowering herbs on the "huyle" (st. 4), and the perfume which seems to initiate the dream, all carry the events into a realm beyond the ordinary. From the narrator's point of view the garden seems to be real and concrete enough. But for the audience, its mystery assumes paramount interest. If they have anticipated a symbolic or allegorical prologue as the proper beginning for a visionary quest, readers will be prepared to translate the mysterious overtones into spiritual meaning.

If the narrator of the prologue is understood as a *figura* of self-love, then the garden of stanza 1 in which the jeweler loses his pearl ("[his] happe and al [his] hele") can only suggest an Englished Eden, the place of Adam's and Everyman's primal joy and primal sin of pride.[10] There man learned to know and desire perfect beauty, and there he fell by assuming he could be judge and master of that perfection, not its servant. For Adam, for Everyman, for the jeweler and the reader, the result of such presumption is deprivation and anguish. The jeweler's character as well as his notions of the pearl, revealed in stanza 1, both complicate and reinforce this interpretation of the garden image. Describing his pearl, the

---

[8] *Sermones in Cantica Canticorum* XXIII, trans. by a religious of C.S.M.V., *On the Song of Songs* (London, 1952), p. 63.

[9] C. A. Luttrell, "*Pearl*: Symbolism in a Garden Setting," *Neophilologus* (April, 1965), pp. 160–176.

[10] For an illuminating discussion of the garden imagery of the proem in relation to medieval notions of the Garden of Eden, see P. M. Kean, *The Pearl: An Interpretation* (New York, 1967), pp. 31–35.

bereft narrator alludes explicitly though briefly to the parable of the pearl
of great price: his pearl is set "sengeley in synglere" and is "wythouten
spot."[11] Yet he has lost the pearl to which he ought to have clung were it
the pearl of price (the kingdom of heaven). Furthermore, the narrator is
a jeweler, not the merchant of the biblical parable.

By reversing and altering the familiar scriptural story, the poet teases
the reader's imagination into greater activity. The narrator is not a merchant who sets out to buy, own and sell pearls, but a jeweler who has cus-
tody of jewels. He should therefore be expected to follow the instructions
of his patron-prince. He would set the special pearl and then return it to
its owner. But instead this jeweler loses the gem in a garden. The parallels between the narrator's loss of his precious pearl in the garden and
Adam's loss of heaven and happiness in the Garden of Eden are quite
exact. In both cases, the precious possession is held in trust; in both cases,
carelessness causes the loss. The loss results in misery, a darkening of the
intellect and a weakening of the will as well as a knowledge of death.
And, of course, both of the losses take place in a garden.

In stanza 2, the garden has undergone a transformation. No longer a
place of bliss, it has become mere "clot" and "moul." With this verbal
metamorphosis of the "erbere" the poet defines a second stage in the garden's history. Here the jeweler faces death and decay unadulterated and
unrelieved, the terrible lot of fallen man. Desolate, emotion driven, he is
Everyman in an unredeemed world, mourning in a garden with no color
and no detail but a grave mound. Yet mysteriously, as he grieves, songs
float to him through the air. As they interrupt and contradict the pathetic
movement of the stanza, the songs are a puzzle both for the narrator and
the reader. Are they the delusive songs of the poetic muses who soothed
Boethius in his sorrow? Or a prefiguration of the birds of the earthly
paradise, or the harpists of the New Jerusalem?

But within the cosmic temporal order outlined in the prologue, the
meaning of the songs can be clarified. If the reader is attending to the
history of the garden, the mysterious music conveys that same sense of
harmony which encouraged fallen mankind to await a savior through
the darkness of the Old Testament. Though he cannot understand the
songs fully, the narrator, like the Old Testament prophets, listens and is
comforted. Rhabanus Maurus sees just such purpose in the Old Testament
song of Anna: "'My heart rejoices in the Lord,' said Anna, which signifies

[11] J. B. Fletcher rightly stressed the importance of this parable for interpreting
Pearl in his article, "The Allegory of the *Pearl*," *JEGP*, xx (1921), p. 2.

grace, or the Church of Christ, the city of the great King."[12] Likewise the song of Moses is "very full of presages of the future and the mysteries of Christ."[13] One commentary on Ezekiel's song suggests the function of healing. "This song well suits him who after a long sickness of the spirit returns to reason from the snares of the devil and is healed of the weight of sins, and studies to restore himself in sacred virtues and to speak the praise of God not only with his voice but also with his heart and his acts."[14] But such songs as these are fleeting. The narrator interprets the singular phenomenon as only one of many sad songs which have occurred to him as he has pondered the disgrace of a soul marred by "moul." He continues to mourn his shining white pearl beneath the earth: the last two lines of stanza 2 withhold any promise of hope.

By contrast, the garden "spot" of the third stanza is not strictly speaking an actual scene, but a mirage superimposed on the darkened garden of stanza 2. It is governed not by the mournful "I" but the imperative "mot":

Þat spot of spyseȝ mot nedeȝ sprede,
Þer such rycheȝ to rot is runne;
Blomeȝ blayke and blwe and rede
Þer schyneȝ ful schyr agayn þe sunne.
Flor and fryte may not be fede
Þer hit doun drof in moldeȝ dunne;
For vch gresse mot grow of grayneȝ dede;
No whete were elleȝ to woneȝ wonne.
Of goud vche goude is ay bygonne;
So semly a sede moȝt fayly not,
Þat spryngande spyceȝ vp ne sponne
Of þat precios perle wythouten spotte. (25–36)

Here the jeweler imagines flowering herbs spreading over the grave. Pale yellow, blue and red flowers appear, brightly shining in the sun. The pearl

[12] *PL* cxii, 1098: " 'Exultavit cor meum in Domine,' dicat ergo Anna, quae interpretatur gratia, Ecclesia videlicet Christi, civitas regis magni."

[13] *PL* cviii, 967: "Carmen istud quod Moyses in testimonium Israel decantavit, non simplicem tantummodo historiam sonat, sed spiritali intelligentia plenissimum est. Partim enim secundum historiam, Israelitarum pro beneficiis opulentissime sibi a Domino collatis, exprobrat perfidiam. Partim per allegoriam, de mysteriis coelestibus sanctam instruit Ecclesiam."

[14] *PL* cxii, 1094: "Potest enim hoc canticum bene convenire his qui post longam aegritudinem animarum resipiscunt a diaboli laqueis, et de peccatorum gravitudine sanantur, et student se virtutibus sacris recuperare, et laudes Dei non solum voce, sed etiam corde et actu pronuntiare."

has become a seed and produces plants burgeoning through the very "rot" that had marred its beauty in stanza 2. This garden of the narrator's dreams is extraordinary indeed, a miracle of transformation. Human death participates in and finds new life through the creative action of nature. It is fitting that the grieving narrator who looks only to his misery does not find himself in this imagined scene but remains outside it at his desolate gravesite, bound to his bereft state.

Instead, in his place, at the very center of the stanza, is St. John's figure of a grain of wheat falling into the earth. Familiar as they were with the systematic scriptural interpretations provided for them by the Fathers and sermon writers, medieval readers would have recognized the emblem of dead grain as a symbol of Christ's death. Rhabanus Maurus, for instance, gives the simplest and most common explanation for the scriptural verses, identifying the grain with Christ: " 'Unless a grain of wheat die,' as Christ when he fell by the death of the flesh into the earth, he filled all the world with a great harvest."[15] Hugh of St. Victor develops the significance of the harvest more fully, using it to show the relationship between Christ's death, resurrection, salvation and Last Judgment. After embellishing Rhabanus' simple analogy between Christ and the wheat, he goes on to show how the same image also figures in the vision of the Apocalypse and the procession of the hundred and forty-four thousand blessed.[16]

[15] *PL* cxii, 938: *"Frumentum, Christus, ut in Evangelio:* 'Nisi granum frumenti mortuum fuerit,' quod Christus, dum morte carnis in terram cecidit, totum mundum multiplici messe replevit."

[16] *PL* clxxv, 760–761: *"Nisi granum frumenti cadens in terram, mortuum feurit: ipsum solum manet (Joan.* xii). Omnibus est manifestum de grano frumenti, quod dum in terram cadit nisi moriatur, id est humore terrae humectetur et tale quale prius fuit esse desinat, et per alterationem vegetationis aliud fiat, solum manet et fructum nullum affert. *Si autem fuerit mortuum,* id est pinguedine et humiditate terrae putrefactum, statim herbam germinat, stipulam roborat, spicas, aristas, paleas, grana format et multum fructum affert; quia, sicut in alia parabola dicitur, sive trigesimum, sive sexagesimum, sive centesimum (*Matth.* xiii), sic Christus in terram cadens per humanitatem, fert fructum multum moriens per passionem. Nihil namque nobis nasci contulisset, nisi moriendo nos redimere potuisset. De hoc fructu, et profectu per Psalmistam ait: *Singulariter sum ego donec transeam* (Psal. cxl). Singulariter enim fuit, donec transiit; quia, donec mortem gustavit, fructum humanae redemptionis non perfecit. Sed moriendo fructum ex se multiplicavit, quia omnes ad vitam aeternam praedestinatos redemit. Per hunc denique fructum, designantur patriarchæ, prophetæ, evangelistæ, apostoli, martyres, confessores, virgines et omnes electæ animæ, quotquot fuerunt ab initio justificandae per gratiam redemptionis, et quotquot erunt in fine beatificandae per gloriam remunerationis. Sanctus quoque Joannes evangelista hunc fructum exprimit, ubi ait: *Audivi numerum signatorum centum quadraginta quatuor millia signati ex omni tribu filorum* Israel

The *Pearl* poet relies on his readers not only to recognize this traditional explication but to contemplate it through his emblem. At the center of the prologue, in the middle of stanza 3, he has his narrator unwittingly announce the solution to his soul's dilemma. The image of the grain of wheat expresses, though only by suggestion, the timeless moment of Christ's coming and death, reaching before and after in history from the Creation of Man to the Apocalypse, made possible by the falling into the earth (human flesh and the tomb) of the Son of God.

In the fourth stanza, the poet allows his narrator to discover yet a further change in the garden but still without grasping its meaning. Here, by noticing the *appearance* of the place, the jeweler unknowingly figures forth its actual transformation through Christ's (and the pearl's) death and resurrection into the apocalyptic "erbere" of the New Jerusalem. Entering the garden in August in a "hyȝ seysoun," the jeweler mentions that it is the harvest time and then he observes flowering herbs on his pearl's "huyle."[17] But even as he delights in the fragrance of the herbs, he ignores

---

(*Apoc.* vii). Et deinceps: *Post haec vidi turbam magnam, quam dinumerare nemo poterat, ex omnibus tribubus, et populis, et linquis, stantes ante thronum.* Per centum namque quadraginta quatuor millia signatorum ex omni tribu filiorum Israel, designavit eos quos divina Providentia ad vitam praedestinatos ante adventum Redemptoris, per praecedentia sacramenta redemptionis ad salutem praeparavit. Per turbam autem magnam, quam dinumerare nemo poterat, quam vidit ex omnibus tribubus et linguis, et populis, illos insinuavit quos post adventum Redemptoris gratia superna justificat et salvat: de qua turba recte dicitur, quam dinumerare nemo poterat, quia pauci erant qui ante adventum Christi justificabantur ad comparationem eorum, qui post adventum ejus justificantur. Ante adventum etenim ejus notus tantum in Judaea Deus. Modo vero omnes gentes plaudunt manibus, jubilant *Deo in voce exsultationis* (*Psal.* lxxv). *O quam mirabile!* (*Psal.* xlv). Istud est granum, quod facit fructum trigesimum in conjugatis; sexagesimum in continentibus; centesimum in virginibus."

[17] "Huyle" has usually been taken as an alternative spelling for "hylle" in *Pearl*, translating the scriptural Latin "mons" and "collis." But Gordon argues that the form, "huyle" (and "hyul," l. 1205) may represent a different word found in modern southeast Lancashire dialect as "hile," meaning "a thick cluster of plants" and also a "mound." Yet another meaning for "huyle" is suggested by reference to two dialect words recorded by Wright in his *English Dialect Dictionary* (1902). *Huylle*, a dialect word of the Shetland and Orkney Islands, is defined by Wright as "a word applied to anything which does not justify appearances." *Hyul*, the second spelling in the *Pearl* manuscript is recorded by Wright as a verb and substantive used in the North and West Midland counties meaning (as a verb) "to conceal, cover, wrap up" and (as a substantive) "an outer covering," "a covered outbuilding," "clothes," "the body." Both *huylle* and *hyul* are related to the verb *hülen*

their relationship to the resurrection of his pearl. With his usual impulsive response to aesthetically pleasing sense impressions, he forgets his grief, and, echoing the "woneȝ" (barns) of stanza 3, he declares:

Þer wonyȝ þat worþly, I wot and wene,
My precious perle wythouten spot. (47–48)

But the audience, following the metaphoric verbal developments of the pearl and of the garden, may realize that both have undergone a miraculous change: like the scriptural grain of wheat, the pearl has died and reappeared as a new spice in a garden totally renewed and ready for harvest.

At the beginning of stanza 4, the jeweler specifies the time of his return to the garden (August and a "hyȝ seysoun"). Medieval readers would recognize that it is (according to patristic exegesis) the very season which Christ had named for the Last Judgment and the final joy of the blessed.

---

meaning "to cover up, to cover from sight, to hide" recorded in the OED as a ME. form derived from the Norse. Stratmann (*A Middle English Dictionary*, 1951) gives a fuller etymological history for the verb: hülen, v., *Goth.* huljan, *OLG* (bi-) hullean, *OHG* hullen, *ON* hylja, meaning "to cover, conceal." Related to the same verb is the common substantive *hull* (ME. *hoole, hole, heul*), the reflex of OE. *hulu,* cognate with OHG *hulla,* Ger. *hulle* meaning "covering" or "cloak." The word was frequently used in ME. to signify the outer covering of a piece of grain. For example, Trevisa writes in *Barth.* De P. R. xvii (1398): "Some greyne and sede . . . is ingendred in coddes and holes as it fareþ in benes."

According to the evidence of Wright, OED and Stratmann, the two spellings *huyle, hyul* describing the *Pearl*'s resting place may be understood to represent a single word meaning "an outer covering or dwelling place" with connotations of "concealment" and "false appearances." The peripheral connotation "a shell for a grain of wheat" may also be applied to the word. The relationship of all these meanings to the general context in which the word appears in the *Pearl* is striking. In stanza 3 the jeweler speaks of *woneȝ* meaning "storage barns for harvested grain." In describing the huyle where the pearl was lost in stanza 4, he echoes *woneȝ*: "þer woneȝ þat worþyly, I wot and wene." By the narrator's explicit definition the *huyle* is a dwelling place, therefore, perhaps a periphrastic description for a grave mound. It is closely related to the image of dead grain in stanza 3 and the grain fully ripe of stanza 4. The pearl, as a spice covered by *moul* has, like the grain dying in the earth, produced the spice plants (the spiritual harvest) scattered on the *huyle*. The *huyle hyul* is also an outer covering hiding more than is evident from its appearances. If the connotation "false appearances" is contained in the word, the audience is provided with a direct statement about the jeweler's blindness in interpreting the events before his eyes long before the Pearl Maiden tells him that he has misunderstood his story.

There are also two great feasts to which this final garden scene may be related: the Transfiguration, celebrating the glorification of man through Christ; and the Assumption, recognizing Mary's introduction to the first and highest place among the blessed. Though not usually listed in calendars, a third feast, Lammas, the celebration of the harvest at which the first fruits were offered for the making of hosts, has been suggested by at least one scholar as the "hyȝ seysoun."[18] For the pearl and her death into a new life, all three feasts are significant: her story includes an assumption and a transfiguration and it follows the pattern of Christ's death and resurrection.

In this liturgical environment, at the harvest time, the garden's history enters a new phase. Now full of color ("þat erber grene"), the grave site ("huyle") is covered with flowering herbs—peonies, gromwell, clove gilliflowers, and flowering ginger. In a miraculous realization of the jeweler's fantasy of stanza 3, herbs have sprung up over the grave. They so captivate the mourner's senses that he praises the site as a worthy dwelling place for his pearl.

For the close reader, this garden grave, growing out of the imagery of stanza 3, offers a rich, comic exercise in meditation. On these two stanzas the poet has lavished his exquisitely artful verbal skill, effecting extravagant pictorial transformations to articulate the joy of Christian resurrection. Modern audiences may never be able to appreciate fully the symbolic richness the poet intended in his choices of words and images either in these stanzas or in the poem as a whole. But even a limited understanding assures us that each is placed with extraordinary care in view of a meticulously planned spiritual scheme.

Precious, exotic, healing, sacramental like the pearl, the particular spices which have sprung up on the grave add a new dimension to the lost jewel.[19] No longer merely a stone, the narrator's imagination has made the pearl a "sede" and a source of spices. (Later on, in an incremental development of the imagery, the jeweler will speak of the heavenly Maiden Pearl as "þat special spece," 235.)

Though the narrator does not stop to reflect on the scene of stanza 4, or even to wonder at it, a reflective audience may share some of the poet's

---

[18] See William Knightley, "*Pearl*: the hyȝ seysoun," *MLN* LXXVI (1961), pp. 97–102.

[19] For discussion of the special healing properties of these herbs, see Milton R. Stern, "An Approach to *Pearl*," *JEGP* LIV (1955), pp. 684–692 and P. M. Kean, *The Pearl: An Interpretation*, pp. 75 and 75n.

delight in discovering the sensible and verbal propriety of the herbs he
selected to represent the pearl's miraculous transformation. Of the four
herbs mentioned, the gromwell is most obviously expressive of the pearl's
miraculous resurrection, and its appropriateness has been remarked by
more than one reader. Blooming in England from June until August, and
yielding its seed in August,[20] the gromylyoun "haȝt lewys þat ben ewene
long and a lytyl qwyt flour and a long stalke and it haȝt qwyt seed lyk
a perle ston."[21] Its two Latin names, "lithospermum" (stone-seed) and
"granium," reiterate the poet's verbal alchemy in transforming the pearl
first into "grayneȝ" (st. 3), and then into "sedes." The "clere et resplan-
dissanz" seeds[22] on the gromwell bush of stanza 4 provide a visual evidence of the miraculous change effected by the fruitful earth of the
"erbere."

The ginger and clove gilliflowers which also decorate the grave may
at first appear less significant symbolically, and we might suppose that the
poet simply sought two "g" herbs to alliterate with the rime word "gromylyoun." But a closer look at the whole scene suggests the poet's more
central purpose. First of all, he required herbs of a pungent odor to provide the perfume inducing his narrator's sleep. Both the ginger, with its
"sharp savor,"[23] and the gilliflowers,[24] which "do smell almost like
cloves"[25] would serve that function well. Ginger and gilliflowers were
often linked together both in literature and in cookery, or used separately
as "god spicis" of sharp savor;[26] the gilliflower is further described as giving "odour of grace."[27] Not only for their perfume, but also in their appearance, the gilliflowers and ginger contribute to the poet's symbolic de-

[20] Rembert Dodoens, *A New Herball* (London, 1586), p. 330.

[21] *Agnus Castus. A Middle English Herbal Reconstructed from Various Manuscripts* in *Essays and Studies on English Language and Literature*, vol. VI (Upsala
and Cambridge, Mass., 1950), p. 160.

[22] *Le Livre des simple medecines.* An Old French translation of the *Liber de sim-
plici medecina dictus circa instans de Platearius,* MS. 3113, Bibliothèque Ste. Gene-
viève, Paris (13th century), ed. P. Dorveaux (Paris, 1913), p. 92.

[23] Bartholomaeus Anglicus, *De proprietatibus rerum,* Harvard University, Hough-
ton MS. Lat. 216, bk. XVII, fol. 250v, col. 2.

[24] Kean has quite rightly noted that the "gilofre" of *Pearl* is the clove gilliflower,
not the familiar pink (*The Pearl*, p. 18).

[25] Dodoens, p. 172.

[26] See *Middle English Dictionary*, ed. Kuhn *et al.* (Ann Arbor, 1956–) vol. IV:
1381 Pegge Cook. Recipes, p. 105, Wan yt is thykke, do thereto god spicis of gyn-
gener, galyngale, canal and clowys gilofre.

[27] *MED*: c. 1400 kalex 6786: "þe gylofre, quybibbe, and mace . . . ȝauen odour of
grace."

velopment of the garden. Gilliflowers are red and white, some speckled, fulfilling part of the narrator's hope for "blomeʒ blayke and blwe and rede" in stanza 3, and adumbrating the image of the Lamb at the end of the poem, white except for his red, gaping wound. The ginger, which has a white flower, also has a white root: "And the more whytter it be . . . the more sharper it is and the more better."[28] Perhaps the poet wanted to suggest the image of a white root buried in the earth, thus adding to the pregnant imagery of the gromwell seed, and reminding the reader of the pearl beneath the "huyle."

As for the peonies, scattered between the other herbs, they, like the gilliflowers, are also red and white, and are called *aglaeophotis* for their brilliance of color.[29] But they are also named *pentaboron* because of their five petals,[30] and it is this fact which may have dictated their inclusion in the garden. Of all the herbs in the "erbere," the peonies are the only ones which did not, in fact, bloom or produce their seed during August in England. Hence we must conclude either that the poet's knowledge as an herbalist failed or that he was particularly anxious to provide his garden with a magical herb of five petals. Because the number 5 figures so largely in the numerical structure of the whole poem, we may suppose that the poet intended to use the five-petaled peony, like the gromwell, as a symbol of the Pearl Maiden's rebirth. Perhaps she is to be the number 5 for this poet as Beatrice is the number 9 for Dante.

Even this brief analysis of the flowering herbs chosen by the poet to decorate the garden scene of stanza 4 illustrates how meticulously the poet attended both to the visual and the symbolic effectiveness of his imagery, insisting on the appearance of his images even as he controlled their spiritual import.

The narrator's reaction to this flowering herbal "erbere" of the fourth stanza is misguided not because he does not see and appreciate its concrete, particular presence, but because he fails to understand what it means. He wonders at the beauty of the place:

> ʒif hit watʒ semly on to sene,
> A fayr reflayr ʒet fro hit flot. (45–46)

[28] Bartholomaeus Anglicus, *De Proprietatibus rerum*, trans. John Trevisa (Westminster, 1485).

[29] *Gerard's Herball* (1597) condensed by Marcus Woodward (London, 1927): "And this *Aglaeophotis* of the earth or *Cynospastus* is *Paeonia*; for Apuleius saith, that the seeds or graines of Peionie shine in the nyhttime like a candle" (p. 235).

[30] Isidore of Seville, *Etymologiae*, bk. xvii, in *Pl* clxxxii, 629.

But he does not recognize the presence of grace in its order. On the other hand, for the reader, close meditative attention to the herbal imagery of this stanza, as well as to the imagery of the prologue as a whole, demonstrates beyond doubt that the poet's attention to words and images was neither casual nor unconscious. Indeed, his consummate care in the first five stanzas suggests one of the major themes of the poem, namely, the relationship between words and the Word, between the instability of earthly images and the providential salvation of all images and all creatures through divine mercy, between the forms of art and the form of eternity.

The poet's concern for literal detail and his deft manipulation of metaphor may lead readers to consider a complex analogy between the verbal construct and spiritual purpose. Even as he presents a narrator at odds with human mortality, the poet suggests the nature and purpose of his art as a gateway to a divine "cnawyng." Like Suger's gilded doors at St.-Denis, or the numerical symmetries of the *Vita Nuova* and the *Commedia*, this prologue (as well as the poem as a whole) in all its details may be seen as an attempt to approach the Eternal Artificer through human art. The poet's deliberate verbal ambiguities and richly fluid imagery lead neither to non-meaning nor to total relativity. Instead, these and all the words and images of *Pearl* are to be redeemed and participate through analogy in a realm of absolute being, a realm infinitely superior to all human expressions of it. The verbal poetic form—its *series imaginum*, its elegant word patterning and intricate numerical scheme—can be shown to symbolize the providential order of divinity. Within the poet's artful universe, the narrator's journey from beauty to Beauty may help to direct the reader's ascent through art to God.

But as the poor jeweler wrings his hands in stanza 5 of the prologue he is not aware of the merciful ambiguities in his tragedy. Yet he does recognize his failure to look to Christ; he confesses that his reason, which ought to have brought him peace, has been crippled by a wretched will caught up in woe. An apt parallel for the confused state of prideful man after the Fall, the jeweler's mental conflict will later be eased by the Pearl Maiden's instruction. When she has reformed his will, he will begin to perceive the significance of his history and its place in the scheme of salvation. Without returning to understand the full meaning of the garden of the prologue (as the reader can), he will grasp in a dim way his own participation in the history of mankind—fallen, redeemed and glorified in the New Jerusalem. As he will learn in detail from the maiden, the central fact on which his own story as well as the garden's history depends is precisely the death and resurrection of Christ, figured in the image of dead grain in stanza 3. He will also discover the meaning of human flesh, earth and death as part of the divine plan. But, as is often the case in visionary quests, the narrator does not return to meditate on the details of his journey, and he like his forebears in the quest form, learns just enough to confess his sin and reform his will. The audience, on the other hand, prompted by the poet's art to retrospective meditation, is granted that larger vision which can introduce them to a more complex and therefore more profound experience of the poem's spiritual universe.

Meaning and number

One final aspect of the prologue to which close readers may turn their attention is its numerical organization. No student of *Pearl*, or of the Middle Ages generally, can be unaware of the importance mathematics played in affirming and clarifying the divine order in the cosmos. As speculative arts studied after one had mastered grammar, logic and rhetoric, arithmetic and geometry offered rules of proportion and analogy by which one could discover God's mind in his creation. Finding numbers and figures within the apparent confusions of the sensory world, the spirit could ascend from the multiplicity and variousness of creation toward the purity and truth of divine reason. Such is the simple but profound principle elegantly articulated more than once by St. Augustine and known to every serious medieval student of the liberal arts, which underlies our poet's careful symmetries. He does not reveal the fullness of his elegant numerical scheme until the end. But he sets out the foundations in the prologue as a pleasing, restful counterpoint to the distressing narrative. As the story proceeds, the evolving numerical scheme can help us follow the constancy of the poem's main image—the pearl—through its series of transformations. We may also be better able to define those thematic or spiritual roles which allow for and control narrative movements away from and apparently contrary to the unity of the main symbol.

The "perle," perfectly round, singularly loved and singularly beautiful, provides, as we have seen, an image center for the narrator's grief. It emerges as a unique gem, not only the subject of line 1 (and the poem as a whole) but also of the refrain linking the first five stanzas to each other: "My pryuy perle wythouten spotte." In its singularity, the pearl image serves the function of the pythagorean or neoplatonic monad, a *oneness* from which all subsequent progression emanates. In addition, as the subject of the last lines in all five stanzas of group 1, the "perle" completes as it had begun the poem's first narrative sequence. Through this careful verbal linking, the prologue assumes a formal circularity paralleling the shape of the pearl image as a circle "endeleʒ rounde," and adumbrating the circular form of the poem as a whole. Thus, hovering over the intricate detail of the narrative, the poet imposes an abstract image of unity and perfection in which the human anguish of the jeweler and of Everyman may finally be put to rest.

Three integers besides one also figure forth wholeness or completion in the prologue: twelve, the number of lines in each stanzaic unit; five, the number of stanzas bound together by the linking refrain; and sixty, the total number of lines in the prologue (and in every stanza group but xv which has seventy-two). It would be premature to look for the full significance of these numbers so early in the poem. But simple calculation reveals certain relationships or ratios among these numbers of completion which would have teased the medieval reader by their symmetries. The two lowest parts of 5 —2 + 3— also produce, by multiplication, not only 12, the number of lines in each stanza, but also 60, the number of lines in each stanza group. Two + the perfect number, 10, produces 12, while 2 + 1, the monad, is 3.[31] Further, the sum and multiplication of 2 and 3 produce, respectively, 5 and 6, which multiplied by 12 and 10, respectively, yield 60. The numerical scheme of the prologue, then, is reducible in an abstract way to the primary integers 1, 2 and 3. So close a look at these simple factors may seem trifling at first glance. Yet the poet's careful numerical ordering of lines and imagery throughout his poem suggests that in the prologue he had more than a casual interest in their power and meaning.

As we have seen, stanza 1 deals not only with the pearl's wholeness,

[31] The importance of 10 and 12 in mystical arithmetic was a medieval commonplace. St. Bonaventure, for example, commenting on Apoc. 7:8, says matter-of-factly: "These seals, then are found in a two-fold perfection: a series of twelve, which is a number of abundance, and of a thousand, which derives from a multiplication of ten by itself in a perfect way" (*Collationes in Hexaemeron* XXII, 31, in *Opera Omnia* v, p. 408). For the numerical composition in *Pearl* and its significance, see C. O. Chapman, "Numerical Symbolism in Dante and the *Pearl*," *MLN* LI (1939), pp. 256–259; P. M. Kean, "Numerical Composition in Pearl," *Notes and Queries*, N.S. XII (1965), pp. 49–51; M. S. Røstvig, "Numerical Composition in *Pearl*," *English Studies*, XLVIII (1967), pp. 326–332; Ian Bishop, *Pearl in its Setting* (Oxford, 1968), pp. 27–31.

beauty and singularity, but also with the jeweler's separation from it (her). A duality results which will dominate the rest of the narrative and will be described later by the narrator as the moment when "we in *twynne* wern towen and *twayned*" (251). Not without purpose, then, separation and its grievous consequences becomes the burden of stanza 2: the earth, evil and destructive, has left the narrator joyless, deprived of all "[his] happe and al [his] hele."

How from such duality can unity be recreated? Stanza 3 suggests a solution in the figure of dead grain producing new fruit. Does 3, integrating oneness and separation, divinity and humanity, eternity and mortality in the poetic process, reiterate the theme of resurrection in an abstract form? Does the number 2, then, as duality, the earth, destructive matter, become a force for creativity when combined with 1, as also with the perfect number 10? Most assuredly 12, which governs the number of lines in each stanza as well as of the poem as a whole—1212—is intended to serve a symbolic function, signifying in some way visionary fulfillment, spiritual conversion, and the completion of an eschatological design.

The jeweler's loss, enigmatic and distressing at the start, is slowly resolved by the maiden's unity, wholeness and completeness. Through a series of transformations of "perle," which reflects the jeweler's changing vision of the central image, he will come finally to rest in his maiden's (and the pearl symbol's) constancy in an eternal realm. Though still separated from her (it), he realizes that his own completion lies in her perfection, the solution also rendered in the addition of 1 and 2 (Christ's divinity and incarnation) or 10 and 2 (the heavenly city.) Such analogies between the arithmetical configurations and the carefully arranged verbal imagery of the prologue may appear to some modern readers an irrelevant complication. But for others, these comic (and cosmic) parallels may enrich even as they help to explicate narrative developments.

Fortune's Fool in the Land of "Wele": ii–iv (stanzas 6–20)

Following the prologue and the jeweler's falling asleep, the visionary journey proper begins. Ten stanzas of description "place" the narrator and initiate him into the realm of the spirit. The jeweler tells his audience at once that his "spyryt þer sprang in space" (of time), that his "goste" has undertaken an adventure into a marvelous land.

At this point in his composition, having made it clear that his poem is to be a vision quest, the poet had a number of models for amplification at his disposal. The most familiar, simplest method would have been to provide the prideful jeweler with a guide to lead him through the Valley of Pride to the House of Humility, the Castle of Love, and then, by way of Confession and Contrition, to the New Jerusalem. After faltering under temptations to pride of life, he would have been severely chastised by his heavenly lady and then conveyed to the places of purification and spiritual transformation. But instead, before introducing the sinful narrator to his guide, the *Pearl* poet chooses to set him in the open country of the earthly paradise. There he discovers with joy that delightful land of soft winds, trembling leaves and sweet bird songs in which Dante discovers Beatrice toward the end of *Purgatorio*. The poet's choice was exactly appropriate to his needs and to his craft. It allowed him to decorate and develop the narrative directions and themes established in the prologue, and at the same time to celebrate God's eternal artistry in the mirror of his own poetic virtuosity.

While the *Pearl* master may well have known the earthly paradise of *Purgatorio* xxviii, his delightful country (which the narrator describes in stanzas 6–10) more nearly resembles the *Younger Titurel*'s Grail Temple or the jewellike interior of the Sainte Chapelle. Every detail expresses the artifice of the place, emphasizing its *un*natural and *un*earthly beauty. Light comes not from the sun or moon but from the landscape itself: the cliffs shine with a "glemande glory" which "no mon [myȝt] leuen;" the leaves of the trees sway "as bornyst syluer," the paths the jeweler walks are of shining pearls whose light exceeds the sun's. Even the birds flying through the air are of "flaumbande hweȝ" and the banks of the river meadow burn "as fyldor (gold thread) fyn." When the narrator comes finally to a stream, he discovers precious jewels shining in the stream bed, glowing through the water "as glente þurȝ glas þat glowed and glyȝt," or as "stremande sterneȝ" (stars). The participial present of these adjectives suggests an eternal state of luminiscence. The structure of all five descriptive stanzas is identical: they are built on similes which draw the paradisal scene into comparison with the highest beauties of human nature and human art. The conclusion toward which all the imagery builds is one to which the incredulous narrator himself assents: neither the finest tapestries nor polished silver nor music nor stained glass—nor nature itself—are worthy of comparison "in respecte of þat adubbement."

In this hyperbolic depiction of the earthly paradise the poet allows his visionary jeweler to develop a new order of imagery. Entirely different in character from the world of waking reality, this paradisal country re-

quires a radical adjustment of the imagination to be properly perceived
and interpreted. Caught up into a realm in which the external senses are
useless, reader and narrator alike must restructure their expectations in
order to "see" aright. But here, as in the symbolic prologue proper to such
quests, the poet's imagery, as well as the jeweler's obtuseness, allows a
double vision of the "place," to be perceived in one way by the audience,
in another by the sinful narrator. In this doubleness, the figure of the
earthly paradise serves the meditative development of the whole composition, advancing willynilly the jeweler's wandering journey toward the
New Jerusalem even as it reveals his sin of pride in a new light.

For the reflective reader, the elaborately artificial, gleaming country of
the paradisal land provides the first step in his imaginative ascent toward
visionary wholeness. Through the poet's artful images, the audience can
delight in a shining landscape for the inner senses which, like the material splendor of St.-Denis described by Suger, was to serve as a means of
transport "from this inferior to that higher world in an anagogical manner." The light, the precious jewels, the miraculous bird songs, the crystal
cliffs and silvered leaves belong to that class of anagogical metaphor
through which architects, stonemasons, sermon writers and poets alike
intended to "weave certain spiritual likenesses, and to bring the most pure
meanings of divine wisdom into the sight of the mind." By reflection on
the highest forms of material and human creation, the contemplating soul
might "perceive, at least by a mirror and in an enigma what it could not
at all as yet look upon face to face."[32]

Well aware of the power of imagery to sway and shape the affections
and convert the soul to a state of wonder, the poet lavished his persuasive
art on this first "place" in his reader's ascent to high vision. At this point
he did not choose the resplendent imagery of St. John's heavenly city for
the soul must be prepared by degrees for such a vision. But this country
is an adumbration of it, proportionally related to it as the earthly is related
to the heavenly Jerusalem. Just as the jeweler's affections are altered by
his perception of the paradisal woods, plains and rivers and turned to joy
and wonder—they "garten my goste al greffe forʒete"—so in a fuller, more
abstract and spiritual way could the reader's be:

> For it (contemplation) occurs in affective experience rather than in ra-
> tional consideration. On this level, when the inner senses are renewed

[32] St. Bernard, *Sermones in Cantica Canticorum*, PL xxxii, 745, quoted by Father
Louis Blenckner in an excellent essay, "The Theological Structure of 'Pearl,'" *Tra-
ditio* (1968), p. 68.

in order to perceive the highest beauty, to hear the highest harmony, smell the highest fragrance, taste the highest delicacy, apprehend the highest delights, the soul is disposed to mental elevation through devotion, wonder, and exultation. . . . When this is accomplished, our spirit is made hierarchical to mount upward through its conformity to the heavenly Jerusalem, into which no one enters unless through grace it has descended into his heart, as John saw in his Apocalypse.[33]

The artfully perfect scene in *Pearl* also serves a very precise thematic purpose. It is, as the narrator rightly guesses, the earthly paradise, and its spiritual function exactly parallels that of Dante's divine forest (*Purg.* xxviii) where,

Lo sommo ben, che solo esso a sé piace,
fece l'uom buono e a bene, e questo loco
diede per arra a lui d'etterna pace.

. . . .

Per sua difalta in pianto ed in affanno
cambiò onesto riso e dolce gioco. (91–93; 95–96)

(The Highest Good, who alone is pleasing to Himself,
Made man good and for good, and this place
Gave him as an assurance to him of eternal peace.

. . . .

Through his default, in sighing and weeping,
He exchanged upright laughter and sweet joy.)

The *Pearl* poet, drawing on just these connotations, places his own paradisal landscape immediately following a symbolic rendition of man's fall from Eden. The beautiful country of the jeweler's vision therefore marks a beginning and gives assurance of a return to bliss through God's mercy. While the reader's spirit is being prepared for clearer sight through the poet's masterful anagogical mirroring of God's light, the narrator's grief is eased by his walk past the "holtwodeȝ bryȝt" and "crystal klyffeȝ" and his soul is readied to meet the blissful maiden. The scene as a whole represents a graceful restorative of joy for mankind, a prefiguration and preparation for the greater glory of the New Jerusalem descending from heaven into the human heart.

But even as the poet allows his country of delights to assuage the jewel-

---

[33] St. Bonaventure, *Itinerarium Mentis in Deum*, in *Opera Omnia* v, pp. 306–307, quoted by Blenckner, p. 66.

er's grief and bathe him in bliss, he reminds the audience of this pilgrim's
besetting sin. The jeweler's unbounded delight, coupled with his urgent
desire for "more and more," shapes the third stanza group (ll. 121–180).
Greedy for all the joy available, not only where he is but also on the farther
shore, he aches to cross the water. His unqualified "blysse" confirms for
the reader the real power of the place to light up and transform the spirit.
But like the prologue it also asserts a powerful reminder of the nature of
fallen man, foolhardy and blind in the face of God's presence and order.
Not only does the jeweler entirely forget his former grief over human
death, but he also attributes his experience to fortune, not casually but with
the force of philosophical belief:

> As fortune fares þer as ho frayneʒ,
> Wheþer solace ho sende oþer elleʒ sore,
> Þe wyʒ to wham her wylle ho wayneʒ
> Hytteʒ to haue ay more and more. (129–132)

With equal assurance he will later attribute his initial loss of the pearl to
that same fortune:

> What wyrde hatʒ hyder my iuel vayned,
> And don me in þys del and gret daunger? (249–250)

Only when he has been corrected by his guide will he, like Boethius, learn
that God, not fortune, has governed him both in weal and woe, and that
he can be granted true joy only by divine mercy.

In the meantime, his joy—a superfluity of light-headed emotion—may
quite rightly astonish the reader who recalls the depth of his former misery. The ease with which he is distracted by paradisal beauties reflects
badly on his judgment and his self-awareness. So, too, does his certainty
that he will be able to gain the other side of the stream which, he guesses,
holds "more and more" of that bliss he has already found:

> I hoped þe water were a deuyse
> Bytwene myrþeʒ by mereʒ made;
> Byʒonde þe broke, by slente oþer slade,
> I hoped þat mote merked wore. (139–142)

Though he is afraid of wading in the deep water, he concludes with characteristic bravado:

And euer me þoȝt I schulde not wonde
For wo þer weleȝ so wynne wore. (153–154)

Never doubting his election and right to joy, the narrator impertinently
and ignorantly reduces the nature and power of God's justice as well as
his mercy. Taking the stream to be an ordinary body of water, he supposes
that crossing it will require only that he find the proper ford. He forgets
his mortality even as he had overlooked the necessity of his pearl's death.
How far from this simple delight in given joy is the proper stance for
fallen man who should bow with profound humility and self-abnegation
in the face of totally unmerited reward.

But even as the jeweler verges, all unawares, on his characteristic *hubris*,
he spies still further pleasure, his Pearl Maiden shining artfully across the
stream "as glysnande golde þat man con schere." Seated at the foot of a
crystal cliff, she so stuns the usually articulate jeweler that he can only stare
in dumb wonder.

Encounter and Recognition

The narrator's meeting with the maiden is an adaptation of a device familiar in visionary quests. He responds typically to the sight of his guide,
abashed and dumb. But, in most cases, as Kean has noted,[34] the narrator
at first fails to recognize his guide and needs to "remember" her through
his lady's forceful reminder. Here, by contrast, the jeweler has every confidence in his recognition. In fact, he precedes the reader in identifying the
maid: "I knew hyr wel, I hade sen hyr ere . . . Þe lenger, I knew hyr more
and more" (164–168). But once more the poet provides a double vision.
The riddle he poses for his audience comes nearer to expressing the real
mystery of the situation than does the narrator's glib rendition. For though
the pilgrim in paradise thinks he "knows" the maiden "more and more,"
he will learn to his chagrin that his understanding is sadly incomplete.
As is his wont, he has failed to take account of the "strange place" in
which he finds himself and in which his lady dwells. He had already re-
duced the joyful beauties of paradise to a place like his own fallen earth.
To be sure, it is more artful, brighter, fresher, but the narrator has refused
to recognize the eternal landscape in its own terms even as he will fail to
discern the risen state of the Pearl Maiden or to understand the difference
between earthly and heavenly justice.

[34] *The Pearl*, p. 117.

In the five stanzas of the third stanza group, the narrator, who gives a literal rendition of what he sees, has led readers by degrees to a high pitch of suspense as he hurried along the paradisal paths, drinking in "more and more" of the beauty of the place. Then, at the very peak of his enthusiasm, in a striking dramatic climax, he spies the Pearl Maiden, and by his recognition of her he anticipates certain fulfillment of his dearest hopes. From this point on, it might appear that the tale must proceed to a delightful, if disappointingly superficial conclusion. The jeweler will have his gem and the two will live happily ever after. It is precisely this fairy-tale picture which the jeweler paints for himself when he has gained the courage to address his lady:

> my blysfol beste,
> My grete dystresse þou al todraweȝ.
> To be excused I make requeste;
> I trawed my perle don out of daweȝ.
> Now haf I fonde hyt, I schal ma feste,
> And wony wyth hyt in schyr wod-schaweȝ,
> And loue my Lorde and al his laweȝ
> Þat hatȝ me broȝt þys blys ner. (279–286)

Lacking both the wit and the patience to entertain creaturely uncertainty, he rushes to the simplest, most reductive interpretation of his story. He fails utterly to examine either the meaning of the place or his own silence and confusion in the light of his lady's presence. But the poet, reaching toward an articulation of the mysterious, inexpressible joy of heaven, offers the audience another, more complex reading of the narrator's astonishing experience by directing attention to the very elements which the jeweler chooses to overlook.

In an elaborate chiarascuro of full, controlled description alternating with the silence of awed wonder, the *Pearl* poet reminds the audience that their imagination and intellect are being prepared for revelation beyond the capacity of ordinary perception or expression. Humor as well as a long literary tradition lie in the jeweler's sudden inability to speak at the end of the third stanza group. Stunned into wonder, he begins the fourth stanza group (16–20) with a reiteration of his bemused and dumb-struck state, as if surprised himself by a new emotion for which he can find no words:

> More þen me lyste my drede aros.
> I stod ful stylle and dorste not calle;

Wyth yȝen open and mouth ful clos
I stod as hende as hawk in halle. (181–184)

Yet even as he stumbles in speech, his narrative voice rushes onward to a
detailed description of the maiden's dress. Entirely comfortable with the
decorum of earthly aristocratic adornment, as with the rhetoric of romance, he provides a description which would become the careful eye of
a tailor. He details every aspect of his lady's costume and demeanor, resting his glance at last on the "wonder perle" she wears "immydeȝ hyr
breste." But then there is silence. Confidence and, momentarily, words
fail him:

Bot a wonder perle wythouten wemme
Inmyddeȝ hyr breste watȝ sette so sure;
A manneȝ dom moȝt dryȝly demme,
Er mynde moȝt malte in hit mesure.
I hope no tong moȝt endure
No sauerly saghe say of þat syȝt,
So watȝ hit clene and cler and pure,
Þat precios perle þer hit watȝ pyȝt. (221–228)

At the climactic moment in his description of the maiden, and in direct
contrast to a parallel moment in the previous group when he knew her
quite certainly, the jeweler discovers a pearl which defies his capacities for
expression. His silence presages the more profound quiescence to come in
his acquisition of humility. It also directs the audience to ponder the meaning of this indescribable pearl, all the more wonderful because it exceeds
the competent jeweler's usual categories of judgment.

In his symbolic prologue, the poet had suggested the miraculous presence of divine grace in his comic shifting and transforming of word
meanings and images and in his numerical play. Then, through the "anagogical" imagery of his earthly paradise, he had attempted to shadow forth
the *other*-worldly quality of God's kingdom. Now, by means of a narrative technique which alternates between elegantly controlled rendition and
confused awe, he directs attention in a new way to the mysteries of the
heavenly realm. Though it can be suggested and figured forth for fallen
man through the rich adornments of an earthly court and meticulously
made aristocratic costume, God's kingdom and its bliss will finally transcend all verbalizations and all images. But the thoughtless narrator hurries
past the silence surrounding the wonderful pearl, attempting to diminish

and dispel its mystery by further speech. In the last stanza of this group and in the first four stanzas of group v, the jeweler simply and naively rejoices, believing that his lady-pearl has been returned to him.

THE LESSON OF MEEKNESS: V–VII (STANZAS 21–35)

With the petulance of a wronged and wounded lover, the narrator proceeds in the first stanza of group v to detail his grievances. Not only has he been separated from his beloved, grieving alone at night, but she has done him the unforgivable wrong of enjoying herself all the while in "Paradys erde." The jeweler's confusion is comically apparent to the astute reader who must recognize a serious spiritual flaw in the narrator's interpretation of his story. His conflation of heaven and earth, and of heavenly and earthly joy, his refusal to understand the qualitative difference between eternity and his temporal world, between the maiden's state and his own, and to remember that he is still mortal man only dreaming of eternal joy, richly merit the maiden's formal, gently condescending response to him.

In the second stanza of this group, the Pearl Maiden begins the narrator's visionary schooling in meekness, mortality, mercy and the Kingdom of God. As a prelude to more profound theological instruction, she undertakes to correct the jeweler's general and fundamental mortal failings: his faith in human eyesight, his adherence to the rule of fortune and his refusal to recognize God's sovereignty in the light of his mortality. To his sad complaint she returns a sharp reprimand:

> "Sir, ȝe haf your tale mysetente,
> To say your perle is al awaye,
> Þat is in cofer so comly clente
> As in þis gardyn gracios gaye,
> Hereinne to lenge for euer and play." (257–261)

His fault is a familiar one in visionary questors, and finds its literary source ultimately in Boethius.[35] Just as Philosophia found it necessary to

---

[35] In my comparisons of Boethius and *Pearl*, I have relied on two contemporary Middle English translations of the *De consolatione*: (1) Boethius, *De consolatione philosophiae* (English verse, 1410) British Museum MS. Harley 44; and (2) Geoffrey Chaucer, "Boece," in *Complete Works of Geoffrey Chaucer*, ed. F. N. Robinson (Cambridge, Mass., 1957). Both translations reflect the work of medieval glossators and represent common interpretations of Boethius at the end of the fourteenth and the beginning of the fifteenth century.

"wipe a little his [Boethius's] eien that ben dirked by the cloude of mortel thynges,"[36] so the maiden tells the narrator that he has "mysetente" his tale. The poet's choice of his verb, "mysetente," from the Old French "mesentente" (misunderstood) underscores the fleshly blindness of a narrator who believes only what he sees with his eyes.[37] Like Philosophia, too, the maiden tells the jeweler that fortune, which he believes has robbed him of his treasure, has in fact given him the chance to find true happiness:

> "And þou hatȝ called þy wyrde a þef,
> Þat oȝt of noȝt hatȝ mad þe cler;
> Þou blameȝ þe bote of þy meschef,
> Þou art no kynde jueler." (273–276)

For Boethius, who likewise refused to seek true bliss and trusted in fortune, Philosophia had provided exactly the same lesson:

> Forwhy this ilke Fortune hath departed and uncovered to the bothe the certein visages and eek the doutous visages of thi felawes. Whan she departed away fro the, she took awey hir freendes. . . . Now whanne thow were ryche and weleful, as the semede, with how mochel woldestow han bought the fulle knowynge of thys . . .? Now pleyne the nat of rychesse ylorn, syn thow hast fownden the most precyous kynde of rychesses, that is to seyn, thi verray freendes.[38]

Clearly, the Pearl Maiden, like Philosophia and the host of guides after her, hopes to redirect the jeweler's vision toward spiritual joy and eternal bliss, the *summum bonum* which cannot be seen by mortal eyes or won on Fortune's wheel.

Even as she presents the traditional Boethian counsels, the Pearl Maiden also develops further the central imagery of the poem, reminding reader and jeweler alike to attend carefully to the "place" of her new life and to the transformation she has undergone. Her new setting, she tells the narrator, is a "cofer," a "forser," a "kyste," all boxes made for the storing of valuables, usually kept under lock and key. Her metaphors for her dwelling place accumulate a rich vocabulary of secure, well protected chambers intended for precious goods. Through them, the poet prepares

---

[36] Chaucer, *Works*, "Boece," bk. i, prosa 2, p. 322.

[37] Gordon glosses *mysetente* as "not given proper attention to" from OE *mis*–OF *attendre*. But it seems more likely that the word comes directly from the OF *mesentente* (*malentendu*) meaning "misunderstood."

[38] Chaucer, *Works*, "Boece," bk. ii, *prosa* 8, p. 340.

his audience (by analogy) for that most secure of all chambers, the "corte of the kingdom of God." No longer the gem the narrator has lost, or the flowering herbs of the garden in the prologue, the maiden has become a "perle of prys" precisely suited for such a chamber:

> For þat þou lesteȝ watȝ bot a rose
> Þat flowred and fayled as kynde hyt gef.
> Now þurȝ kynde of þe kyste þat hyt con close
> To a perle of prys hit is put in pref. (269–272)

Behind this imagery, drawing together the "gresse" and the "blomeȝ," the "moul" and the "kynde of Kryste" of the prologue, lies the familiar Old Testament notion found in Isaiah (40: 7) of mankind as dying grass:

> All mankind is grass and all their glory like the flower of the field. The grass withers, the flower wilts, when the breath of the Lord blows upon it. So then the people is the grass. Though the grass withers and the flower wilts, the Word of our God stands forever.

New Testament and Patristic tradition, building on the Old, had reinterpreted the "Word" as the eternal "grass" of Christ's flesh, symbolized in the bread of the Eucharist:

> "The Word was made Flesh," and the prophet says "All flesh is grass." But that grass which the Word was made withered not into hay, nor did its flower fall, "for the Spirit of the Lord abideth forever," so must the grass, the Flesh that he is made be likewise everlasting. For how shall He bestow eternal life, if He Himself did not abide forever? And He says expressly, "If any man eat of this Bread, he shall live forever," and explains moreover, "The Bread which I will give is my Flesh, for the life of the world."[39]

The poet has adapted a rich tradition of sacred imagery, redeveloping its original connections and inspiration in his transplanting.

But despite the maiden's richly weighted glossing of his tale, the narrator continues to miss the point. In his jeweler's response, the poet takes an opportunity to illustrate the comic foolishness of a mortal about to be saved in spite of himself, and to confirm the reader in his judgment of the naive jeweler. The narrator simply will not recognize that his pearl is dead

---

[39] St. Bernard of Clairvaux, *Sermones in Cantica Canticorum*, trans. by a Religious of the C.S.M.V., *On the Song of Songs* (London, 1952), p. 104.

and risen and that her garden is not yet his. He will "wony" with her beyond the waters now that he has found her still alive.

With righteous indignation, the maiden, speaking authoritatively, as-
sails him. She lists his three errors, which have just been vividly dramatized:

> (1) Þou says þou traweȝ me in þis dene,
>   Bycawse þou may wyth yȝen me se;
> (2) Anoþer þou says, in þys countré
>   Þyself schal won wyth me ryȝt here;
> (3) Þe thrydde, to passe þys water fre. (295–299)

This incisive outline of the jeweler's illogic anticipates her plan for lessons
on human blindness, mortality, salvation and creaturely humility in the
next stanza-group (vi).

In addition, it is through the sixth group (perhaps a numerical coincidence) based on the link word, "demen" (to judge), a word with obvious
eschatological overtones, that the jeweler moves a first halting step away
from his prideful habit of judging for himself and thus refusing absolute
submission to the heavenly judge. As we might have expected, the maiden
begins by accusing him of pride ("sorquydryȝe"), of faith in his own
reason, and of refusal to believe Christ's *words*. In those scriptural words
which are alone worthy of belief, she tells him, he will find a touchstone
for all other words. For Christ "lelly hyȝte your lyf to rayse,/ Þaȝ fortune
dyd your flesch to dyȝe" (305–306). Instead of accepting this simple formula, which would explain all that has happened to his pearl and all that
will happen to him, the narrator, like mortal men generally, has embarked
on an elaborate fantasy, trusting his senses and his limited reasoning, setting himself against the very source of his salvation.

To correct his pride and remind him of the necessity of creaturely submission, the maiden once again imitates her forebear, Philosophia, who
had admonished Boethius:

> Allas what ayle fiers men and prowde
> To lyfte vp ther neckes so in vayn?
> This mortall yokke which that ye bere aboute
> Shall payse it doun vnto the grounde ayen.[40]

Using a livelier metaphor to similar purpose, Pearl chides the narrator:

[40] Boethius, Harley 44, fol. 32v.

For þoȝ þou daunce as any do,
Braundysch and bray þy braþeȝ breme,
When þou no fyrre may, to ne fro,
Þou moste abyde þat he schal deme. (345–348)

Her lesson is a hard one. She depicts God's justice as incomprehensible to human reason and uninfluenced by accusations or even by prayer, save through the gift of his mercy.

But the narrator, like other vision questors in such situations, is mollified and confesses his sin. He acknowledges "crystes mersy and Mary and Jon" as the ground of his bliss. The jeweler's failing had been overweening Pride of Life. Through his guide he has been led to confess his fault and to recognize the central truth of his fallen existence: "I am bot mol." The maiden's response takes the form of an absolution, acknowledging her student's movement from pride to humility:

For now þy speche is to me dere.
Maysterful mod and hyȝe pryde,
I hete þe, arn heterly hated here.
My Lorde ne loueȝ not for to chyde,
For meke arn alle þat woneȝ hym nere;
And when in hys place þou schal apere,
Be dep deuote in hol mekenesse. (400–406)

But her absolution is premature. The jeweler, schooled overlong in earthly justice, still harbors resentment for his pearl's high heavenly estate. At the end of stanza group VII, the maiden reminds him of her unmerited preferment, stirring him to the curiosity necessary for the next rhetorical division of the poem:

Þow wost wel when þy perle con schede
I watȝ ful ȝong and tender of age;
Bot my Lorde þe Lombe purȝ hys godhede,
He toke myself to hys maryage,
Corounde me quene in blysse to brede. (411–415)

Though he has confessed his sin and meekly asked to understand her life in heaven, the jeweler still cannot refrain from challenging a justice not based on merit and reward. From this point, the debate moves to a new level of theological and verbal refinement, a level which has called forth adverse criticism from some readers. Yet, as we shall see, such a tactical change is both fitting and necessary.

The poet initiates this subtler movement before he has concluded the jeweler's confession and absolution. He might well have introduced his new subject at the beginning of a new stanza group. But, like Dante's terza rima, his link words offer the audience a key to remembering and memorizing the various rhetorical parts of his compositon. By beginning his systematic treatment of heavenly justice and beatitude under the link word "blysse-blysful," which also concludes the lesson in meekness, he could rely on his readers' remembering the general content of the next six stanza groups by simply recalling the place of 'blysse' as the concatenating link word.

The "Astate" of the Blessed and the Vintner's Justice: VIII–XIII
(stanzas 36–65)

In the next six stanza groups, the maiden begins to develop images of the heavenly court for her newly penitent jeweler. Her poetic method elaborates the aristocratic motif already well established in the tone, language and figures from the very beginning. It is also clearly suited to the jeweler's taste and expectations. But at the same time, narrator and audience alike must come to understand that the ranks and courtesy of heaven are radically different from their earthly counterparts. To comprehend the order and customs of the blessed, they must disabuse themselves of all earthly expectations and move *through* the maiden's courtly metaphors to a whole new realm of values, to a "court" in which souls enjoy perfect but various happiness bound together as a mystical body to the head of Christ. The maiden's oblique language at the beginning of her theological discourse —her play with the words and concepts of "queen," "empress," and "cortaysye"—suggest a possible transition through analogy from the notion of an earthly to a heavenly court. But the leap from earth to heaven is not easy or direct as the poem's riddling, symbolic and figurative language has suggested from the start. The poet's knowledgeable maiden prepares both the jeweler and the audience by degrees of complication to move from the image of the "perle" endlessly round to the perfectly square city of the New Jerusalem (and from 5 to 6).

For medieval readers familiar with contemporary Augustinian and Bradwardian arguments concerning heavenly reward, the maiden's dialogue undoubtedly provided a delightful jeu-d'esprit, counterpointed as it is against the poor jeweler's obtuse worldliness. The first question the narrator asks his Pearl is one befitting a fourteenth-century neopelagian, namely, her rank in the heavenly court.[41]

In reply, the maiden seems at first to blur the usual orthodox distinctions of gradation among the blessed based on relative merit. Dante, by contrast, had carefully related the degrees of happiness enjoyed by his saints to the nature and extent of their holiness. But the maiden declares:

> The court of þe kyndom of God alyue
> Hatȝ a property in hytself beyng:
> Alle þat may þerinne aryue
> Of alle þe reme is quen oþer kyng. (445–448)

And then in characteristically indirect language she adds an apparent paradox. Though all the blessed are kings and queens, Mary remains the empress over all and the "Quen of Cortaysye." She also likens the court of the blessed to the mystical body described by St. Paul:

> Of courtaysye, as saytȝ Saynt Poule,
> Al arn we membreȝ of Jesu Kryst:
> As heued and arme and legg and naule
> Temen to hys body ful trwe and tryste,
> Ryȝt so is vch a Krysten sawle
> A longande lym to þe Mayster of mystre (457–462)

[41] Fourteenth-century theologians argued with vehemence over the question of God's omnipotence versus man's free will. The opposing positions developed by the two major theological camps were not free from the natural psychological phenomenon leading men to force their opponents' views to extremes. Such forcing resulted in a categorizing of the contenders as *pelagii moderni* and *deterministi*. The "modern Pelagians," including thinkers of such eminence as William Ockham and Robert Holcot, contended that human reason is not an instrument capable of understanding the omnipotence of God. They placed emphasis rather on the study of man and examined the power of human will and the conditions surrounding its freedom. The part of God against these *pelagii moderni* was passionately defended by Richard FitzRalph, Thomas Buckingham, John Wyclif and, especially, Thomas Bradwardine. The *deterministi* stressed God's omnipotence to such an extent that the modern Pelagians accused them of theological determinism. Bradwardine and his allies argued that God in his mercy and justice governed every activity of man and his world. They also maintained the omnipotence of his pleasure in the election of the saints and tended to discount any possibility of man's acting meritoriously on his own initiative. They insisted on the need for prevenient grace to move a soul to prayer, penance and final salvation.

This apparent contradiction between equality and difference could be easily enough resolved in two separate but related arguments to be found in St. Augustine and in Bradwardine as well as in Dante: (1) all who are in heaven enjoy total happiness; and (2) souls enjoy this totality in different ways in order to enhance the beauty of God's court through variety. But the maiden eschews doctrinal clarity in order to underscore heaven's mysteries.[42]

And typically, the jeweler fails to grasp the point of his lesson. He can only ask, with his earthly sense of courtly preferment, how a mere child could be made a queen of heaven:

> Þyself in heuen ouer hyȝ þou heue,
> To make þe quen þat watȝ so ȝonge.
> What more honour moȝte he acheue
> Þat hade endured in worlde stronge,
> And lyued in penaunce hys lyueȝ longe
> Wyth bodyly bale hym blysse to byye?
> What more worschyp moȝt he fonge
> Þen corounde be kyng by cortaysé? (473–480)

For answer to so impertinent a question, the Pearl Maiden recounts the parable of the laborers in the vineyard.

The poet's near contemporary, Bishop Bradwardine, had posed a very similar neopelagian question: "Why when one case is different from another, is there the same judgment?" Then, following St. Augustine, he had responded, like the maiden, by pointing to the scriptural laborers:

> Let us recall, therefore, the workers in the vineyard, those who labored all day and those who labored one hour. Surely the case is different in regard to the labor expended, but the judgment is the same in the payment of wages. And did these laborers who murmured hear anything from the master of the house except, "I will it?" ... Thus in the Gospel, our Lord, when he would speak of such a case, says: "I praise you,

---

[42] Dante's heavenly spheres clearly represent various levels of merit for his saints. Bradwardine, following Augustine, suggests a different emphasis in his discussion of gradation in paradise: "Amplius autem diversitas graduum coelestium mansionum coelestis Ecclesiae pulchritudinem conficit & ornatum, sicut sonorum diversitas melodiam perficit dulciorem & colorum varietas picturam efficit pulchriorum" (*De Causa Dei*, bk. 1, chap. 46, p. 435).

Father, Lord of heaven and earth, because you have hidden these things from the wise and prudent and have revealed them to little children."[43]

As the maiden concludes *her* rendition of the parable of the vineyard, she likewise reminds the jeweler that the grace of heavenly reward belongs entirely to the will and gift of God, not to human merit:

> In euentyde into þe vyne I come—
> Fyrst of my hyre my Lorde con mynne:
> I watȝ payed anon of al and sum.
> ȝet oþer þer werne þat tok more tom,
> Þat swange and swat for long ȝore,
> Þat ȝet of hyre noþynk þay nom,
> Paraunter noȝt schal to-ȝere more. (582–588)

Both for the Augustinian Bradwardine and the *Pearl* poet's guide, submissive assent to this incomprehensible justice and mercy of God can best be taught to fallen man through the indirection of parables.

But the maiden's parable has further purpose in terms of the vision quest's double form. Her account of the laborers in the vineyard contributes significantly to the poem's increasingly rich vocabulary concerning heavenly mysteries. The scriptural parable in which "vch man [is] payed inlyche/ Wheþer lyttel oþer much be hys rewarde" reiterates the lesson of the queens and kings of the heavenly court, but this time in terms of work done and reward merited by the laborers. The narrator's complaint heard anew within the context of the scriptural story demonstrates the universality of his attitude, God's awareness of it, and his veiled, parabolic effort to explain the nature of his kingdom to fallen man. As the laborers make their grouchy demand on the Lord, the jeweler's voice becomes a chorus:

> "More haf we serued, vus þynk so,
> Þat suffred han þe dayeȝ hete,
> Þenn þyse þat wroȝt not houreȝ two,
> And þou dotȝ hem vus to counterfete." (553–556)

[43] "Sed cur, inquis, non solum in parvulorum, verum & geminorum seu grandævorum, una eadem causa tam diversum iudicium? Nonne similis quaestio est, cur in diversa causa iudicium idem? Recolamus igitur illos operarios in vinea, qui tota die laboraverunt, & eas qui unica hora; nempe causa diversa est impensi laboris, & tamen idem iudicium in redditione mercedis; Nunquid & hi aliud audierunt murmurantes a Patrefamilias nisi hoc volo? . . . Confitebor tibi Pater Domine coeli & terrae, qui absconditi haec a sapientibus & prudentibus, & revelasti ea parvulis." (*De causa Dei*, bk. ii, chap. 14, pp. 515–516).

The *Pearl* poet seems to have been particularly intrigued by the special quality of opacity in the scriptural parables dealing with the mystery of God's kingdom. In his paraphrase of this story of the laborers, and the parables of the pearl of great price and the little children to follow, he offers almost no glossing of the text. Instead he expects the obtuse narrator as well as the audience to interpret the "sothful gospel":

> Ryʒtwysly quo con rede,
> He loke on bok and be awayed. (709–710)

For the poet, the parables provided ideal surrogates for his own (through the maiden's) voice, introducing a new degree of authority and truth about heaven without reducing the central mysteries of God's mercy and justice to simple doctrinal formulas. Because the words are God's the poet's verbal composition is raised to a new plane of certainty and truth. From this point until the very end of the poem, the poet increasingly depends on scriptural paraphrase. But here he prefers the parabolic word, as he will later prefer the symbolic figures of St. John. The jeweler's spiritual acuity and readiness for mystery continue to require demonstration, and, in addition, the mystery of heaven's "property" itself defies total verbalization.

In terms of the story, we discover that the maiden's reticence in speaking directly to the obtuse jeweler is richly merited. For though the narrator has listened to the word of God in the parable, he still refuses to understand. In response to the parable of the laborers, while he shows respect for the scriptural word by quoting the Old Testament 'Sauter,' he stubbornly objects:

> Now he þat stod þe long day stable,
> And þou to payment com hym byfore,
> Þenne þe lasse in werke to take more able,
> And euer þe lenger þe lasse, þe more. (597–600)

His literal obtuseness gives the poet cause to pursue his doctrinal explorations. At last, through the maiden, he focuses explicitly on Adam's sin, the history of fallen and redeemed mankind, and the transcendent wonder of God's mercy and justice (ll. 600–660).

Fifteen stanzas (36–50) have carried us to this point in the theological argument, that is, to its exact center. Like Dante, the *Pearl* poet seems to have constructed his composition so that its deepest lesson emanates from its central point, radiating outward to illuminate the whole narrative.

Here, for the first time, in stanza group xi—which coincidentally concludes at stanza 55, line 660, merging the key integers 5 and 6 (and their parts or factors 2 and 3)—the poet presents the essence of his argument:

> For þe grace of God is gret inoghe. (612)

The "more" and "less" which had governed the irritable narrator's notions of justice through the first six hundred lines are resolved in the next sixty lines. Precisely at the poem's arithmetical center—lines 606–612—the Pearl Maiden describes the incomprehensible superabundance of God's graceful "enough":

> Queþer-so-euer he dele nesch oþer harde:
> He laueʒ hys gyfteʒ as water of dyche,
> Oþer goteʒ of golf þat neuer charde.
> Hys fraunchyse is large þat euer dard
> To Hym þat matʒ in synne rescoghe;
> No blysse betʒ fro hem reparde,
> For þe grace of God is gret inoghe. (606–612)

From a theoretical point of view, nothing more need be said. So great a saving gift must, ideally, override all human concern for self, all love of earthly good. Understanding its import, the narrator should rise with joy to the vision of God.

But the narrator does not grasp its significance. His particular character as cantankerous lover of this world, certain of his judgments, requires more than simple statements for proper understanding and full repentance. His spiritual blindness once again allows the maiden to refine her lesson and also to lead her pilgrim finally to the conclusion proper to visionary quests—a sight of the New Jerusalem. Knowing well that she must expand her argument in order to effect the jeweler's conversion, the maiden proceeds with further explication. In the central group, xi, she amplifies her description of God's "enough" by describing Adam's fall, Christ's doleful death, and the sacrament of baptism:

> Þe blod vus boʒt fro bale of helle
> And delyuered vus of þe deth secounde;
> Þe water is baptem, þe soþe to telle,
> Þat folʒed þe glayue so grymly grounde,
> Þat wascheʒ away þe gylteʒ felle
> Þat Adam wyth inne deth vus dround.
> Now is þer noʒt in þe worlde rounde

Bytwene vus and blysse bot þat he wythdroʒ,
And þat is restored in sely stounde;
And þe grace of God is gret innogh. (651–660)

Then, as if reading the narrator's querulous mind, she goes on in group
XII to explain the superiority of the innocent babe to the repentant adult
sinner. Augustine had used just such a comparison often and to great
advantage in his defense of grace against the Pelagians. Indeed, the Augustinian example of infant death as a strategic argument for grace without merit may perhaps have suggested *Pearl*'s story.

In any case, the maiden does not allow the question of infant salvation
to drop easily. Like Augustine, she supports God's mercy toward "inno-
sents" by referring to the parable of the little children. This new parable,
introduced coincidentally at the end of the twelfth stanza group at stanza
60, concludes the defense of her own salvation and initiates a new movement. When it is carried into the thirteenth stanza group, Christ's story
of the little children merges gracefully with yet another parable and a new
theme. Because the Pearl Maiden came to the kingdom as a little child,
following the scriptural story, she inherited that bliss "þat con not blynne,"
the pearl of price for which the merchant sold all his goods.

Up to this point, the maiden has been at great pains to teach the narrator the necessity of her own death and the high beauty of her place in
heaven. Now she intends to lead him beyond himself, to "transhumanize"
him as Beatrice did Dante, so that he can see beyond her to that kingdom
which is "wemleʒ, clene, and clere." For this new lesson concerning the
kingdom, she presents a story which had lain beneath the surface of the
jeweler's proud boasting from the first stanza. But unlike the poem's jeweler who has *lost* his gem, the scriptural jeweler had gone out, forsaking
all he owned to "bye hym a perle watʒ mascelleʒ." The maiden properly
counsels her own narrator to imitate his scriptural exemplar:

I rede þe forsake þe worlde wode
And porchace þy perle maskelles. (743–744)

On such advice will the jeweler, like early monastic visionaries, give over
his worldly loves and expectations in order to seek the kingdom of God?
Not yet. For he must know more about the maiden's "astate" (and allow
the poet to complete his numerical composition).

The narrator's deliberate inability to understand the "bok" properly, his
ignorance of the intricate congruence of the two parables interwoven by

the maiden reflects the poet's artful dependence on the traditional naiveté of the visionary pilgrim. The jeweler's "unseeing" is by now habitual and comic—a shortcoming which cannot be overcome even by the most meticulous and gracefully devised explanations. Closer in this respect to the lover of the *Roman de la Rose* than to Dante's pilgrim, he provides a perfect foil for the maiden's complex parabolic discourses on the unimaginable wonder of the heavenly kingdom. No St. John in his visionary journey, the poor jeweler sees but does not fully understand what he learns in his dream. At this point, in the midst of group XIII, the slow-witted narrator can acknowledge the maiden's superhuman beauty, unequaled in Pygmalion's art or Aristotle's philosophy. But he still asks what power has granted this unearthly, unmatched lady her place in heaven.

His question leads the maiden to elaborate on the nature of the heavenly kingdom, intermingling images from Solomon's Song of Songs and St. John's Apocalypse. The Lamb, she says, called her from the world with Solomon's words to be his wife, washing her garment first with his blood:

> Cum hyder to me, my lemman swete,
> For mote ne spot is non in þe. (763–764)

The reader may well pause here, at the end of group XIII, to delight in the complementary series of scriptural images juxtaposed in mosaic-like order: the small child at Christ's knee, the perfect pearl sought by the jeweler, the Lamb whose blood paradoxically washed the garment white, the maiden herself as the lady of Solomon's love song. For him, the elegant congruences of these images may call forth a complex meditation, preparing him to "see" the final images of St. John's heavenly Jerusalem in a way quite different from the jeweler's.

But for the narrator, the maiden's speech provokes only further puzzlement. How can she "both makelleʒ" and "maskelleʒ" (they are *his* words, not hers), have usurped the place of all others in the heavenly kingdom. As usual, the poet allows his jeweler this obvious backsliding into old error in order to carry the lesson forward, this time to its proper end.

PROLOGUE TO THE VISION OF PEACE: XIV–XVI (STANZAS 66–81)

With the beginning of group XIV, at stanza 66 (another numerical coincidence) the maiden introduces the poem's final movement and a new image—a figural representation of the heavenly Jerusalem. Such a conclusion has been anticipated, not by the unsuspecting narrator but by the poet's art: in his choice of the visionary quest to frame his narrative; in his careful ordering of imagery in the prologue; in his dextrous manipulation of scriptural parables of the kingdom; and finally in his allusion to the eschatological figure of the Lamb. Like Dante, the *Pearl* poet has made close readers aware from the start that a human understanding of heavenly bliss can only be approached by stages, and that such experiences cannot be described by a simple univocal use of human language. In his manipulation of words, images and meanings, in his richly suggestive landscapes, in his paraphrase of riddling parables, in his numerical wizardry, he has relied heavily on indirect, multivalent modes of verbal discourse.

To add to this comic complexity of expression, in stanza group xv, the poet, who has already demonstrated his delight in numerical riddling, introduces a puzzle for his readers. Instead of the usual five stanzas, this group contains six. Could this be a scribal error, as some critics have suggested, or does it contribute to the poet's scheme? If the poet required an extra stanza to meet a need for 1212 lines, why should he have placed it here? Perhaps the answer to these questions must remain the poet's secret. But, given some sense of his scheme thus far, we may make certain speculations. First of all, it is in this stanza group that the maiden first offers to show the jeweler St. John's heavenly city and gives him a taste for its beauty by a direct paraphrase from Revelation. We move explicitly from the Pearl Maiden's speech to St. John's. Secondly, in the *sixth* stanza of the group, the jeweler penitently confesses his own creaturely weakness and his maiden's blessedness in an action reminiscent of other visionary questors:

To Krysteʒ chambre [thou] art ichose.
I am bot mokke and mul among,
And þou so ryche a reken rose,
And bydeʒ here by þys blysful bonc
Þer lyueʒ lyste may neuer lose. (904–908)

Because he has understood at last the miracle of the pearl's eternal "chambre" and her everlasting life as a fresh rose, the new convert is able to ask a favor: to know more of the New Jerusalem.

From 5 to 6, from the perfectly round pearl to the perfectly square city, from the blessed guide to the source of blessedness: thus the anomalous sixth stanza of group xv may represent by comic analogy the incorporation of circle and square, of human sanctity within the vision of God's oneness. Such a conjecture may appear whimsical. Yet the problem of the squared circle, a metaphor for God's complex simplicity, clearly interested poets as well as theological gymnasts of the later Middle Ages. The transformed Dante, about to see his final vision at the end of canto xxxiii, compares his puzzled state to that of the "geometer who sets his whole mind to squaring the circle and in his thinking fails to find that principle." Bishop Bradwardine, the *Pearl* poet's contemporary, likewise examines solutions to this problem in his *Geometria Speculativa* as a means to discover God.

Yet, if he offers such multivalence of possibility in approaching the nature of bliss, the poet also teaches the essential difference between words, figures and numbers used to describe beatitude and the ecstatic experience itself. Even as the narrator moves toward his final vision, the maiden embarks on an excursion on the relationships between words and meanings. As she prepares the jeweler to glimpse the New Jerusalem, she carefully explains the difference between the earthly and heavenly cities, both signified by the same word, "Jerusalem." She also underscores the distance between earthly representations of the heavenly city and heaven itself. For authority she calls not on her own "seeing" and "cnawyng" but on that of St. John. She further insists, patiently, that the distinction between the old and new Jerusalem turns on the fact of fleshly death:

> Of motes two to carpe clene,
> And Jerusalem hyȝt boþe nawþeles—
> Þat nys to yow no more to mene
> Bot "ceté of God," oþer "syȝt of pes":
> In þat on oure pes watȝ mad at ene;
> Wyth payne to suffer þe Lombe hit chese;
> In þat oþer is noȝt bot pes to glene
> Þat ay schal laste wythouten reles.
> Þat is þe borȝ þat we to pres
> *Fro þat oure flesch be layd to rote,*
> Þer glory and blysse schal euer encres
> To þe meyny þat is wythouten mote. (949–960)

Her argument is crucial to the jeweler's lesson. He must come to understand the absolute necessity of human death as the fee of entry to the "ceté of God." As he approaches a vision of St. John's eschatological figures, the maiden reminds him that he "may not enter wythinne hys tor" though he

may "þurȝ grea favor" have a "syȝt" of it. Through the death of Christ in
the Old Jerusalem, Everyman has been granted the possibility of coming
at last to the most secure chamber of God's love in heaven. Through grace,
the mediation of St. John's prophetic figures, and his own degree of pre-
paredness, he may anticipate that final blessedness by gazing, in life and
in time, on a shadow and likeness of it. Such are the necessary modifications and possibilities concerning temporal separation and eternal union
which preface the jeweler's entry to the last fifteen stanzas of the vision
proper.

THE VISION "AS JOHN DEUYSED": XVII–XIX (STANZAS 82–96)

Pearl culminates, like other poems of the quest tradition, in an eschatological vision. Fifteen stanzas are given over to a richly detailed paraphrase
of St. John's prophecy. But the *Pearl* poet depends, like a number of his
predecessors, on the symbolic distance from full vision provided by the
scriptural figures. His narrator wonders at the literal appearances of his
mystical "syȝt," speaking for instance, of the hide of the Lamb: "Bot a
wounde ful wyde and weete con wyse/ Anende hys hert, þurȝ hyde to-
rente" (1135–1136). At every turn, the poet underscores the *pictorial* rather
than the spiritual aspect of the vision, keeping both narrator and reader
from the inner chamber of the kingdom. In certain respects, his descriptions resemble those of thirteenth- and fourteenth-century illuminators of
the Apocalypse. Indeed, one image in the poetic vision may well owe its
inspiration partly to the illuminator's art: the heavenly city itself. The
narrator sees the city "al of brende golde bryȝt/ As glemande glas burnist
broun" (989–990). In distinctly medieval fashion beneath the city, he
discerns the foundations rising in steps, each step a single gem. The wall
rises and then the city above the foundations. Another image, that of the
jeweler viewing the heavenly city from across a stream, has no direct
parallel in the scriptural text, but one can be found in a number of the
illuminated manuscripts. St. John is pictured walking along a stream,
either alone or with an angel. On the other side of the water is the heavenly city of the New Jerusalem. So in *Pearl*:

> If I þis mote þe schal vnhyde,
> Bow vp towarde þys borneȝ heued,
> And I anendeȝ þe on þis syde
> Schal sve, tyl þou to a hil be veued. (973–976)

In his descriptions of the apocalyptic vision, the poet even chooses words drawn from the illuminators' craft. Not only is the city 'brende golde'; the horns of the Lamb are 'red golde cler'; and the wall of jasper gleams as 'glayre,' the white of egg used in making illuminations.

While the standard illustrations are infused with the poet's imaginative power, he nevertheless takes pains to maintain a distance afforded by scripture and the traditional iconographic formulae. The narrative and thematic rationale for such reticence is clear. Throughout his adventure, the pilgrim, unlike Dante's retrospective narrator, has been unable to penetrate symbols, figures and parables without assistance and even then only partially. As he reviewed the pearl's loss in the garden, he had wrestled with the "kynde of kryst," and refused comfort. In the midst of what would eventually be recognized as divinely ordained circumstances, he had remained blind and deaf. Only through the Pearl Maiden's explication of scriptural parables could the jeweler *begin* to understand the significance of the maiden's death. Then, when he had partly grasped the meaning of the vineyard parable in terms of his own situation, and of the pearl parable in relation to heavenly reward, he could be brought to confront images of the heavenly city. But despite his careful preparation, he remains able to note only visual impressions; he cannot perceive their spiritual significance. Seeing the Lamb, all white except for a gaping, bleeding wound, he declares with naive indignation: "Alas, þoȝt I, who did þat spyt?" (1138) Because of lingering "fatnesse of herte and greuouseness of eres," and despite the maiden's instruction, he must still look to the figures but not to their meanings.

The Conclusion: xx (stanzas 97–101)

Not until he has been denied a deeper vision of the New Jerusalem in the coda to his dream can he recognize that all the events both in and out of the vision are part of a divine scheme, the meaning of which has escaped him. When he awakens from vision on his "huyle" he understands at least that what he had called ill fate is in fact the divine will: "So wel is me in þys doel-doungoun/ Þat þou art to þat Prynseȝ paye" (1187). The narrator's concluding resignation sums up both his fault and his lesson:

To þat Prynceȝ paye hade I ay bente,
And ȝerned no more þen watȝ me gyuen,
And halden me þer in trwe entent,

As þe perle me prayed þat watʒ so þryuen,
Aʒ helde, drawen to Goddeʒ present,
To mo of his mysterys I hade ben dryuen. (1189–1194)

Had he but accepted God's will and rested in it with "trwe entent," that is, with true understanding, he might have entered more deeply into the meaning of the eschatological vision, even to the heart of the mystery. As it is, the pilgrim must be content with partial vision and partial knowledge, still plagued by earthly desire and temptations to possession.

But this is as it should be. For the jeweler's miraculous vision is only a beginning. Through it, he, like his early monastic forebears, is converted to meekness and a desire for his savior, whom he now must seek resignedly. What remains is the difficult ascent from desire to desire until he has purified his soul and made it ready for the fullness of bliss.

> And thou shalt cast out of thine heart all such sins, and sweep thy soul clean with a besom of dread of God, and with water of thine eye wash it; and so shalt thou find thy drachma Jhesu. He is drachma. He is penny, and He is thine heritage. This drachma will not so lightly be found as it may be said; for this work is not of one hour nor of a day, but many days and years with mickle sweat and swink of the body and travail of the soul. And if thou cease not; but seek busily, sorrow and sigh deep, mourn still, and stoop low till thine eye water for anguish and for pain, for thou hast lost thy treasure Jhesu . . . And if thou find Him as I have said . . . as a shadow or glimmering of Him, thou mayest if thou wilt call thy friends to thee for to make mirth with thee and melody, for thou hast found thy drachma Jhesu.[44]

Like Walter Hilton, the *Pearl* poet, insists on the difficulties attending the quest for "ghostly knowing." The narrative outcome of *Pearl* reflects the poet's practical, sober assessment of man's limited ability to approach divine mysteries.

And yet such knowing is possible:

> *"Seek then that thou hast lost, that thou might find it."*
> Nevertheless forasmuch as thou hast not yet seen what it is fully, for thy ghostly eye is not yet opened, I shall tell one word for all which thou shalt seek, desire and find, for in that word is all that thou has lost. This

---

[44] Walter Hilton, *The Scale of Perfection*, ed. E. Underhill (London, 1948), I, 48, pp. 117–118.

word is Jhesu. I mean not this word Jhesu painted upon the wall, or
written with letters on the book, or formed by lips in sound of the
mouth, nor feigned in thine heart by travail of thy mind; for on this
manner-wise, may a man out of charity find Him. But I mean Jhesu ...
all goodness, endless wisdom, love and sweetness, thy joy, thy worship
and thine everlasting bliss, thy God, thy Lord and thy salvation.[45]

This close meditation on the Word, a stage of contemplation proposed by
Hilton for those who seek perfection, is very like the one which the *Pearl*
poet finally offers his readers through the form of his poem. But with a
profound sense of comic propriety he had hidden the ultimate step in his
spiritual quest behind a variety of masks: in his cumulatively rich images
of the pearl "endeles round," in the circularity of the verbal structure, beginning and ending with the pearl prepared for the prince's pleasure, in
the maiden's simple description of heavenly bliss—"We þurʒoutly hauen
cnawyng"—in the several parables of the kingdom and in the careful
numerical order built on 1, 2, 3, and 12.

With a gentle smile, he disappoints expectations on the narrative level
in order to force readers beyond the story to his elaborate poetic artifice.
Through his purposeful manipulation of the narrator's *historia*, the *Pearl*
poet has asked his audience to return again and again to the heart of the
mystery: "But what is the kingdom of heaven *really* like?" The answer
to which many visionary quests had already pointed was partly that the
essence of the kingdom cannot be known to man in time. The condition
for heavenly bliss is death:

> Fro þat oure flesch be layd to rote,
> Þer glory and blysse shall euer encres
> To þe meyny þat is wythouten mote. (958–60)

Therefore all verbal forms for expressing its nature must finally be inadequate. Christ spoke in parables about the joy of heaven partly because of
the spiritual blindness of his listeners, but also, the *Pearl* poet suggests, because only the blessed "þurʒoutly hauen cnawyng." Yet *Pearl*, like the
Vita Nuova and the *Commedia*, also holds out the promise, characteristic
of the later medieval visionary perspective, that men can approach the joy
and wisdom of heaven before death while still alive and in time. The *Pearl*
master has cloaked his meditation on the kingdom of God in manifold
guises, mingling elements of literary tradition in new and surprising

[45] *Scale* 1, 46, pp. 111–112.

ways. Through a form borrowed from well-known predecessors, he, like Dante, has tested the limits to which his art can be pressed in approaching the nature and beauty of beatitude. By adapting the traditional double form of the visionary quest to ingenious new purpose, he has led his most attentive readers to grasp the spiritual framework informing his jeweler's narrative. Through verbal and numerical patterning, he demonstrates how a profoundly moving and humanly devastating event can be transformed to share in divine order and oneness.

The *Pearl* poet makes great demands on his ideal reader, at the same time giving those with limited spiritual insight their portion of understanding and pleasure in a poignant, lively story. Like the narrator, even the ideal reader is the victim of earthly expectations and faith in sense experience, a perennial problem for fallen man. Like the narrator, he may tend to accept the story in all its immediacy, high emotion and dramatic charm and fail to discover the directions toward which the story leads. But for those who take the time, the poet has provided a complex meditation on divine oneness. In a spiraling movement, the reader who seeks may come finally to "see" spiritually the meaning of the poet's fourteenth-century parable of the kingdom of heaven:

> The Kingdom of heaven is like a Prince who goes out in search of pearls pleasing to his taste. When he has come upon gems suitable for his judgment, he brings them to his domain and there provides them with an exquisite gold setting.

If he perceives the spiritual reality taught by the parable of *Pearl* in all its verbal and arithmetical facets then the poem itself will have become like the "perle" of the opening stanza, a thing of beauty "endeles round" with the capacity to lead the reader toward a "privy cnawyng" of God.

Such a reader may surpass the jeweler-narrator's experience and join the poet who speaks *Pearl*'s last stanza of simple contentment and praise. There, he will find set out the "easy" formula for becoming a pearl pleasing to the prince while yet alive in time:

> To pay þe Prince oþer sete saȝte
> Hit is ful eþe to þe god Krystyin;
> For I haf founden hym, boþe day and naȝte,
> A God, a Lorde, a frende ful fyin.
> Ouer þis hyul þis lote I laȝte,
> For pyty of my perle enclyin,
> And syþen to God I hit bytaȝte

In Krysteʒ dere blessyng and myn,
Þat in þe forme of bred and wyn
Þe preste vus scheweʒ vch a daye.
He gef vus to be his homly hyne
Ande precious perleʒ vnto his pay. (1200–1212)

This last stanza, in which the poet speaks *in propria persona* marks a
radical leap from the jeweler's faltering resignation of the previous stanza.
By comically appropriate juxtapositon, and potent ellipsis, the English
master implies the great distance between a new convert awakening from
a single vision, and the visionary blessedness of Christ's habitual friends
in the world, those who find him daily in the miracle of the Eucharist—
a wafer endlessly round which contains the whole mystery of human salvation.

SIX

WILL'S DARK VISIONS OF PIERS THE PLOWMAN

Both *Pearl* and *Piers Plowman* were produced in the latter half of the fourteenth century,[1] and both participate in the great theological debates and spiritual difficulties of that period. But the two poets differ widely, though they use a common literary tradition, conventions, and techniques. As if retreating to an earlier, calmer time, the *Pearl* poet devises elaborate symmetries to represent a simple, almost sweet trust in divine providence. By contrast, Langland's long, wandering work—the last great visionary quest of the Middle Ages—clearly defines a final stage in the mode's history.[2] In a poem which, like *Pearl*, ostensibly describes the way to salvation, the poet of *Piers* paradoxically chooses to emphasize late fourteenth-century theological skepticism: he takes pains to satirize the decadence of the established church, the proliferation and confusion of its teaching, and the moral formlessness of political and social life.

The artistic order Langland manages in his poem reflects a near breakdown of a familiar form in the face of impossible worldly pressures.[3] Yet

[1] The dating of both poems remains conjectural. The dialectal evidence of the poems in B.M. MS. Cotton Nero A.x suggests a date between 1360 and 1390 for *Pearl*. The first version of *Piers* is usually dated about 1362. Internal evidence points to a date of 1376–77 for the B-text. The last (C-text) version is generally assigned to the 1390s.

[2] Spenser's *Faerie Queene* must be regarded as a consciously archaic, humanized manifestation of the visionary quest form. It should be studied as a Renaissance translation of the mode described in Chapter Four along lines already suggested by Rosamund Tuve (*Allegorical Imagery* [Princeton, 1966]).

[3] Several early critics of *Piers* have recorded their dismay at apparent confusion and digressions in the longer versions of the poem. Manly, for example, (*Cambridge History of English Literature*, 1908) says of the B-text:

> Some scholars have regarded the poem as unfinished; others, as showing by the nature of its ending the pessimism of its author. It is true that it ends unsatis-

the poet also posits, perhaps more forcefully than ever before, that eschatological idealism which is a hallmark of the later medieval visionary quest.
Piers (and Langland) war against human failure and boldly point the
way on a journey to an ultimate historical moment beyond the chaos of
the contemporary world. Langland's is finally a complex mode which
defies even as it employs the themes and techniques of the quest form.[4]
His poetic voice represents a decisive, irreversible shift in perspective from
the sureness of a soul *in aevo* to the linear uncertainties of a spirit *in
medias res*, desperately dreaming of finality. Yet the tough-minded, hard
won, unifying optimism hidden in Langland's art may be, in its way,
no less potent than the *Pearl* poet's for those who will "loke on boke and
rede aryʒt." And this is particularly true for the contemporary reader.

TRADITION AND FORM

The continental visionary quests of thirteenth-century France were, as we
have seen, intended as guidebooks for the sinning Christian, preparing
him expressly for Easter and the celebration of man's redemption. Their
purpose was formally hortatory and their final success was explicitly the
conversion of the listener to prayer, penance and a life of humility. Led
by a dreaming narrator, the audience would encounter the deadly sins,
pass through the houses of confession and mercy and arrive finally before

---

factorily, and that one or more visions might well have been added; but it may be
doubted whether the author ever could have written an ending that would have
been artistically satisfactory. He had . . . no skill in composition, no control of his
materials or his thought (II, 28).

Langland's merit, Manly concludes, lies in his sincerity:

The very lack of control, which is his most serious defect as an artist, serves to
emphasize most convincingly his sincerity and emotional power, by the inevitable-
ness with which at every opportunity he drifts back to the subjects that lie nearest
his heart (II, 29).

Such an evaluation, negative as it is with regard to *Piers'* aesthetic unity, is not
unreasonable and must be accounted for in any effort to describe Langland's unique
artistry.

[4] Dorothy Owen (*Piers Plowman*, London, 1912), Morton Bloomfield (*Piers Plowman as a Fourteenth Century Apocalypse*, New Brunswick, 1962) and Ann Wood
(*Long Will and his Dreams*, unpublished Harvard diss., 1970) have provided three of
the most useful and illuminating studies of Piers' generic kinship. The last of these,
together with Elizabeth Kirk, *The Dream Thought of Piers Plowman* (New Haven,
1972), I came upon too late for them to be of use in the present essay, but the first
two have provided invaluable assistance.

the throne of the Lamb in the New Jerusalem. At least some of the vision quests were explicitly intended to be read aloud over the course of several days but the poems are equally suited to silent meditation.[5] The poet's task, like the sculptor's or the illuminator's, was to mark as clearly and forcefully as possible the way to salvation through examination of conscience, contrition, confession, and a firm purpose of amendment. The stance of the listener or reader was to be a meditative one. With devotion and concentration he would hold the *series imaginum* in his mind, helped by the "places" in which he found the images. Day by day during Holy Week he would review the state of his soul, recall the mercy of God, and look forward to the great feast of the Resurrection.

In its basic outline, *Piers Plowman* follows the pattern of its continental kin, setting out cumulatively enriching materials for a thorough examination of conscience. The B-text (which will serve as the basis for this study) can be divided into seven sections, providing seven interrelated readings, each sixty to ninety minutes in length.

1st Meditation	Prologue and Passus I–IV	Introduction of Holichurch and Lady Mede; the "places" of Truth and Falsehood; lessons concerning society's reform according to reason and conscience.
2nd Meditation	Passus V–VII	Procession and repentance of seven deadly sins; introduction of Piers, the honest plow-

---

[5] Langland's poem, like Dante's, may well have been intended to be read and meditated silently. Its complexities, together with the fact of the highly personalized character of Will as model for the quest, would suggest that the poem was to serve the private prayer life of the solitary reader. But the question requires more thorough study of the text and manuscripts. Certainly there are clear precedents both for penitential exercises intended to be read aloud and those to be studied and glossed silently by the reader. On the one hand, Guillaume de Deguileville's long and popular vision poem, *Le Pèlerinage de Vie Humaine* (1330–32 and 1355) provides directions for oral reading to a community over the course of several days (see ll. 5055–5066; 9046–9054; 11,395–11,406). By contrast, Dante's *Commedia*, with the poet's several addresses to his *readers*, was clearly intended for silent meditation. (See esp. L. Spitzer, "The Addresses to the Reader in the *Commedia*," *Italica* XXXII (1955), pp. 143–165, and E. Auerbach, *Literary Language and its Public in Late Antiquity and in the Middle Ages* trans. R. Manheim [New York, 1965], pp. 297–317). For study of the question with regard to *Piers Plowman*, see J. A. Burrow, "The Audience of *Piers Plowman*," *Anglia* LXXV (1957), pp. 373–384.

		man, as an example of truth and social love in human garb; Piers' pardon sent from Truth.
3rd Meditation	Passus VIII–X	*Vita Dowel*: a personified excursion into Will's soul and the meaning of "Doing Well."
4th Meditation	Passus XI–XII	Will's vision of his moral life from its beginning; introduction of Imaginatif as guide and prophet.
5th Meditation	Passus XIII–XIV	Conclusion of *Vita Dowel*: theological banquet of Clergy and Scripture, Conscience, Patience and Will; Patience's and Conscience's encounter with Haukyn, the Active Man, guilty of all sins of fleshly concupiscence, saved at last by repentance and God's mercy.
6th Meditation	Passus XV–XVII	*Vita Dobet*: Anima's anatomy of Church history; the Tree of Charity and reappearance of Piers; emergence of Faith, Hope and Love in human history.
7th Meditation	Passus XVIII–XX	Conclusion of *Vita Dobet*: Christ's passion, death and harrowing of hell; the *Vita Dobest*: the life of "unity-holichurch" born of Christ's death and resurrection; initiation of conflict with Antichrist.

As the narrator, Will moves through his visions, we can follow (albeit with difficulty) his gradual discovery of the way to repentance and spiritual perfection. At the end of the *Vita Dobet* (xviii), after he has dreamed of Christ's redemption, he determines, as the audience should, to go off to Easter Mass: "Ariseth and reuerenceth goddes resurrexioun,/ And crepeth to the crosse on knees and kisseth it for a Iuwel," (427–428; k-d 427–428) he orders his wife and daughter.[6]

But while Langland used the basic form of the continental penitential quest aimed at converting souls for the Easter feast, he turned it to more complex use. Not only concerned with the conversion of the individual soul, he also studies with prophetic urgency the need for converting the whole society.[7] His narrator is both Everyman of all ages and fourteenth-century fallen man (perhaps quite like himself) moving toward an imminent and much-needed eschaton. Langland extends and complicates Will's field of vision to include not only his own soul but the entire world, both immediate and cosmic; and he designs his narrative to encompass all time in man's search for the Trinity, to be fully revealed at the end of the present age. In this widening of perspective, Langland shared with prophets, poets, historians and artists of the later Middle Ages a sense of the special importance of his own place in the history of salvation.

Like Joachim of Fiore,[8] St. Francis of Assisi, St. Dominic, the designers of many an illustrated Apocalypse, Dante, and his own later contemporary, St. Vincent Ferrer, the poet could imagine for his audience the com-

---

[6] In this discussion, I am assuming single authorship for the whole of the b-version though there is certainly some justification for the possibility of several authors. But in such a case, these hypothetical authors would have had to comprise an unusually close fellowship of like-minded religious reformers who understood the complex thematic and narrative directions set by the a-text and could see them to a fitting and significant conclusion. Not only a thorough knowledge of vernacular vision-quest literature and a subtle sense of the narrator's character and role, but also close contact with later medieval prophetic tradition would have been required of them all. All quotations are from the b-text, ed. W. W. Skeat, *The Visions of Will Concerning Piers the Plowman* (Oxford, 1886). Although the new edition by G. Kane and E. T. Donaldson (*Piers Plowman: the B Version* [London, 1975]) appeared too late for use in this study, line references to the new edition (K-D) follow those to Skeat in the text.

[7] Professor Bloomfield was the first to demonstrate the social nature of Will's quest. He argues persuasively that Langland's social concern is traceable to older monastic ideals of a utopia on earth (*Piers Plowman*, 1962).

[8] In 1938, W. H. Wells first suggested a comparison between Langland's historical schema and Joachim of Fiore's prophetic descriptions of an Age of the Spirit ("The

pletion of God's historical revelation to man: the coming and defeat of
Antichrist, a short time of peace on earth, and then the eternal Sabbath.
At the end of Passus xix, the questing Will shows us in vision an histori-
cal movement toward the conversion of the world to Unity-Holichurch.
After Christ's resurrection, the apocalyptic harvest of the faithful becomes
a critical concern (B. xix, 314–330).

Once a personified house of humility has been built, Conscience and
Kynde Wit draw all Christians to it:

> There nas no Crystene creature that kynde witte hadde,
> Saue schrewes one suche as I spak of,
> That he ne halpe a quantite holynesse to wexe.
> Somme þorw bedes-byddynge and somme þorw pylgrymage,
> And other pryue penaunce and some þorw penyes-delynge.
> And thanne welled water for wikked werkes,
> Egerlich ernynge out of mennes eyen.
> Clennesse of the comune and clerkes clene lyuynge
> Made Vnite holicherche in holynesse to stonde.
>
> (B. xix, 370–378; K-D, 372–380)

Even as this passage was being read by the faithful of the late fourteenth
century, Vincent Ferrer had begun preaching of just such an age of peace
near at hand:

> Aquarius figures the eleventh state of this world after the death of Anti-
> christ, since then the sun of justice will be in Aquarius, for then all gen-
> erations of the infidels will be baptized. Oh, there will be such a pressure
> for baptism, there will not be enough priests. Then the prophecy of
> Ezekiel will be completed: I will take you from among the peoples. I
> will gather you from the whole world and lead you into your land.[9]

For Langland, both the perfection of the human race, and its converse,
total degradation in love of the world had to be realized before mankind

---

Philosophy of Piers Plowman," *PMLA*, LIII (1938), pp. 339–349. More recently, Professor Bloomfield has pointed to analogies without committing himself to insistence
on direct influence. See *Piers Plowman*, Appendix I, 157–160.

[9] Quoted by Marjorie Reeves in the *Influence of Prophecy in the Later Middle
Ages* (Oxford, 1969):

> Aquarius . . . et figurat undecimum statum mundi huius futurum post mortem
> Antichristi, quia tunc sol iustitiae erit in aquario: nam tunc omnes generationes
> infidelium baptizabuntur. O qualis pressura erit ad baptismum, non sufficient
> clerici! . . . Tunc complebitur prophetia Ezechielis: Tollam quippe vos de genti-
> bus et congregabo vos de universis terris et adducam vos in terram vestram, scilicet
> ecclesiam militantem . . . (171).

would enter the city of peace. In this last stage of human history, the good would be ruled by the Holy Spirit in an ideally spiritual church. Then Christ, who bridged the gap between fallen man and divine truth, would be joined by man renewed, spiritually free and living fully a life of unity and brotherhood. Then,

> . . . kynde loue shal come ʒit and conscience togideres,
> And make of lawe a laborere suche loue shal arise,
> And such a pees amonge the peple and a perfit trewthe,
> That Iewes shal wene in here witte and waxen wonder glade,
> That Moises or Messie be come in-to this erthe,
> And haue wonder in here hertis that men beth so trewe.
>
> (B. III, 297–302; K-D, 299–304)

It is in expectation of this moment that Langland measures Will's final achievement and extends the traditional form of his poem almost to the breaking point.

The First Meditation: Prologue and Passus i–iv

The Prologue

Langland begins his prologue, as we might have expected, by introducing his narrator. The protagonist's spiritual blindness at the opening of *Piers* is comparable to that of *Pearl's* jeweler, though the particulars differ. With a guilelessness characteristic of souls unaware of their moral plight, Will presents himself as a wanderer who has given up all attachment to social forms, dressed himself in the costume (or disguise) of a shepherd-hermit, and begun a search for wonders "in this worlde:"

> In a somer seson whan soft was the sonne,
> I shope me in shroudes as I a shepe were,
> In habite as an heremite vnholy of workes,
> Went wyde in this world wondres to here. (1–4; K-D, 1–4)

In a swift juxtaposition of significant images—the hermit's habit, the shepherd's shrouds, and the journey or pilgrimage—Langland's Will unwittingly draws together a rich, coherent framework through which the reader may both judge the wanderer's serious flaws and anticipate the necessary directions of the visionary poem.

A long and venerable tradition attached to the English hermit—including hermits roaming over the Malvern hills where Will locates his own adventures.[10] Theirs was preeminently the responsibility of "seeing" and interpreting divine omens. While monastic writers habitually traced their lineage to Old and New Testament prophets—Elias, Eliseus, John the Baptist—hermits, who preferred the wilderness and solitude to human companionship, had particularly arrogated the prophetic role to themselves. Will, then, should have been especially fitted by virtue of the dress he had assumed, to interpret visions and lead Christians toward salvation. But his habit is a disguise. He has taken on the outer dress of eremitic life, yet has apparently given no thought to its meaning for his soul.

Such inattention to spirit in favor of outward show is not unusual in this world, as Langland will fully demonstrate in the prologue. But it has particular significance for those who profess to practice the highest Christian life. The earliest and most influential monastic literature had insisted on the importance of the monk's clothing as a sign of his spiritual state and a means of entering into God's mysteries.[11] John Cassian devotes the first chapter of his seminal *Institutes* to a consideration of monastic dress as it reveals a man's special election and responsibility, "for when we have seen the external ornament, then we can explain their inner conditon."[12] Thus Will's costuming himself as a hermit reveals the possibility of a high vocation as prophet, but a possibility which our hero has carelessly—even unconsciously—rejected.

The narrator's second description of his garb—a shepherd's shroud—further defines the nature of his irresponsibility and seems to place him in an especially condemned class of spiritual drifters. St. Benedict had called attention to them in his rule: they were the "sarabaites" who are "without a shepherd, outside the Lord's flocks, but enclosed in their own."[13] So Will, taking upon *himself* the dress and role of shepherd,

---

[10] See M. R. Clay, *The Hermits and Anchorites of England* (London, 1914), pp. 146 ff.; D. Knowles, *The Monastic Orders in England* (Cambridge, 1963), p. 78.

[11] See P. P. Oppenheim, O.S.B., *Das Mönchskleid im Christlichen Alterum* (Freiburg, 1931), pp. 229–246.

[12] Joannes Cassianus, *De institutis cœnobiorum*, ed. M. Petschenig, CSEL XVII (Vienna, 1888), I, I, p. I.

[13] *Benedicti regula*, ed. R. Hanslik (Vienna, 1960), p. 18; see also J. Leclercq, "Le poem de Payen Bolotin contre les faux Ermites," *Revue Benedictine* LXVIII (1958), esp. p. 77:

> Ordinis expers, ordo nefandus, pellibus agni
> Cum sit amictus, uult reputari religiosus,
> Nec tamen actis religionem testificatur. (1–3)

rejects the true shepherd, Christ, as well as his surrogates, St. Peter and the abbot.

Finally, as a "wanderer," Langland's narrator falls into yet another class of false hermits decried by Benedict and often castigated in later spiritual literature. He is a "gyrovagus"—one of those who "all their life long, ever restless and never stationary, . . . are slaves of their own moods and love of luxury."[14] While Will's pleasures are simple, they, rather than spiritual discipline, guide him. As a wanderer seeking wonders "in *this* world," he rejects the central and necessary pilgrimage of the soul *from* this world toward the heavenly city.[15]

Will's attachment to this world also bears a clear resemblance to the singular fault of literary visionaries from the *De consolatione philosophiae* onward. Boethius, who created Will's most famous and authoritative ancestor in this plight, had defined the foolishness of taking up such aimless worldly wandering. But he had also demonstrated that it is an inevitable activity for Everyman confronted with himself in the world. Boethius, Huon de Méri's wandering soldier, *Amant* of the *Roman de la Rose*, Pearl's jeweler, Langland's shepherd—all have expected to find wonders in the world in neglect of the world within, the "treuth in hert," which is the only proper object of human searchings.

Like his comrades-in-quest, Will is sleepy and fallen, totally unprepared to discover Truth in his heart or to infuse it into the social order. He has gone out to hear "wondres," he tells us, but the day is so lovely and the sound of the stream where he lingers so enticing that he falls asleep:

> Ac on a May mornynge on Maluerne hulles
> Me byfel a ferly of fairy me thou3te;
> I was wery forwandred and went me to reste
> Vnder a brode banke bi a bornes side,
> And as I lay and lened and loked in the wateres,
> I slombred in a slepyng it sweyued so merye.
> (B. *Prol.* 5–10; K–D, 5–10)

Yet like his literary forebears and contemporaries, this slightly absurd, slightly comic seeker after wonders also possesses just those qualities re-

---

[14] *Benedicti regula*, p. 19; Morton Bloomfield was the first to call attention to Will's similarities to Benedict's *gyrovagi* (*Piers Plowman*, pp. 24–25 and 69–71).

[15] The motif of the hermit (and Everyman) as pilgrim in this world was an ancient one to which Will apparently pays no heed as he sets off in search of wonders. See J. Leclercq, "Monachisme et pérégrination du IXe au XIIe siècle," *Studia Monastica* III (1961), pp. 33–52.

quired to study a soul's halting movement toward grace—openness, optimism, above all, a *willingness* to see wonders.

But besides casting Will as Everyman of all time in his fallen state, Langland has also wedded him to his own historical moment in England of the later 1300s. As a Christian living in the evening of the world he cannot rest content with the salvation of his own soul. He has no choice but to accept his responsibility to convert society according to the ancient Christian and monastic ideals of social unity. By God's grace and the demands of his own time, Will must become a prophet. He is to discover the world in its absolute truth and falsehood. As he examines the fabric of history, he will learn how the three persons of the Trinity have been revealed to man through time and this temporal learning process will constitute an important basis for the long narrative. He will also perceive the arrival of Antichrist on the threshold of the eschaton. For in these last days of the world's history, absolute Truth and Falsehood have already begun to prepare for their final apocalyptic battle. Thus complexly characterized, Will is to serve as a filter for all our perceptions of his visionary experience. As a fallible self-deceiving pilgrim, he is not to be trusted entirely. Yet because he is also a prophet, his visions assume, at times, an authority and stability not unlike that of the scriptural prophets. Langland leaves it to the audience's judgment to discern and distinguish.

Will begins his first vision in the prologue as he reports the appearance of a surrealistic, nightmarish setting:

> . . . I was in a wildernesse wist I neuer where,
> As I bihelde in-to the est an hiegh to the sonne,
> I seigh a toure on a toft trielich ymaked;
> A depe dale binethe a dongeon there-inne,
> With depe dyches and derke and dredful of sight.
> A faire felde ful of folke fonde I there bytwene,
> Of alle maner of men the mene and the riche,
> Worchyng and wandryng as the worlde asketh.
>   (B. *Prol.* 12–19)

This scene bears some resemblance to the sun-capped hill and fearful valley of Dante's opening vision in the *Commedia*. But in its simplicity and symbolic directness, it more closely parallels an iconographical scheme which appears in contemporary Anglo-Norman and English Apocalypses. Illustrations show a tower on a hill next to which Christ in glory sits in a mandorla. At the bottom of the hill is a great hole with the feet of a fiend disappearing into the abyss and the seven-headed beast directing his progress. On either side stand the people of the world, those on the right dead, those on the left alive and militant (Fig. 22). But whereas the Apocalypse illustrators give the scene clear eschatological significance, Langland witholds direct interpretation. Instead he relies on Will's pregnant silences to initiate a tone of unspecified anxiety—even terror—which will dominate the whole prologue.

In the next portion of the opening vision, the narrator's eyes take us from this panoramic overview to a close penetrating look at the folk who people the field. Good and evil members of human society appear in rapid succession, "worchyng and wandryng as the worlde asketh" (19). A melée of minstrels and merchants, farmers and hermits, pursue their manifold interests chiefly according to the dictates of greed. So great is the pressure of concrete detail in this catalogue that it seems scarcely reducible to the spiritual function proper to such prologues. The proud in their finery, worthless and false beggars, lying jongleurs, anchorites at home in prayer and penance, friars, parsons selling benefices in London to escape the penury imposed by the plague—all move confusedly across Will's field of vision.

Yet if we move back somewhat from Will's report, the crowded details in this scene assume a shape which is not without contemporary parallels. We have already seen how scriptural commentators and designers of illustrated Apocalypses had been able to discover in the traditional eschatological scenes images of the society which had begun to embody them. Langland's illustrations likewise emphasize a dynamic tension between St. John's apocalyptic prophecy and the events of present history. Through Will's bitter, satiric comment on the vivid scene, the poet first exemplifies Everyman's dismay from the beginning of time, pondering the cruelty of his race, its injustice and avarice, aware in a bewildered way of a better society, but little able to effect it. Then his narrator imposes an eschatological interpretation on empirical experience, as if driven by desperation. His critique rises to an authoritative and prophetic level. With the assurance of a Wyclif, Will (certainly speaking for Langland and embodying with a vengeance the late medieval visionary perspective) condemns the greed and hypocrisy of clergy and laity alike. He calls at last on the judgment of Doomsday for comfort against his distress and anger:

> drede is at the laste
> Lest crist in consistorie acorse ful manye.
>
> (B. *Prol.* 98–99; K-D, 98–99)

Then, as if an inner curtain had been lifted, we are carried by the narrator's vision abruptly from the foreground of the fair field to its eternal presence in heaven and hell. Under the aegis of apocalyptic "dred," Will is given a glimpse of the Church's real power when it was ruled by Peter and the cardinal virtues, and then its failure in a court governed by imperfect cardinals:

> I parceyued of the power that Peter had to kepe,
> To bynde and to vnbynde as the boke telleth,
> How he it left with loue as owre lorde hight,
> Amonges foure vertues the best of alle vertues,
> That cardinales ben called and closyng ʒatis,
> There crist is in kyngdome to close and to shutte,
> And to opne it to hem and heuene blisse shewe.
> Ac of the cardinales atte Courte that cauʒt of that name,
> And power presumed in hem a pope to make,
> To han that power that Peter hadde inpugnen I nelle;
> For in loue and letterure the eleccioun bilongeth,
> For-thi I can and can nauʒte of courte speke more.
>
> (B. *Prol.* 100–111; K-D, 100–111)

Through this abrupt shift from concrete detail to abstract "power," from creatures named to names, Langland deftly defines a twofold concern of the narrative: the movement inward and heavenward and the movement through time. For his complex literary and spiritual goal, the poet required terms to instruct the soul in its eternal aspect and also to represent humankind's historical progress toward salvation. Personifications and emblems could fill the first requirement: the tower, the dungeon and field, the cardinal virtues, Truth and Holichurch, Falsehood and Lady Mede, Conscience, Kynde Wit, Reason, Scriptures, Imaginatif, Gluttony, Lechery and the whole cast of abstract subjects depict the qualities or "places" for which their names stand eternally hovering over all human history as well as entering into it. On the other hand, the large troop of exemplary and scriptural personages—Will, cardinals, plowmen, minstrels and hawkers drawn from the streets, cathedrals, monasteries and courts of fourteenth-century England, angels, Abraham, Moses, Christ, Piers—meet the second need. Through them Langland shows the gradual historical realization of eternal good and evil at many points in time all through the course of salvation history. His complex intermingling of a double terminology allows the poet to reveal the qualities of Truth and Falsehood in abstract definition and also in individual souls within time's flow.

Langland also uses this twofold vocabulary to represent movements toward an historical merging of the temporal and eternal in anticipation of the grand apocalyptic conflict. When Truth has been fully realized in history and Antichrist has appeared as a man, then the final battle can be fought. In his stylistic entwining of "ideas" and history, Langland can prepare souls not only for a spiritually effective Easter but also for this last conflict. Will's double voice (or Langland's superimposed on Will's) in the prologue—as sleepy wanderer and doomsday preacher reviling the evil of the world—parallels the poem's verbal duality. The poet seems equally drawn by Everyman's lethargy and blindness and his paradoxical capacity to imagine a millennial society on earth.

Moving from Christ and the Church to Civil Justice, Langland now sets before Will's dreaming mind yet another mode of discourse and a bizarre tableau in which a Lunatic, a Goliard and an Angel teach the King what he must do in order to rule justly. This jarring sequence, as well as the fable of the belling of the cat which follows, belong to that enigmatic dream-art characteristic of prophetic and satiric literature. The narrative becomes riddling and parabolic: dark conceits cloak utopian idealism as well as cynical commentary on the actual King's and Commons' failures. At this point, the B-text poet prefers allusive drama to didactic glossing and does not interpret. Who are the Lunatic, the Goliard and the Angel? On what authority do they offer the King instruction?

The poet refuses to gloss the cat-rat fable. As Will says, "What this meteles (dream) bemeneth ȝe men that be merye,/ Deuine ȝe, for I ne dar bi dere god in heuene!" (208–209) This whole complex inner dream from cardinals to cats, which carries the audience from surfaces to intimations of metaphysical order and disorder, does not clarify attainable goals but imposes a tone of mysterious foreboding and disturbing dissonance on the world of appearances. It also demonstrates that Will (and perhaps mankind generally), may have serious difficulty understanding pregnant dreams and prophecies.

As abruptly as it had begun, this metaphysical interlude ends, and Will returns the audience to his shallower vision of the field of folk. He describes a sample of civil population passing before him, those who rule and judge and those who toil with their hands. His last glimpse of the field in the prologue offers us a devastating image of society's pettiness and godlessness. Workers call out their empty salute, "Dieu vous saue, Dame Emme," and concentrate on their stomachs:

> Cokes and here knaues crieden, 'hote pies, hote!
> Gode gris and gees gowe dyne, gowe!'
> Tauerners vn-til hem tolde the same,
> 'White wyn of Oseye and red wyn of Gascoigne,
> Of the Ryne and of the Rochel the roste to defy.'
>
> (B. *Prol.* 225–229; K-D, 226–230)

For the audience who has looked on all the visionary scenes of the prologue from a late fourteenth-century perspective, the falsehood Will perceives in the busy field has special significance. It is not only an evil time but the worst of times, for "þe moste myschief on molde is mountyng wel faste" (67). The utter materialism of a world concerned with wine and hot pies instead of the bread and wine of the Eucharist can only presage the emergence of Antichrist and apocalyptic conflict. An urgency imposed by imminent cataclysm accounts for Will's (and the poet's) tone of anger culminating in these last lines of harsh alliteration and sharp monosyllables.

Passus I–IV

> What this montaigne bymeneth and the merke dale,
> And the felde ful of folke I shal ȝow faire shewe.
>
> (B. I, 1–2; K-D, 1–2)

If the reader has shared Will's confusion in the prologue and has also attended to the poet's urgent concern, he will be prepared to seek the intricate gloss on the opening scenes, which comprises the next four passus and completes the first day's reading. But even as Langland offers clarification through his series of personified instructors in the next several passus he continues to eschew simple explication in favor of lively dramatization. He chooses always to emphasize the function of linear narrative *in the process of* revealing eternal truth.

First of all, Will, like other literary visionaries, spies a lovely lady coming down from a castle. In her opening address to him, the lady echoes both the reprimands of Boethius' Philosophia and the hard lesson of the Apocalypse glosses:

> '. . . Sone! slepestow? sestow this people,
> How bisi thei ben abouten the mase?

The moste partie of this poeple that passeth on this erthe,
Haue their worschip in this worlde thei wilne no better;
Of other heuene than here holde thei no tale.'

(B. I, 5–9; K-D, 5–9)[16]

Then, without revealing her identity, she interprets the omnitemporal significance of the tower and dungeon Will had seen in the prologue. "The
toure vp the toft . . . Treuthe is there-inne," she explains. The "truth" she
details is not mystical but ethical, concerned with the regulation of this
world's goods and maintenance of just social order. Her scheme for
moral truth falls under the rubric "mesure is medcyne":

Who-so trewe is of his tonge and telleth none other,
And doth the werkis ther-with and wilneth no man ille,
He is a god bi the gospel agrounde and aloft,
And ylike to owre lorde bi seynte Lukes wordes.

(B. I, 88–91; K-D, 88–91)

This simple, stern definition of "treuth" corresponds closely to the opening of St. Benedict's rule.[17] Such a coincidence is not surprising when we

---

[16] Thus Philosophia had condemned Boethius for his sleeping, dulled mind (bk. I,
poem I). Contemporary Apocalypse glosses preached in words nearly approximating
these used by Holichurch: "Þe most partie of the world folowe antecrist and his deci-
ples þat now given hem to flesslich likynges" (Elise Fridner, An English Fourteenth
Century Apocalypse Version with a Prose Commentary [Lund, 1961], p. 145).

[17] St. Benedict opens his handbook for monks with admonitions directly echoed
by Langland's Holichurch:

Exurgamus ergo tandem aliquando excitante nos scriptura ac dicente: Hora est
nos de somno surgere; et apertis oculis nostris ad deificum lumen adtonitis auribus
audiamus, diuina cotidie clamans quid nos admonet uox dicens: Hodie si vocem
eius audieritis, nolite obdurare corda uestra; et iterum: Qui habet aures audiendi,
audiat, quid spiritus dicat ecclesiis. Et quid dicit? Uenite, filii, audite me, timorem
domini docebo uos. Currite, dum lumen uitae habetis, ne tenebrae mortis uos con-
prehendant. Et quaerens dominus in multitudinem populi, cui haec clamat, opera-
rium suum iterum dicit: Quis est homo, qui uult uitam et cupit uidere dies bonos?
Quod si tu audiens respondeas: Ego, dicit tibi deus: Si uis habere ueram et per-
petuam uitam, prohibe linguam tuam a malo et labia tua ne loquantur dolum;
deuerte a malo et fac bonum, inquire pacem et sequere eam. Et cum haec feceritis,
oculi mei super uos et aures meae ad preces uestras, et antequam me inuocetis,
dicam uobis: Ecce adsum. Quid dulcius nobis ad hac uoce domini inuitantis nos,
fratris carissimi? Ecce pietate sua demonstrat nobis dominus uiam uitae. Succinctis
ergo fide uel obseruantia bonorum actuum lumbis nostris per ducatum evangelii
pergamus itineraria eius, ut mereamur eum, qui nos vocauit in regnum suum, ui-

remember that the visionary quest as a literary form originated in the
monasteries. Both St. Benedict and Langland make measure and good
works the basis for heavenly bliss. For both of them these two counsels
should govern man in the first stage of his spiritual development and
provide a framework for the most fundamental examination of conscience.

But Langland also grounds his first spiritual instruction in a grand historical and eschatological context. According to his narrative scheme, this
initial aspect of Truth belongs preeminently to the Age of the Father:

> For he is fader of feith fourmed ȝow alle,
> Bothe with fel and with face and ȝaf ȝow fyue wittis
> Forto worschip hym ther-with the while that ȝe ben here.
> And therfore he hyȝte the erthe to help ȝow vchone
> Of wollen, of lynnen of lyflode at nede,
> In mesurable manere to make ȝow at ese.
>
> (B. I, 14–19; K-D, 14–19)

---

dere. In cuius regni tabernaculo si uolumus habitare, nisi illuc bonis actibus curri-
tur, minime peruenitur. Sed interrogemus cum propheta dominum dicentes ei:
Domine, *quis habitauit in tabernaculo tuo aut quis requiescit in monte sancto tuo?*
Post hanc interrogationem, fratres, audiamus dominum respondentem et ostenden-
tem nobis uiam ipsius tabernaculi dicens: *Qui ingreditur sine macula et operatur
iustitiam; qui loquitur ueritatem in corde suo; qui non egit dolum in lingua sua;
qui non fecit proximo suo malum; qui opprobrium non accepit aduersus proximum
suum. (Benedicti regula, Prol.* 8–27, pp. 3–5).

An even more exact parallel for this Benedictine text occurs a little later in Passus III
as Concience defines the truth which brings heavenly reward:

> 'There aren two manere of medes my lorde, with ȝowre leue.
> That one, god of his grace graunteth in his blisse
> To tho that wel worchen whil thei ben here.
> The phophete precheth ther-of and put it in the sautere,
>   *Domine quis habitabit in tabernaculo tuo?*
> "Lorde, who shall wonye in thi wones and with thine holi seyntes,
> Or resten on thi holy hilles?" this asketh Dauid;
> And Dauyd assoileth it hymself as the sauter telleth,
>   *Qui ingreditur sine macula, et operatur iusticiam,*
> Tho that entren of o colour and of on wille,
> And han wrouȝte werkis with riȝte and with reson;
> And he that ne vseth nauȝte the lyf of vsurye,
> And enfourmeth pore men and pursueth treuthe.'
>
> (B. III, 230–240; K-D, 231–241)

During this "time," in the poetic narrative and also in human history, man must learn how to refer all his actions to the creator whom he worships at a distance. Like "treuth," the Father of Falsehood who dwells in the dungeon also belongs, for the moment, to the Old Testament, though we shall eventually see how he spans all history. But now he is shown to derive from the time of Adam and Cain (B. I, 61–70). These "places" of Truth and Falsehood thus historically and metaphysically defined by Will's guide will stand through the rest of the poem as two poles against which to judge all the poetic action. Remembering the images of the tower and the dungeon and the significance accorded them, Will and the reader alike may be able to bring together the manifold appearances of good and evil represented throughout the long narrative. Only then can they fully grasp both the historical and eternal import of the two emblems.

But who is the lady who knows the meaning of the visionary prologue. Will asks her finally "What she were witterli that wissed me so faire" (B. I, 73). Like Dante and the *Pearl* poet, Langland not only enjoys riddles but also uses them to effective purpose. Before he reveals his lady's identity, the poet identifies her as wise, stern and concerned. Then he allows her to give her name and to describe herself in Boethian language:

'Holicherche I am . . . thow ouȝtest me to knowe,
I vnderfonge the firste and the feyth tauȝte,
And brouȝtest me borwes my biddyng to fulfille,
And to loue me lelly the while thi lyf dureth.'
                    (B. I, 75–78; K-D, 75–78)

Will abruptly kneels before her and, like the jeweler of *Pearl* to his maiden, meekly asks her to help him save his soul. This image—Will's first gesture within his visionary quest—offers an initial model of repentance. As he kneels and prays, the aimless wanderer has become (for the moment) a seeker for truth and salvation:

Thanne I courbed on my knees and cryed hir of grace,
And preyed hir pitousely prey for my synnes,
And also kenne me kyndeli on criste to bileue,
That I miȝte worchen his wille that wrouȝte me to man;
'Teche me to no tresore but telle me this ilke,
How I may saue my soule that seynt art yholden?'
                    (B. I, 79–84; K-D, 79–84)

Because the guide is Holichurch, this action must be regarded as a sacramental one. It also indicates the social nature of Will's quest for perfection. Only through the Church on earth can he learn how to win heaven. Likewise, the whole Christian community must find its salvation in and through the sacramental agency of its mother the Church. Though Holichurch leaves Will in the midst of Passus II not to return to the dramatic action again, she will hover in a hidden, riddling way over the whole narrative. As St. Augustine had argued, hers is the role of preserving and protecting God's covenant with man from the beginning of time and prefiguring the peace of the heavenly city. In addition, the character of Holichurch had a more immediate interest for a visionary poet in the evening of the world. In contemporary commentaries on the Apocalypse, she was recognized as the principal subject of St. John's prophecy:

> E est sa matire en ceste livere especiaument le estat del eglise de Asye, e generaument tutte seinte Eglise, nomement ceo ke ele sueffre en ceste vie, ceo ke ele receivera en l'autre. Sa intention est de amonester a patience, kar, tut seient les labures et les tribulations de ceste vie grevus a suffrir, il passent aucun hore, e le guerdon durra sanz fin.[18]

> (The matter of this book is especially the state of the Church of Asia, and generally, of all Holichurch: What she suffers in this life and what she will receive in the other. Its intention is to admonish to patience because although the labours and tribulations of this life are painful to endure, they pass in an hour and the reward will last without end.)

Like such Apocalypse glosses, and like Gothic cathedral sculpture, Langland's poem undertakes to analyze the whole history of the Church in anticipation of the Apocalypse. For his social and historical purpose, Holichurch, rather than the mystical Grace-Dieu of Deguileville's poem, or Dante's Beatrice, or the *Pearl* poet's mysterious maiden, must be the guide as well as the goal of the narrator's quest.

As he draws us from the "treuth" of Passus I to a new episode in Passus II, Will remains on his knees in his penitential pose. With reverence, he asks how he can know Falsehood and he thereby precipitates

---

[18] Fridner, *A Fourteenth-Century Apocalypse*, p. 4:
And specialich/ þe Matier of þis book draweþ to þe chirches of Asye. And/ comunelich of al holy chirche namelich þat it suffreþ in þis lyue/ & þat it shal resceyue in þat oþere. He entent is to amo/ nesten to be pacient for þorouȝ þouȝt alle pe tribulaciouns & þe an/ guisshes ben hard & stronge forto suffren sumtyme. & þerfore/ þe mede is endeles.

Holichurch's further instruction, not by doctrine but the indirection of drama. The dream images of moral evil which now pass through Will's imagination and balance the expositon of "treuth" are partly caricatures based on the actual courtiers, clergy and commons of contemporary England. But they are equally related to the text and commentaries for St. John's Apocalypse. Mede herself is an Englished fourteenth-century image of the Whore of Babylon:[19]

> I loked on my left half as the lady me taughte,
> And was war of a womman wortheli yclothed,
> Purfiled with pelure the finest vpon erthe,
> Y-crounede with a corone the kyng hath non better.
> Fetislich hir fyngres were fretted with golde wyre,
> And there-on red rubyes as red as any glede,
> And diamantz of derrest pris and double manere safferes,
> Orientales and ewages enuenymes to destroye.
> Hire robe was ful riche of red scarlet engreyned,
> With ribanes of red golde and of riche stones.
>   (B. II, 7–16; K-D, 7–16)

For Langland, as for many a contemporary artist, the Whore of Babylon has moved irretrievably from the pages of Scripture into the midst of his own society. When Langland introduces her into his narrative, she is not yet mounted on the back of the beast, but she is to wed the worldly, contemporary False Fickle-Tongue through the agency of Favel (B. II, 41–42).

To give even greater point to his witty, amusing, but savage depiction of the elegantly dressed Mede's struggle for power against Reason and Conscience, Langland "places" Will and the reader on the road to Westminster and in its chambers. In this choice, he transforms the more commonly used visionary routes to hell and its halls into the present social world: contemporary England has become an inferno. At the same time, the poet dramatizes the absurdity of falsehood in his extravagantly personalized caricatures of evil of which this example is typical:

> Thanne was Falsenesse fayne and Fauel as blithe,
> And leten sompne alle segges in schires aboute,
> And bad hem alle be bown beggeres and othere,

---

[19] Robertson and Huppé have exhaustively explored the relationship between Mede and the Whore of Babylon in their *Piers Plowman and Scriptural Tradition* (Princeton, 1951).

To wenden wyth hem to Westmynstre to witnesse this dede.
Ac thanne cared thei for caplus to kairen hem thider,
And Fauel fette forth thanne folus ynowe;
And sette Mede vpon a schyreue shodde al newe,
And Fals sat on a sisoure that softlich trotted,
And Fauel on a flaterere fetislich atired.

(B. II, 157–165; K-D, 158–166)

In such pictures as this, Langland has out-Chaucered Chaucer. The color-ful procession to Canterbury has been translated into a searing satire with none of the blandishments of outward disguise to soften its impact. No audience could be confused about Langland's attitude toward the false-hood of a materialistic society. His images of Mede's wedding procession as well as the events at Westminster must arouse both amusement and disgust in reader and dreamer alike and cause them to judge severely the scenes at hand. Through the lively drama of Lady Mede betrothed to Fals, traveling to Westminster to win the King's approval, Langland reminds his audience of the ease with which desire for earthly reward enters into the hearts of the court as well as the commons. At all times in human history, as this instance illustrates, Mede slyly unbalances the good order of the commonweal.

Like Holichurch, Lady Mede will disappear from the dramatic action shortly. But her presence will continue throughout the long narrative in a wide variety of guises until she assumes her final form at Antichrist's coming in Passus xx. Like the truth taught by Holichurch, this first form of falsehood imaged in Lady Mede—the desire for earthly reward coupled with an unwillingness to work—has special reference to the Age of the Father and the first stages of spiritual regeneration. For in those first days of restoration, God required only that Adam and Eve should work hon-estly by the sweat of their brow and live in social concord, justice and love. Here in Passus II, then, the poet delineates man's fundamental sin against the Old Law—earthly greed and a failure to live honestly. He also presents his first mnemonic set-piece—a charter wittily linking various sins with alliterating titles of earthly power and possession:

And Fauel with his fikel speche feffeth bi this chartre
To be prynces in pryde and pouerte to dispise
To bakbite, and to bosten and bere fals witnesse,
To scorne and to scolde and sclaundere to make,
Vnboxome and bolde to breke the ten hestes;

And the erldome of enuye and wratthe togideres,
With the chastelet of chest and chateryng-oute-of-resoun,
The counte of coueitise and alle the costes aboute.

(B. II, 78–85; K-D, 79–86)

.   .   .   .

And al the lordeship of lecherye in lenthe and in brede,
As in werkes and in wordes and waitynges with eies.

(B. II, 88–89; K-D, 89–90)

This and the other set pieces in *Piers* may seem overly ingenious to some
modern readers. But for Langland's penitential purpose they clearly had
great import. They are in every case placed strategically to force the audience into a pointed, easily memorable study of their sins or the right way
to salvation. Lest the reader forget the basic lessons of contrition, confession and purpose of amendment proper to all vision quests, the poet places
his memory houses at useful intervals from beginning to end of the
B-text.

From definitions of truth and falsehood in their Old-Testament, social
sense (I–II), Langland moves Will and the audience to meditation on a
model earthly order led by an ideal king (III–IV). Conscience and Reason
become the protagonists as they urge the King to banish troublesome
Mede from the kingdom and end her deceptions. The narrative logic—
from definition to exemplification—is clear indeed in these four passus
and must elicit our delight in the symmetries of absolute good and evil
thus analytically exposed.

For a moment near the end of Passus II, the King had begun to act
in the manner proposed by Reason and Conscience and to predict a
utopian society. He had cast out Fals according to Conscience's dictates
(B. II, 192–204). But he still requires substantial counsel before true justice
and order can be achieved. With a bold idealism, Conscience prophesies
just such a perfect kingdom at the end of Passus III:

I Conscience knowe this for kynde witt me it tauȝte,
That resoun shal regne and rewmes gouerne;
And riȝte as Agag hadde happe shul somme.
Samuel shal sleen hym and Saul shal be blamed,
And Dauid shal be diademed and daunten hem alle,
And one Cristene kynge kepen hem alle.
Shal na more Mede be maistre, as she is nouthe,
Ac loue and lowenesse and lewte togederes,

Thise shul be maistres on molde treuthe to saue.
And who-so trespasseth ayein treuthe or taketh aȝein his wille,
Leute shal don hym lawe and no lyf elles.
Shal no seriaunt for here seruyse were a silke howue,
Ne no pelure in his cloke for pledyng atte barre.
Mede of mys-doeres maketh many lordes,
And ouer lordes lawes reuleth the rewmes.
Ac kynde loue shal come ȝit and conscience togideres,
And make of lawe a laborere suche loue shal arise,
And such a pees amonge the peple and a perfit trewthe,
That Iewes shal wene in here witte and waxen wonder glade,
That Moises or Messie be come in-to this erthe,
And haue wonder in here hertis that men beth so trewe.
(B. III, 282–302; K-D, 284–304)

In a parallel movement at the end of Passus IV, the lively discourse between Reason and the King which precipitates the trial of Mede also brings the utopian meditation to a momentary realization:

The kynge called Conscience and afterwardes Resoun,
And recorded that Resoun had riȝtfullich schewed,
And modilich vppon Mede with myȝte the kynge loked,
And gan wax wrothe with lawe for Mede almoste had shent it,
(B. IV, 171–174; K-D, 171–174)

.   .   .   .

Mede shal nouȝte meynprise ȝow bi the Marie of heuene!
I wil haue leute in lawe and lete be al ȝowre Ianglyng,
And as moste folke witnesseth wel wronge shal be demed.
(B. IV, 179–181; K-D, 179–181)

These extraordinary visions (or should they be called fantasies?) of a perfect Christian order assume conviction and apocalyptic urgency because they have been forged from scathing anatomies of current political scandal. The world has so far forgotten simple obedience to Moses' law and the order of just love that only cataclysm and renovation can follow.

The Second Meditation: Passus v–vii

Langland's abrupt transition from the first to the second dream—and from prophetic idealism to human failure and divine mercy—turns on a familiar topos: like the narrator of *Pearl*, Will the dreamer has awakened from sleep just as he is about to witness a further episode in the miraculous conversion of the court. Had he slept "sadder," he says, he might have seen more. But instead, he has awakened to babble on his beads—a poor substitute for the higher state of vision, but one which happily leads him back to sleep. This amusing, very human image of Will strikes a theme for the ensuing narrative. Unlike *Pearl's* jeweler, Will is granted more than one chance (chiefly because he would not otherwise be saved). Langland ties his movement toward conversion ineluctably to a process worked out in his own time and place. Only through time can anagogical experiences—visions of divine justice and mercy—begin to shape and transform his actual fallen world, informing it at least temporarily with hope and purpose.

Will's second vision of the field of folk moves the dreamer and the audience from the perspective of apocalyptic "dred" to a glimpse of God's mercy and the power of repentance. With a fresh remembrance of the first day's exercise to build on, readers, led by the narrator, must now consider Tynne the Tynker, Hogge the nedler, Pernel, Thomas, Watt, and their own souls in their concrete, pathetic singularity. In the dramatic episodes of Passus v, vi and vii we have again a clear definition of Langland's central purpose: to encourage his audience to examine their souls in their own ways and in terms of their own failings, and then to repent.

Will's second dream begins with Reason's sermon on the signs of Doomsday which serves to recapitulate the prophetic, apocalyptic overtones of the first vision. Immediately then, the figure of Repentance enters:

Thanne ran Repentance and reherced his teme,
And gert Wille to wepe water with his eyen.
(B. V, 61–62; K-D, 60–61)

His entrance, together with Will's penitentially tearful response, initiates the kindly, sympathetic, often humorous tone which will shape this day's meditation. One by one the deadly sins are removed from Prudentius' *Psychomachia* and placed in the taverns, market-places, cottages and convents of Langland's English countryside. There, full of fault, weak and unwilling to enforce strict spiritual discipline, the poet allows them to be saved only at the last minute by Repentance's stern, simple command. Poor Glutton, for instance, who sets out "to go to schrifte," is unhappily waylaid by his besetting fault. Beton the brewer offers him good ale, "peper" and "piones," a pound of garlic and a farthing's worth of fennel seed. Showing no resistance, Glutton stops in the tavern in a scene reminiscent of Raoul's *Songe d'Enfer* and is cheerfully welcomed by a crowd of confrères. After good revelry, he falls down drunk to be carried home by his wife and daughter.

Then Repentance addresses him, inspiring guilt and a renewed desire for shrift:

> 'This shewyng shrifte,' quod Repentance, 'shal be meryte to the.'
> And thanne gan Glotoun grete and gret doel to make
> for his lither lyf that he lyued hadde,
> And avowed to fast 'for hunger or for thurst
> Shal neuere fisshe on the Fryday defien in my wombe,
> Tyl Abstinence myn aunte haue ʒiue me leue;
> And ʒit haue I hated hir al my lyf-tyme.'
>
> (B. V, 385–391; K-D, 378–384)

Because this, and all the dramatic conversion experiences—as well as the whole poem—are directed toward Easter, they must point inevitably to their source not in dread but in love. The passus ends, as we might have expected, with a glorification of mankind's *felix culpa*. Paradoxically, as Langland's visionary drama vividly demonstrates, it is through human sin that the glory of Easter is made possible. Repentance briefly rehearses the story of Christ's death which brought hope to the world. In response, the sinning souls, now forgiven, conclude with a shout of praise:

> A thousand of men tho thrungen togyderes;
> Criede vpward to Cryst and to his clene moder
> To haue grace to go with hem Treuthe to seke.
>
> (B. V, 517–519; K-D, 510–512)

Within the careful rhythmic structure of Langland's narrative, the sterner, more abstract images of social order and prophecy in the first four passus are now given human substance and complexity by the joyful (if temporary) personal spiritual triumph of sinners through repentance and love.

Because they have thus repented, Langland now allows the great host of souls who peopled Passus v to prepare to seek Truth. Simultaneously he introduces the audience and Will to Piers the Plowman for the first time. Like the wise hermits of the romance tradition, Piers, who has seen fifty winters digging and delving in the service of Truth, enters the story at just the right moment. For at least two reasons, an encounter between the pilgrims and Piers is inevitable at this point in the visionary narrative. First of all, only those who have repented *can* seek St. Truth. For the moment, because of their contrition, these pilgrims have chosen a course leading to salvation. Secondly, Piers is a fitting guide for them because, as Langland has already demonstrated in Passus I and II, the first stage in spiritual development requires the proper ordering of oneself in the material world and this the plowman has clearly done. Hence he provides an ideal example and leader for humankind as he works out his salvation under the Old Testament rubric, *mesure is medcyne*.

But Langland also gives Piers a new lesson to teach. Through his character, teaching and actions, the poet will begin to move the narrative toward the unveiling of an Age of the Son. But only in the course of time. For the moment, the plowman's Manor House of Mercy (B. V, 594–637), through which the pilgrims must pass, provides a decisive thematic shift. It also offers the audience a second mnemonic set-piece by which to "place" their spiritual progress. With careful deliberation, Piers matches parts of Mercy's manse with alliterating virtues requisite for salvation. Its walls are of wit to keep will out. The "kirneles" are Christendom which saves kind. The building is buttressed with believe-or-you-won't-be-saved.

Yet finally it is mercy itself, not human merit, to which Piers directs the pilgrims:

> Mercy is a maydene there, hath myʒte ouer hem alle;
> And she is syb to alle synful and her sone also;
> And thoruʒe the helpe of hem two (hope thow none other),
> Thow myʒhte gete grace there bi so thow go bityme.
> (B. V, 644–647; K-D, 635–638)

The lesson remains allusive and prophetic. Both the plowman and his questing souls (as well as Will and the narrative style) still remain in the Age of the Father. The truth of Christ's coming can be presented only through allegory, not as history. Not until Mercy has become Mary and her "sone," Christ, will a new ethic be established for the pursuit of truth. One may think particularly in "dark" passages like this (as in the earlier prophecies of Reason and Conscience) of the familiar iconographical figures of "Synagogue" who sees the shadows of things while "Ecclesia" sees images of truth.

In the meantime, Piers, the good farmer of the Old Testament and the first stage of spiritual regeneration, must set about plowing the literal half-acre given into his care by God (B. VI, 4–6). Placed as he is in Langland's narrative *after* the exposition of the seven deadly sins, the plowman begins his social mission with a thorough-going naiveté concerning the fallen human condition. But he is a naif very different from Will. Piers is concerned and committed from the start. He intends to change the world. Though he has a great deal to learn about human weakness, he will not fail in his dedication to finding St. Truth. With pain he discovers the lovelessness and laziness of his fellow workers and watches the decline of order, measure and honest labor. Hunger rather than love becomes the goad to action (B. VI, 167–332).

It is within this sorry context—like Noah's world before the flood and Everyman's in the fair field—that Langland has Truth send Piers his famous pardon: "Dowel, and haue wel and god shal haue thi sowle,/ And do yuel, and haue yuel, and hope thow non other/ But after thi ded day the deuel shal haue thi sowle" (B. VII, 113–114; K-D, 116–118). At first this seems a sensible and fair lesson taken as it is from the Athanasian Creed. Yet, when a priest reads it aloud, he declares that it is no pardon. And then Piers, in a rage, tears the pardon up. The plowman's action is singular and inexplicable within its immediate context. Even the priest's odd rejection of a gift from Truth (and his implicit denial, therefore, of Truth's power) does not seem to warrant what amounts to a spiritual transformation in Piers.

Precisely because it does not accord with the narrative logic—or the reader's expectations—this scene has rightly called abundant critical attention to itself.[20] But if we understand Piers as a dedicated pilgrim (in Old Testament fashion) learning to take on prophetic responsibility, the action becomes clearer. In a momentary flash of luminous understanding, the plowman is allowed to see what neither Will nor the pilgrims nor the audience can. Because Truth (God) has sent the pardon, he will also provide fallen man with the power (grace and mercy) necessary for doing good and avoiding evil. The plowman's response to the priest suggests these directions. He quotes in Latin the psalmist's praise of God: "If I should walk in the valley of the shadow of death, I shall fear no evil for you are with me." In the face of the priest's worldly certainty concern-

---

[20] Rosemary Woolf gives a brief summary of major (though always conflicting) interpretations of this scene. Her close and careful reading offers a valuable alternative to my conclusions: "The Tearing of the Pardon" in S. S. Hussey, ed., *Piers Plowman: Critical Approaches* (London, 1969), pp. 50–75.

ing justice and his patent lack of hard experience, Piers sees, as if through a sudden illumination, the centrality of God for human salvation. Totally exasperated, he cries out:

I shal cessen of my sowyng . . . and swynk nouȝt so harde,
Ne about my bely-ioye so bisi be namore!
(B. VII, 118–119; K-D, 122–123)

In this speech, Langland marks Piers' spiritual "letting go." His transforming revelation is as dramatic in its power as the conversion experience of a Paul or an Augustine. And it allows the poet to introduce a transcendent order of perception, a visionary way of "seeing" his complex anatomy of mercy, merit, penance and salvation.

Abruptly the plowman has been moved from the role of compassionate laborer managing God's temporal kingdom to that of Davidic prophet:

Of preyers and of penaunce my plow shal ben herafter,
And wepen whan I shulde slepe though whete-bred me faille.
The prophete his payn ete in penaunce and in sorwe,
By that the sauter seith so dede other manye.
(B. VII, 119–122; K-D, 124–127)

In the conclusion to his diatribe, Piers prophesies a new age in the history of the world, the awakening of spiritual love. This new spirit will go beyond the meting out of material goods, turning man instead to dependence on God for material sustenance:

And, but if Luke lye he lereth vs bi foules,
We shulde nouȝt be to bisy aboute the worldes blisse;
Ne solliciti sitis he seyth in the gospel,
And sheweth vs bi ensaumples vs selue to wisse.
The foules on the felde who fynt hem mete at wynter?
Haue thei no gernere to go to, *but god fynt hem alle.*
(B. VII, 124–129; K-D, 129–135; italics mine)

Here the poet directs the noble farmer very clearly away from self-reliance and hard-working responsibility. To bring spiritual perfection to those in his care, Piers will look no longer to himself but to divine intervention through prayer and penance. At this point in the soul's reformation, Langland's narrative articulates a singular movement toward the historical realization of a perfect society. Already adumbrated in the prophecies of Reason and Conscience and in the teaching of Repentance, the poet provides the coming Age of the Son with a concrete prophet in the developing image of Piers the Plowman.

But Will (and perhaps the audience) is not yet spiritually prepared to appreciate Piers' discovery of new directions. As in *Pearl*, the poet has the ignorant narrator push his own, and our, instruction forward. Will awakens because of the noise of Piers' argument and then he undertakes to contemplate his dream. He thinks of the enigmatic visions of Nebuchadnezzar and Joseph, observing that they were fulfilled in history. But, as he considers his own dream, he, like the priest, overlooks his need for perceiving God's saving mercy and misses the prophetic import of Piers' dramatic action. Here, at the conclusion of the second reading, the audience must exercise its own judgment, examining closely the distance between the drama of the vision and Will's assessment of it.

THE THIRD MEDITATION: PASSUS VIII–X

Langland propels Will into his third vision and the third reading through the concluding double vision of Passus VII. Piers, the good plowman, has learned the need for penance and prayer. On the other hand, the ignorant Will, awakening from his dream, and unable to interpret it, believes he must find "Dowel" as his source of salvation. But what *is* Dowel? The answer has already been offered in Piers' actions and his prophecy. But the pilgrim's penchant for questioning leads him to roam the highways into what seems to be a new poem in its mode and more personal focus.[21]

The poet "places" Will "by a wilde wildernesse" and a "wode-syde," being lulled to sleep by the melody of birds. Here we are reminded not only of the scene of the prologue, but also of Huon de Méri's *Tournoiement Antechrist* and the *Roman de la Rose*. The secular, russet-robed Will, like his forebears, cannot resist the urge to wander without direction until he is gripped by the marvelous. This time, as he falls asleep, he is greeted by the "merveillousest meteles . . . that euer dremed wyȝte in worlde" (B. VIII, 68–69).

As this opening sequence of the dream suggests, Langland intends to carry us now from the cosmic movements of history into a comic yet profound probing of Will's slowly emergent inner life. Such an abrupt

[21] It is quite possible that the *Visio* and the *Vita* originally existed as separate poems. But their natural affinities have clearly been developed and woven into a complex, single fabric by the poet's ingenuity.

shift has been anticipated in the stylistic juxtaposition of visionary levels in the prologue and also in the jarring conversion of Piers. We must now enter the complex realm of the struggling psyche in order to prepare for further historical revelations.

Will's introduction to self-knowledge begins with an encounter with personified Thought and Wit—his *own* thought and wit or intelligence, which can instruct as well as entangle.[22] The poor, bewildered narrator who thinks he must understand Dowel to be saved, finds himself debating at great length with his spirit's ghostly presences:

> Thouȝte and I thus thre days we ȝeden,
> Disputyng vppon Dowel day after other,
> And ar we were ywar with Witte gan we mete.
> He was longe and lene liche to none other,
> Was no pruyde on his apparaille ne pouerte noyther,
> Sadde of his semblaunt and of soft chiere.
>
> (B. VIII, 112–117; K-D, 117–122)

Through such comic personifications of Will's "semblables," Langland exaggerates and thereby calls attention to those mental processes and spiritual forces which participate in the salvation process. In the successive lessons preached by Thought, Wit, Study, Clergy, Scripture and Imaginatif in the next five passus, the poet will seem to be showing his basic saving lessons on well-doing *ad nauseam*. It is as if he were addressing a class of dullards who need to hear the same instructions over and over in order to learn. But, of course, Will *is* just such a spiritual dullard who fitly bears the standard of fallen man. And this realization guides us to one of Langland's principles of organization. The dreamer listens without understanding. Instead of seeking to perform good deeds as Piers has done, he, like many a scholar, waits to know more. Both Thought and Wit help Will along by defining in various ways the three "do's." But only spiritual discipline can lead him to action.

A third mnemonic set-piece dominates Passus IX and serves as an emblem (related to the tower of Truth) for the whole *Vita Dowel*. Langland has Wit devise an alliterative castle by which we are to understand our humanity as an image of God (1–65). Dowel, Wit explains, lives in

---

[22] For a valuable study of the development of such self-allegorization in later medieval vernacular literature, see Charles Muscatine, "The Emergence of Psychological Allegory in Old French Romance," *PMLA*, LXVIII (1953), pp. 1160–1182.

a castle made of the four earthly elements. Nature has given him a beloved called Anima who dwells in the heart. Conscience is the constable
of the castle. To make his point more precise, Wit glosses his own figure.
The castle is called caro (the flesh) "as much to mene as man with a
soule" (49). Anima is the spirit who roams over the whole body but
makes her home in the heart. And Conscience (Inwit) who lives in the
head, keeps flesh and spirit in rule and reason. So obvious and lengthy
a mnemonic artifice may seem unnecessarily simple minded even for Will.
Yet here, as throughout the long narrative, Langland demonstrates how
profoundly impressed he is not only with human dullness but also creaturely wandering, forgetfulness and inattention. Man (both himself and
his audience) requires the most explicit help in finding his way to salvation.

It is within the context of this "safe" castle that Will begins to receive
prophetic definitions of the three "do's" which form the moral basis for
his instruction and the poem's narrative.

> Dowel, my frende, is to don as lawe techeth,
> To loue thi frende and thi foo leue me, that is Dobet.
> To ʒiuen and to ʒemen bothe ʒonge and olde,
> To helen and to helpen is Dobest of alle.
> And Dowel is to drede god and Dobet to suffre,
> And so cometh Dobest of bothe.
>
> (B. IX, 199 204; K D, 202 208)

Like the Trinity, Dowel, Dobet and Dobest can mean many things as we
soon learn.[23] But finally all three are to be realized as a total unifying
experience when the soul is fully formed in the image of the Triune God.
Taken together they can offer protection in a variety of ways against
"wikked Wille" whose "dedliche synnes" make Dowel depart from his
dwelling.

The lesson preached at this point and throughout the poem is as simple

---

[23] It is no wonder that scholars have sought greater certainty than Piers seems to
offer in his definition of the meaning of Dowel, Dobet and Dobest. For
discussion of this problem, see H. W. Wells, "The Philosophy of Piers Plowman,"
PLMA, LIII (1938), pp. 339–349; E. T. Donaldson, *Piers Plowman: the C-Text and
its Poet* (New Haven, 1949); T. P. Dunning, "Structure of the B-Text of Piers
Plowman," *RES*, n.s. VII (1956), pp. 225–237; and S. S. Hussey, "Langland, Hilton
and the Three Lives," *RES*, n.s. VII (1956), pp. 132–150.

as it is powerful and it mirrors instructions to be found in many a monastic treatise. But of course, all these lessons are only a fabric of words. Not until Will and mankind generally have turned such directives into action can the visionary goal of human perfection be realized.

In the meantime, Will's failure as a disciplined truth-seeker is brought abruptly to the fore at the beginning of Passus x. In one of his most amusing pedagogical disguises, Langland enters the scene as Dame Study, Wit's wife. Shrewish, irritable, formidable, she severely chastises Wit for scattering his knowledge willy nilly. Like a mistress of novices, she intends to keep a close watch on spiritual truth. With a prophetic ardor reminiscent of the poet's voice in the prologue and the firm teaching of Holichurch, she decries the common scorn for the simple preaching of holy scripture (B. x, 32–37). Study also sounds a warning note to Will and his ilk who spend three days with thought but do no deeds of mercy:

God is moche in the gorge of thise grete maystres,
Ac amonges mene men his mercy and his werkis.
(B. x, 66–67; K-D, 67–68)

In fact, her caveat also extends to the poem itself as Langland argues over and over. Its words will only serve truth if it leads to *actions* of love and mercy.

Before Will leaves, Study has impressed him not with the importance of ample scholarship, but of intellectual restraint and love. "Don't know more than you should," she advises, paraphrasing St. Augustine. Finally, she preaches love as the essence of her rule:

For-thi loke thow louye as longe as thow durest,
For is no science vnder sonne so souereyne for the soule.
(B. x, 205–206; K-D, 210–211)

Her lessons complement the earlier Old Testament message of Holy Church, "mesure is medcyne." As usual, we find that for Langland human perfection lies in practicing the strictest discipline and following the simplest of rubrics.

Clergy's lesson to Will is likewise simple and the most explicitly monastic lesson of the poem:

For if heuene be on this erthe and ese to any soule,
It is in cloistere or in scole be many skilles I fynde;

For in cloistre cometh no man to chide ne to fiȝte,
But alle is buxumnesse there and bokes to rede and to lerne.

                              (B. X, 300–303; K-D, 305–308)

But even as Clergy holds this ancient religious ideal up for praise, it is being rudely inverted by its contemporary practitioners as Langland has been demonstrating from the start. Hence Clergy (yet another of Langland's disguises) concludes his lesson with a prophecy. In it he reminds Will and the audience of the urgently necessary apocalyptic hope which underlies the whole poetic structure:

Ac there shal come a kyng and confesse ȝow religiouses,
And bete ȝow, as the bible telleth for brekynge of ȝowre reule,
And amende monyales monkes and chanouns,
And putten hem to her penaunce *ad pristinum statum ire,*
And barounes with erles beten hem thorugh *beatus-virres* techynge.

                              (B. X, 317–321; K-D, 322–326)

As he carries forward Langland's anagogical purpose, Clergy predicts that a perfect king will awaken Cain and that Dowel will destroy evil. But as revolutionary as this prophecy is, poor Will misunderstands. Clergy must go on to explain—as Christ explained to the Pharisees and the Pearl Maiden to the jeweler—that a spiritual kingdom requires a visionary king quite unlike wealthy earthly rulers.

When Clergy has completed his explication of simple poverty and Christian love—lessons Will has already heard but does not remember— we find that the narrator has sunk yet further into a comic befuddlement. "This is a longe lessoun," he declares, "and litel am I the wyser;/ Where Dowel is, or Dobet derkelich ȝe shewen" (372–373). He announces his confusion with a sense of moral outrage and righteousness reminiscent of the *Pearl* narrator. And like the *Pearl* jeweler, he proceeds to outline his own understanding of divine justice and mercy. In this first extended demonstration of his own religious knowledge, he sounds like an angry, distraught sophomore. Yet Will's shadowboxing with God's ways contains enough elements of truth to lead an astute audience back in memory to Piers' fateful tearing of his pardon. For in this excursion, Will notes to his amazement that God has saved sinners and poor plowmen and damned clever clerks all in accordance with an incomprehensible mercy. Like the *Pearl* poet, Langland allows his narrator's sadly human exposition of divine justice and mercy to fall short of truth even as it reaches toward the paradoxical mystery of God's merciful justice (B. X, 469–475).

The Fourth Meditation: Passus xi–xii

The next two passus of meditation and the next reading turn on Scripture's scornful condemnation at the beginning of xi:

"multi multa sciunt, et seipsos nesciunt."
[many know many things and do not know themselves.]

(B. XI, 2; K-D, 3)

Will now reveals his difficulties in a new light:

Tho wepte I for wo and wratth of her speche,
And in a wynkyng wratth wex I aslepe.

(B. XI, 3–4; K-D, 4–5)

In his tearful, angry reaction to Scripture he demonstrates both pride and fear. Self-knowledge seems terrifying—even as fearful as the world outside. But the poet as *deus ex machina* mercifully softens the pain of self-discovery, encapsulating it in the ambiguities and enigmas of a new dream. Through a "merueillouse meteles," he will teach Will how he has coveted the world, indulged in self-love, and avoided the poverty and penance necessary to salvation. The personifications of the new vision introduce him, as if for the first time, to his own life—forty-five years of sin and negligence. Placed at the center of the B-text version of *Piers*, this close anatomy of Will's (and Everyman's) moral life provides an exacting model for personal assessment.

As Will is introduced to his own spiritual worthlessness, Langland provides materials both for a powerful internal crisis and the stirring of guilt necessary for penance. Will's vision unveils the futility of Fortune's wiles and leaves him nothing. His condition precisely illustrates one described by St. Anselm and familiar to Everyman:

Alas, unfortunate that I am, one of the miserable children of Eve, separated from God. What have I undertaken? What have I actually done? Where was I going? Where have I come to? To what was I aspiring? For what do I yearn? 'I sought goodness' [Ps. cxxi.9] and, lo, 'there is confusion' [Jer. xiv.19]. I yearned for God, and I was in my own way. I sought peace within myself and 'I have found tribulation and sadness' in my heart of hearts [Ps. cxiv.3]. I wished to laugh from out the happiness of my soul, and 'the sobbing of my heart, [Ps. xxxvii.9] makes me cry out. I hoped for gladness and, lo, my sighs come thick and fast.[24]

[24] St. Anselm, *Proslogion*, trans. M. J. Charlesworth (Oxford, 1965), p. 113.

Because he is an image of fallen Everyman, Will engages in no such insightful inner dialogues. Yet he does recognize his emptiness and anx-
iously acknowledges his need for divine help and assurance:

> And in a were gan I waxe and with my-self to dispute,
> Whether I were chosen or nouȝt chosen; on Holicherche I thouȝte,
> That vnderfonge me atte fonte for one of goddis chosen;
> For Cryste cleped vs alle come if we wolde.
>
> (B. XI; 111–114; K-D, 116–119)

As he turns to the Church and Christ's promises, he acknowledges at
last that Mercy alone—the fruit of Contrition—can overcome man's debt
to God. Scripture heartily agrees with him for "*Misericordia eius super
omnia opera eius* [*est*]" (134).

Now, having dramatized Will's objective "sight" of his empty, godless
life and his discovery of spiritual need, Langland can move to a new level
of exploration. For the first time, he can allow his pilgrim to ponder
images of his savior:

> For owre ioye and owre hele Iesu Cryst of heuene,
> In a pore mannes apparaille pursueth vs euere,
> And loketh on vs in her liknesse and that with louely chere,
> To knowen vs by owre kynde herte and castyng of owre eyen,
> Whether we loue the lordes here byfor owre lorde of blisse.
>
> (B. XI, 179–183; K-D, 185–189)

As Langland develops his incrementally enriched vision of a human,
saving Christ, he will build on this image, emphasizing the Lord's likeness to Everyman—his exemplary relationship to the poor, the down-trod-
den, the simple and the holy. He is to be studied in a typically fourteenth-
century way as a continuing mysterious presence for mankind, realizing
in his person and his history the prophetic dreams of lunatics and plowman, Holichurch, Conscience and Reason (B. XI, 224–234). This entire
sequence—Will's realization of his need and the ensuing images of a
compassionate Christ—provides a suggestive parallel for the much earlier
scene of Piers' revolutionary tearing of the pardon. But Will's conversion
is neither so long lasting nor so thorough as the plowman's.

In the very next scene, as the dreamer surveys a cosmic landscape—the
world and all its creatures—he marvels to learn that the cause of earthly
corruption is human irrationality. With a tone of comic patience born of
infinite experience, Reason explains why God allows unreason. She also

serves to introduce Will directly to his own earthly arrogance—a fault
which is very like the *Pearl* narrator's. This pride is responsible not only
for his wandering dimness of sight and lack of attention, but also for the
prolific verbal repetitions of the poem:

> 'For-thi I rede,' quod Reson 'rewle thi tonge bettere,
> And ar thow lakke eny lyf loke if thow be to preyse!
> For is no creature vnder Criste can formen hym-seluen;
> And if a man miʒte make hym-self goed to the poeple,
> Vch a lif wold be lakles leue thow non other!
> Ne thow shalt fynde but fewe fayne for to here
> Of here defautes foule by-for hem rehersed.'
>
> (B. XI, 378–384; K-D, 386–393)

Through Reason, Langland here defines the human need for his poem,
as also for its length. Few men care to look directly at their faults "by-for
hem reherse," and they cannot effect reform themselves. Therefore the
poet, directing the penitential meditation, must offer image after image of
human sin and repentance until even those as recalcitrant as Will suffer
for shame.

Will's personal, if passing, embarrassment for his besmirched humanity in the course of Passus XI allows Langland to introduce a major new
character. Assuming yet another guise, he illuminates once more (and in
a tone of voice not unlike Holichurch's) that anagogical force which
has been propelling Will toward spiritual renovation in spite of himself
from the beginning. Will has just awakened at the end of XI, put to shame
by Reason for asking to know too much. But in self-congratulatory tones
he also announces that he now knows what "Dowel" is. At this point,
"one loked on me, and axed/ Of me, what thinge it were?" (400–401) It
is Imaginatif, as Will soon learns, who sternly chastises him for his chat-
ter and arrogance:

> 'Haddestow suffred,' seyde 'slepyng tho thow were,
> Thow sholdest haue knowen that Clergye can and conceiued
>   more thorugh Resoun;
> For Resoun wolde haue reherced the riʒte as Clergye saide,
> Ac for thine entermetyng here artow forsake;
>   *Philosophus esses, si tacuisses.'*
>   (If you could keep silent, you would be a philosopher.)
>
> (B. XI, 403–406; K-D, 413–417)

Together with Piers, Imaginatif is perhaps the poet's most ingenious and thematically significant creation. Like Piers, he is carefully placed to assert the spiritual goal of Will's journey. At the beginning of xii, he tells the dreamer explicitly that he has "folwed the in feithe this fyue and fourty wyntre,/ And many tymes have moeued the to thinke on thine ende" (3 4).

Not surprisingly, Imaginatif's first practical function is to reassert the claim of the divinely instituted Holichurch as a necessary vehicle to salvation. Since Holichurch's disappearance from the narrative, Clergy has been spoken of in disparaging "crabbed" words and Will has made easy game of corruption among the religious orders. But now Imaginatif teaches him that one can find a reliable route to heaven best through those human instruments which have been divinely inspired—the Church, the sacred books, the writings of the Fathers. As Professor Bloomfield has suggested, Langland makes this new teacher a "vehicle of divine assurance and truth" in the face of worldly and ecclesiastical corruption.[25] Like Dante's "mente" or enlightened memory, Imaginatif serves to raise the mind from the confusion and error of empirical experience toward an awareness of its eternal goal. It is he who continually shapes and regulates the evidence of the external senses by reference to an inner spiritual authority—one higher far than reason. Like the Lunatic of the Prologue, like Holichurch, Reason and Conscience in the opening meditations, and like Piers, Imaginatif points with a prophetic confidence, unsupported by scrutiny of the fallen world, to a divine scheme whereby man will be saved in spite of his blindness.

At the same time, Imaginatif (and Langland as prophetic poet) also chides the loquacious, verbally oriented pilgrim for "making" his own book about Dowel, Dobet and Dobest. He reminds the audience that Will's writing is a way of avoiding the Christian action necessary for salvation:

> 'And thow medlest the with makynges and myʒtest go sey thi sauter,
> And bidde for hem that ʒiueth the bred; for there ar bokes ynowe
> To telle men what Dowel is Dobet, and Dobest bothe,
> And prechoures to preue what it is of many a peyre freres.'
>
> (B. XII, 16–19; K-D, 16–19)

---

[25] For Bloomfield's interpretation of Imaginatif, see his *Piers Plowman*, Appendix III, pp. 170–174.

This poem belongs to a far lower order than the sacred canon and its commentaries.[26] Yet, Will who "seigh wel he sayde me soth," must defend his own spiritual slowness and his adherence to worldly uncertainties. He must continue to use the verbal security of his poem as a crutch and go on seeking. Once again, Langland's pilgrim-narrator illustrates the personal confusion and self-deception as well as the worldly delight in proliferating verbal formulas which keep Everyman from carrying forward God's plan for salvation. Imaginatif, like the other prophets of the poem, disappears from the scene as mysteriously as he had appeared. But like the other major anagogical figures, he can also be felt as a continuing presence in the narrative, guiding Will toward an eschatological perspective.

THE FIFTH MEDITATION: PASSUS XIII–XIV

Happily enough, the opening of Passus XIII offers Will and his audience yet another dream and the opportunity to discover new aspects of "truth." After wandering "many a ȝere after," musing (but without understanding) on Imaginatif's lessons, Will, now dressed "in manere of a mendynaunt," again falls asleep. Langland delights in adorning his dreamer in a variety of symbolic costumes as if clothes might create the illusion of making the man. Just as he tries out many doctrinal definitions, so Will puts on a number of quasi-religious robes in the hope of making his way heavenward. We can observe by the narrator's own evidence of his long and fruitless wandering, however, how little he has discovered by himself, what a time-waster he can be, and why he requires close surveillance by a guiding divinity. Will's sad falling off from the strength and certainty of Imaginatif's prophecy demonstrates beyond doubt that his only hope for salvation lies in further visions. Only by being *given* glimpses of divine purpose in the midst of his fragmented, undirected history, will he be able to turn from his time-bound wandering to contrition, confession and, above all, a firm purpose of amendment. But not yet.

In his new dream, Will is led to a "place" familiar in vision quests— a dining hall at Court where Conscience is master of ceremonies and where Clergy and Conscience, Scripture and Patience are to eat with Will.

---

[26] Langland's low opinion of poetic "makynges" provides an obvious contrast for Dante's view of his "sacred poem" in its relationship to Scripture.

Langland's metaphoric banquet must present a significant strain for the
modern imagination, and it was certainly intended to pose a riddle even
for medieval audiences. Though banquets are a commonplace in medieval
visionary quests, Langland has given his fresh point to further his complex spiritual purpose. The allegorical feast, which consists of the Church
Fathers and the four evangelists, as well as a sauce, *post mortem*, and
a sour loaf of *agite penitenciam* (do penance), contains in its diet all that
Will needs for salvation. It is, in effect, an extravagant (and perhaps
overly ingenious) extension of Imaginatif's lesson concerning Will's need
for divine instruction and sacramental confession.

Through the entire meal, Patience, who is dressed as a pilgrim (an
oblique echo of Piers) looks on the feast. Meanwhile, Will, who is ever
the literalist, impatiently and self-righteously resents the Doctor's lusty
appetite. Finally, helped by Conscience and Patience, he asks the Doctor
his favorite question, "What is Dowel . . . Is Dowel any penaunce?" (102)
Clergy's first answer, like the poem's early lessons and the pardon sent
by Truth, counsels self-reliance: "Do non yuel to thine euenecrystene
nouȝt by thi powere" (104).

But, as we have already learned, such advice by itself is impracticable
for fallen man. Consequently, Conscience, who has to silence a chattering
Will, asks the question again. This time, the Doctor answers as Imaginatif had taught:

'Dowel,' quod this doctour 'do as clerkes techeth,
And Dobet is he that techeth and trauailleth to teche other,
And Dobest doth hym-self so as he seith and precheth.'
                    (B. XIII, 115–117; K-D, 116–118)

The Doctor then goes on to recall a lesson higher still—one which he had
learned from Piers Plowman. For the first time since his leave-taking in
Passus VII, Piers comes to the fore as the center around which all doctrine
and all human action must turn:

For one Pieres the Ploughman hath impugned vs alle,
And sette alle sciences at a soppe saue loue one,
And no tixte ne taketh to meyntene his cause,
But *dilige deum* and *domine, quis habitabit*, etc.
                    (B. XIII, 123–126; K-D, 124–127)

As the audience may well observe, such lessons as these, simple as they
may appear, are hemmed around by mystery. What, for example, do
clerks teach? And who precisely is Piers Plowman? What does the coun-

sel, "love God," mean? Why is David's famous psalm about righteousness and salvation quoted without a gloss? Though readers and listeners may first discard Langland's complex framing devices to nod approval at familiar lessons, a closer look at all the components of the scene suggests no such easy solution. Though "treuth" is implied in the personified figures, in the prophetic character of Piers, in the lessons taught by the Doctor, it is also hidden by the uncertainties of human time, bound ineluctably to Langland's narrative (and to the limited perceptions of the fallen world).

Despite the complexity of the narrative—or perhaps because of it—the figure of Piers continues to hold out the promise of spiritual understanding and salvation. The exemplary plowman alone maintains concrete hope of truth—not through "science" but through his deeds: "Thanne passe we ouer til Piers come and preue this in dede" (132).

The very mention of Piers' name at the banquet prompts Patience to speech. Gently he recalls his meeting with Love and the lesson she gave him—to love thine enemy as thyself (142–143). Through his simple espousal of Love's doctrine, Patience becomes the hero of the piece, surpassing the Doctor as a master of truth. With a convincing certainty, Conscience, whom we have learned to trust, whispers in Clergy's ear:

'Me were leuer, by owre lorde and I lyue shulde,
Haue pacience perfitlich than half thy pakke of bokes!'
                    (B. XIII, 200–201; K-D, 200–201)

Langland establishes a clear hierarchy of values in this intricate dialogue and sets patient love above the intellectual guides espoused by Imaginatif in Passus XII. But he like Imaginatif will not dismiss Clergy entirely from the quest. For at last all those who have shared in this allegorical banquet must work in consort to lead Will (and the human race) to St. Truth. Thus the Doctor reminds Conscience that religious instruction will be required before the total conversion of the world can be realized. Conscience readily agrees:

'That is soth . . . so me god helpe!
If Pacience be owre partyng felawe and pryue with vs both,
There nys wo in this worlde that we ne shulde amende,
And confourmen kynges to pees and al kynnes londes,
Sarasenes and Surre and so forth alle the Iewes
Turne in-to the trewe feithe and in-til one byleue!'
                    (B. XIII, 205–210; K-D, 205–210)

But, as Conscience and Patience have also demonstrated, the diet of Clergy taken by itself remains too rich for ordinary mortals. Before such social hopes as this can be realized, Conscience must follow the paths of the pilgrim, Patience.

The reason for such a course is made clear in the very next scene. For the first character whom Patience and Conscience encounter in their search is a very ordinary fallen man-on-the-street. He lacks even Will's unbridled curiosity concerning things spiritual. Haukyn the Minstrel and Wayfarer sings his songs and peddles his bread through all Christendom, thinking very little of his eternal life. While Will may mull over theological formulations, Haukyn, or *Activa-Vita* as he names himself, is simply busy making earthly ends meet. In his limited vision and patently unintellectual confusions, he offers Langland an opportunity to explore the extent of human failure in its homeliest, least cerebral manifestations. During this long scene, which comprises nearly two passus (xiii–xiv), Will is scarcely in evidence. It is as if Haukyn is part of himself—concupiscence-of-the-flesh, now seen without the affectations of spiritual musings and lofty dialectic.

Langland's dense description of Haukyn the Active Man can be compared in its power to Shakespeare's depictions of Falstaff. The two characters share a ribald love of petty evil and a gross but endearing openness. But Haukyn, in the service of Langland's eschatological purpose, represents fleshly weakness in its essence more clearly and anatomically than Falstaff. Through the image of Haukyn, guilty of every sin, wearing the spotted, worn robe of Christendom, the poet provides a model for self-examination which must appeal variously to the various kinds of sinners who study it. The covetous, the gluttons, the lechers, the proud, the envious—all will find a place in Haukyn's description of himself.

But in Haukyn the audience will also find a model for repentance. At last *Activa-Vita*, under the tutelage of Conscience and Patience, learns the steps to proper penance:

> 'And I shal kenne the,' quod Conscience 'of contricioun to make,
> That shal clawe thi cote of alkynnes filthe,
> > *Cordis contricio*, etc.:
> Dowel shal wasshen it and wryngen it thorw a wys confessour,
> > *Oris confessio*, etc.:—
> Dobet shal beten it and bouken it as briȝte as any scarlet,
> And engreynen it with good wille and goddes grace to amende the,

And sithen sende the to satisfaccioun for to sowen it after,
      Satisfaccio dobest.
(B. XIV, 16–21; K-D, 16–22)

Contrition of heart, Confession by mouth, Satisfaction—these three actions pave the way to Haukyn's and Everyman's salvation.

Langland seizes the opportunity of Haukyn's impending confession to recapitulate the lessons of the first five meditations. Patience and Conscience, who have found Haukyn out, offer him a catechism on poverty, charity, justice and faith. The cumulatively enriching scenarios which have provided Will's instruction up to this point can now be recalled by simple summary. The poet's pedagogical method of manifold repetition leading to such epitomes as this suggests a belief that mankind learns slowly and with great difficulty how to perceive the path to heaven. Only now, in this sermon to Haukyn, after a great deal of talk and thirteen passus, do the poet's instructions seem to bear fruit in action, not for Will but for *Activa-Vita*. With the force of full conviction, Haukyn concludes the *Vita Dowel* by performing the first stage of Penance, true contrition:

'Allas!' quod Haukyn the actyf man tho 'that, after my Crystendome,
I ne hadde ben den and doluen for Doweles sake!
So harde it is,' quod Haukyn 'to lyue and to do synne.
Synne suweth vs euere,' quod he and sori gan wexe,
And wepte water with his eyghen and weyled the tyme,
That euere he ded dede that dere god displesed;
Swowed and sobbed and syked ful ofte,
That euere he hadde londe or lordship lasse other more,
Or maystrye ouer any man mo than of hym-self.
(B. XIV, 320–328; K-D, 322–331)

He concludes his sorrowful speech with an exemplary cry for mercy, weeping and wailing.

During these last two passus, Will has been scarcely in evidence save for brief comments to indicate his continuing presence. Nor has he been affected by the sinner's moving contrition. Still confused, still seeking, he moves to a new arena and a new variation on his problem. What is Dobet? Though solutions to his question have been explored over and over by the actions and lessons of the poem he has not yet adverted to the necessity of *doing* for himself. But as is typical in vision quests, his spiritual lassitude encourages further development of the narrative and therefore its devotional lessons. As Langland's expressive poetic structure illustrates, it is precisely Will's (as well as the poet's and Everyman's) commitment to such temporal unfolding and to temporal events which prevents his turning to the inner self and Christian action.

The Sixth Meditation: Passus xv–xvii

At the beginning of Passus xv, Will has nearly gone mad. His searching for Dowel has led him into the direst confusion:

> Ac after my wakyng it was wonder longe,
> Ar I couth kyndely knowe what was Dowel.
> And so my witte wex and wanyed til I a fole were.
>
> (b. xv, 1–3; k-d, 1–3)

No longer the carefree seeker after wonders who had set out eagerly on his quest, Will is now strained almost beyond his rational capacities. He has been overwhelmed (as the audience may well be) by the impossibility of seeing truth clearly through the multifold filters of the dream, the personified abstractions and the enigmatic figures and voices. We have been forceably shown that Will's personal search intersects human history at a moment when Church and society alike lack reasonable order. We have been convinced by the difficulties of the narrative as well as Will's own blindnesses that "the moste meschief on molde is mountyng wel faste." No wonder then that the dreamer's search for certainty of belief and standards for action nearly destroys him. Indeed, in the face of such odds, one cannot but marvel at the tenacity of his faith. For Langland's recalcitrant but willing narrator contends against an impossibly diffuse, materialistic, casuistical society.

Indeed, the poetic structure now suggests that Will and his audience may expect escape from the poem's and the world's labyrinthine verbal and moral deceptions only by way of vision and spiritual transformation. From time to time in the course of his dreams, Will has been shown prophecies of a coming historical moment when king and Church will know and follow truth, and when "love will be leader." In the teaching of the Lunatic and Holichurch, Piers, Patience, Clergy, Reason, Conscience and Imaginatif, a luminous hope has shone round devastating images of human sin and weakness. Now, as the *Vita Dobet* begins, Langland once more figures the urgent need for such social hopes—this time in the image of Will's near insanity.

The world through which "long Will" has been seeking St. Truth rejects his madness out of hand:

That folke helden me a fole and in that folye I raued,
Tyl Resoun hadde reuthe on me and rokked me aslepe.

(B. XV, 10–11; K-D, 10–11)

And Will is left once again with his dreams. While at first these "meteles" had provided a chance pleasure, they have now become a saving necessity—a means of retreat from the pressures imposed by his difficult quest.

Under the aegis of Reason, Will's next dream moves him one step nearer to the spiritual vision which alone can save him. Before him a creature appears, a shape-shifter who represents man's life force. Anima incorporates in herself all the lively energy through which man can know, love and serve either God or the world. This strange creature, whose powers can lead to bliss or perdition, takes the responsibility of pointing Will toward the root of the world's dilemma. At the foundation of all human failure, and Will's failure in particular, she finds the corruption of the Church. To demonstrate her point, she anatomizes the history of Holichurch from its founding until the present. The lives of the twelve apostles, the desert Fathers, and the early missionaries who converted England stand in exemplary contrast to their contemporary successors. Once, anchorites and hermits, monks and friars were peers to the apostles. Anthony, Dominic, Francis of Assisi, Benedict and Bernard all represented the Church's best ideals. They lived in "lowe houses" and through them grace grew. In her glowing descriptions the earlier Church is characterized by simple patience and love.

Against such an example, she can only offer the severest indictment of current clerical practice. Like Dante, Langland (through Anima) traces the cause for the Church's weakness to the Donation of Constantine. His remedy is simple:

A medecyne mote ther-to that may amende prelates,
That sholden preye for the pees; possessioun hem letteth,
Take her landes, ȝe lordes and let hem lyue by dymes.
If possessioun be poysoun and inparfit hem make,
Good were to dischargen hem for holicherche sake,
and purgen hem of poysoun or more perile falle.
ȝif presthod were parfit the peple sholde amende,
That contrarien Crystes lawe and Crystendome dispise.

(B. XV, 524–531; K-D, 562–569)

From the start, Langland has placed Holichurch and Mede in opposition. Now, through Anima, he proposes to separate them in practice. But how then is Ecclesia to thrive?

Anima offers us an answer in Passus xvi, filtered as usual through personifications and the enigmatic figure of Piers. At the same time, she also initiates a final revolutionary movement in the pilgrim's spiritual education. For here begins the historical realization of Piers' spiritual mission, one which is to have great significance both for the true Church and for Will. The simple plowman, who had so dramatically withdrawn from the field at the end of Passus vii to devote himself to prayer and penance, now appears anew as a gardener. According to Anima, he has become the guardian of the Tree of Charity. Such a role is fitting indeed. Piers had already been cast as the manifest symbol of God's loving covenant with man. Appearing briefly in the *Visio* and merely mentioned in the *Vita Dowel,* he had imaged Divine Love *as it has appeared* to fallen man throughout his history. Now as gardener for the great flowering tree, he anticipates a still fuller realization of divine love in human time—and in Langland's narrative.

The Tree of Charity itself, by which Anima introduces Passus xvi and the *Vita Dobet* proper, is another mnemonic figure, cousin to the Charter of Sin (ii), the Manor House of Mercy (vi) and the Castle of Caro (ix). Like those images, this tree provides a summary focus for the narrative lessons to follow. Planted by God in the human heart, and cultivated by Piers, it also offers ample material for reflection on the instruction of the whole poem. It names opaquely, though memorably, those simple actions that are necessary for salvation:

> 'Mercy is the more ther-of the myddel stokke is Reuthe.
> The leues ben Lele-Wordes the lawe of Holycherche,
> The blosmes beth Boxome-Speche and Benygne-Lokynge;
> Pacience hatte the pure tre and pore symple of herte,
> And so, thorw god and thorw good men groweth the frute Charite.'
>
> (B. XVI, 5–9; K-D, 5–9)

This witty Tree of Love depends for its life on God's mercy though its fruit is good action. In the remaining passus, Will is to perceive the drama of the tree trunk, Mercy, transformed into human flesh and entering the fallen world. The tree itself, which lists the names of the saving virtues, can only articulate relationships. It does not represent the essence of goodness. For man, this must be found in Christ's history.

With Piers as gardener for the extraordinary tree, Langland begins to draw Will slowly toward the drama of Christ's entry into human time. Both narrator and audience have already learned through the confusing experience of the poem how difficult it is to find salvation when they must depend on prophecies, authorities and intimations. Now as the narrative moves us toward the fulfillment of prophecy, the lessons become simpler, the way clearer. Though the plowman's instruction is still indirect and riddling, he allows the narrator to study at last the triune Deity which has made goodness possible in the world from the time of Adam. Piers' gloss for the three pillars supporting his Tree of Charity not only provides a mnemonic trinitarian image, but it also identifies the movements of the whole poem. As the first part of the poem had depicted the Age of the Father and preached control of the flesh (I-XIV), so the tree's first pillar represents *potencia Dei-patris* and affords strength against the "wykked wynde" of the world. The second pillar, paralleling the emergence of Piers and the prophecies of Christ in the narrative (VI-XIII) depicts *sapiencia Dei-patris*,

> That is, the passioun and the power of owre prynce Iesu,
> Thorw preyeres and thorw penaunces and goddes passioun in mynde.
>
> (B. XVI, 37–38; K-D, 37–38)

Finally, the third pillar, *liberum arbitrium*, is the Holy Spirit whose presence has been apparent in the narrative chiefly through the prophetic figures Will has met. This third power is to provide Piers' total liberation from the devil's power (XIX-XX):

> 'Ac whan the Fende and the Flesshe forth with the Worlde
> Manasen byhynde me my fruit for to fecche,
> Thanne *Liberum-Arbitrium* laccheth the thridde plante,
> And palleth adoun the pouke purelich thorw grace
> And helpe of the holy goste and thus haue I the maystrie.'
>
> (B. XVI, 48–52; K-D, 48–52)

The time of grace here described, in which Piers will have "maystrie," is no less than confirmation of a future peace—and a holy kingdom in which all mankind will live in harmony and love. Such a moment has been adumbrated in the course of the narrative. But it is still to come.

In the meantime, Piers must introduce Will to the whole history of salvation, particularly to those events which lead directly to the incarnation, passion and death of the Savior. Nowhere is the Lenten nature of this meditative poem more apparent than in the concluding lessons. Will himself notes that it is Lent. He speaks of meeting Abraham on a "Mydlenten Sondaye," (172) of witnessing the Palm Sunday procession, and going off to Easter Mass. Furthermore, Piers chooses, as if quite consciously, to follow in a general way the liturgical patterns of the Sundays of Lent in teaching Will about Old Testament prophecy and New Testament fulfillment. Indeed, the text of these four passus might well be considered a moving gloss for the Lenten liturgy.

Piers gives Will a dramatic outline or blueprint of Christ's history—his incarnation through the Holy Spirit and his public life—the miracle of the loaves and fishes, the casting out of the money changers from the temple, the Holy Thursday meal and Judas' betrayal. When he has concluded with a description of Good Friday and Christ's death on Calvary, Will abruptly wakes up. Clearly the narrator is not quite ready for the full force of "seeing" the Christian exemplar face to face. Yet, although he tells us he is still an "ydiote," Will has found a goal for his wanderings which cannot help but lead him to salvation:

> I awayted after faste,
> And ȝede forth as an ydiote in contre to aspye
> After Pieres the Plowman; many a place I souȝte.

> (B. XVI, 169–171; K-D, 169–171)

Not long ago, the narrator had been a "lorel" and a "fole" with little hope of making his way to truth. Now in his first full confrontation with Piers he has suddenly become an avowed disciple. This inner transformation at the plowman's hand is no less dramatic in its effect than the simultaneous entrance into the narrative of scriptural characters and events of a kind William Blake would use centuries later. Faith, who now appears to Will, is also Abraham, representing for mankind the truth of the Trinity and the power to sacrifice bread and wine before Christ's coming. In direct conversation with the ancient Father of Faith, Will learns how the Trinity came to visit Abraham and why he holds the children in his bosom. At the end of the passus, Will and Abraham together look forward to the coming of the *Agnus Dei* who will loose them from hell.

Spes, or Hope, who rushes in on Abraham and Will even as they are "hoping," announces at the beginning of Passus XVII that he is "a spye," that is, a scout who is looking for a "knyȝte." Like Abraham, he knows a good deal about the Trinity, and furthermore he espouses the prophetic law of Christian love. Unhappily, Will cannot support Hope's doctrine of love. To him it seems impracticable in the world he knows so well. But even as he goes forward disputing with Hope, a Samaritan on a mule appears. Now Langland has Will discover *in actio* the scriptural story of the Good Samaritan transformed into a parabolic account of Faith, Hope and Love and anticipating Christ's appearance on Calvary. Here the poet figures forth the pressure and tension of gradual, prophetic discovery. Will begins to see the emergence of love on earth even as the late prophets of the Old Testament did. Through examples and glimmerings, he perceives the power love has to transcend all other virtues and overcome all sin. In this instance, the Good Samaritan stops to help the wounded, naked man whom Faith and Hope had passed by, and a profoundly impressed Will asks to be his groom. But, like Faith and Hope, the Samaritan provides only a foreshadowing. He continues Will's lesson on the Trinity through the well-known mnemonic images of the fist and of the taper, and he shows especially how the flame of Christ's mercy will bring men joy:

> And as the weyke and fyre wil make a warme flaumbe
> For to myrthe men with that in merke sitten,
> So wil Cryst of his curteisye and men crye hym mercy,
> Bothe forȝiue and forȝete and ȝet bidde for vs
> To the fader of heuene forȝyuenesse to haue.
>   (B. XVII, 239–243; K-D, 242–247)

Finally, when he has finished his instruction on Christ's mercy—filtered through his homely comparisons—the Samaritan disappears "as wynde," leaving Will to awaken, puzzled once more.

THE LAST MEDITATION: PASSUS XVIII–XX

The image Will now paints of himself presents a sharp contrast to his earlier poses. No longer dressed as a hermit or a mendicant friar, he has assumed a costume "wolleward and wete-shoed," which underscores both the penitential lessons he has learned and the transformed nature of his vagabond life.[27] He has been wandering, he tells us, "al his lyf-tyme,"

[27] Skeat notes the connotation of "wolleward," signifying penitential garb comparable to a hair shirt: "The sense of the word is clearly—with wool next to one's body, or, *literally*, with the body towards wool. It is well discussed and explained by Nares, who says—'Dressed in wool only, without linen, often enjoined in times of superstition by way of penance'" (*Piers Plowman*, vol. II, pp. 247–248).

and when he stops to sleep it is because he is "wery of the worlde." It is also Lent. Just as Will's garb suits his penitential condition, so, too, his dream is exactly appropriate for this liturgical time. As he looks into his new vision, Will perceives a Palm Sunday procession with young children and he hears hymns being sung and played on organs and, in the midst of the crowd, "one semblable to the Samaritan and some-del to Piers the Plowman" (B. XVIII, 10). The figure on the mule is, of course, the long-awaited Savior who had been anticipated in the characters of Piers and the Samaritan and who mysteriously includes both of them in his miraculous presence. He is absolute Goodness come, as Abraham tells Will, to wage war against "the foule fende and Fals-dome and Deth" (28). The Tower of Truth and the Dungeon of Falsehood—allegorical emblems at the beginning of the poem—have at last assumed concrete meaning in the images of Jesus and his slayers.

From an omnitemporal perspective—including the Old Testament and the eschaton—Langland moves us gracefully to a close "shewynge" of the miraculous passion and death from a temporal human standpoint. There are, for instance, those who do not believe that Jesus is "goddes sone" and "saide he was a wicche." Then, too, there is the blind Longinus who willingly drives his spear into Christ's side. Longinus' restored vision serves as a powerful commentary on Will's situation: the pilgrim himself has undergone just such a transformation, miraculously blessed with spiritual sight through Piers.

The vision to which the dreamer is party in the scenes which follow is remarkable indeed. He (and the audience) witness, as if it were a piece of contemporary history, Jesus in the process of redeeming the world. His betrayal, passion and death all enter our imagination as drama. Finally, Truth, in a tone of awe, introduces a last miraculous event: the Prince of Peace has come to harrow hell. Nowhere in the poem is Langland's dramaturgical skill more apparent than in the dialogue he creates between Lucifer and Christ. In his role as conqueror, Jesus finally declares to his enemy:

> The bitternesse that thow hast browe brouke it thi-seluen,
> That art doctour of deth drynke that thow madest!
> For I, that am lorde of lyf loue is my drynke,
> And for that drynke to-day I deyde vpon erthe.
>
> (B. XVIII, 361–364; K-D, 363–366)

He also promises a final apocalyptic triumph as the necessary end to this sacrificial action:

I fauȝte so, me threstes ȝet for mannes soule sake;
May no drynke me moiste ne my thruste slake,
Tyl the vendage falle in the vale of Iosephath,
That I drynke riȝte ripe must *resureccio mortuorum*,
And thanne shal I come as a kynge crouned with angeles,
And han out of hell alle mennes soules.

(B. XVIII, 365–370; K-D, 367–372)

For a moment, as this grand harrowing of hell is completed, the world is at peace. Love, Peace and Truth, who serve as glossators on the scene, explain its universal anagogical significance. Together they conclude by hymning Easter songs of praise, triumph and joy:

Pees, and Pees here *per secula seculorum.*
  Misericordia et veritas obuiauerunt sibi; iusticia et
    pax osculate sunt.
Treuth tromped tho, and songe '*Te deum laudamus*';
  And thanne luted Loue in a loude note,
    Ecce quam bonum et quam iocundum, etc.

(B. XVIII, 421–423; K-D, 421–423)

In their songs, Langland has managed to create an image of luminescent joy precisely suited to his Easter purpose. In its way their celebration is as total as Dante's final paradisal vision.

In the context of this awesome atmosphere, Will responds with homely piety:

riȝt with that I waked,
And called Kitte my wyf and Kalote my douȝter—
'Ariseth and reuerenceth goddes resurrexioun,
And crepeth to the crosse on knees and kisseth it for a Iuwel!'

(B. XVIII, 425–428; K-D, 425–428)

Then at the beginning of Passus XIX, the thought of the Eucharistic feast draws Will himself to Mass. But during the offertory, before the consecration of the host, he falls asleep once again.

Now the full nature of his transformed and transforming vision becomes apparent. Like St. Gregory the Great, like Lancelot in the *Queste*, like the visionary friar near the end of the *Fioretti*, Will sees in his dream the present figure of the bloody Savior:

> sodeynly me mette,
> That Pieres the Plowman was paynted al blody,
> And come in with a crosse bifor the comune peple,
> And riȝte lyke in alle lymes to owre lorde Iesu.
>
> (B. XIX, 5–8; K-D, 5–8)

But even now, Will cannot rest with simple vision; he must seek to understand his "seeing." Who is this figure? Is he Piers or Christ or Jesus?

His scholastic questions allow a kneeling Conscience to explain at length Christ's new role as King. He is now conqueror as well as savior. In his discourse, Conscience brings into focus once again the essentially penitential purpose of all the poem's lessons (B. XIX, 59–64). He shows the development of the Savior's name leading to his institution of the sacrament of penance. From the time when he was an infant born in Bethlehem until the wedding feast at Cana, he was called "Jesus," and he "did well." Then, when he had entered alone on his spiritual mission, healing the deaf and dumb, he was called "fili David, Iesus," "doing better" even until the moment when he died on the cross. At last, when he arose from death, he had become "Christus resurgens." Under this name, he established "Dobest," and gave the world its only satisfactory pardon:

> Dobest he tauȝte,
> And ȝaf Pieres power and pardoun he graunted
> To alle manere men mercy and forȝyfnes,
> Hym myȝte men to assoille of alle manere synnes,
> In couenant that thei come and knowleche to paye,
> To Pieres pardon the Plowman *redde quod debes.*
> Thus hath Pieres powere be his pardoun payed,
> To bynde and to vnbynde both here and elles-where,
> And assoille men of alle synnes saue of dette one.
>
> (B. XIX, 177–185; K-D, 182–190)

Here at last is the fulfillment and explanation of Piers' dramatic tearing of the first pardon in Passus VII. His prophetic conversion to prayer and penance presaged God's much-needed saving gift of mercy and forgiveness. Through Christ's sacrifice, the sacrament of penance is instituted and placed in Piers' care. The good plowman—God's presence in the world from Adam to Apocalypse—has assumed his penultimate role as guardian of Holy Church.

Now, as he had first done in the opening passus, Will kneels down. Once again he assumes a pose of filial respect as he witnesses the founding of the Church through the coming of the Holy Spirit:

> 'Knele now,' quod Conscience 'and if thow canst synge,
> Welcome hym and worshipe hym with *"veni, creator spiritus."* '
> Thanne songe I that songe and so did many hundreth,
> And cryden with Conscience 'help vs, god of grace!'
>
> (B. XIX, 204–207; K-D, 209–212)

Here at last the dreamer himself utters his penitential plea for mercy, following in the footsteps of the sinners of Passus v and of Haukyn, the Minstrel.

With a purity and clairvoyance possible only to a visionary perspective, the poet next projects an ideal image of Holy Church, one which echoes St. Augustine's definition of the omnitemporal city of God:

> There nas no Crystene creature that kynde witte hadde,
>
> . . . .
>
> That he ne halpe a quantite holynesse to wexe.
> Somme thorw bedes-byddynge and somme thorw pylgrymage,
> And other pryue penaunce and some thorw penyes-delynge.
> And thanne welled water for wikked werkes,
> Egerlich ernynge out of mennes eyen.
> Clennesse of the comune and clerkes clene lyuynge
> Make Vnite holicherche in holynesse to stonde.
>
> (B. XIX, 370–378; K-D, 372–380)

The secular realm, too, is ordered according to perfect justice. At the end of Passus XIX, the King promises to rule the Commons and defend Church and Clergy:

> ... sith I am ʒowre aller hed I am ʒowre aller hele,
> And holycherche chief help and chiftaigne of the comune.
> And what I take of ʒow two I take it atte techynge
> Of *spiritus iusticie*.
>
> (B. XIX, 468–471; K-D, 471–474)

The early prophetic visions of Reason and Conscience (Passus III and IV) are finally grounded securely in the context of Christ's redemption.

But although such joy can be fully imaged in the celebration of the original Easter and Pentecost, it remains a hard-won commodity in the fallen world, and it will not be totally realized until the final apocalyptic battle has been waged. Consequently, Will must awaken from his dream at the beginning of Passus xx to continue his wandering. He is left an exile in the world, physically and spiritually needy, and fully aware of his plight. But he has also found a new security. The near despair, the confusions, the verbal labyrinths in earlier movements of the journey have been replaced by a sober confidence vested in the person and action of the Savior coming in Piers' armor. Though he has had no blinding mystical vision of the Godhead, Will has entered into the heart of Christ's saving Manor House of Mercy, now called Unity-Holichurch. What remains is to await with diligence the coming of Antichrist so that all that has been seen in the concluding passus may bear its fruit in history.

Need confirms Will's new spiritual security in one of the poem's most lyrical passages. The narrator has now become "semblable" to Christ:

> So nedy he [Christ] was, as seyth the boke in many sondry places,
> That he seyde in his sorwe on the selue rode,
> "Bothe fox and foule may fleighe to hole and crepe,
> And the fisshe hath fyn to flete with to reste,
> There nede hath ynome me that I mote nede abyde,
> And suffre sorwes ful sowre that shal to Ioye tourne."
> For-thi be nouȝte abasshed to bydde and to be nedy;
> Syth he that wrouȝte al the worlde was wilfullich nedy,
> Ne neuer none so nedy ne pouerere deyde.
>
> (B. XX, 41–49; K-D, 42–50)

With such assurance, Will once more falls asleep, this time to dream prophetically of the coming apocalyptic conflict.

In his vision, he sees Antichrist, dressed as a man, mingling with Church and society. His last "seeing" recapitulates the *Visio's* disturbing picture of society and allows us to understand those opening images in a fuller, more formally complete way. Now we may confidently interpret the corruptions in Church, Commons and Court as signs of imminent cataclysm. Clearly the fiend is abroad, preparing his army to attack Unity-Holichurch:

> Antecryst cam thanne and al the croppe of treuthe
> Torned it vp so doune and ouertilte the rote,

And made fals sprynge and sprede and spede mennes nedes;
In eche a contre there he cam he cutte awey treuthe,
And gert gyle growe there as he a god were.
Freres folwed that fende for he ʒaf hem copes,
And religiouse reuerenced hym and rongen here belles,
And al the couent forth cam to welcome that tyraunt,
And alle hise, as wel as hym saue onlich folis;
Which folis were wel leuer to deye than to lyue
Lenger, sith leute was so rebuked.

(B. XX, 52–62; K-D, 53–63)

Will, who had pictured himself as a fool much earlier, now slyly finds that "folis" comprise the remnant of the Good.

As the passus and the dream proceed, this intermingling of the self and the cosmic apocalyptic battle becomes at once more complex and clear. As in Huon de Méri's much earlier *Tournoiement Antechrist*, the historical conflict between Christ and Antichrist is shown to be an extension of the individual's struggle for salvation. In a complex coda, Will becomes at once a spectator at the apocalyptic conflict, and an image of Everyman at the end of his life. Old Age and Death confront him and he turns to Kynde for good counsel. "Lerne to loue," Kynde preaches, "and leue of alle othre" (207). With this, the narrator properly betakes himself "thorw Contricioun and Confessioun" until he comes to "Vnite" (212). Arriving there, he discovers the constable, Conscience, whose task it is to save Christians and who is sorely besieged by Antichrist's seven giants, the seven deadly sins. In the personifications of his last dream, Will perceives his own salvation in the midst of a general eschatological struggle.

But Will does not see the salvation of the world. At the end of his vision, Conscience, overwhelmed by worldly corruption, becomes the protagonist. As he looks on the "enchantments" by which Friars have deluded the people and given them false pardons, he declares:

I wil bicome a pilgryme,
And walken as wyde as al the worlde lasteth,
To seke Piers the Plowman that Pryde may destruye.

(B. XX, 378–380; K-D, 380–382)

Like the conclusions of the *Vita Nuova* and *Pearl*, this final statement is principally the promise of a new beginning. Another quest must be made though the goal will remain the same. Conscience will now seek the enigmatic Piers from the point at which Will has stopped. And in this further adventure, which will continue as far and as long as the world lasts, the simple plowman will doubtless appear in new garb, perhaps that of the angelic king prophesied by Joachim of Fiore and anticipated by Dante. At the same time, further visions (and further readings of Langland's long poem) should issue in ever-deepening understanding of the way to that full experience of spiritual peace toward which all the spiritual quests of the later Middle Ages have directed their protagonists and their audiences.

INDEX

Adso, Abbot, author of *Libellus de ortu et tempore Antichristi*, 72n

Aevum, definition of, 38-40; and visionary perspective, 39-40, 43-44

Agnus Castus, 171n

Alain de Lille, 142

Albertus Magnus, 92n; and art of memory, 91

Alcuin, *Commentariorum in Apocalypsin*: Ambrose Autpert's influence on, 6-7; exegetical method in, 8, 20, 59; intellectual vision in, 7, 17; St. John in, 8; Tychonius' influence on, 6

Alexander of Bremen, 16n, 17, 20; *Expositio in Apocalypsim*: New Jerusalem and contemporary spirituality in, 29; St. John in, 54; spiritual illumination in, 28-29

Alexander, J.J.G., 65n

Anagogical imagery, in *Pearl*, 79, 151-52, 178-79, 183; in spiritual quests, 151-52; in Trinity College Apocalypse, 76-77

Anagogical narration, 51-53; Hugh of St. Victor's definition of, 52n

Anagogical vision, and art, 40-44, 48-50, 53-54, 76-77, 178; in Dante's *Commedia*, 42-43, 115, 152; *Vita Nuova*, 115, 118, 122-23; in Richard of St. Victor, 37-38, 117

Anagogy, definitions of, in Dante. 41-43; as mode of experience, 35-38; in scriptural exegesis, 36

Angers, Tapestries of Apocalypse, designed by Hennequin of Bruges, 82&n

Anselm, St., *Proslogion*, 237

Anselm of Havelburg, 17, 19n; *Dialogues*: seven seals in, 19; seventh seal in, 20; spiritual progress through history in, 20; *status* of pale horse and contemporary spirituality in, 19-20

Anthony, St., of the desert, 247

Antichrist, in Berengaudus' commentary, 11, 72n; in *Hortus Deliciarum*, 80n; in Huon de Méri, 130; in illustrated Apocalypses, 72-76, 72n, 78-81, 78n, 130, Figs. 19, 20; in *Liber Floridus*, 80n; in non-Berengaudus commentary, 78nn; in *Piers Plowman*, 224, 256-57

Apocalypse of St. John, Beatus illustrations for, 8, 60-64; Carolingian illustrations for, 56-60; and Church in fourteenth-century glosses, 222; commentaries on: Alcuin, 6-8; Alexander of Bremen, 28-29; Ambrose Autpert, 6, 7, 9n, 19n; Anselm of Havelburg, 19-20; Beatus, 8, 21, 60-64, 61n, 76, 125; Bede, 5-6, 21, 22, 110; Berengaudus, 9-12, 67-68, 70-76, 72n, 78-81, 80n; Bruno of Segni, 12-15; Haimo of Auxerre, 8-9, 17, 55n, 59; Joachim of Fiore, 25-29; Richard of St. Victor, 20-25, 35-38, 76-77; Rupert of Deutz, 15-19; early Christian interpretations of, 4&n; early medieval commentaries on, 4; historical interpretation of, 9-13, 17, 19-20, 23-29, 54, 55, 78-81; ima-

Library of Congress Cataloging in Publication Data

Nolan, Barbara, 1941–
  The Gothic visionary perspective.

  Includes index.
  1. Apocalyptic art. 2. Arts, Gothic. I. Title.
NX650.A6N64   700'.9'02   76–56241
ISBN 0–691–06337–0